Basic Skills and Strategies
for College Reading

BASIC SKILLS AND STRATEGIES FOR COLLEGE READING

A TEXT WITH THEMATIC READER

Jane L. McGrath

Paradise Valley Community College

Prentice
Hall

UPPER SADDLE RIVER, NEW JERSEY 07458

Library of Congress Cataloging-in-Publication Data

McGrath, Jane L.
    Basic skills and strategies for college reading: a text with thematic reader/Jane L. McGrath.
      p. cm.
    Includes index.
    ISBN 0-13-087483-3
      1. College readers.   2. Reading (Higher education)—Problems, exercises, etc. I. Title.

PE1122.M267 2002
808'.0427—dc21   2001036719

Editor in chief: Leah Jewell
Acquisitions editor: Craig Campanella
Assistant editor: Vivian Garcia
Editorial assistant: Joan Polk
VP/Director of production and manufacturing: Barbara Kittle
Senior managing editor: Mary Rottino
Production editor: Kari Callaghan Mazzola
Project liaison: Randy Pettit
Marketing manager: Rachel Falk
Marketing assistant: Christine Moodie
Prepress and manufacturing manager: Nick Sklitsis
Prepress and manufacturing buyer: Ben Smith
Electronic page makeup: Kari Callaghan Mazzola and John P. Mazzola
Interior design: John P. Mazzola
Cover director: Jayne Conte
Cover design: Bruce Kenselaar
Cover art: The Image Bank

This book was set in 10/12 New Century Schoolbook by Big Sky Composition
and was printed and bound by Banta Company.
The cover was printed by Phoenix Color Corp.

© 2002 by Pearson Education, Inc.
Upper Saddle River, New Jersey 07458

Printed in the United States of America
10 9 8 7 6 5 4 3 2 1

ISBN 0-13-087483-3

Pearson Education LTD., London
Pearson Education Australia PTY, Limited, Sydney
Pearson Education Singapore, Pte. Ltd
Pearson Education North Asia Ltd, Hong Kong
Pearson Education Canada, Ltd., Toronto
Pearson Educación de Mexico, S.A. de C.V.
Pearson Education—Japan, Tokyo
Pearson Education Malaysia, Pte. Ltd
Pearson Education, Upper Saddle River, New Jersey

BRIEF CONTENTS

CONTENTS

THEME 2   OUR FIRST AMENDMENT FREEDOMS   200

THEME 3   DRUGS, ALCOHOL, AND TOBACCO   248

PREFACE

Basic Skills and Strategies for College Reading is for college students in a first-level reading course. The text focuses on the essential reading skills necessary for effective comprehension.

The content and structure of this text, like the next-level text, *Building Strategies for College Reading*, are guided by the research on the "best ideas for teaching developmental reading." These principles closely mirror the findings of N. Stahl, M. L. Simpson, and C. G. Hayes—as outlined in their 1992 article "Ten Recommendations from Research for Teaching High Risk College Students" in *Journal of Developmental Education* 16 (1)—and include the following:

1. Adopt a cognitive-based philosophy, assuming that students are active participants and in control of their own learning—capable of becoming effective independent learners.
2. Use a course model that stresses transfer of skills to authentic college classes.
3. Help students realize that "the fundamental avenue to college success is the ability to quickly expand their vocabulary, and that students must immerse themselves totally in the language of the academy."
4. Teach learning strategies that have been research-validated and insure students know how to choose among them and use them.
5. Systematically train students to select and use appropriate strategies.
6. Use reliable, process-oriented assessment procedures rather than relying too much on standardized tests.
7. Broaden the students' conceptual background knowledge.
8. Teach students to plan, monitor, and evaluate their own learning.

The text provides authentic reading tasks to help prepare students to meet the demands of the texts and tasks they will encounter in future classes. The paragraphs and multi-paragraph expository pieces come from texts, magazines, and newspapers. Subject areas include computers, the Internet, personal finance, music, communications, personal development, environmental science, sociology, health occupations, earth science, career exploration, geography, psychology, biology, art, English, history, health, American government, and human relations.

I hope students will see themselves as active participants in the reading process—readers who can set and accomplish reading and study goals and objectives.

ORGANIZATION

The text has two main parts—six instructional chapters and three thematic reading units—plus the Appendix, Glossary, Suggested Answers, and Index sections.

The six chapters provide instruction in the essential reading skills necessary for effective comprehension. These skills include previewing, understanding vocabulary, identifying and understanding main ideas, identifying major and minor supporting details, identifying the way an author organizes details and/or sentences, distinguishing between facts and opinions, making valid inferences, and determining a thesis.

The development of each chapter is true to instructional design principles: explanations, examples, and practice—lots of practice. The explanations are concise with a constant emphasis on application to college material. The sequence of development and instructional language encourages students to connect and integrate the new skills and information they are learning with what they already know.

Students can self-check odd-numbered exercises with the Suggested Answers section at the end of the book, while even-numbered exercises and Putting It All Together exercises can be used to monitor progress.

Each chapter begins with a Chapter Preview and Chapter Focus and ends with a review section that includes a summary of key ideas and the objectives self check. After the review, students have the opportunity to test their skills in Putting It All Together. For more practice, students can complete the Crossword Puzzle, Log on to the Web, and Ideas for Writing and Discussion sections.

The three thematic reading units each include a full textbook chapter—personal development, American government, biology—plus related articles on the unifying topic.

Each theme begins with an introduction to the topic and the readings. Each reading is followed by vocabulary and comprehension questions. The themes end with three activities to encourage students to continue reading and thinking about the topic: Crossword Puzzle, Log on to the Web, and Ideas for Writing and Discussion.

Because the thematic approach supplies multiple exposures to a topic, it provides a scaffolding of knowledge that allows students to handle more sophisticated material than isolated readings. This approach also encourages a more meaningful and connected understanding of a topic and promotes critical thinking as students view a topic from several perspectives.

Although many of the ideas in the Appendix may help students prepare for and take any type of test, the ideas are specifically intended for standardized reading tests, for which students cannot study specific content. Tips for preparing for and taking content exams are available on the Companion Website at <www.prenhall.com/mcgrath>.

SUMMARY OF KEY FEATURES

- The content and structure of this text are guided by the research on the "best ideas for teaching developmental reading."
- The focus is on instruction in the essential reading skills necessary for effective comprehension.
- The logical development of each chapter—explanations, examples, practice—helps students progress smoothly.
- The sequence of development and instructional language encourages students to connect and integrate the new skills and information they are learning with what they already know.

- The text provides authentic reading tasks to help prepare students to meet the demands of the texts and tasks they will encounter in future classes.

- Students read a variety of high interest paragraphs and multi-paragraph expository pieces from texts, magazines, and newspapers. Subject areas include computers, the Internet, personal finance, music, communications, personal development, environmental science, sociology, health occupations, earth science, career exploration, geography, psychology, biology, art, English, history, health, American government, and human relations.

- The three thematic reading units each include a complete textbook chapter—personal development, American government, biology—plus articles, with questions, on the unifying topic.

- End-of-chapter and end-of-theme Web exercises direct students to Internet sites appropriate to a specific content-related task. In addition, students can gain additional vocabulary and comprehension practice on the Companion Website at <http://www.prenhall.com/mcgrath>.

- Students can self-check odd-numbered exercises with the Suggested Answers section at the end of the book, while even-numbered exercises and Putting It All Together exercises can be used to monitor progress.

- The Preparing For and Taking Standardized Reading Tests section in the Appendix may help students prepare for and take any type of test, but is specifically for standardized reading tests where students cannot study specific content.

Jane L. McGrath
Paradise Valley Community College

ABOUT THE AUTHOR

Jane L. McGrath earned her undergraduate degrees in education and mass communications and her Ed.D. in reading education from Arizona State University. During her more than twenty-five years with the Maricopa Colleges, McGrath taught a variety of reading, English, journalism, and computer applications courses. McGrath has received Innovator of the Year honors from the Maricopa Colleges and the League of Innovation in Community Colleges. She has also received Outstanding Citizen awards from the cities of Phoenix and Tempe for her community service work. McGrath now combines talents with her husband Larry on a wide range of writing and computer projects from travel articles to cookbooks to technical pieces for the high-performance automotive industry. She is a member of the National Association of Developmental Educators and the College Reading and Learning Association.

BASIC SKILLS AND STRATEGIES
FOR COLLEGE READING

PREVIEWING TEXTBOOKS

CHAPTER PREVIEW

Objective

This chapter will develop your ability to preview textbooks to become familiar with their special features and aids.

Sections

1.1 Previewing a Textbook

1.2 Table of Contents

1.3 Preface

1.4 Author Information

1.5 Index

1.6 Appendix

1.7 Glossary

CHAPTER FOCUS

The word "preview" means to "look at or see in advance." In reading, the term preview means to survey, or examine, reading material in an orderly way *before* you begin to read.

Previewing gives you an overall picture of what you are going to read and gives you the chance to make connections between what you know and what you are going to read.

Previewing is like looking at a completed jigsaw puzzle before you try to fit the individual pieces together.

SECTION 1.1   PREVIEWING A TEXTBOOK

Previewing a textbook takes only a few minutes and it gives you a head start on successful reading. By knowing about the textbook, its author, and its aids before you start to read the first chapter, you can improve your comprehension and reduce your frustration. To preview a text, look at features and aids such as the following:

AT THE FRONT OF THE TEXT	AT THE BACK OF THE TEXT
Title Page	Glossary
Table of Contents	Appendix or Appendices
Preface	Index
Author Information	Answer Key

Practice your previewing skills in these exercises.

SECTION 1.2   TABLE OF CONTENTS

A table of contents is located in the first few pages of a textbook. It lists the titles, and often the subtitles, of the chapters and the page numbers on which they begin. Reading a table of contents gives you an overview of the topics and a picture of how they relate to one another.

CONTENTS

■ EXERCISE 1.1

Use the excerpt on the left, from the Contents of *Student Resource Guide to the Internet* by Cynthia B. Leshin, to answer these questions.

1. On what page would you begin reading to find out what it means to be "on the Internet"? _____

2. In which chapter would you look for information on how to use an Internet browser? _____

3. On what page does the Glossary (Geek Speak) begin? _____

4. How many appendices does the text have? List the title(s).

   _____

   _____

5. List the titles of the first three major sections in Chapter 2.

   _____

   _____

   _____

■ EXERCISE 1.2

Use the Contents in *this* textbook to answer these questions.

1. Where did you find the Contents? (List the page numbers.) _____

2. On what page does the Glossary begin? _____

3. How many thematic reading units are there? List the titles.

   _____

   _____

   _____

4. On what page would you begin reading to learn how to find the thesis of a multi-paragraph reading selection? _____

SECTION 1.3   PREFACE

Within the first few pages of some textbooks is an introductory letter from the author called the preface.

Reading a preface gives you information about the book such as who it is written for, what the author hopes readers will accomplish, and how the book is organized.

PREFACE

The Internet is a powerful medium for finding information, sharing information, and interacting with others. These capabilities offer new ways to access resources for school, college preparation, career planning, and finding a job. Some of the ways that you will find the Internet valuable as a tool for success in school, for improving your grades, and in preparing for a career include:

- finding the latest information on a subject for research papers;

- collecting data from others online;

- collaborating with others who share your research interests;

- cross-cultural exchanges with Netizens worldwide;

- meeting and learning from subject matter experts on virtually any topic;

- access to resources such as dictionaries, encyclopedias, and library catalogs worldwide;

- access to literature such as the classics and novels;

- access to news publications and electronic journals with resources for researching their databases for past articles or stories;

- access to databases of diverse information at universities, and government agencies; and

- learning about companies by visiting their Web sites.

In addition to helping you succeed in school, your understanding and knowledge about how to use the Internet provides you with important skills that employers value. In a time of rapid global change, companies realize that the Internet has an important role in their future. Most companies do not totally understand how the Internet will or can fit into their success, therefore they are looking for bright, knowledgeable, and enthusiastic individuals who will help pioneer this new electronic frontier. Many companies, in fact, are turning to the Internet to find

■ EXERCISE 1.3

Use the excerpt on the left, from Leshin's *Student Resource Guide to the Internet*, to answer these questions.

1. Leshin says the Internet is a powerful medium for _____

2. Leshin lists ten ways you will find the Internet a valuable tool. List the two most important to you today.

   _____

   _____

3. In addition to helping you succeed in school, how does Leshin think understanding the Internet will help you? _____

   _____

■ EXERCISE 1.4

Use the Preface in *this* textbook to answer these questions.

1. For whom did I write this book?

   _____

2. How do I want students to see themselves as they work through the text?

   _____

3. How is the book organized?

   _____

   _____

SECTION 1.4   AUTHOR INFORMATION

The author's name and school affiliation is often listed on the first page of the book, called the title page. Additional information about the author is sometimes included in a special About the Author section.

Reading about the author can give you information about his or her credentials to write the book.

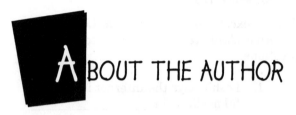

ABOUT THE AUTHOR

Cynthia Leshin is an educational technologies specialist with her doctorate in educational technology from Arizona State University. Dr. Leshin has her own consulting company—XPLORA. She consults with businesses and schools interested in learning about and implementing technology-rich environments for student success, improved learning, and customer support.

She has authored ten books for Simon and Schuster including *Internet Adventures—Step-by-Step Guide to Finding and Using Educational Resources; Netscape Adventures—Step-by-Step Guide to Netscape Navigator and the World Wide Web; Management on the World Wide Web;* and seven discipline-specific Internet books with Internet-based learning activities. She has also written a book, *Instructional Design: Strategies and Tactics.* Her expertise in educational psychology and theories of learning provides her with a unique background for translating complicated technical information into an easy-to-use, easy-to-understand, and practical learning resource.

Dr. Leshin has taught computer literacy and Internet classes at Arizona State University West and Estrella Mountain Community College. She has taught college-accredited Internet classes using distance learning technology for Educational Management Group, a Simon & Schuster company. The Internet serves as a tool for teaching and communicating with her students.

In Dr. Leshin's "other life" she rides mountain bikes and races for Cannondale's HeadShok team. She also enjoys organic gardening, hiking, skiing, scuba diving, and exploring southwestern trails with her three dread-locked Puli dogs and her husband, Steve.

■ EXERCISE 1.5

Use the excerpt on the left, from Leshin's *Student Resource Guide to the Internet*, to answer these questions.

1. What subjects has Leshin taught? Where has she taught?

   _____

   _____

   _____

   _____

2. In what field is Leshin's doctorate?

   _____

■ EXERCISE 1.6

Use the About the Author section in *this* textbook to answer these questions.

1. Is what field is McGrath's doctorate?

   _____

2. What information about McGrath did you find most interesting?

   _____

   _____

   _____

SECTION 1.5   INDEX

An index is an alphabetical list of the topics covered in the book and their page numbers. Names and titles of readings are sometimes included. If a text has an index, it is located at the end of the book.

Using the index can save you time when you need to locate specific information.

INDEX

ABC.com, 54
Academic institutions home pages,
    181–82
Access date, 109
ActiveX, 20, 43
Address. *See* URLs
Address location field, 22
Administrative address, 59–60
Adobe Acrobat reader, 45, 192
Airlines on the Web, 198–99
Algorithm, relevance ranking, 90
All Business Network, 144
AlphaWorld, 71
Alta Vista, 79, 91
Alternative Entertainment Network,
    54
*American Psychological Association
    (APA) Publication Manual*, 110
America Online (AOL), 16, 55, 70
America's Job Bank, 135
    exploring job opportunities on,
        150–53
Andreessen, Marc, 5
Animation, 42
Apollo, 145
Apple QuickTime Plug-In, 45
Applets, 42
Archeological link, 92–93
Argus Clearinghouse, 86
ARPANET, 4
Artists Underground, 54
Art online resources, 93
ASCII text, 140, 141
Ask An Expert, 100
AT&T College Network, 135, 164

Audio, streaming, 42
AudioNet, 54
Auto Channel, 54
Awesome List, 28

Banners, scrolling, 43
Bartlett's Familiar Quotations, 100
Berners-Lee, Tim, 5
Best Bets for Extending Your Search:
    Other Internet Job Guides,
    132–33
Best of the Web, 28
Beyond Mail, 7
Bookmarks, 25, 26, 82
    adding to folder, 31
    copying, 31–32
    deleting, 32
    exporting and saving, 32–33, 39
    importing, 33–34
    modifying name of, 31
    organizing (Netscape Navigator)
        28–31; (Internet Explorer)
        34–36, 37
    saving favorite Web sites, 28–36
    using Internet Explorer, 34–36, 37
    using Netscape Navigator, 28–34
Boolean logic, 84
Boolean operators, 82
Boston Globe, 136
Britannica Online, 100–1
Brown University, 182
Browser(s), 5, 6, 9, 11, 13, 42
    basics of, 20–4
    customizing, 39–41
    integration with desktop, 20

■ EXERCISE 1.7

Use the excerpt on the left, from Leshin's *Student Resource Guide to the Internet*, to answer these questions.

1. On what pages will you find information about importing bookmarks? _____

2. If you want to find information on "address," what other topic do you need to see? _____

■ EXERCISE 1.8

Use the Index in *this* textbook to answer these questions.

1. On what page will you find information on using context clues?

    _____

2. If you want to find information on "transition words," where do you need to look? _____

SECTION 1.6   APPENDIX

An appendix is a special section that contains extra or supplemental information. If a text has an appendix, it is located toward the end of the book. The plural of appendix is appendices.

Always check the appendices to see if the information is useful to you.

FINDING WEB SITES THAT HAVE MOVED

The Internet is a dynamic and rapidly changing environment. Information may be in one place today and either gone or in a new location tomorrow. New sites appear daily; others disappear. Some sites provide forwarding address information; others will not. As you travel in cyberspace and find that a resource you are looking for can no longer be found at a given Internet address, there are several steps you can take to find if the site has a new address.

- Check for a new Internet address or link, often provided on the site of the old address.

- Shorten the URL.

    The format for a URL is: **protocol//server-name/path**

    Try deleting the last section of the URL (path), so that the URL ends with the domain name or server name (com, edu, net, org). For example, you may be looking for NASA's links to astronomy sites. Take the original URL provided for the site, in this case **http://quest.arc.nasa.gov/lfs/other_sites.html,** and delete the last part of the address. **lfs/other_sites.html** leaving **http://quest.arc.nasa.gov.** You will most likely get to NASA's Home Page and can navigate to the specific topic or category you are looking for.

- Type in a company name for the URL.

    Companies usually use either their name, some part of their name, or an abbreviation as their domain name that becomes their URL. Netscape 2.02 and 3.0 accept abbreviated Net addresses, without the **http://www.** prefix. If you type a single word as your URL, Netscape adds the prefix **http://www.** and the suffix **.com.** For example, to connect to Netscape's Home

■ EXERCISE 1.9

Use the excerpt on the left, from Leshin's *Student Resource Guide to the Internet*, to answer this question.

1. What information is in this appendix?

    _____

    _____

■ EXERCISE 1.10

Use the appendix in *this* textbook to answer this question.

1. How many appendices does *this* text contain? List the title(s).

    _____

SECTION 1.7   GLOSSARY

If a text has its own dictionary—called a glossary—it is located toward the back of the book.

Using the glossary is helpful because it gives the meanings of words specific to the context.

GEEK SPEAK

ActiveX: Microsoft's response to Java was the *ActiveX* development platform. This technology makes it possible for Web programmers to create and for Web surfers to view moving and animated objects, live audio, scrolling banners, and interactivity. The *ActiveX* technology—available in Microsoft Internet Explorer—allows viewing of many plug-in applications without first downloading and installing the required plug-in. *ActiveX* lets desktop applications be linked to the World Wide Web, for example, programs such as Word can be viewed directly from Explorer.

administrative address: The email address used for sending requests to listservs for either text documents or subscriptions to a mailing list.

anonymous FTP: The method used in file transfer protocol that allows Internet users to log into an FTP server as an unregistered user. Before browsers were used for FTP, users connecting to an FTP server would have to log in by entering a login name and password. The login name was anonymous; the password, your email address.

---

bit: A single-digit number, either a 1 or a 0, that represents the smallest unit of computerized data.

bookmarks: A feature providing the user with the opportunity to mark favorite pages for fast and easy access. Netscape's bookmarks can be organized hierarchically and customized by the user through the Bookmark List dialog box.

Boolean operators: Phrases or words such as "AND," "OR," and "NOT" that limit a search using Internet search engines.

browser: A client program that interprets and displays HTML documents.

client: A software program assisting in contacting a server somewhere on the Net for information. Examples of client software programs are Gopher, Netscape, Veronica, and Archie. An Archie client runs on a system configured to contact a specific Archie database to query for information.

compression: A process by which a file or a folder is made smaller. The three primary purposes of compression are to save disk space, to save space when doing a backup, and to speed the transmission of a file when transferring via a modem or network.

cookie: Cookie technology allows the storage of personal preferences for use with Internet information and communication tools. A text file is created of a user's preferences, saved in their browser's folder, and stored in RAM while the browser is running. For example, a popular Web audio site, Timecast, allows users to select their personal audio preferences to be played with RealAudio. These personal preferences are saved in a browser folder called a *cookie file*. When the user connects to the site, the server at that site looks for the cookie file on the user's computer to find their specifications.

delayed-response media: Internet communication tools that require time for an end-user to respond (e.g., electronic mail, listservs, and newsgroups).

digerati: A community of diverse professionals—computer scientists, film makers, designers, engineers, architects, artists, writers, musicians—who are becoming increasingly wealthy through their creative and innovative use and exploration of digital technology. Louis Rossetto and Jane Metcalfe (*Wired* magazine) were the first to give a name to these digital elite whom they believed were becoming the most powerful people on earth.

domain name: The unique name that identifies an Internet site. Names have two or more parts separated by a dot such as **xplora.com.**

finger: An Internet software tool for locating people on the Internet. The most common use is to see if an individual has an account at a particular Internet site.

■ EXERCISE 1.11

Use the excerpt on the left, from Leshin's *Student Resource Guide to the Internet*, to answer these questions.

1. In Leshin's book, what does the word *bookmark* mean?

    _____

2. In Leshin's book, what is a *cookie*?

    _____

■ EXERCISE 1.12

Use the Glossary in *this* textbook to answer these questions.

1. In *this* textbook, what does *paragraph* mean?

    _____

2. In *this* textbook what does the word *inference* mean?

LOOKING AHEAD   Strategies you can use to preview a multi-paragraph reading assignment such as a text chapter or a magazine article are included in Chapter 6.

CHAPTER REVIEW

SUMMARY OF KEY IDEAS

- To preview means to survey, or examine, reading material in an orderly way *before* you begin to read.
- Previewing gives you an overall picture of what you are going to read and gives you the chance to make connections between what you know and what you are going to read.
- During preview you examine a text's features and aids that can give you a head start on good comprehension, such as the title page, table of contents, preface, author information, glossary, appendix, index, and answer key.

PUTTING IT ALL TOGETHER

Use a textbook from another class or a text you borrow from your college's learning center to answer these questions.

1. List the title and author of the text.
2. List the page numbers of the table of contents.
3. List the title of each chapter.
4. List the aids the book contains such as preface, glossary, index, and answer key and the page numbers on which they appear.
5. Who is this book written for? If there isn't a preface, write your prediction about the book's purpose.
6. What does the author hope readers will accomplish?
7. List two pieces of information about the author.
8. How many appendices does the text contain? List the title(s).
9. When do you think you might use the information in the appendix?
10. If there is a glossary, list the first and last word entries. If the text uses another method to define words, such as in the margins, please describe it.

LOG ON TO THE WEB

A variety of Internet sites give readers an opportunity to preview books before they buy them. For example, e-bookstores such as Amazon.com and bn.com often post a summary of a book's content, reviewer's comments, and even a sample chapter. College textbook publishers like Prentice Hall post information about each of their books. The Web pages typically include the table of contents, a description of the intended reader, information about the author, and a description of print and electronic supplements.

For the purpose of this Web assignment, assume you are a member of a committee assigned to find out what textbooks are available in one of your favorite subject areas, such as psychology, general business, or computer applications. To begin your search, log on to Prentice Hall's academic catalog at <http://www.prenhall.com/list_ac/index.html>.

Go to the list of texts available in your subject area and select one text to preview. Go to that textbook's homepage and read all the information available on the text and the author.

Write down: (1) the name of the text, (2) who the text is written for, (3) how many chapters the book contains, (4) a description of any aids the book contains, such as a glossary, (5) a description of any print and electronic supplements for the book such as a Companion Website or CD, and (6) what you discovered about the author.

IDEAS FOR WRITING AND DISCUSSION

A. Visit your college learning center and interview a tutor or staff member to discover their best advice on how to be successful in your classes. Describe how you can use the advice.

B. List and explain the skills, attitudes, and behaviors you think are most important to college success.

CHAPTER 2

UNDERSTANDING WORDS

CHAPTER PREVIEW

Objectives

- Use the context to help define words and phrases.
- Use the parts of a word to help define it.
- Use a dictionary and/or a glossary to define words and phrases.
- Use other resources for defining words and phrases.
- Remember the meanings of words and phrases.

Sections

CHAPTER FOCUS

Words are important. They are the raw material we use to write everything from e-mail messages and memos to letters, stories, and essays. Therefore, when you don't understand a word an author uses, you may not understand what he or she is writing about.

There are several resources you can use to help define a word. However, just finding a definition isn't always enough. To understand an author's specific meaning for a word, you must look at the word in context—how it is used with the other words in the sentence and surrounding sentences. This is because words take on meaning from their context.

For example, *run* is a common everyday word. However, if a friend asks you to define *run*, you'd need to know which *run* she means: for example, *run* as in "the player hit a home run," or "she had a run in her pantyhose," or "he was going to run to the store," or "she was going to run for office." Once you know the context—the situation or the rest of the words—you could give a good definition.

Like *run*, many words have more than one meaning.

Example   Think about the definitions of the word *medium* in these sentences.

1. The Internet is a powerful <u>medium</u> for finding information.
2. Copper is a good <u>medium</u> for conducting heat.
3. I asked for my hamburger to be cooked <u>medium</u>—more than rare, but less than well-done.
4. At the state fair we saw a fortune teller and a <u>medium</u> to try to communicate with my dead uncle's spirit.
5. The artist used watercolors on cloth as the <u>medium</u> for her work.

Explanation   Understanding the way the word is used with the other words in the sentence helps you understand the specific meaning of *medium*.

In sentence 1, *medium* is a means of communication.

In sentence 2, *medium* is something that carries energy.

In sentence 3, *medium* is an intermediate amount.

In sentence 4, *medium* is a person who channels communication between the earthly world and spirits.

In sentence 5, *medium* is the technique and material used by an artist.

Therefore, whatever resource you use to define a word, always make sure the meaning you select makes sense in the author's context. The more words you understand, the more accurately and completely you will understand the author.

SECTION 2.1   USING CONTEXT CLUES TO DEFINE WORDS AND PHRASES

Authors often provide clues to help you understand words and phrases. This means you can often figure out a word's meaning just by using the author's clues. Unless a sentence is very difficult, using context clues can be a quick and efficient way to help ensure a correct definition.

For example, in Sentence 3 above, I said "I asked for my hamburger to be cooked <u>medium</u>—more than rare, but less than well-done." Even though you knew what *medium* meant, the punctuation (—) was a clue that more information was coming. Then, "more than rare, but less than well-done" explained it was an amount in between rare and well-done.

Authors often use punctuation marks, such as a dash, colon, parenthesis, or comma, to call attention to a context clue.

Another technique authors use is to directly state a definition for the unfamiliar word.

Example   A <u>liquid asset</u> is cash or any other asset that can be converted to cash with a minimum amount of trouble and no loss in market value. (Winger and Frasca, *Personal Finance*)

Explanation   In this sentence Winger and Frasca directly state that the definition of *liquid asset* is "cash or any other asset that can be converted to cash with a minimum amount of trouble and no loss in market value."

Example   <u>Portamento</u>—sliding or gliding from one tone to the next—is extensively used in American Black music, both vocal and instrumental. (Brooks, *America's Black Musical Heritage*)

Explanation   In this sentence Brooks defines the musical term *portamento* as "sliding or gliding from one tone to the next" and sets it off with dashes.

Sometimes authors help you understand a word or phrase by giving an example or an explanation.

Example   <u>Ordinary contractions</u>—can't, haven't, isn't—can be used in most current magazine articles. (McGrath, *Magazine Article Writing Basics*)

Explanation   To help my writing students understand what I mean by *ordinary contractions* I give three examples and set them off with dashes.

Example   Using <u>Hypertext Markup Language</u> (HTML), the programming language used to create a Web page, formats the text of the document and specifies links to other documents. (Leshin, *Student Resource Guide to the Internet*)

Explanation   In this sentence Leshin uses commas to set off her explanation that *Hypertext Markup Language* is "the programming language used to create a Web page."

Occasionally, authors use the opposite of the unfamiliar word as a clue.

Example   The expensive, high-end recreational vehicles (RVs) that roam today's highways offer luxuries most <u>stationary homeowners</u> would envy. (Kronemyer, "Living on the Road," *Active Times*)

Explanation   In this sentence Kronemyer makes it clear that *stationary homeowners* are the opposite of those who own RV homes. Since RVs move from place to place, stationary homes are houses and apartments built to stay in one place.

Authors also combine context clues to help you understand the meaning of a word or phrase.

Example   <u>Nonverbal behavior</u> plays a strong, necessary role in interpersonal relationships. So much can be "said" by a smile, hug, or handclasp that words are often not needed. (Barker and Barker, *Communications*)

Explanation   To define *nonverbal behavior*, Baker and Baker give examples, "a smile, hug, or handclasp," and an explanation, "words are often not needed."

Word meanings you figure out using context clues are not wild guesses. They are the logical result of combining all the information about the word an author provides. We call this process *making an inference*. An inference is a sensible, reasoned conclusion based on the information you are given.

LOOKING AHEAD   Strategies you can use to make valid inferences, as well as practice exercises, are included in Chapter 5.

■ EXERCISE 2.1: USING THE CONTEXT TO HELP DEFINE WORDS AND PHRASES

Use the author's context clues to discover the meaning of the underlined words and phrases in these sentences. Circle the best definition.

Example   The tornado left only <u>devastation</u> in its path. The town—homes, buildings, cars—was completely destroyed.

      a. flooding

      b. total destruction

      c. construction

      d. trees

Explanation   From the examples "homes, buildings, and cars" being completely destroyed, we can infer the town was totally destroyed.

1. A decision to <u>terminate</u>—fire—an employee should never be made on the spur of the moment.

      a. limit

      b. confine

      c. fire

      d. hire

2. <u>Aseptic</u> means germ free, or without disease-producing organisms.

      a. disease germs

      b. bacteria

      c. a cut or injury

      d. without germs

3. A <u>savvy</u> consumer, one who shops around, can often find remarkably good buys on clothing.

      a. lazy

      b. sharp

    c.   foolish

    d.   unaware

4. In gaming <u>meccas</u> such as Las Vegas, Atlantic City, and Reno, the gambling options are unlimited.

    a.   casinos

    b.   buildings

    c.   centers of activity

    d.   churches

5. The Central Library offers a monthly lecture series in <u>conjunction</u> with the college to make the best use of expert speakers and facilities.

    a.   working together

    b.   working separately

    c.   cultural

    d.   competition

6. Employees who think products are more important than customers <u>hinder</u>, rather than help, sales.

    a.   increase

    b.   hurt

    c.   help

    d.   assist

7. Before making a large purchase, consumers should make sure they are dealing with a <u>reputable</u> company, one that is known for good products and customer service.

    a.   famous

    b.   dishonest

    c.   large

    d.   honest

8. In addition to providing meaning and purpose in our lives, spending time helping others may have a <u>positive effect</u> on our health.

    a.   good influence

    b.   unknown result

    c.   harmful result

    d.   limiting outcome

9. Early hunter-gatherer settlements were never large and were of <u>relatively short duration</u> because, as one area was "picked over," the tribe was forced to move on.

    a.   family-oriented

    b.   clean

    c.   inferior

    d.   for a brief time

10. As farmers left the countryside in search of work in new factories, whole villages were <u>abandoned</u>, while nearby factory towns swelled into big cities.

    a.   looted

    b.   defended

    c.   deserted

    d.   full

■ **EXERCISE 2.2: USING THE CONTEXT TO HELP DEFINE WORDS AND PHRASES**

Use the author's context clues to discover the meaning of the underlined words and phrases in these sentences. Write the definition.

1. <u>Leadership</u> (the process of influence) can originate from a number of sources. (Manz and Neck, *Mastering Self-Leadership*)

   _____

   _____

2. There is some form of <u>measurement</u> or evaluation for every job. (Chapman and O'Neil, *Your Attitude Is Showing*)

   _____

   _____

3. "Although we have not received many complaints about Internet scams, they are <u>abundant</u>," she said. (Holstein, "How to Avoid Con Artists," *The Arizona Republic*)

   _____

   _____

4. <u>Acculturation</u> is the process by which a certain people are influenced by a foreign culture. (Brown, *The Art of Rock and Roll*)

   _____

   _____

5. In Tanzania, women and girls in rural villages may have to walk miles to collect the water—often polluted—that they will use for drinking, cooking and washing. Similar <u>treks</u> of increasing length must be taken to collect the firewood for cooking. (Nebel and Wright, *Environmental Science*)

   _____

   _____

6. At the end of the glacier, tidal action causes '<u>calving</u>': A slab of ice breaks off, and an iceberg is born. (Whelan, "Ice Police Cry, 'Stop That Berg!'" *Wall Street Journal*)

   _____

   _____

7. A variety of <u>domestic</u> and business applications form the foundation of personal computing. Domestic applications include maintaining an up-to-date inventory of household items; storing names and addresses for a personal mailing list; maintaining records for, preparing, and sending personal income tax returns; creating and monitoring a household budget; keeping an appointment and social calendar; handling household finances.... (Long and Long, *Computing*)

   _____

   _____

8. Some Internet search engines permit the use of <u>Boolean operators</u> (words such as "and," "or," and "not") to restrict the search. (Leshin, *Student Resource Guide to the Internet*)

   _____

   _____

9. A loan's <u>balloon payment</u> is usually the last installment payment, and it is for an amount much greater than the other monthly payments. (Winger and Frasca, *Personal Finance*)

   _____

   _____

10. The meals you eat away from home generally contain more fat and less fiber, iron and calcium. Thus, they tend to be <u>less nutritious</u>. (Heilman, "Health Tips," *Active Times*)

    _____

    _____

11. It all started with the "smiley" figure that shows someone is happy or telling a joke. Now a new language is developing as clever people use computer keystrokes to create <u>emoticons</u>, symbols that convey thoughts and emotions. (Macionis, *Sociology*)

    _____

    _____

12. When you understand the <u>primitive</u> beginnings of medicine, you appreciate the advances made during the past 5,000 years. (Badasch and Chesebro, *Introduction to Health Occupations*)

    _____

    _____

13. Because Earth is related to all other objects in space, the science of <u>astronomy</u>—the study of the universe—is very useful in probing the origins of our own environment. (Lutgens and Tarbuck, *Foundations of Earth Science*)

    _____

    _____

14. Identifying an object, act, or person by name so that she, he, or it can be referred to in communication is known as <u>labeling</u>. (Barker and Barker, *Communication*)

    _____

    _____

15. For now, reaching 100 is still considered news. Of the 273 million people in the United States, only 70,000 are <u>centenarians</u>. But in the next 50 years, as science extends the span of human life, 100th birthdays will become more common. (Warshofsky, "The Methuselah Factor," *Modern Maturity*)

    _____

    _____

■ **EXERCISE 2.3: USING THE CONTEXT TO HELP DEFINE WORDS AND PHRASES**

Using one of your texts, identify five sentences with unfamiliar words where the author provides a context clue. Copy the sentences onto a sheet of notebook paper, underline the unfamiliar words, and write the definitions.

SECTION 2.2   USING THE PARTS OF A WORD TO HELP DEFINE IT

Another strategy you can use to help understand a word is to examine the parts of the word. A strategy is an action you select to achieve a particular goal.

For example, some words are made by combining two components that are words themselves—*commonplace, headache, policeman.* You can often define these compound words by defining each individual word.

You can also look for a root word and any prefixes and/or suffixes. The root is the basic part of a word. A prefix can be added to the beginning of a root word and/or a suffix can be added at the end of a root word to make other words. Prefixes and suffixes change the meaning of the root word. A suffix can also change the way a word can be used in a sentence and its part of speech.

By Jeff Stahler, The Cincinnati Post, Newspaper Enterprise Association

Knowing the meanings of word parts—roots, prefixes and suffixes—helps you unlock and understand the meanings of whole families of words. For example, knowing that the Latin root *manus* means "hand" can provide a clue to the meaning of the words built with the root, such as *manual* (doing physical work with the hands) and *manuscript* (written by hand).

However, because many of our roots, prefixes, and suffixes come from the ancient Latin, Greek, and Anglo-Saxon languages, the changes in spelling and meaning over the years can make using this strategy a challenge. For example, since the word *manufacture* is made from the root *manus*, manufacture should mean "make by hand." Although that definition was accurate many years ago, today manufacture generally means "making something by any means, but especially with machinery."

Nevertheless, knowing even a few word parts can help unlock the meanings of many unknown words.

Example
Everyone agrees that hiring an employee is a <u>multistep</u> process.
The college offers an excellent <u>multicultural</u> program for future teachers.
Before you can experience <u>multimedia</u> Web sites, you need to install some basic plug-ins.

Explanation   Knowing that the prefix *multi* means "many," you are better able to understand the sentences.

The following table lists some common word parts and their definitions.

ROOTS			
aud, aur	hear	*literate, literatus*	able to read/write
annus (ennal)	year	*manus*	by hand
carcin	cancer	*mille*	1,000
cardio	heart	*mit*	send
chrono	time	*mor, mort*	die
cred	belief	*nom, nomen*	name
demos	the people	*pathy*	feeling
divers	different	*phob*	fear
duc, duct	lead, make, shape	*psycho*	mind, soul
geron, geras	aging, old age	*port*	carry
graph, graphy	writing, record	*scribe, script*	write
hyper	more than normal	*spec*	see

PREFIXES			
ante-	before	*micro-*	small
anti-, contra-	against	*mal-*	badly, inadequate
auto-	self	*mis-*	wrongly
bi-	two, both	*mono-*	one, single
bio-	living organisms	*multi-*	many
circum-	around	*para-*	beside, beyond
con-	with	*poly-*	many
contra-	against	*post-*	after, behind
dis-	not or away	*pre-*	before, in front of
ec-, eco-	habitat	*pro-*	in favor of, ahead of
em-, im-	to give	*proto-*	original; chief
en-	to make; cause	*pseudo-*	false
ex-	out of	*re-*	again
hemi-	half	*retro-*	backward
hyper-	excessive, more than	*quadri-, quadr-*	four
hypo-	low, less than	*semi-*	half
il-, in-, ir-	in/into or not	*sub-*	under, below
inter-	among, between	*super-, supra-*	above
intra-	within, inside	*tele-, trans-*	across, over a distance
macro-	large	*ultra-*	super, excessive
mega-	large	*un-, non-*	not
mal-	bad	*uni-, mono-*	one

SUFFIXES			
-able, -ible	able to	*-graphy*	writing or science
-al	characterized by	*-ism*	manner of action
-ance, -ancy	action, quality, amount	*-less*	without
-ence, -ency	action, quality of	*-logy*	oral/written expression
-er, -or, -ist	one who	*-ly*	like
-fy	make, form into	*-ment*	action
-ful	full of	*-ology*	study of

■ **EXERCISE 2.4: USING THE PARTS OF A WORD TO HELP DEFINE IT**

Use your understanding of common word parts to discover the meaning of the underlined words in these sentences. Circle the best definition.

> ***Example***   It's possible to be <u>hypersensitive</u> to anything in your diet.
>
>> a.   dislike
>> b.   undersensitive
>> c.   oversensitive
>> d.   enjoy

> ***Explanation***   The prefix *hyper* means more than normal. Therefore, you can be more sensitive than normal or "oversensitive" to anything in your diet.

1. Although many considered his actions old-fashioned, he lived by a strict <u>creed</u>.
   a.   aging
   b.   set of beliefs
   c.   perfection
   d.   set of mistakes

2. During her second year of medical studies, she decided to specialize in <u>geriatrics</u>.
   a.   problems of aging people
   b.   problems of children
   c.   problems of the skin
   d.   problems of the eyes

3. There was much fear and excitement at the start of the new <u>millennium</u>.
   a.   year
   b.   century
   c.   thousand-year period
   d.   golden age

4. The college encouraged <u>intramural</u> sports activities.
   a.   team games
   b.   contact sports
   c.   games played with teams from other colleges
   d.   games played among teams within the college

5. Recent legislative actions have targeted certain sweepstakes promoters and <u>telemarketers</u>. Telemarketers are people who:
   a. sell products by mail
   b. sell products over the phone
   c. sell products at flea markets
   d. sell products door-to-door

6. The business owner hired a new accountant when he discovered thousands of dollars had been <u>misappropriated</u>.
   a. wrongly used
   b. given away
   c. hidden
   d. saved

7. She thought cigar smoke was quite <u>disagreeable</u>.
   a. sweet-smelling
   b. harmful
   c. pleasant
   d. unpleasant

8. Many children throughout the world are <u>malnourished</u>.
   a. poor
   b. without enough to eat
   c. in foster homes
   d. without access to education

9. In the future we will see more <u>proactive</u> approaches to the way diseases are detected and treated, such as early detection and prevention.
   a. using technology to help
   b. fearful
   c. acting before a problem happens
   d. limited

10. Behavioral techniques have proved successful in treating <u>phobias</u>, especially simple and social phobias.
    a. temptations
    b. a fondness for
    c. fears
    d. accidents

■ **EXERCISE 2.5: USING THE PARTS OF A WORD TO HELP DEFINE IT**

Use your understanding of common word parts to unlock the meaning of the underlined words in these sentences. Write the definition.

1. Experts would tell baby boomers that the only thing they have to fear is <u>gerontophobia</u> itself. (Lague, "The Longevity Masters," *Modern Maturity*)

   _____

   _____

2. Goals are generally more effective for managing our immediate behavior if they are specific and challenging, yet <u>achievable</u>. (Manz and Neck, *Mastering Self-Leadership*)

_____

_____

3. Psychosocially healthy people recognize that there are others whose needs are greater than their own. They <u>enrich</u> the lives of others. (Donatelle and Davis, *Access to Health*)

_____

_____

4. Because geographers are trained in a broad range of topics, they are particularly well equipped to understand <u>interactions</u> between people and their environment. (Rubenstein, *An Introduction to Human Geography*)

_____

_____

5. We cannot determine if someone is <u>chronologically</u> 80 years old, yet biologically 60. There is no one-size-fits-all span for human life. (Warshofsky, "The Methuselah Factor, *Modern Maturity*)

_____

_____

6. Although prominent public figures may have great <u>credibility</u>, their statements should not keep us from asking our own questions. (Davis and Palladino, *Psychology*)

_____

_____

7. Ill-timed self-disclosures (telling about ourselves, our values, attitudes, and beliefs) can result in others seeing us as <u>maladjusted</u>. (Bittner, *Each Other*)

_____

_____

8. The inventory of e-mail devices is growing as more people, even techies, seek fast and <u>portable</u> ways to e-mail. (Dreyfuss, *Simply e-mail*)

   _____

   _____

9. To strive for something difficult, to go beyond what's called for in everyday life, becomes <u>empowering</u>.... (Beckley, director of Alpine Ascents International travel company)

   _____

   _____

10. In the late 1960s, jeans acquired an image of youthful independence in the United States, as young people adopted a style of clothing previously associated with low-status <u>manual</u> laborers and farmers. (Rubenstein, *An Introduction to Human Geography*)

    _____

    _____

■ **EXERCISE 2.6: USING THE PARTS OF A WORD TO HELP DEFINE IT**

Using a text from one of your other classes, identify five unfamiliar words where your understanding of common word parts helps you unlock the meaning. Copy the sentences containing the words onto a sheet of notebook paper, underline the unfamiliar words, and write the definitions.

SECTION 2.3   USING A DICTIONARY TO DEFINE WORDS AND PHRASES

We often use a dictionary to check the spelling of a word. It's also a good source for definitions. That makes using a dictionary another good strategy for finding the meaning of an unfamiliar word.

In addition to definitions, a dictionary includes the pronunciation, history, and parts of speech of the word. A word entry may even include synonyms and antonyms. Synonyms are words and phrases that have the same or nearly the same meaning. Antonyms are words that mean the opposite.

Dictionaries are not all the same. The more familiar you are with the content and layout of yours, the easier it will be to use.

The annotated graphic at the top of page 22 shows material from page 311 in *Webster's New World Dictionary, Third College Edition*, which contains the words from *Corpus Christi* to *Corrode*. As you study the annotated graphic, notice how much information beyond the definition is given for the word *Correct*.

Definitions In this dictionary, definitions are arranged in historical order, so the more recent or common meanings may be near the end of the entry.

Corpus Christi / corrode ← **Guide Words** at the top of a page give the first and last word entries on that page.

Pronunciation tells how the word is most commonly used by English speakers. Symbols used are explained in a "Key to Pronunciation." (See below)

Word History (Etymology) tells how the word came into English, using symbols such as ME for Middle English and < for "derived from."

Main Entry All main entries are listed in strict alphabetical order. If the word can be spelled more than one way, all variations are listed.

cor·rect (kə rekt′) *vt.* ⟦ ME *correcten* < L *correctus*, pp. of *corrigere* < *com-*, together + *regere*, to lead straight, rule: see RECKON ⟧ **1** to make right; change from wrong to right; remove errors from **2** to point out or mark the errors or faults of **3** to make conform to a standard **4** to scold or punish so as to cause to rectify faults **5** to cure, remove, or counteract (a fault, disease, etc.) —*vi.* to make corrections; specif., to make an adjustment so as to compensate (*for* an error, counteracting force, etc.) —*adj.* **1** conforming or adhering to an established standard; proper *[correct* behavior*]* **2** conforming to fact or logic; true, accurate, right, or free from errors **3** equal to the required or established amount, number, price, etc. —**cor·rect′-able** *adj.* —**cor·rect′ly** *adv.* —**cor·rect′ness** *n.* —**cor·rec′tor** *n.*

Part-of-Speech Labels When a word is used as more than one part of speech, long dashes introduce each different part of speech.

Synonyms/Antonyms Some dictionaries list words that mean the same as and words that mean the opposite of the main word.

SYN.—**correct** connotes little more than absence of error *[a correct* answer*]* or adherence to conventionality *[correct* behavior*]*; **accurate** implies a positive exercise of care to obtain conformity with fact or truth *[an accurate* account of the events*]*; **exact** stresses perfect conformity to fact, truth, or some standard *[the exact* time, an *exact* quotation*]*; **precise** suggests minute accuracy of detail and often connotes a finicky or overly fastidious attitude *[precise* in all his habits*]* See also PUNISH —**ANT. wrong, false**

Key to Pronunciation The key at the bottom of a dictionary page shows how the symbols sound.

at, āte, cär; ten, ēve; is, ice; gō, hôrn, look, tool; oil, out; up, fur; ə *for unstressed vowels, as* a *in* ago, u *in* focus; ′ *as in* Latin (lat′′n); chin; she; zh *as in* azure (azh′ər); thin, *the*; ŋ *as in* ring (riŋ) *In etymologies:* * = unattested; < = derived from; > = from which ☆ = Americanism   **See inside front and back covers**

Since you usually find several definitions for a word, you must read through the definitions to find the one that best fits the context. Keep in mind, however, that because of writing style differences and language changes, a dictionary definition probably won't fit word-for-word into the sentence you're reading. When that happens, put the definition into your own words and try that in the sentence to be sure it makes sense.

Example   Which dictionary definition best fits the word "critically" in this sentence?

We want you to be able to evaluate <u>critically</u> the information you read and hear in the media and elsewhere. (Davis and Palladino, *Psychology*)

criti·cal (krit′i kəl) *adj.* **1** tending to find fault; censorious **2** characterized by careful analysis and judgment *[a sound critical* estimate of the problem*]* **3** of critics or criticism **4** of or forming a crisis or turning point; decisive **5** dangerous or risky; causing anxiety *[a critical* situation in international relations*]* **6** of the crisis of a disease **7** designating or of important products or raw materials subject to increased production and restricted distribution under strict control, as in wartime **8** *a)* designating or of a point at which a change in character, property, or condition is effected *b)* designating or of the point at which a nuclear chain reaction becomes self-sustaining —**crit′i·cally** *adv.* —**crit′i·cal′ity** (-kal′ə tē) or **crit′i·cal·ness** *n.*

Explanation   Definition 2 is the most appropriate. The authors are saying they want you to think about and objectively judge—consider both the merits and faults of—the information you read and hear.

USING A GLOSSARY

A glossary, like the one in the back of this text, is an in-book dictionary. It includes an alphabetical listing of the text's important, difficult, and technical words and phrases. A glossary is a quick, easy-to-use resource because it only lists the specific meaning of the word as it is used in the book. Content area texts often contain glossaries.

Example   Assume you are reading Politsoke's *Music* text for your Introduction to Music class. You come to this sentence with the unfamiliar word *accidentals*.

In classical music, at least before Beethoven, <u>accidentals</u> tend to appear as surprising touches or as part of a predictable change of key. (Politsoke, *Music*)

Compare the definitions for the word *accidental* you would find if you looked it up in *Webster's New World Dictionary* and in the glossary in Politsoke's Music text.

The entry in *Webster's New World Dictionary*:

ac·ci·den·tal (ak′sə dent″l) *adj.* ⟦ME < LL *accidentalis*: see prec. ⟧ **1** happening by chance; fortuitous **2** belonging but not essential; attributive; incidental **3** *Music* of an accidental —*n.* **1** a nonessential quality or feature **2** *Music a)* a sign, as a sharp, flat, or natural, placed before a note to show a change of pitch from that indicated by the key signature *b)* the tone indicated by such a sign —**ac′ci·den′tal·ly** *adv.*

The glossary entry in Politsoke's *Music* text:

accidental   Sharp, flat, or natural sign before a note indicating that the pitch is not to be played as it normally would be in a given key, but is to be altered according to the sign.

Explanation   The glossary entry is specific to the way Politsoke is using it, whereas the dictionary provides all possible definitions.

However, not all books provide a glossary and even those that do sometimes won't provide enough information, so you may still need to use a dictionary.

■ EXERCISE 2.7: USING A DICTIONARY TO DEFINE WORDS AND PHRASES

Decide which dictionary definition best explains the underlined words. Underline the correct dictionary definition and write the meaning.

Example   Up to 90 percent of allergic reactions while eating are <u>triggered</u> by a handful of foods: eggs, soybeans, wheat, milk, fish, nuts, and shellfish.

trig·ger (trig′ər) *n.* ⟦earlier *tricker* < Du *trekker* < *trekken*, to draw, pull: see TREK ⟧ **1** a small lever or part which when pulled or pressed releases a catch, spring, etc. **2** in firearms, a small lever pressed back by the finger to activate the firing mechanism **3** an act, impulse, etc. that initiates an action, series of events, etc. —*vt.* **1** to fire or activate by pulling or pressing a trigger **2** to initiate (an action); set off *[the fight that triggered the riot]* —☆**quick on the trigger** [Colloq.] **1** quick to fire a gun **2** quick to act, understand, retort, etc.; alert

Answer   *Triggered* means <u>caused by.</u>

Explanation   In the example sentence, *triggered* is used as a verb (action word), not a noun (name of person, place, or thing). Of the two verb definitions given, the second one fits this context.

1. Desert landscapes frequently appear <u>stark</u>. (Lutgens and Tarbuck, *Foundations of Earth Science*)

   stark (stärk) *adj.* 〚ME *starc* < OE *stearc*: see STARE〛 **1** *a)* stiff or rigid, as a corpse *b)* rigorous; harsh; severe *[stark* discipline*]* **2** sharply outlined or prominent *[one stark* tree*]* **3** bleak; desolate; barren *[stark* wasteland*]* **4** *a)* emptied; stripped *[stark* shelves*]* *b)* totally naked; bare **5** grimly blunt; unsoftened, unembellished, etc. *[stark* realism*]* **6** sheer; utter; downright; unrelieved *[stark* terror*]* **7** [Archaic] strong; powerful —*adv.* in a stark manner; esp., utterly; wholly *[stark* mad*]* —**stark′ly** *adv.* —**stark′ness** *n.*

2. The <u>angle</u> from which an object is photographed can often serve as an author's comment on the subject matter. (Giannetti, *Understanding Movies*)

   an·gle[1] (aŋ′gəl) *n.* 〚ME & OFr < L *angulus*, a corner, angle < Gr *ankylos*, bent, crooked: see ANKLE〛 **1** *a)* the shape made by two straight lines meeting at a common point, the vertex, or by two planes meeting along an edge (see DIHEDRAL, SPHERICAL ANGLE) *b)* SOLID ANGLE **2** the space between, or within, such lines or planes **3** the measure of this space, expressed in degrees, radians, or steradians **4** a sharp or projecting corner **5** an aspect, as of something viewed or considered; point of view *[to* examine a problem from all *angles]* **6** [Colloq.] *a)* a motive *b)* a tricky method for achieving a purpose —*vt., vi.* -**gled**, -**gling 1** to move or bend at an angle or by means of angles **2** [Colloq.] to give a specific point of view to (a story, report, etc.) —**SYN.** PHASE[1]

3. To be part of the solution to preventing hate and bias crimes you can support educational programs designed to <u>foster</u> understanding and appreciation for differences in people. Many colleges now require diversity classes as part of their academic curriculum. (Donatelle and Davis, *Access to Health*)

   fos·ter (fôs′tər, fäs′-) *vt.* 〚ME *fostren* < OE *fostrian*, to nourish, bring up < *fostor*, food, nourishment < base of *foda*, FOOD〛 **1** to bring up with care; rear **2** to help to grow or develop; stimulate; promote *[to foster* discontent*]* **3** to cling to in one's mind; cherish *[foster* a hope*]* —*adj.* **1** having the standing of a specified member of the family, though not by birth or adoption, and giving, receiving, or sharing the care appropriate to that standing *[foster* parent, *foster* brother*]* **2** designating or relating to such care —**fos′ter·er** *n.*

4. World War I proved a <u>watershed</u> for many aspects of American art and life, and certainly for music. (Politoske, *Music*)

   wa|ter·shed (-shed′) *n.* **1** a ridge or stretch of high land dividing the areas drained by different rivers or river systems ☆**2** the area drained by a river or river system **3** a crucial turning point affecting action, opinion, etc.

5. If you speak below your listeners' educational level, they more than likely will be not only bored but also angry when they discover they are being <u>patronized</u>. (Baker and Baker, *Communications*)

   pa·tron·ize (pā′trən īz′, pa′-) *vt.* -**ized**′, -**iz′ing 1** to act as a patron toward; sponsor; support **2** to be kind or helpful to, but in a haughty or snobbish way, as if dealing with an inferior **3** to be a regular customer of (store, merchant, etc.)

6. A <u>compress</u> and a soak are both moist applications in which water touches the skin. They can be either warm or cold. A compress is a localized application. A soak can be either localized or general. (Wolgin, *Being a Nursing Assistant*)

> **com·press** (kəm pres′; *for n.* käm′pres′) **vt.** ⟦ME *compressen* < OFr *compresser* < LL *compressare* < L *compressus,* pp. of *comprimere,* to squeeze < *com-,* together + *premere,* to PRESS[1]⟧ to press together; make more compact by or as by pressure —**n.** **1** a pad of folded cloth, sometimes medicated or moistened, for applying pressure, heat, cold, etc. to some part of the body ☆**2** a machine for compressing cotton bales —**SYN.** CONTRACT —**com·press′i·bil′i·ty** *n.*

7. The Chicago Bulls' first shoe deal with Converse, while exceedingly <u>modest</u> in comparison to today's mega–shoe deals, filled a need for our young club. (Colangelo, *How You Play the Game*)

> **mod·est** (mäd′ist) **adj.** ⟦Fr *modeste* < L *modestus,* keeping due measure, modest < *modus:* see MODE⟧ **1** having or showing a moderate opinion of one's own value, abilities, achievements, etc.; not vain or boastful; unassuming **2** not forward; shy or reserved *[modest behavior]* **3** behaving, dressing, speaking, etc. in a way that is considered proper or decorous; decent **4** moderate or reasonable; not extreme *[a modest request]* **5** quiet and humble in appearance, style, etc.; not pretentious *[a modest home]* —**SYN.** CHASTE, SHY[1] —**mod′est·ly adv.**

8. Poor listening creates <u>friction</u> and misunderstanding in both personal and professional relationships. (Watson in Baker and Baker, *Communications*)

> **fric·tion** (frik′shən) **n.** ⟦Fr < L *frictio* < pp. of *fricare,* to rub: see FRIABLE⟧ **1** a rubbing, esp. of one object against another **2** disagreement or conflict because of differences of opinion, temperament, etc. **3** *Mech.* the resistance to motion of two moving objects or surfaces that touch —**fric′tion·less adj.**

9. We have <u>ample</u> testimony that artists themselves tend to look upon their creations as living things. (Janson and Janson, *A Basic History of Art*)

> **am·ple** (am′pəl) **adj.** **-pler** (-plər), **-plest** (-pləst) ⟦ME & OFr < L *amplus,* prob. < **amlos* < IE base **am-,* to contain⟧ **1** large in size, extent, scope, etc.; spacious; roomy **2** more than enough; abundant **3** enough to fulfill the needs or purpose; adequate —**SYN.** PLENTIFUL —**am′ple·ness** *n.*

10. The first step in investigating a biotic community may be to simply <u>catalogue</u> all the species present. Species are the different kinds of plants, animals, and microbes.

> **cat·a·log** or **cat·a·logue** (kat′ə lôg′, -läg′) **n.** ⟦Fr *catalogue* < LL *catalogus* < Gr *katalogos,* a list, register < *katalegein,* to reckon, list < *kata-,* down, completely + *legein,* to say, count: see LOGIC⟧ a complete or extensive list, esp. ☆*a)* an alphabetical card file, as of the books in a library *b)* a list of articles for sale, school courses offered, items on display, etc., usually with descriptive comments and often with illustrations *c)* a book or pamphlet containing such a list *d)* a long list, as of warriors, rivers, or ships, characteristic of the classical epic —**vt., vi.** **-loged′** or **-logued′, -log′ing** or **-logu′ing** **1** to enter in a catalog **2** to make a catalog of —**SYN.** LIST[1] —**cat′a·log′er, cat′a·logu′er, cat′a·log′ist,** or **cat′a·logu′ist** *n.*

■ **EXERCISE 2.8: USING A DICTIONARY TO DEFINE WORDS AND PHRASES**

Use your dictionary to define the underlined words. Write the definition that fits the context.

1. Fun is an <u>integral</u> part of most high school students' lives.

    _____

    _____

2. Other composers developed a percussive rhythmic style with sharp, constantly changing <u>accents</u>. (Politoske, *Music*)

    _____

    _____

3. A basic difference, however, is that while psychologists focus on the individual, sociologists look at the person's <u>web</u> of social relationships. (Macionis, *Sociology*)

    _____

    _____

4. Being aware of the various steps of good listening has little value unless we can manage the steps with skill and <u>consistency</u>. (Bittner, *Each Other*)

    _____

    _____

5. Computers are very good at <u>digesting</u> facts and producing information. (Long and Long, *Computers*)

    _____

    _____

6. <u>Matter</u> is all around us. Almost everything we see, touch, taste, or smell is matter. (Miller and Levine, *Biology*)

    _____

    _____

7. Maps often are the best way to present information such as population <u>density</u>. (Rubenstein, *An Introduction to Human Geography*)

    _____

    _____

8. The word "style" is derived from *stilus*, the writing instrument of the ancient Romans. Originally, it referred to <u>distinctive</u> ways of writing: the shape of the letters as well as the choice of words. (Janson and Janson, *A Basic History of Art*)

    _____

    _____

9. From bridge and chess to Trivial Pursuit and Scrabble, games are enjoying a <u>renaissance</u> in digital form. (Arar, *Computer Games for Grownup Kids*)

    _____

    _____

10. Computer technology is having a <u>profound</u> effect on physically challenged people. (Long and Long, *Computers*)

    _____

    _____

■ EXERCISE 2.9: USING A DICTIONARY OR GLOSSARY TO DEFINE WORDS AND PHRASES

Using a text from one of your other classes, identify five sentences with unfamiliar words. Copy the sentences onto a sheet of notebook paper and underline the unfamiliar words. Use either the glossary or a dictionary to find the definitions. Write the definitions.

USING A THESAURUS

A thesaurus is a book of words and their synonyms. Synonyms are words and phrases that have the same or nearly the same meaning. A word's synonyms can often help you figure out the meaning of the word.

For example, compare this entry in Roget's 21st Century Thesaurus for "correct" with the dictionary entry on page 22.

correct, *adj.* true, actual, factual, accurate (TRUTH); proper, free of error, unmistaken, appropriate, legitimate (PROPRIETY, RIGHT).
correct, *v.* remedy, rectify, right, repair, redress, adjust, revise, edit (CURE, RIGHT, IMPROVEMENT, RESTORATION); undeceive, set right, set straight (INFORMATION); punish, penalize, discipline (PUNISHMENT).

■ **EXERCISE 2.10: LOG ON TO THE WEB**

Several dictionaries and thesauruses are now available online. There are even a few Web sites devoted to defining baffling terms. When you have the time and the access, you can log on and find definitions, synonyms, and antonyms. Use a search directory/engine to locate the resources you need, or try these:

> http://www.m-w.com/netdict.htm
> http://www.dictionary.com/
> http://www.facstaff.bucknell.edu/rbeard/diction.html
> http://www.whatis.com

SECTION 2.4   DEFINING WORDS AND PHRASES WHILE READING

When you're reading passages other than practice material, strategies for defining unfamiliar words will not be as obvious as for the example words in the practice sentences. To understand the variety of material you're required to read, you'll need to use the strategies flexibly. By that I mean you'll need to choose the strategy or strategies that best fit the situation.

For example, when you come to a word that you don't understand, you might first look for any context clues you can use. On the other hand, if you recognize a part of the word, perhaps that is all the clue you need. Or, you might start by looking it up in the dictionary and fitting the meaning back into the context.

Read this passage from *Computers*, by Long and Long.

> Few will argue that we are rapidly approaching the age of automation, an era when invisible computers participate in or help us with nearly all we do. (Long and Long, *Computers*)

How you define the words in this sentence depends on factors such as how many words were unfamiliar, your experience with computers, how much time you have, and your knowledge of word parts such as *auto* and *in*.

The same is true whenever you read. You choose the best way to define each word.

Even familiar words can cause comprehension problems. For example, some words are confusing because they sound like another word.

THE FAMILY CIRCUS

5-4
©2000 Bil Keane, Inc.
Dist. by King Features Synd.

"That's not a jet. It's just a plain plane."

■ **EXERCISE 2.11: DEFINING FAMILIAR WORDS THAT ARE EASILY CONFUSED**

In these sentences use the most appropriate strategies to decide which word best fits the context of the sentence. Circle your answer.

1. a. Log on to the Web (cite, sight, site) listed on page 2 of your syllabus.
   b. If you want an "A" on your paper, you must correctly (cite, sight, site) the author's information.
   c. From the balcony the sunset was a magnificent (cite, sight, site).

2. a. If I accurately measured each (angle, angel) of the triangle, the answer would be correct.
   b. The gift shop had a wonderful music box with an (angle, angel) on top.

3. a. We can leave when (your, you're) ready.
   b. Is this (your, you're) jacket?

4. a. To receive your free copy of the book, send a request on company (stationary, stationery).
   b. The art museum's garden exhibit included both (stationary, stationery) pieces and displays with moving pieces called mobiles.

5. a. By signing this contract you agree to (accept, except) the terms and interest charges.
   b. You can access all of the newspaper's information online (accept, except) the comics.

■ **EXERCISE 2.12: DEFINING UNFAMILIAR WORDS AND PHRASES**

Using the strategies you decide are most appropriate, define the underlined words and phrases. Write the definitions.

1. <u>Chronic drinkers</u> are more likely than others to have histories of violent behavior. (Donatelle and Davis, *Access to Health*)

   _____

   _____

2. In his inaugural address Herbert Hoover told the American people that the years ahead were "bright with hope." He was <u>expressing the optimism</u> that many Americans felt, and he and they apparently had good reason for their sunny expectations. (Unger, *These United States*)

   _____

   _____

3. Throughout the past hundred years, people have <u>lamented</u> that nobody writes letters anymore. ("A Century of Eureka Moments," *Wall Street Journal*)

   _____

   _____

4. Perhaps the <u>prototypical</u> American composer of the period was
    the German-trained Edward MacDowell (1860–1908), a man
    once regarded as America's greatest composer. (Politoske, *Music*)

    _____

    _____

5. During the past <u>decade</u>, the subject of domestic violence has fi-
    nally grabbed our attention. (Donatelle and Davis, *Access to
    Health*)

    _____

    _____

6. As <u>inevitable</u> as it may seem today, the zipper was anything but
    an overnight success. (Grunwald and Adler, Introduction to
    Clarke Sales Company Manager's Letter, *Letters of the Century*)

    _____

    _____

7. The term ore <u>denotes</u> useful metallic minerals that can be mined
    at a profit. (Lutgens and Tarbuck, *Foundations of Earth Science*)

    _____

    _____

8. This book is about what I believe. Of course, what I (or anyone
    else) believe is the <u>culmination</u> of many things: family and faith
    and experience, education and intuition, all mixed together to
    provide a share of knowledge and—hopefully—a touch of wis-
    dom. (Colangelo, *How You Play the Game*)

    _____

    _____

9. The earth <u>intercepts</u> only a <u>minute</u> percentage of the energy
    given off by the sun—less than one two-billionth. (Lutgens and
    Tarbuck, *The Atmosphere*)

    _____

    _____

10. As a business owner you must be familiar with the growing list
    of federal laws that <u>supersede</u> state statutes and guarantee vari-
    ous forms of job-security protection. (McGrath and McGrath,
    "Firing Employees," *Performance Racing Industry*)

    _____

    _____

■ **EXERCISE 2.13: DEFINING UNFAMILIAR WORDS AND PHRASES**

Using the strategies you decide are most appropriate, define the underlined words and phrases. Write the definitions.

1. In previous years, more employees worked alone and therefore did not have to concern themselves with the <u>interpersonal relationships</u> that are necessary to achieve high standards of excellence in a modern business enterprise. (Chapman and O'Neil, *Your Attitude Is Showing*)

   _____

   _____

2. Jazz, one of the few distinctly American types of music, was <u>derived</u> from a variety of sources. (Politoske, *Music*)

   _____

   _____

3. Nineteenth-century cities looked much more <u>rustic</u> than they would later on, with rural areas rarely more than three miles away. (Hertz and Klein, *Twentieth Century Art Theory*)

   _____

   _____

4. Assume that ten reporters who work for a magazine in San Diego, California, are <u>collaborating</u> on a story about that city's best restaurants. (Macionis, *Sociology*)

   _____

   _____

5. Nonverbal messages usually <u>complement</u> verbal messages. (Barker and Barker, *Communication*)

   _____

   _____

6. A <u>sedentary</u> lifestyle, alcohol abuse, tobacco, and caffeine are known contributors to osteoporosis. (Rosenfeld, *Live Now, Age Later*)

   _____

   _____

7. The earth's atmosphere is unlike that of any other body in the solar system. No other planet is as <u>hospitable</u> or exhibits the same life-sustaining mixture of gases as the earth. (Lutgens and Tarbuck, *The Atmosphere*)

   _____

   _____

8. Hundreds of studies have sought to identify what it is that <u>differentiates</u> effective managers from ineffective ones. (Robbins, *Training in Interpersonal Skills*)

    _____

    _____

9. A place having two or more local names presents a <u>quandary</u> to <u>cartographers</u> who need to give the place a label on the map. (Rubenstein, *An Introduction to Human Geography*)

    _____

    _____

10. The most striking works of Paleolithic art are the images of animals <u>incised</u>, painted, or sculpted on the rock surfaces of caves, such as the wonderful *Wounded Bison* from the cave at Altamira in northern Spain. (Janson and Janson, *A Basic History of Art*)

    _____

    _____

■ EXERCISE 2.14: DEFINING UNFAMILIAR WORDS AND PHRASES

Using the strategies you decide are most appropriate, define the underlined words and phrases. Write the definitions.

1. Emotionally unhealthy people are much more likely to let their feelings overpower them than are emotionally healthy people. Emotionally unhealthy people may be <u>highly volatile</u> and <u>prone</u> to <u>unpredictable</u> emotional outbursts and to inappropriate, sometimes frightening responses to events. An ex-boyfriend who becomes so angry that he begins to hit you and push you around in front of your friends because he is jealous of your new relationship is showing an extremely unhealthy and dangerous emotional reaction. Violent responses to situations have become a problem of <u>epidemic</u> proportions in the United States. (Donatelle and Davis, *Access to Health*)

    _____

    _____

    _____

    _____

    _____

2. Folk music, soul music, jazz, country, rock—whatever the style, popular music plays an <u>overwhelming</u> part in the daily lives of most Americans. The origins of any popular music are deep in the human spirit, and its history reaches back to the earliest ages. Today, it has a far greater <u>commercial market</u> in America than does "classical" music, and it has a significant role in the film industry. Through video, popular music is also closely <u>allied</u> to visual arts, and it is at the edge of <u>emerging</u> computer technologies. (Politoske, *Music*)

   _____

   _____

   _____

   _____

   _____

   _____

3. <u>Primitive</u> human beings had no electricity, few tools, and poor shelter. Their time was spent protecting themselves against <u>predators</u> and finding food. They were <u>superstitious</u> and believed illness and disease were caused by supernatural spirits. In an attempt to heal, tribal doctors performed ceremonies to <u>exorcise</u> evil spirits. They used herbs and plants as medicines. Some of the same medicines are still used today. (Badasch and Chesebro, *Introduction to Health Occupations*)

   _____

   _____

   _____

   _____

   _____

   _____

4. We might be much better off to try positive <u>adaptations</u> to stress. Physical exercise tends to prepare the body for stressful situations and creates in some people a <u>tension-relieving mechanism</u>. Under a doctor's care we might develop a jogging program or a <u>strenuous</u> exercise program. Some form of relaxation may also help us to <u>alleviate</u> stress. Sitting quietly in pleasant surroundings or going for a walk in the park or the country are all ways of alleviating stress. Cutting down on the amount we eat and cutting back or stopping the intake of caffeine or other stimulants may also be solutions to handling stress. (Bittner, *Each Other*)

   _____

   _____

   _____

   _____

   _____

   _____

5. Communication is <u>central</u> to the learning process. Words, gestures, and other <u>symbols</u>, or things that stand for other things, are used to <u>transmit</u> ideas through symbolic communication. Only human beings have the ability to develop and use symbols with which to communicate. This ability <u>enables</u> humans to learn ideas from others and to teach them to new generations. Culture, that combination of ideas, inventions, and objects, is both understood and transmitted because of this ability to communicate. (Rose, Glazer, and Glazer, *Sociology*)

_____

_____

_____

_____

_____

_____

6. The year is 2005. Computers are <u>invisible</u>; that is they are built into our <u>domestic</u>, working, and external environment. Imagine this <u>scenario</u>. Your invisible computer is preprogrammed to awaken you to whatever stimulates you to greet the new day. The wake up call could be the sound of your favorite music, a vibrating bed, or any of hundreds of video information or entertainment options, such as your favorite network morning program, today's weather, a stock report, a production status report for the evening shift at your place of employment, the movie of your choice, or a to-do list for the day. Suppose your wake up choice is the <u>latter</u>—a to-do list for the day. Besides listing the events of your day, your invisible computer might verbally emphasize important events…. (Long and Long, *Computers*)

_____

_____

_____

_____

_____

_____

SECTION 2.5   REMEMBERING WORDS AND PHRASES

Unless you actively work at remembering new words and phrases, you will have to rediscover the meaning each time you see the word.

UNDERSTANDING

Being able to remember something often depends on how thoroughly you learned it in the first place. You must *get*, or understand, something before you can *forget* it. Sometimes when we say "I forgot," what we mean is "I didn't understand it."

By understanding, I mean your ability to translate words and information into ideas that make sense to you. Something that doesn't make sense to you is hard to learn. The more understandable information is to you, the easier it is to learn.

There is not one best method for remembering everything. However, applying several of your senses will help: See it, say it, hear it, write it.

REVIEWING AND USING

Regular review, spaced over time, is critical to remembering new words and information. Rather than one two-hour study session, plan short but frequent study sessions. Begin a session by reviewing some of the words you've already learned and then tackle new ones.

You also have to use new information to remember it. In fact, it's been estimated that you must use a new word at least ten times before it's really *yours*. Try to use a few new words in your writing and conversations each day.

ONE STRATEGY FOR LEARNING THE MEANINGS OF WORDS AND PHRASES

One strategy for learning—understanding and remembering—new words and phrases is to make flashcards.

Write the word and sentence (context) on the front of a 3 x 5 index card. Also note the class and/or text page number.

Davis, p. 36

foster

To be part of the solution to preventing hate and bias crimes you can support educational programs designed to foster understanding and appreciation for differences in people.

On the back of the card write the definition (the one that most closely fits the way the word was used in your original sentence). You can also write a sentence with a personally meaningful context.

to help to grow or develop; stimulate; promote

My health class was designed to foster healthier living.

Use the cards at various moments during the day to review and test yourself. Sometimes, look at the word and try to recall the definition. At other times, look at the definition and try to recall the word.

Once in a while as you go through the cards, sort them into two stacks: *know* and *don't know*. The next time you review, use only the *don't know* stack to concentrate your study.

CHAPTER REVIEW

SUMMARY OF KEY IDEAS

- Words are the building blocks of everything we write. Therefore, it's important to understand the meaning of words and phrases.
- Words take on meaning from their context—how they are used with the other words in the sentence and surrounding sentences.
- To understand an author's specific meaning for a word, you must consider the word's context.
- There are several strategies you can use to figure out the meaning of a word. These strategies include using the author's context clues, breaking the word into parts, looking it up in a dictionary or other resource book, and asking someone for help.
- To remember information you must use it and review it often.

SELF CHECK

- I can use the context of the sentence to help define words and phrases.
- I can use the parts of the word to help define it.
- I can use a dictionary to define words and phrases.
- I can use other resources, such as a thesaurus, to help define words and phrases.
- I can remember the meanings of new words and phrases.

PUTTING IT ALL TOGETHER

Using the strategies you decide are most appropriate, define the underlined words and phrases. Write the definitions.

1. Recent <u>immigrants</u> are <u>not distributed uniformly</u> through the United States. One-fourth are clustered in California, one-fourth in New York and New Jersey, one-fourth in Florida, Texas, and Illinois, and one-fourth in the other forty-four states. Coastal states were once the main entry points for immigrants because most arrived by ship. Today, nearly all arrive by motor vehicle or airplane. California and Texas are the two most popular states for entry of motor vehicles from Mexico, and these six states have the country's busiest airports for international arrivals. (Rubenstein, *An Introduction to Human Geography*)

   _____

   _____

2. Violence in American society is a topic that <u>garners</u> much interest, concern, and debate in this country. How police respond to violence, especially police use of force, is of particular concern to many of us. (Hurtt, "Use of force limited")

    _____

    _____

3. The <u>proceeds</u> from the sale of gifts and raffle tickets for prizes will help to fund the wildlife center's mission of <u>rehabilitating</u> injured animals and returning them to the wild.

    _____

    _____

    _____

4. Cameron Judd's novel *Firefall* is set in 1884. The story begins one night as a meteor falls from the sky to <u>demolish</u> a Montana mining town.

    _____

    _____

5. Scientists who launched the Galileo probe on its 2.7 billion-mile mission to explore Jupiter may send the craft on a final flight—a <u>kamikaze plunge</u>. Yes, NASA may deliberately crash the spacecraft into Jupiter or one of its icy moons in 2002.

    _____

    _____

6. Although everyone loves fresh flowers, there's no question that silk flowers can make an impression nearly <u>indistinguishable</u> from the real thing. Best of all, you don't have to spend a fortune to enjoy gorgeous floral arrangements year-round.

    _____

    _____

7. Owning a house requires a lot of work—lawns to mow, roofs to repair, and leaky faucets to fix. So, when a job demands most of your time and your schedule is <u>erratic</u>, renting an apartment instead of owning a home may be sensible.

    _____

    _____

8. The home of the future will be smarter, cleaner, and more
    <u>serene</u>, thanks to a new generation of stylish appliances and fur-
    niture that make use of fresh designs and modern technology.
    For example, the home office will be upgraded from an extra
    bedroom where the computer was stored to a <u>sanctuary</u> with
    comfortable custom furniture in soothing colors, wood tones, and
    glass. (Adapted from Koenenn, "Smart Houses")

    _____

    _____

    _____

9. Considering all your options means more than taking stock of
    the <u>pros</u> and <u>cons</u> of any given choice, although that's a good
    first step. In addition to reviewing the positive and negative
    points, think about a third one: the <u>neutral</u> reasons. (Adapted
    from Carter and Troyka, *Majoring in the Rest of Your Life*)

    _____

    _____

    _____

    _____

10. One of the things the founders of our nation most feared was
    <u>centralized</u> government power. Indeed, our Constitution and our
    Bill of Rights were written <u>explicitly</u> to <u>ensure</u> that power rested
    with the people and that no single branch of government—
    whether the executive, legislative, or judicial—gains a <u>monopoly</u>
    of power. (McClenaghan, *Magruder's American Government*)

    _____

    _____

    _____

    _____

CROSSWORD PUZZLE

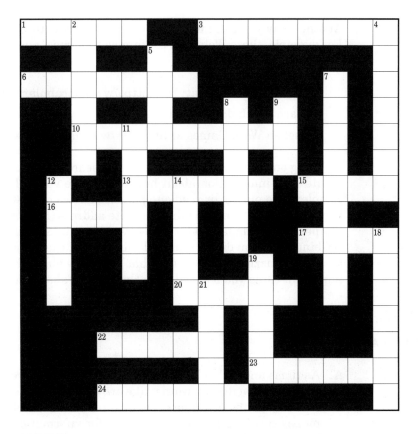

ACROSS

1 more than enough
3 household
6 germ free
10 your best reasoned conclusion
13 word part added to end of a root word
15 basic part of a word
16 hinder
17 positive
20 bleak; desolate; barren
22 point of view
23 ten-year period
24 not extreme

DOWN

2 word part added to the beginning of a root word
4 how words are used together in a sentence
5 to terminate
7 study of the universe
8 improve
9 a network
11 to help to grow
12 savvy
14 phobias
18 means
19 set of beliefs
21 journeys

WORD LIST (NOT ALL USED)

ample
angle
aseptic
astronomy
centenarians
context
contractions
creed
decade
denotes
deserted
disagreeable

domestic
enrich
fears
fire
foster
friction
glossary
good
hurt
incised
inference
modest

optimism
portable
prefix
primitive
root
sharp
stark
stationary
strategy
suffix
treks
web

LOG ON TO THE WEB

Another way you can improve your vocabulary is to work, and play, with words. For example, these Web sites contain word games, puzzles, and links to information about vocabulary.

> Vocabulary University® at http://www.vocabulary.com
>
> Learn Vocabulary Syndicate® at http://www.syndicate.com
>
> English Word Games at http://www.nanana.com/wordgames.html

Log on to one of these sites or use a search directory/engine to locate another site with information about how to improve vocabulary. Play one word game, complete one puzzle, or read one person's advice on how to improve your vocabulary. Then, write down (1) the complete address (http://www. ...), (2) the name of the person or company who sponsors and maintains the site, (3) a sentence describing what you did or read, (4) the name of the person or company who wrote the game, puzzle, or advice, (5) what you know about the writer, and (6) the most important thing you learned from the activity about improving your vocabulary.

IDEAS FOR WRITING AND DISCUSSION

A. As times and technology change, so do the words we use to describe them. We invent new words, like *extreme sports* and *e-commerce*. We also change the meaning of "old" words. For example, to *surf* now means spending time online looking for information, and *uninstall* can mean being fired or laid off from a job.

   What are some other words that have come into English or changed meanings during the past two years? How do you think the changes happen?

B. When you look words up in the dictionary you often find definitions that are labeled *old-fashioned*, *archaic*, or *obsolete*. Although all three terms point out a definition that is not used in today's language, each term has a slightly different meaning.

   What do the different labels mean? Why do you think definitions become old-fashioned, archaic, and obsolete?

C. Think back over all the words you read this week. Select two words you think are unusual or that you didn't completely understand. Find out all you can about the words, such as meanings, parts of speech, and history. Write down the resources you use and what you discover.

READING PARAGRAPHS

CHAPTER PREVIEW

Objectives

- Distinguish between general and specific words and ideas.
- Identify the main idea of a paragraph, whether it is directly stated or implied.

Sections

3.1 Distinguishing between General and Specific Words and Ideas
3.2 Identifying the Topic of a Sentence
3.3 Identifying and Understanding Main Ideas

CHAPTER FOCUS

Reading is more than understanding individual words. Reading is an active thinking process of understanding an author's ideas.

The basic unit of writing authors use to express their ideas is the sentence. A well-written sentence contains one general idea. Understanding individual sentences is important. Most of the time, however, you read groups of sentences that have been combined into a paragraph.

In a paragraph, the sentences fit together to support and explain one main idea. A main idea is often called an *umbrella idea* because it covers everything in the paragraph. In other words, a main idea ties the sentences together.

When you are reading for learning, your purpose will almost always include understanding a paragraph's main idea. If you don't understand the main idea, you have nothing to tie the paragraph's bits and pieces of information together. Without knowing the main idea, it is difficult to understand and remember the paragraph's information.

SECTION 3.1   DISTINGUISHING BETWEEN GENERAL AND SPECIFIC WORDS AND IDEAS

Key to understanding the groups of words and sentences we read is figuring out how they relate to one another. One important relationship is the level of specificity: determining whether one word or idea is more *general* or more *specific* than another. The label *general* means broad, comprehensive, including everything. The label *specific* means limited, individual, narrow.

To see how these labels apply to everyday words and ideas, consider this list of terms:

Thanksgiving   New Year's Eve   holidays   Labor Day

In this list, the term "holidays" is more general because it includes all the other terms. The terms "Thanksgiving," "New Year's Eve," and "Labor Day" are specific terms because they are limited, individual examples of holidays.

Consider these two examples.

Example 1   Think about these two terms. How are they related to each other? Which one is general? Which one is more specific?

basketball player   athlete

The more general term is _____

The more specific term is _____

Explanation   Athlete is the general or comprehensive term for people who excel in many kinds of sports. A basketball player is more specific because it is an individual example of one kind of athlete.

Example 2   Consider the relationships among these four terms. To decide which term is most general, ask yourself "Who or what is this group of terms about?" Your answer will tell you which term is the most general.

computer   telephone   office equipment   copy machine

The most general term is _____

Explanation   In this example, "office equipment" is the more general term because it covers, or includes, all the other terms. A computer, telephone, and copy machine are more specific because they are individual examples of office machines.

■ EXERCISE 3.1: GENERAL AND SPECIFIC WORDS AND IDEAS

The words in each group are related. Look at the relationships among the words. Decide which word is more general than the other three. Underline the most general word in each group—the word that answers "Who or what is the word group about?"

Example   jazz   rock and roll   <u>music</u>   country

Explanation   Music is underlined because it is the most general word; jazz, rock and roll, and country are specific kinds of music.

1. animal   cat   dog   horse
2. dime   quarter   money   dollar
3. trout   fish   tuna   shark
4. soda   coffee   tea   drink
5. fabric   silk   wool   cotton
6. basketball   tennis   sport   cycling

■ **EXERCISE 3.2: GENERAL AND SPECIFIC WORDS AND IDEAS**

The words in each group are specific examples of a general idea. In the space provided, write the general idea that connects them—a word or phrase that can answer the question "Who or what is the word group about?"

Example fear   happiness   love   <u>*emotions*</u>

Explanation   Fear, happiness, and love are connected because they are each a specific type of emotion or feeling.

1. pie   cake   ice cream   _____

2. earring   necklace   pin   _____

3. cocker spaniel   poodle   golden retriever   _____

4. runner   boxer   soccer player   _____

5. dish washer   blender   microwave   _____

6. desk   table   bed   _____

■ **EXERCISE 3.3: GENERAL AND SPECIFIC WORDS AND IDEAS**

Each of the words listed represents a general idea. In the spaces provided, write two specific examples of the general word.

Example crime   <u>*robbery*</u>   <u>*assault*</u>

Explanation   Crime is the general word; robbery and assault are specific kinds of crime.

1. vehicle   _____   _____

2. occupation   _____   _____

3. food   _____   _____

4. clothing   _____   _____

5. medicine   _____   _____

6. drinks   _____   _____

IDENTIFYING DIFFERENT LEVELS OF SPECIFICITY

Unfortunately, figuring out the relationship among a group of words or ideas isn't always as uncomplicated as the previous exercises make it seem. This is because words can change in specificity: Words can be general sometimes and specific at other times. Stated another way, words can play different roles in different sentences. In the same way words take on their definition from their context, words take on their role (whether they are general or specific) from their context.

Also, there is not always an equal number of general and specific terms in a list or paragraph. The number of relationships among groups of words or among sentences in a paragraph can vary greatly. For example, several words or sentences can be at the same level of specificity, each can be at a different level, or there can be a mixture. Therefore, the question you always need to ask is "What are the relationships among *this* group of words or ideas?"

In the previous example with the terms *athlete* and *basketball player*, you determined that *basketball player* was the more specific term.

But what happens when we add *Michael Jordan* as a third term? What are the relationships among these three terms? Which one is the most specific?

basketball player   athlete   Michael Jordan

The most specific term now is   _____

Explanation   In relation to one another, *athlete* is still the more general, or comprehensive term for people who excel in many kinds of sports. A *basketball player* is still a specific example of one kind of athlete. However, *Michael Jordan* is the most specific term because he is a specific example of a basketball player.

What are the relationships among the terms when we add *tennis player*? Arrange them from most general to most specific.

basketball player   athlete   Michael Jordan   tennis player

_____

   _____

   _____

     _____

Explanation   In relation to one another, *athlete* is the more general, or comprehensive term for people who excel in many kinds of sports; *basketball player* and *tennis player* are at the same level of specificity because they are both specific examples of athletes; *Michael Jordan* is a more specific term because he is an example of a basketball player.

It is often helpful to write the information in a way that shows the relationships. One common way to do this is to use the structure of an informal outline: to indent specific information under the more general. An indent is a tab or space from the margin. Using this format, the previous example would look like this:

athlete
    tennis player
    basketball player
       Michael Jordan

■ EXERCISE 3.4: GENERAL AND SPECIFIC WORDS AND IDEAS

The words in each group are related. Each word is at a different level of specificity. Arrange the words from most general to most specific.

Example   soup   liquids   chicken-noodle

liquids
    soup
       chicken-noodle

Explanation   Liquids is the most general word (it answers the question, "What is the group about?") Soup is an example of a liquid and chicken-noodle is an example of a soup.

1. round object   baseball   ball

    _____

    _____

    _____

2. running shoe   athletic shoe   footwear

    _____

    _____

    _____

3. movie   entertainment   *Star Wars*

    _____

    _____

    _____

4. food   corn   vegetable

    _____

    _____

    _____

5. Arabian   horse   animal

    _____

    _____

    _____

6. athlete   golfer   Tiger Woods

    _____

    _____

    _____

SECTION 3.2   IDENTIFYING THE TOPIC OF A SENTENCE

A well-written sentence contains one general idea. The general idea, often called the *topic*, answers the question, "Who or what is the author writing about?"

Consider these two examples.

Example 1   Read this sentence and determine the topic.

Each year, food allergies cause about 125 deaths and more than 1,000 near fatalities in the United States. (Good Housekeeping Institute)

The topic is _____

Explanation   The topic of this sentence—the term that answers the question "who or what is the author writing about?"—is *food allergies*.

Example 2   Read this sentence and determine the topic.

Liars tend to fidget, perspire, wring their hands or otherwise let their bodies betray their words. (Webb, *How to Tell When Someone's Lying*)

The topic is _____

Explanation   The topic of this sentence—the term that answers the question "who or what is the author writing about?"—is *people who lie*.

■ **EXERCISE 3.5: IDENTIFYING THE TOPIC OF A SENTENCE**

Each sentence contains one general idea (topic) that answers "Who or what is the author writing about?" In each sentence underline the word(s) that represent the topic.

Example   No one knows how long <u>romantic love</u> can last or why it goes away.

Explanation   Romantic love is underlined because it is the topic, the most general idea, in the sentence. The other two ideas—how long it can last and why it goes away—are too specific.

1. The sundial came into use around 1500 B.C. to measure the passage of time.
2. It is estimated that lightning strikes the earth about 100 times every second.
3. Protect yourself from the sun's rays by wearing sunscreen, protective clothing, and sunglasses.
4. College costs have risen constantly for the past ten years.
5. A clever con artist is a good actor who pretends to be a nice guy.
6. You can find information on any subject in a library.
7. Climate has always had a big effect on life in America.
8. Being able to speak well often means you will get more attention and better grades in school.
9. A dictionary is a good source for proper word meanings and pronunciations.
10. A solar eclipse occurs when the moon passes between the earth and sun.

■ **EXERCISE 3.6: IDENTIFYING THE TOPIC OF A GROUP OF SENTENCES**

Each group of sentences shares one general idea (topic). After reading a group of sentences, underline the word or phrase that best expresses the topic.

Example

1. Harriet Beecher Stowe wrote *Uncle Tom's Cabin*, a forceful book against slavery.
2. Several romantic novels, short stories, and religious poems were written by Harriet Beecher Stowe.
3. Harriet Beecher Stowe was born in 1811 and died in 1896.
   a. writers
   b. <u>Harriet Beecher Stowe</u>
   c. *Uncle Tom's Cabin*

Explanation   The term *writers* (a) is too general because the three sentences only talk about the one writer, Harriet Beecher Stowe. The title of her book, *Uncle Tom's Cabin* (c), is too specific because it is only one of her writings.

GROUP **1**

1. The Strait of Dover separates England from France and the European continent.
2. One of the busiest maritime routes in the world is the Strait of Dover, which connects the English Channel and Atlantic Ocean with the North Sea.
3. The Strait of Dover is about 34 km (about 21 mi.) wide.
   a. ocean shipping routes
   b. you can't drive from England to France
   c. the Strait of Dover

GROUP **2**

1. Armistice Day, now called Veterans Day, was proclaimed in 1919 to commemorate the end of World War I.
2. We now observe Veterans Day in the United States to honor all those, living and dead, who served with the armed forces in wartime.
3. Veterans Day is known in Canada as Remembrance Day and in Great Britain as Remembrance Sunday.
   a. World War I
   b. Veterans Day
   c. holidays

GROUP **3**

1. A primary example of Art Deco design in the United States is the interior of Radio City Music Hall in New York City, designed by Donald Deskey in 1931.
2. Art Deco is a style of design used in furniture, jewelry, textiles, and interior decor that was popular in the 1920s and 1930s.
3. Art Deco declined in popularity in the late 1930s, but it is now enjoying a comeback.
   a. Art Deco design
   b. popular design styles
   c. Radio City Music Hall

GROUP **4**

1. Sir Edmund Hillary, with his Nepalese Sherpa guide, was the first mountain climber to reach the summit of Mount Everest, the world's highest peak.
2. The sport of mountain climbing began in eighteenth-century Europe when people wanted to climb Mont Blanc, the highest peak of the Alps.
3. World-class climber Chris Bonington describes several major mountain-climbing expeditions in his book *The Climbers: A History of Mountaineering*.
   a. popular mountains to climb
   b. Sir Edmund Hillary
   c. mountain climbing

GROUP **5**

1. Steven Spielberg's early movies include *Jaws* (1975), *Close Encounters of the Third Kind* (1977), *E.T.* (1982), and, of course, the Indiana Jones series: *Raiders of the Lost Ark* (1981), *Indiana Jones and the Temple of Doom* (1984), and *Indiana Jones and the Last Crusade* (1989).
2. Hollywood's Academy of Motion Picture Arts and Sciences produces the Academy Awards show each year to recognize people who create the best movies.
3. Movies, also called feature films, are produced in three stages: preproduction, production, and postproduction.
   a. movies
   b. Steven Spielberg
   c. Oscars

GROUP **6**

1. Recent research indicates that the cholesterol in eggs is not as harmful as once thought.
2. The number of eggs eaten by Americans hit an all-time low in 1991.
3. Scrambled eggs are once again a popular breakfast item.
   a. scrambled eggs
   b. eggs
   c. cholesterol in eggs

SECTION 3.3   IDENTIFYING AND UNDERSTANDING MAIN IDEAS

A paragraph is a group of sentences that fit together to support and explain one main idea. The main idea includes two elements:

1. The topic—the who or what the author is writing about
2. The controlling thought—what the author wants you to know or understand about the topic

Readers often mistake the topic for the main idea. But the topic is only one part of the author's main idea.

Consider these two paragraphs. The topic in each paragraph is the same, but the controlling thoughts are very different.

PARAGRAPH **1**

I found my first gray hair this morning. Clerks and cashiers are starting to call me "Ma'am." I didn't recognize half of the musicians nominated for this year's Grammy Awards and I actually blushed at the language in the movie we saw last night. Getting older is better than the alternative, but it certainly isn't any fun.

Explanation   Who or what am I writing about? *Getting older* is the topic. What do I want you to understand about *getting older*? *That it's no fun* is the controlling thought. Therefore, the main thought—the combination of the topic and the controlling idea—is *getting older isn't any fun.*

PARAGRAPH **2**

Whoever said "The best is yet to come," was certainly right. From a never-ending list of people to see, places to go, and things to do, I now have the freedom to choose what to do and when to do it. The friends I've made over the years are truly wonderful. Every day is a gift just waiting for me to enjoy it. Getting older has so many advantages.

Explanation   Who or what am I writing about? *Getting older* is the topic. What do I want you to understand about *getting older*? *That it has many advantages* is the controlling thought. Therefore, the main idea—the combination of the topic and the controlling thought—is *getting older has many advantages.*

To fully understand a paragraph, it is important to identify and understand the main idea, not just the topic.

■ EXERCISE 3.7: IDENTIFYING THE CONTROLLING THOUGHT OF A PARAGRAPH

In each paragraph the topic is underlined. Circle the controlling thought—what the author wants you to know or understand about that topic. When you combine the topic and the controlling thought, you have the main idea of the paragraph.

Example

A variety of over-the-counter products are now available to help people <u>stop smoking</u>. One product is a special filter that reduces the amount of nicotine from each cigarette. There is also chewing gum that contains nicotine. It helps quitters slowly cut down on cigarettes. In addition, arm patches that slowly release nicotine into the body are available.

Explanation   The topic—what the paragraph is about—is *stopping smoking.* The controlling thought—what I want you to know about the topic of stopping smoking—is *there are a variety of over-the-counter products now available to help.* Therefore, the main idea—the combination of the topic and the controlling thought—is: *There are many over-the-counter products available to help people stop smoking.*

1. Many people find it very hard to stop <u>smoking</u>. Some are addicted to the nicotine. Others find it difficult just to break the habit of smoking. Still others are caught up in the social aspects of smoking. They want to fit in with their friends.

   Therefore, the main idea is _____

   _____

2. <u>Weather</u> has a big influence on our lives. It affects our everyday activities, our jobs, and our health and comfort. The weather often controls what we wear. Sometimes, it even influences where we can and can't go.

   Therefore, the main idea is _____

   _____

3. Looking for a *Star Wars* action figure or something to brighten up your living room? No problem. Just log on to your computer, join an auction, and bid for it. There are hundreds of general and specialized <u>online auction sites</u>.

   Therefore, the main idea is _____

   _____

4. The <u>2000 Arena Football League</u> season will be played after all. Last week the owners canceled the season because of problems with the players' organizing committee. However, this week owners and players have decided to work out their differences. They will begin to negotiate an agreement next week.

   Therefore, the main idea is _____

   _____

5. Some say you see a bigger variety at the mall. Others prefer the supermarket. A few think the library is the best place. You also hear a lot about airport lounges and art galleries. The fact is, no matter where you are, <u>people-watching</u> is fun.

   Therefore, the main idea is _____

   _____

6. <u>Technology</u> is rapidly changing the way we communicate. In fact, the present era is called the Information Age because so many changes are happening so rapidly. Starting in the past century, people began developing new forms of communication— the telegraph, the telephone, and the radio. In the past few decades, the invention of many more ways to store, retrieve, and transmit information has created an information explosion.

   Therefore, the main idea is _____

   _____

7. In <u>Salzburg, Austria,</u> you can still visit the places that were used in the movie version of *The Sound of Music* in 1964, starring Julie Andrews and Christopher Plummer. For example, you can walk through the Mirabell Gardens where Maria and the children danced around the statue of Pegasus, the winged horse, as they sang the "Do-Re-Mi" song. You can also visit the Leopoldskron Castle, which was used as the setting for the von Trapp family home, and you can see the Mondsee Cathedral where scenes of the marriage of Maria to the Baron were shot.

   Therefore, the main idea is _____

   _____

8. Today's households seem to have one thing in common: Nobody wants to make dinner. The stay-at-home soccer moms, the two-career couples, and the army of singles are too busy, too tired, or too unmotivated to spend hours each week shopping, planning meals, and cooking. But everyone has to eat. That is why deli, restaurant, and grocery <u>takeout meals</u> are the food industry's fastest growing segment.

   Therefore, the main idea is _____

   _____

9. Willie Morris's autobiographical novel, <u>*My Dog Skip*</u>, is a nearly perfect piece of bedtime reading for kids and their parents. Each chapter is a self-contained story. The descriptions of World War II–era Mississippi are lush and dreamlike. The activities of the central canine character, who is smarter, faster, and just plain better than any other dog, will capture the attention of readers of all ages.

   Therefore, the main idea is _____

   _____

10. The <u>salt cedar</u>, or tamarisk tree, is a serious threat to native plants and wildlife across much of the Southwest. One way it forces out other plants and animals is by using large amounts of water. For example, one salt cedar alone can use 200 gallons of water a day, more than the amount used by a small family. It also adds large amounts of salt to the soil and rivers. The trees now cover more than 1 million acres.

    Therefore, the main idea is _____

    _____

IDENTIFYING STATED MAIN IDEAS

In exposition, an author often states the main idea in the first sentence of the paragraph. This is helpful because it clearly focuses your attention on the author's message and prepares you for the rest of the paragraph.

However, the main idea sentence—also called the topic sentence—can appear anywhere in a paragraph. It can be in the middle of the paragraph (tying the beginning and ending together), at the end of the paragraph (as a summary), or even split between two sentences in the paragraph.

No matter where the main idea/topic sentence is located, your strategy for identifying and understanding the main idea is the same:

1. Identify the topic by answering the question "Who or what is the author writing about?"
2. Clarify the controlling thought by answering "What does the author want me to know or understand about the topic?"
3. Combine the topic and controlling thought and identify the main idea/topic sentence.

Consider these two examples.

Example 1   Read this paragraph and then practice the three steps: (1) identify the topic, (2) clarify the controlling thought, (3) combine them and identify the main idea/topic sentence.

[1]A well-balanced diet contains all the necessary vitamins. [2]This means that most people do not need to take vitamin supplements in order to stay healthy and keep their body working well. [3]In fact, the body quickly eliminates many of these high-dosage supplements without using them.

Who or what am I writing about? (the topic) _____

What do I want you to understand about the topic? (controlling thought)

_____

_____

Therefore, the main idea of this paragraph is stated in sentence(s) _____

> ***Explanation***   Who or what am I writing about? *Vitamins*. What do I want you to understand about *vitamins*? *That a well-balanced diet contains the ones we need*. Therefore, in this paragraph, the main idea is stated in sentence 1.
>
> ***Example 2***   Read this paragraph and determine the main idea.
>
> [1]Vitamins are organic compounds the body requires to work effectively, to protect health, and to assure proper growth in children. [2]Vitamins help us form hormones, blood cells, nervous-system chemicals, and genetic material. [3]They also help produce hundreds of important chemical reactions throughout the body. [4]Without vitamins, many of these reactions would slow down or stop. [5]However, the complex ways in which vitamins act on the body are still unclear.

Who or what am I writing about? (the topic) _____

What do I want you to understand about the topic? (controlling thought)

_____

_____

Therefore, the main idea of this paragraph is stated in sentence(s) _____

> ***Explanation***   Who or what am I writing about? *Vitamins*. What do I want you to understand about *vitamins*? *They are important, but we don't know how they work*. Therefore, in this paragraph, the main idea is split between sentences 1 and 5.

■   EXERCISE 3.8: IDENTIFYING A STATED MAIN IDEA

Each of these paragraphs contains a stated main idea. The main idea answers: "Who or what is the author writing about?" *and* "What does the author want me to know about the what or who?" For each paragraph, write the number of the sentence(s) that contains the main idea.

1.   [1]Adobe is an ancient building material. [2]Peruvians and Mesopotamians knew at least 3,000 years ago how to mix adobe—three parts sandy soil to one part clay soil—and box and mold it into bricks. [3]The Walls of Jericho, the Tower of Babel, Egyptian pyramids, and sections of China's Great Wall are adobes. [4]So are more modern structures like Spain's Alhambra, the green mosques of Fez and Marrakech, and the royal palace at Riyadh. (Steinhart, *Dirt Chic*)

The main idea is stated in sentence(s) _____

2. [1]The earliest device created to measure the passage of time was the sundial. [2]It measured the sun's shadow. [3]The water clock was an improvement over the sundial since it didn't depend on the sun. [4]Once the art of glass making was perfected, the hourglass was created to mark the passage of time with sand. [5]People created several ways of keeping track of the passage of time before the invention of the modern clock.

The main idea is stated in sentence(s) _____

3. [1]Parents don't have total control over a child's life. [2]They don't produce little robots who act on adult wishes at the press of a button. [3]Children are also socialized by their peers, those of their own age group with whom they share experiences. [4]In their peer group, children learn to play, compete, and fight. [5]They practice grown-up roles, exchange secrets, interact with others, and explore the world. (Rose, Glazer, and Glazer, *Sociology: Understanding Society*)

The main idea is stated in sentence(s) _____

4. [1]Drugs differ in the ways in which they affect the body. [2]Some drugs kill bacteria and are useful in treating disease. [3]Other drugs affect a particular system of the body, such as the digestive or circulatory system. [4]Among the most powerful drugs, however, are the ones that affect the nervous system in ways that change behavior. (Miller and Levine, *Biology*)

The main idea is stated in sentence(s) _____

5. [1]Eating healthy is easy. [2]Increase your intake of fruits, vegetables, and whole grains and reduce your intake of fatty meats and whole-milk dairy products. [3]Choose small portions of veal, skinless poultry, and fish instead of high-fat beef. [4]Make meats the sidedish to pasta, beans, and veggie-based main dishes. [5]Also, steam or broil food instead of frying. (Lincoln Health Network, *Well Worth It*)

The main idea is stated in sentence(s) _____

6. [1]Physical attractiveness greatly influences the early impressions that others form of us. [2]Physically attractive people are viewed more positively than are less attractive people, a phenomenon referred to by psychologists as the halo effect. [3]In a study by Bersheid and Walster (1972), subjects were shown pictures of men and women of varying degrees of physical attractiveness and were asked to rate their personality traits. [4]The physically attractive people were viewed as more sensitive, kind, interesting, strong, poised, modest, sociable, intelligent, witty, honest, more sexually responsive, happy, successful, and less socially deviant than were the average-looking people. [5]Although beauty is a factor in initial acquaintance, more substantial personal qualities become important later in a relationship. (Alexander, *Adjustment and Human Relations*)

The main idea is stated in sentence(s) _____

RESTATING THE MAIN IDEA USING YOUR OWN WORDS

To be sure you understand the author's meaning, it is a good idea to rephrase the main idea/topic sentence using your own words. For example, in one of the paragraphs about vitamins, you determined the main idea was a combination of these two sentences: "Vitamins are organic compounds the body requires to work effectively, to protect health, and to assure proper growth in children," *and* "However, the complex ways in which vitamins act on the body are still unclear." To be sure you understand the meaning of the sentences you could rephrase them like this: *Our bodies require vitamins to stay healthy, but we aren't sure how they work.*

Consider this example.

Example   Rephrase this topic sentence using your own words.

"A well-balanced diet contains all the necessary vitamins."

_____

_____

Explanation   One possibility is: If we eat a well-balanced diet we get all the vitamins we need.

WHAT TO DO WHEN MAIN IDEAS ARE IMPLIED (UNSTATED)

Authors do not always state the main idea of a paragraph. When this happens, the author wants you to add together the information from all the sentences and infer, or put together, the main idea. The author implies; you infer.

Like defining a word through context, to infer an unstated main idea you combine what the author does say, the author's clues, and your own knowledge. Inferring a main idea is not just making a wild guess. Inferring requires your best reasoned conclusion based on the information you are given. Strategies you can use to make valid inferences and practice exercises are included in Chapter 5.

Your basic strategy for identifying an implied main idea is:

1.   Identify the topic—ask who or what the author is writing about.
2.   Identify the controlling thought—ask what the author wants you to know about the topic.
3.   Combine the topic and controlling thought into a main idea statement.

If you aren't sure you have identified the main idea of a paragraph, try this: After each sentence of the paragraph, read your main idea sentence. It should be more general than all the other sentences. The main idea sentence will sum up and unify all of the other sentences of the paragraph.

Consider these two examples.

Example 1   In this paragraph the main idea is not stated in any one sentence. However, when you add together what is stated—the topic and controlling thought—you can infer the main idea.

[1]In the vast, dry Arizona desert, it's not easy to come by a cool drink of water, a natural swimming pool and a fishing hole all in one place. [2]But for thousands of birds, the area surrounding the Colorado River—the Imperial National Wildlife Refuge—provides just that. (Jones, *Taking Refuge*)

Who or what is Jones writing about? (the topic) _____

What does Jones want you to understand about the topic? (controlling thought) _____

_____

_____

Therefore, the main idea of this paragraph is _____

_____

_____

_____

Explanation   Who or what is Jones writing about? *Arizona's Imperial National Wildlife Refuge.* What does Jones want you to understand about the Imperial National Wildlife Refuge? *That it provides a wonderful natural habitat for birds.* Thus we can infer the main idea is: *Arizona's Imperial National Wildlife Refuge provides a wonderful natural habitat for birds.*

Example 2   Read this paragraph. Identify the topic and the controlling thought, then state the main idea in your own words.

[1]It is estimated that the average American who enters the workforce today will change careers, not just jobs, five to seven times. [2]This means that training for work should emphasize transferable skills, not simply specific knowledge and particular skills. [3]Examples of nonspecific, and thus transferable, skills include time management, personnel management, and self-management skills. [4]A specific skill, such as the ability to take dictation, can become outdated. (Alexander, *Adjustment and Human Relations*)

Who or what is Alexander writing about? (the topic) _____

What does Alexander want you to understand about the topic? (controlling thought) _____

_____

_____

Therefore, the main idea of this paragraph is _____

_____

_____

_____

Explanation   Who or what is Alexander writing about? *Americans can plan on changing careers several times.* What does Alexander want you to understand about *Americans changing careers several times*? *That the best preparation is learning general skills that can be applied to several careers, rather than job-specific skills.* Thus we can infer the main idea is: *Because Americans are likely to change careers several times, the best preparation is to learn general skills that can be applied to several careers, rather than job-specific skills.*

■ **EXERCISE 3.9: IDENTIFYING AN IMPLIED MAIN IDEA**

The main idea in each paragraph is implied. Following each paragraph are three possible main idea statements. Circle the letter of the sentence that best expresses the main idea. Remember, the main idea answers both: "Who or what is the author writing about?" *and* "What does the author want me to know about the who or what?"

1. The biggest challenges facing small businesses have traditionally been taxes, government regulations, and access to money. But a recent study finds a bigger problem in this day of low unemployment rates—a labor shortage. The Small Business Administration (SBA) study found that about half of small businesses are looking to hire someone and most of them are having trouble finding good people. (Small Business Administration, *Labor Shortages and Related Issues in Small Businesses*)

    a. Small businesses often have problems with taxes, laws, and money.

    b. The unemployment rate is at an all-time low.

    c. Currently, the biggest problem for small businesses is finding good workers.

2. Mexico still has a small population of wolves, with somewhat larger populations—perhaps twenty to twenty-five thousand—remaining in Alaska and Canada. The largest concentrations of wolves still in the lower forty-eight states are in northeastern Minnesota (about one thousand) and on the Isle Royale in Lake Superior (about thirty). There is a very small wolf population in Glacier National Park in Montana and a few in Michigan's Upper Peninsula. Occasionally lone wolves show up in the western states along the Canadian border.... (Adapted from Lopez, *Of Wolves and Men*)

    a. The number of wolves in North America has gotten smaller over the years.

    b. The largest concentration of wolves in the lower forty-eight states is in northeastern Minnesota.

    c. About twenty to twenty-five thousand wolves remain in Alaska and Canada.

3. There's no question that word-processing programs streamline the writing process. But there's a tendency to give those programs more credit than they deserve. After all, a computer is pretty stupid. It's just a tool, kind of like a screwdriver. A good screwdriver does the hard work, but you still have to pick out the right screw for the job. It's the same when you use the computer as a tool to help you write. You still have to supply the key ingredient for good writing—the thinking that underlies it. (Chan and Lutovich, *Can a Computer Improve Your Writing?*)

    a. Although a computer can help in some ways, good writing still requires good thinking.

    b. A computer is just a tool like a screwdriver.

    c. A word-processing program makes some parts of the writing process easier.

4. Employees should have a clear idea of what they are trying to accomplish in their jobs. Further, managers have the responsibility for seeing that this is achieved by helping employees to set work goals. These two statements seem obvious. Employees need to know what they're supposed to do, and it's the manager's job to provide this guidance. Simple? Hardly! (Robbins, *Training in InterPersonal Skills*)

   a. Employees need to know what they're supposed to do in their jobs.

   b. It is a manager's job to help employees know what they're supposed to do.

   c. A manager's responsibility for helping employees set work goals isn't as simple as it seems.

5. Individuals and companies are purchasing small, inexpensive microcomputers for a variety of business and domestic applications. The growth of this general area, called personal computing, has surpassed even the most adventurous forecasts of a decade ago. Some high-tech companies actually have more personal computers than telephones. (Long and Long, *Computing*)

   a. Personal computing is becoming so popular that it is growing even faster than predicted.

   b. Companies are purchasing microcomputers for a variety of business applications.

   c. The personal computer is more popular than the telephone.

6. Six billion is an enormous number, impossible to imagine in any context. Yet sometime during 1999 the human population on Earth reached and began surpassing 6 billion people. The United Nations projects continued population growth well into the twenty-first century, and there is no reason to doubt that our numbers may well reach 9 billion before the middle of the century—a 50 percent increase in 50 years. Virtually all of the increase will be in the developing countries, which are already densely populated and straining to meet the needs of their people for food, water, health, shelter, and employment. (Nebel and Wright, *Environmental Science*)

   a. In 1999 the human population on Earth reached and began surpassing 6 billion people.

   b. The human population of Earth is growing so fast it is becoming difficult to meet the needs of all the people.

   c. There will probably be 9 billion people on Earth before the middle of this century—a 50 percent increase in 50 years.

■ EXERCISE 3.10: IDENTIFYING THE MAIN IDEA

Write the main idea of each paragraph. Remember, whether the main idea is stated or implied, it answers both: "Who or what is the author writing about?" *and* "What does the author want me to know about the what or who?"

1. [1]A hockey player rushing up ice travels at more than twenty-five miles an hour; a slap shot hurls a frozen rubber disc toward a goalie at one hundred miles an hour. [2]Everything that happens

in hockey—passing, stickhandling, checking, shooting—happens fast. (Greenfield, "The Iceman Arriveth")

_____

_____

_____

2. [1]Acadia National Park in Maine offers visitors a variety of wonderful scenery. [2]Established as a national park in 1919, it includes a rugged coastal region of great natural beauty with the highest land on the eastern seaboard. [3]It consists of most of Mount Desert Island, parts of Isle au Haut, and a number of other islets, as well as the tip of the Schoodic Peninsula. [4]The coast is characterized by wave-eroded granite cliffs. [5]The inland portion of the park is forested with spruce and fir, and contains lakes and mountains carved by glacial action. (McGrath and McGrath, "Travel Treasures")

_____

_____

_____

3. [1]Of all the skills we are taught in high school and college, few receive less emphasis than listening skills. [2]Instead, we concentrate most of our time on speaking and becoming good senders of communication. [3]But our success as senders is directly tied to our ability to understand the total communication process, and that involves listening. [4]Listening involves much more than just "hearing" what someone is saying. [5]In fact, being a good listener often requires greater skill than being a good speaker. (Bittner, *Each Other*)

_____

_____

_____

4. [1]When you set a purpose for reading, you focus your attention on the specific parts of the assignment you need to understand. [2]Without setting goals you are saying that everything in the assignment is of equal value and that you want to learn it all in complete detail. [3]Although this total-mastery approach may be necessary in a few reading assignments each term, most times it will just lead to frustration and information overload. [4]Setting a purpose each time you read can make you more effective and efficient. (McGrath, *Understanding Diverse Viewpoints*)

_____

_____

_____

5. [1]There seems to be no limit to the number of individuals a single person is capable of recognizing. [2]An adult living in a large city probably sees millions of faces over a lifetime, and can recognize

thousands of them, even if he cannot assign names to them. [3]Not even the passage of decades clouds the memory for faces. [4]Psychologists have shown people photographs cut from their high school yearbooks fifteen years after graduation, and they were able to match 90 percent of the faces with the correct names. [5]Nearly fifty years after graduation, the accuracy only dropped to 70 percent. (Brownlee, "What's in a Face")

_____

_____

_____

6. [1]What is a budget? [2]Put very simply, a budget is any plan—simple or complex—that expresses your financial goals and how you will allocate your limited resources to achieve them. [3]A budget can be so simple that you keep it on the back of an envelope and monitor your monthly progress with checkmarks. [4]Or it can be as complex as the one the federal government prepares each year, detailing how almost $2 trillion will be spent. (Winger and Frasca, *Personal Finance*)

_____

_____

_____

■ EXERCISE 3.11: IDENTIFYING THE MAIN IDEA

Write the main idea of each paragraph. Remember, whether the main idea is stated or implied, it answers both: "Who or what is the author writing about?" *and* "What does the author want me to know about the what or who?"

1. [1]Led Zeppelin was an incredibly important band from 1968 until 1983. [2]The two most important members were probably Jimmy Page, recognized by everyone for his influence on rock guitar players, and the vocalist Robert Plant. [3]While Jimi Hendrix may be credited as rock's most significant guitar player and the first influence leading toward heavy metal, Led Zeppelin should be considered the first great heavy metal band. [4]Led Zeppelin has also influenced the mythology of heavy metal, since Jimmy Page believes in exotic philosophies; this clearly comes through their song lyrics and playing style. (Brown, *The Art of Rock and Roll*)

_____

_____

_____

2. [1]Tornadoes and hurricanes are nature's most awesome storms. [2]Because of this status, they are logically the focus of much well-deserved attention. [3]Yet, surprisingly, these dreaded events are

not responsible for the greatest number of weather-related deaths. [4]That distinction is reserved for lightning and flash floods.

_____

_____

_____

3. [1]Online investing is fast, easy, cheap, and puts you totally in charge—which gives it the appeal of a good video game. [2]If you use it sensibly, you'll invest more efficiently. [3]But if you forget that each mouse click is a real financial decision, you quickly can dig yourself into a hole. (Brenner, "The Smart Way to Invest Online," *Parade*)

_____

_____

_____

4. [1]A well-known proverb states: "The best potential in 'me' is 'we.'" [2]The underlying message in this proverb is critical for good team work: For you to reach your ultimate potential at school and/or at work, you must work with your team and not against it. [3]If team members focus only on themselves and the credit they receive rather than focusing on the success of the team as a whole, both the team member's performance and the team's overall performance will suffer. (Adapted from Manz and Neck, *Mastering Self-Leadership*)

_____

_____

_____

5. [1]You are unique. [2]No one in the world likes exactly the same music, food, movies, books, clothes, colors, or people as you do. [3]While you may find a lot in common with others, you alone possess your unique personality. (Carter and Troyka, *Majoring in the Rest of Your Life*)

_____

_____

_____

6. [1]The *curve of forgetting*, discovered by German psychologist Hermann Ebbinghaus in the late 1800s, shows that our memory for learned material is best right after the learning session. [2]As time passes, we forget more and more. [3]This basic finding has been reproduced numerous times since Ebbinghaus discovered it. [4]For example, Jenkins and Dallenbach (1924) found that subjects recalled the most when they were tested immediately following learning. [5]In their experiment, the subjects learned a list of 10 nonsense syllables and then were asked to recall the list

1/2, 2, 4, and 8 hours later. [6]One-half hour following the initial training session, the subjects were able to recall half of the list; their performance became worse as time passed. [7]The *curve of forgetting* research is clear: You can expect your best recall shortly after a learning session. (Adapted from Davis and Palladino, *Psychology*)

CHAPTER REVIEW

SUMMARY OF KEY IDEAS

- Understanding individual words and sentences is important. However, it is equally important to understand paragraphs. A paragraph is a group of sentences that fit together to support and explain one main idea.
- When you are reading for learning, you almost always need to understand a paragraph's main idea. This is because the main idea is the general or *umbrella idea* that ties all the sentences and bits and pieces of information together.
- Key to understanding groups of words and sentences is figuring out how they relate to one another. One important relationship is the level of specificity—is one word or idea more *general* or *specific* than another.
- An author often states the main idea in the first sentence of the paragraph. However, the main idea can appear anywhere in a paragraph. In addition, authors do not always state the main idea of a paragraph. When this happens, the author wants you to infer the main idea.
- Whether the main idea is stated or implied, your strategy for identifying and understanding the main idea is the same:
  1. Identify the topic by answering the question "Who or what is the author writing about?"
  2. Clarify the controlling thought by answering "What does the author want me to know or understand about the topic?"
  3. Combine the topic and controlling thought into a main idea statement.
- To be sure you understand the author's idea, it is a good idea to rephrase the main idea using your own words.

SELF CHECK

- I can distinguish between general and specific words and ideas.
- I can identify the main idea of a paragraph, whether it is directly stated or implied.

PUTTING IT ALL TOGETHER

Fill in the blanks following each paragraph.

1. [1]You may think of communication only in terms of conversations with friends. [2]But communication goes far beyond that. [3]Communication is the <u>transmission</u> of information and meaning from one individual to another. [4]The <u>central concept</u> here is meaning. [5]Communication is only successful when both parties understand not only the information communicated but also the meaning of that information. (Donatelle and Davis, *Access to Health*)

    transmission means _____

    a central concept is_____

    _____

    Main idea _____

    _____

2. [1]American artist Mary Cassatt (1844–1926) possessed both <u>superb</u> technical skill and great talent. [2]Her dedication and devotion to the highest standards for her art helped her overcome the "handicap" of being a woman. [3]As an American in Paris, at a time when Paris was the center of the art world, she absorbed the best innovations in her <u>contemporary</u> world of painting. [4]Cassatt developed an independent style based on precise draftsmanship, refined color sensibility, and a gift for creative compositions. (Slatkin, *Women Artists in History*)

    superb means _____

    contemporary means _____

    Main idea _____

    _____

3. [1]No matter how much we look at the events of our lives with <u>optimism</u>, we all find that troubles will at times dim our path. [2]Part of life involves dealing with disheartening events from loneliness, depression, or unfair treatment at the hands of others, to the loss of a loved one. [3]It is to our advantage to learn how to face these troublesome times in our lives. [4]Most important is for us to get past them and not to let their pain <u>hinder</u> us in such a way that we are too discouraged to go on. (Alexander, *Adjustment and Human Relations*)

    optimism means _____

    hinder means _____

    Main idea _____

    _____

4. [1]People travel for a variety of reasons: study, work, leisure, and to volunteer. [2]Regardless of the motivation, experiencing the world offers <u>immense</u> personal and professional rewards. [3]By <u>venturing</u> out of your safe, familiar environment, you gain

insights about humanity and about yourself. [4]Your understanding of other cultures expands along with your self-awareness, important elements in developing a healthy worldview. (Carter and Troyka, *Majoring in the Rest of Your Life*)

immense means _____

venturing means _____

Main idea _____

_____

5. [1]A quiet but powerful revolution is reshaping the United States. [2]The number of elderly people—women and men aged sixty-five and over—is increasing more than twice as fast as the population as a whole. [3]Between 1970 and 1996, while the overall U.S. population rose 31 percent, the number of seniors climbed by 69 percent, and the number over age eighty-five <u>soared</u> by 167 percent. [4]This "graying" of the United States promises <u>profound</u> effects. (Macionis, *Sociology*)

soared means _____

profound means _____

Main idea _____

_____

6. [1]You can have the best coach in the world, someone who knows the game [tennis] inside out and is an excellent teacher. [2]But he or she can only help to a certain point. [3]After that, it's up to you to produce the <u>mental side</u>, to carry out what the coach has said. [4]My dad taught me how to play the game, but I taught myself to win. [5]<u>Embracing</u> his belief that the one who works the hardest will do the best started me on the road to success. (Evert Lloyd, *Chrissie: An Autobiography*)

mental side means _____

embracing means _____

Main idea _____

_____

7. [1]Understanding what someone is saying often involves much more than listening and speaking. [2]It is often what is *not* actually said that may speak louder than any words. [3]Rolling your eyes, looking at the floor or ceiling when speaking rather than <u>maintaining</u> eye contact, body movements, hand gestures—all these nonverbal clues influence the way we interpret messages. [4]Researchers have found that only 7 percent of the meaning of a message comes from the words spoken. [5]An <u>astounding</u> 93 percent of the meaning comes from nonverbal cues. (Donatelle and Davis, *Access to Health*)

maintaining means _____

astounding means _____

Main idea _____

_____

8. [1]Vote-by-mail elections have stirred a growing <u>controversy</u>. [2]<u>Critics</u> fear that the process threatens the principle of the secret ballot. [3]They worry about fraud, and especially the possibility that some voters may be subjected to undue pressures when they mark their ballots. [4]Its supporters say that it can be as fraud-proof as any other method of voting. [5]They also cite this fact: The process increases voter turnout in local elections and, at the same time, reduces the costs of conducting them. (McClenaghan, *Magruder's American Government*)

controversy means _____

critics are _____

Main idea _____

_____

9. [1]In the very distant past, life on Earth was far different from what it is today. [2]Most people lived in small tribes and family groups that hunted animals and gathered plants for food. [3]Because these groups were small and almost always on the move, their effects on the environment were minimal. [4]Natural processes could easily <u>restore depleted</u> food sources and break down wastes once the humans moved on. (Miller and Levine, *Biology*)

restore means _____

depleted means _____

Main idea _____

_____

10. [1]Your body movement and posture can send powerful <u>nonverbal</u> clues. [2]For instance, how you walk is often a strong <u>indicator</u> of how you feel. [3]When you have a problem, you may walk very slowly with your head down and your hands clasped behind your back. [4]You may even pause to kick a rock on the ground. [5]On the other hand, when you feel especially proud and happy, you may walk with your chin raised, your arms swinging freely, and your legs somewhat stiff—with a bounce in your step. (Adapted from Barker and Barker, *Communication*)

nonverbal means_____

indicator means _____

Main idea _____

_____

CROSSWORD PUZZLE

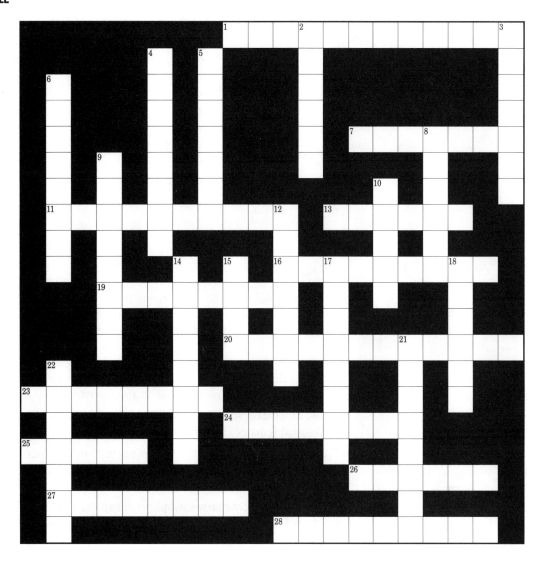

ACROSS

1   a connection between
7   impressive
11 amazing
13 block or obstruct
16 not spoken
19 divide
20 transfer
23 significant
24 home and family
25 fundamental
26 sanctuary
27 stress
28 accepting

DOWN

2   influence
3   an old saying
4   huge
5   not stated
6   reword
8   excellent
9   absolute maximum
10 make reasoned conclusion
12 broad and comprehensive
14 joined together
15 very large
17 without meaning
18 opposite of passive
21 limited and narrow
22 feared

WORD LIST

active	emphasis	refuge
affect	enormous	relationship
allocate	general	rephrase
astounding	hinder	specific
awesome	implied	superb
basic	infer	transmission
combined	nonsense	ultimate
domestic	nonverbal	vast
dreaded	profound	
embracing	proverb	

Log on to the Web

Practice good reading skills on current reading material by logging on to one of these sites or use a search directory/engine to locate a 'zine or online version of a print magazine with information that interests you.

Addicted to Noise at <http://www.addict.com> is a music 'zine that contains daily music news, album and concert reviews, and music columns by some of rock's most famous writers.

Salon at <http://www.salon.com> is one of the Web's most popular 'zines and features original content daily.

Parenting Toolbox at <http://www.parentingtoolbox.com> is designed for nontraditional families and provides articles and advice on raising good kids.

Backpacker at <http://www.bpbasecamp.com> is the online version of *Backpacker Magazine*. It includes news, features, and daily tips for hikers.

Creative Seasoning Network at <http://www.creativeseasoning.com> is a 'zine that focuses on growing and using herbs and spices as well as interesting bits about their history.

Read a paragraph or short selection with the specific purpose of understanding the main idea. Print out the paragraph or short selection you read and write down: (1) the complete address (http://www. ...), (2) the name of the person or company who sponsors and maintains the site, (3) the name of the person who wrote information you read, (4) what you know about the writer, (5) the main idea of the paragraph.

Ideas for Writing and Discussion

A. Since the 1960s when people started wearing T-shirts with messages like, "Keep on Truckin'," the T-shirt has become a walking billboard of individual expression. "The T-shirt is like a camera," says Scott Fresener, the author of *The T-Shirt Book*, "providing a photo of your thoughts."

If you were to design a T-shirt, what would it say? Why would you select that message?

B. In the past two days, how many times have you smiled at someone? How many positive thoughts have you enjoyed? How many times have you said something like "thank you" or "I appreciate your help" and how many times have you done something for someone else so that they could make a comment like that to you?

Behaviors like these reflect your attitude. How important do you think a positive attitude is to your success in school, work, and life.

C. Make a list of three tasks and activities you consider to be *active*. Then list three tasks and activities you consider to be *passive*. Consider the differences in your behavior when you complete activities on the two lists.

What are some of the reasons why effective reading must be an *active* rather than a *passive* activity?

MORE ABOUT READING PARAGRAPHS

CHAPTER PREVIEW

Objectives
- Distinguish among major details, minor details, and irrelevant details.
- Identify the pattern(s) of organization authors use to develop the details.
- Identify signal words and phrases.

Sections

CHAPTER FOCUS

If authors only wrote main idea statements, paragraphs would be only one sentence long. That means there wouldn't be any details to support or explain the idea. Without details, we wouldn't have any information to help us understand the main idea or give us the opportunity to learn more about the idea. Fortunately, authors do write more than main ideas. They almost always explain, expand, and support their ideas with a variety of details.

SECTION 4.1   IDENTIFYING MAJOR AND MINOR DETAILS

Early in Chapter 3 you discovered that knowing the relationships among words and sentences is important. Specifically, you found that distinguishing between general and specific words and ideas helped you identify an author's main idea. Now, let's consider another important aspect of the relationships among groups of words and sentences: how details support and explain a main idea.

Because a paragraph can have any number of sentences, it can have any number of details. There are two general categories of details that support main ideas: major details and minor details.

A *major detail* is a specific piece of information that directly supports and explains the main idea.

Example   In a previous exercise you determined that sentence 1 is the main idea of this paragraph about Acadia National Park. Now, look at the other sentences.

[1]Acadia National Park in Maine offers visitors a variety of wonderful scenery. [2]Established as a national park in 1919, it includes a rugged coastal region of great natural beauty with the highest land on the eastern seaboard. [3]It consists of most of Mount Desert Island, parts of Isle au Haut, and a number of other islets, as well as the tip of the Schoodic Peninsula. [4]The coast is characterized by wave-eroded granite cliffs. [5]The inland portion of the park is forested with spruce and fir, and contains lakes and mountains carved by glacial action.

Explanation   Sentences 2, 3, 4, and 5 contain specific examples to directly support and explain the main idea that Acadia National Park offers visitors "a variety of wonderful scenery." Thus they are called major details.

A *minor detail* is a very specific piece of information that supports and explains a major detail.

Example   Consider the relationships among the three sentences in this revised paragraph about Acadia National Park.

[1]Acadia National Park in Maine offers visitors a variety of wonderful scenery. [2]Established as a national park in 1919, it includes a rugged coastal region of great natural beauty with the highest land on the eastern seaboard. [3]For example, the park's Cadillac Mountain is 1,530 feet above sea level.

Explanation   Sentence 1 is still the main idea and sentence 2 still contains a major detail. However, the information in the new sentence 3 is a specific piece of information that supports and explains "the highest land on the eastern seaboard" in sentence 2. Therefore, sentence 3 is a minor detail.

In addition to major and minor details, some paragraphs contain information that is interesting, and sometimes important, but does not support or develop the main idea. This type of information is called *irrelevant* to the paragraph.

Example   Consider the relationships among the four sentences in this revised paragraph about Acadia National Park.

[1]Acadia National Park in Maine offers visitors a variety of wonderful scenery. [2]Established as a national park in 1919, it includes a rugged coastal region of great natural beauty with the highest land on the eastern seaboard. [3]The inland portion of the park is forested with spruce and fir, and contains lakes and mountains carved by glacial action. [4]It was known as Lafayette National Park from 1919 to 1929.

Explanation   Sentence 1 is still the main idea. Sentences 2 and 3 contain major details that directly support and explain the main idea. The information in the new sentence 4 is interesting and important, but irrelevant to this main idea.

Although the relationships among sentences may not be this obvious in real paragraphs, you can use the same strategy to figure them out:

Does the information directly support and explain the *main idea*?
If yes, it's a major detail. If no,
Does the information support and explain a *major detail*?
If yes, it's a minor detail. If no, it's probably irrelevant to this main idea.

Example   Look again at this paragraph on the devices people created to mark the passage of time. Earlier, you determined the main idea is stated in the last sentence. Now, decide the role of each of the other sentences: major detail, minor detail, or irrelevant.

[1]The earliest device created to measure the passage of time was the sundial. [2]It measured the sun's shadow. [3]The water clock was an improvement over the sundial since it didn't depend on the sun. [4]Once the art of glass making was perfected, the hourglass was created to mark the passage of time with sand. [5]People created several ways of keeping track of the passage of time before the invention of the modern clock.

Sentence 1 _____

Sentence 2 _____

Sentence 3 _____

Sentence 4 _____

Sentence 5 _____

Explanation   Sentence 1 is a major detail because it directly supports and explains the main idea by giving the sundial as an example of "several ways of keeping track of the passage of time." Sentence 2 is a minor detail because it supports and explains the major detail in Sentence 1 by telling how a sundial works. Sentences 3 and 4 are major details because they directly support and explain the main idea by giving additional examples of "several ways of keeping track of the passage of time."

■ Exercise 4.1: Identifying Major, Minor, and Irrelevant Details

The main idea is underlined in each paragraph. Determine the role of each of the other sentences: major detail, minor detail, or irrelevant.

Example

[1]<u>Studies show that keeping a positive attitude pays off</u>. [2]Research has found that individuals with positive outlooks do better in school, their careers, and personal lives than pessimists. [3]In one study, for instance, insurance salespeople who had positive outlooks sold 56 percent more insurance than less optimistic coworkers. (Bruce and Foley, "Is It Time for an Attitude Adjustment?" *USA Today*)

Sentence 2 _____

Sentence 3 _____

Explanation   Sentence 1 is the main idea. It tells us what the authors are writing about—"keeping a positive attitude," and what they want us to know about keeping a positive attitude—that it pays off. Sentence 2 is a major detail because it directly supports and develops the main idea by giving an example of how keeping a positive attitude pays off: Research shows people who have it do better in school, their careers, and personal lives. Sentence 3 is a minor detail because it directly supports and develops the major detail by giving an example of how they do better in their careers.

1. <u>[1]By staying on top of things from day to day, you can make housework easier and more manageable.</u> [2]For example, teach the family the beauty of hanging up clothes when they take them off. [3]Throwing them on the floor creates more laundry and more work. [4]To save time, try cleaning a drawer or dusting the blinds while you talk on the phone. (Pinkham, *TIPical Mary Ellen*)

   Sentence 2 _____

   Sentence 3 _____

   Sentence 4 _____

2. <u>[1]Shy people tend to lack social skills.</u> [2]They avoid eye contact and are inclined to withdraw when spoken to. [3]They show little interest or vitality, and they pause too long in conversations. [4]Many have not learned how to meet others. [5]For instance, they have not learned how to start a conversation and keep it going or how to end social encounters. [6]Most shy people have social anxiety. [7]For example, they fear being evaluated, embarrassed, ridiculed, rejected, and found inadequate. (Alexander, *Adjustment and Human Relations*)

   Sentence 2 _____

   Sentence 3 _____

   Sentence 4 _____

   Sentence 5 _____

   Sentence 6 _____

   Sentence 7 _____

3. <u>[1]Tomorrow, a new wave of technologies will emerge that will continue to cause radical changes in our lives.</u> [2]For example, if you're in the market for a new home, you will spend less time in the seat of a realtor's car because you will be able to "visit" any home for sale in the country via computer from the comfort of your home. [3]All you will need to do is select a city and enter your criteria to take advantage of the ultimate real estate multi-list. [4]The electronic realtor will then list those houses that meet your criteria, provide you with detailed information on the house and surrounding area, then offer to take you on a tour of the house—inside and out. [5]After the electronic tour, you will be able to "drive" through the neighborhood, looking left and right as you would in your automobile. (Long and Long, *Computers*)

   Sentence 2 _____

   Sentence 3 _____

   Sentence 4 _____

   Sentence 5 _____

4. [1]Everyone copes with stress in different ways. [2]For some people, drinking and taking drugs helps them to cope. [3]Others choose to get help from counselors. [4]Still others try to keep their minds off stress or to engage in positive activities such as exercise or relaxation techniques. (Donatelle and Davis, *Access to Health*)

Sentence 2 _____

Sentence 3 _____

Sentence 4 _____

5. [1]Positive reinforcers are events or stimuli such as food, water, money, or praise that are presented after the target response occurs. [2]For example, a real estate agent earns a commission for each house she sells; the commissions reinforce her for selling as many houses as possible. [3]Your little brother is allowed to watch cartoons on Saturday morning after he has cleaned his room; as a result, he cleans his room every Saturday. [4]You have been praised for receiving good grades on psychology tests; the praise should encourage you to study even harder. (Davis and Palladino, *Psychology*)

Sentence 2 _____

Sentence 3 _____

Sentence 4 _____

6. [1]Every rock contains clues about the environment in which it formed. [2]For example, some rocks are composed entirely of small shell fragments, which tells Earth scientists that the particles came from a shallow marine environment. [3]Other rocks contain clues that indicate they formed from a volcanic eruption, or deep in the Earth during mountain building. [4]Thus, rocks contain a wealth of information about events that have occurred over Earth's long history. (Lutgens and Tarbuck, *Foundations of Earth Science*)

Sentence 2 _____

Sentence 3 _____

■ **Exercise 4.2: Identifying Main Ideas and Major, Minor, and Irrelevant Details**

Read each paragraph. Determine the main idea and write it in the space provided. Then, decide the role of each sentence. Label each sentence as one of the following:

- main idea (or part of the main idea)
- major detail
- minor detail
- irrelevant information

1. [1]The demand for registered nurses (RNs) is on the upswing. [2]Two of the reasons for the increase are our aging population and more hospitalized patients who are older and acutely ill. [3]However, as the demand is increasing, nursing school enrollments are declining. [4]For example, enrollments of nursing school students in entry-level bachelor's degree programs fell 4.6 percent in the fall of 1999. [5]Most RNs in the United States are women. (Medical Press Corps News Service)

Main idea _____

Sentence 1 _____

Sentence 2 _____

Sentence 3 _____

Sentence 4 _____

Sentence 5 _____

2. [1]Setting specific, reasonably difficult goals improves performance. [2]A major reason is that when we guide our lives with goals, we tend to focus our efforts in a consistent direction. [3]Without goals, our efforts may become scattered in many directions. [4]We may keep trying, but without goals we will go nowhere unless we happen to receive more than our share of luck. (Adapted from DuBrin, *Human Relations*)

Main idea _____

Sentence 1 _____

Sentence 2 _____

Sentence 3 _____

Sentence 4 _____

3. [1]Many factors influence when we eat, what we eat, and how much we eat. [2]Sensory stimulation, such as smelling, seeing, and tasting foods, can entice us to eat. [3]Social pressures, including family traditions, social events that involve eating, and busy work schedules, can also influence our diets.... [4]Cultural factors also play a role in how we eat. [5]People from Middle-eastern cultures tend to eat more rice, fruits, and vegetables than does the typical American. [6]The Japanese eat more fish.... (Donatelle and Davis, *Access to Health*)

Main idea _____

Sentence 1 _____

Sentence 2 _____

Sentence 3 _____

Sentence 4 _____

Sentence 5 _____

Sentence 6 _____

4. [1]As people age, physical changes occur in the body. [2]These changes affect many body systems. [3]In addition, there are many role changes that occur in aging persons. [4]These work, family, and social changes affect many aspects of both physical and mental health. (Adapted from Badasch and Chesebro, *Health Occupations*)

Main idea _____

Sentence 1 _____

Sentence 2 _____

Sentence 3 _____

Sentence 4 _____

5. [1]The key to a healthy, well-balanced diet is eating the correct amounts of a variety of essential foods. [2]These essential foods are divided into six groups on *The Food Guide Pyramid*. [3]If you eat the recommended number of portions of food from each group on the pyramid every day, your diet will be adequate for good health. [4]The number and size of portions will depend on the age, size, and activities of the individual. (Wolgin, *A Nursing Assistant*)

Main idea _____

Sentence 1 _____

Sentence 2 _____

Sentence 3 _____

Sentence 4 _____

6. [1]Your choice of a bank is usually determined by a variety of factors. [2]Perhaps the most important of these is convenience. [3]In addition, the range of services provided by the bank is also often considered. [4]Finally, what the bank charges to service the account and what it offers in interest on average balances must be evaluated. [5]Shop around to find a checking account that fills your needs best. (Winger and Frasca, *Personal Finance*)

Main idea _____

Sentence 1 _____

Sentence 2 _____

Sentence 3 _____

Sentence 4 _____

Sentence 5 _____

SECTION 4.2   IDENTIFYING THE WAY AN AUTHOR ORGANIZES DETAILS AND/OR SENTENCES

Because a paragraph can contain any number of sentences and have any number of major and minor details, authors try to organize them in a way that will best help the reader understand them. In textbooks, the ways authors use to organize information are predictable and identifiable. Not every paragraph uses just one recognizable pattern of organization. However, when you can identify the way the author develops the details, it prompts you to become a more active and successful reader.

For instance, if you determine an author has developed a paragraph using comparison (similarities) and contrast (differences) you can actively look for the ways the author thinks two or more things, ideas, or people are the same and/or different. On the other hand, if you discover the author is using time order (listing details in the order in which they happened or will happen), you know to look for a sequence of times and dates.

Fortunately, identifying an author's pattern of organization is not a guessing game. Authors generally use signal words and punctuation marks as clues to their organization. Common examples include phrases like *for example, for instance, however,* and *on the other hand.*

Words like these, often called transitions, help you understand an author's ideas by signaling the author's direction of thought or shifts in viewpoint. They also alert you to particular types of information to help you figure out the relationships among different kinds and levels of information. There are many words, phrases, and punctuation marks that can be clues. Consider these two examples.

Example 1   As you reread this paragraph by Alexander from a previous exercise, notice the two signal phrases. Identify what they signal.

> ¹Shy people tend to lack social skills. ²They avoid eye contact and are inclined to withdraw when spoken to. ³They show little interest or vitality, and they pause too long in conversations. ⁴Many have not learned how to meet others. ⁵<u>For instance</u>, they have not learned how to start a conversation and keep it going or how to end social encounters. ⁶Most shy people have social anxiety. ⁷<u>For example</u>, they fear being evaluated, embarrassed, ridiculed, rejected, and found inadequate. (Alexander, *Adjustment and Human Relations*)

The phrase in sentence 5 signals _____

The phrase in sentence 7 signals _____

Explanation   The signal phrase "for instance" helps you figure out the relationship of sentence 5 to sentence 4 (5 gives an example of 4), and "for example" is a clue to the relationship of sentence 7 to sentence 6 (7 gives an example of 6).

Example 2   Identify the signal phrase Carter and Troyka use in sentence 3 and what it signals.

> ¹You make decisions every day. ²Some of them are insignificant, such as whether you wear a blue shirt or a red shirt. ³On the other hand, some decisions are crucial to your future, such as where you will attend college or what major you choose. (Carter and Troyka, *Majoring in the Rest of Your Life*)

The signal phrase in sentence 3 is _____

The phrase signals _____

Explanation   The phrase "on the other hand," signals a change in direction of thought from the previous sentence. Sentence 2 is about insignificant decisions. Sentence 3 is changing to significant decisions.

Six common ways, or patterns, textbook authors use to organize details that support and explain main ideas are the following:

- examples or listing
- comparison and/or contrast

- time order or steps in a sequence
- definition
- classification
- cause and effect

In addition, authors often combine two patterns.

ORGANIZING USING EXAMPLES OR LISTING

Using a specific, relevant example or a listing of examples is one of the most common ways authors organize information to support and develop a main idea. Authors also often use examples in combination with other patterns of organization such as definition and classification.

Words and punctuation that may signal examples include the following:

for example
to illustrate
for instance
such as
specifically
namely
the abbreviations i.e. and e.g.
punctuation marks like the dash [—] and colon [:]

Words that signal a continuation of thought or list include the following:

and
too
in addition
moreover
or
also
another
furthermore
as well as
besides
in other words

Topic sentences such as these alert you to read for examples or lists:

The best strategy for staying warm is to rely on an old mountaineering technique known as layering, a method that helps the body maintain a comfortable balance between heat generated and heat lost. For example, the first layer....

(*You would read for details that give examples of what's in each layer.*)

There are many examples of how most of our closely held beliefs are those we got while growing up.

(*You would read for details that give examples of beliefs we got from parents and others who influenced us while growing up.*)

Practice   Identify Manz and Neck's main idea and how they use an example to develop and support that idea.

[1]Most of our activities possess what we would consider both pleasant and unpleasant characteristics. [2]A runner, for example, can think about heat and sweat, sore muscles, exhaustion, blisters, and a score of other things most people would consider unpleasant; or, a runner can think about praise from others for his or her excellent physical condition, of a potentially longer life due to improved health, and the feeling of power and strength that accompanies a conditioned runner's stride. [3]Both types of thoughts are available to a runner, and the type the runner chooses will significantly affect his or her enjoyment of the activity. (Manz and Neck, *Mastering Self-Leadership*)

_____

_____

Explanation   The main idea is "the aspects of an activity we choose to focus on—pleasant or unpleasant—influence how much we will enjoy it." Sentence 2 gives specific examples of how thinking about the pleasant or unpleasant characteristics of running will influence how much the runner enjoys running.

ORGANIZING USING COMPARISON AND CONTRAST

Authors can develop and support their main idea by giving the likenesses, the differences, or both the likenesses and differences between or among things or ideas or people. By having us look at two or more things, ideas, or people, authors help us see similarities we hadn't seen before or notice the unique features of each more clearly.

Words that may indicate comparisons or likeness include the following:

similarly
like
the same as
compared to
in the same way
likewise
parallels
resembles
equally
just as

Words that may indicate a change in thought or a contrast include the following:

but
yet
on the other hand
however
instead
nevertheless
on the contrary
unlike
in contrast to

whereas

in spite of

although

conversely

different from

rather than

just the opposite

Topic sentences such as the following alert you to watch for likenesses and/or differences:

Despite the differences between a computer and WebTV, they are alike in some ways.

(You would read for details that tell how a computer and WebTV are alike.)

While both African and American Black music contain an absolute regularity of pulse, the character of the rhythm of the two musics shows marked differences. (Brooks, *American Black Musical Heritage*)

(You would read for details that give the differences in the rhythm of the two musics.)

Both oral and written communication involve the creation and sending of messages. However, they differ in a number of ways. (Barker and Barker, *Communication*)

(You would read for details that give the differences between oral and written communication.)

There are many similarities between watching a movie and watching a play. However, there are also startling differences.

(You would read for the ways watching a movie and a play are the same and the ways they are different.)

Practice   Determine Stassel's main idea and what she compares and/or contrasts to develop and support that idea.

[1]Since "A is for Alibi" was published in 1982, Sue Grafton has been working her way to Z, chronicling the adventures of Kinsey Millhone, a tough, unpretentious private detective. [2]With sixteen books completed and only ten to go, Grafton and her fictional alphabet sleuth have a lot in common. [3]Both have an all-purpose long-sleeved black dress, which Millhone uses to blend in at cocktail parties, courthouse proceedings, and funerals. [4]They stay physically fit. [5]Both are squeamish about needles, have a strong attachment to their purses, and are expert at telling white lies. (Adapted from Stassel, "Grafton Keeps Mystery Alive")

_____

_____

Explanation   The main idea is "writer Sue Grafton and her fictional character Kinsey Millhone have a lot in common." Stassel supports and develops that idea in sentences 3–5 with specific details on how they are alike. Both have an all-purpose long-sleeved black dress, stay physically fit, are squeamish about needles, have a strong attachment to their purses, and are expert at telling white lies.

Practice   Determine Pirsig's main idea and what he compares and/or contrasts to develop and support that idea.

[1]You see things vacationing on a motorcycle in a way that is completely different from any other. [2]In a car you're always in a compartment, and because you're used to it you don't realize that through that car window everything you see is just more TV. [3]You're a passive observer and it is all moving by you boringly in a frame.

[4]On a cycle the frame is gone. [5]You're completely in contact with it all. [6]You're *in* the scene, not just watching it anymore, and the sense of presence is overwhelming. [7]That concrete whizzing by five inches below your foot is the real thing, the same stuff you walk on, it's right there, so blurred you can't focus on it, yet you can put your foot down and touch it anytime, and the whole thing, the whole experience, is never removed from immediate consciousness. (Pirsig, *Zen and the Art of Motorcycle Maintenance*)

_____

_____

Explanation   The main idea is "you see things vacationing on a motorcycle in a way that is completely different from any other." Pirsig's details in sentences 2–7 describe the differences between seeing things from a car and seeing things from a motorcycle.

ORGANIZING USING TIME ORDER OR STEPS IN A SEQUENCE

When authors want you to understand the order in which something has happened or will happen, or how to do something, they describe the sequence of steps followed or the behaviors needed to complete the process.

Words that signal time include the following:

previously

earlier

meanwhile

later

eventually

in the past

in the future

before

at present

Words and punctuation that may indicate a process or steps in a sequence include the following:

first, second, third ...

next

then

finally

eventually

following this

steps

at the start

to begin

initially

during the next hour, day, year

specific times or dates

Topic sentences such as these can alert you to a sequence of activities:

The interview, like any research, is a time-consuming process that involves a number of steps.

(*You would read for details that give the steps.*)

A caterpillar passes through many stages on its journey to become a butterfly.

(*You would read for the details that describe the stages.*)

Practice   Determine the main idea and the sequence of steps the details give to develop and support that idea.

[1]To bring out the beauty of a gem diamond, a number of processes are necessary. [2]These processes, which include cleaving, sawing, cutting, and polishing, are usually known collectively as diamond cutting and are the most exacting and difficult techniques of lapidary art. [3]The first step in cutting a diamond is the careful examination of the stone when the expert cutter determines the cleavage planes of the diamond and decides how the stone can best be divided by cleaving and sawing. [4]The rough diamond is then marked with lines of India ink as a guide for the later operations.

[5]The stone is then firmly cemented into a wooden holder and the holder firmly mounted in a vise. [6]The cutter then holds a cleaving iron, an instrument like a heavy, blunt knife, on the line and parallel to the cleavage plane of the diamond. [7]The stone is cleft by striking the iron with a light blow of a hammer. [8]In present-day practice, diamonds are sawed more often than they are cleaved. [9]The saw is a thin metal disk, the edge of which is charged with a mixture of diamond dust and oil.

[10]The final step in the cutting of a diamond, called polishing, consists of forming the facets of the finished stone. [11]For the polishing process the gem is held firmly in a mount called a dop. [12]Diamonds are most often cut in the form of brilliants with a total of 58 facets. [13]Facets are formed on a flat, horizontally revolving cast-iron wheel that is charged with a mixture of diamond dust and oil. [14]The stone in its dop is held against the surface until the facet is formed. [15]In the course of polishing, the stone is moved many times in its dop to present new surfaces to be polished. (Adapted from *Funk & Wagnalls New Encyclopedia*)

_____

_____

Explanation   The main idea is "to bring out the beauty of a gem diamond, a number of processes are necessary." The steps in the process are: (1) stone is carefully examined to determine the cleavage planes, (2) diamond is marked with lines of India ink, (3) stone is firmly cemented into wooden holder and holder firmly mounted in vise, (4) cutter cleaves (strikes) or saws along the marked cleavage plane of the diamond, (5) the gem is held firmly in a mount called a dop, (6) the stone in its dop is held against the surface of a flat, horizontally revolving cast-iron wheel until a facet is formed, and (7) the stone is moved many times in its dop to present new surfaces (total of 58 for a brilliant cut) to be polished.

ORGANIZING USING DEFINITION

Authors often need to clarify a definition or explain their personal interpretation of the meaning of a term or concept. Rarely, however, do they just state a definition. To help readers fully understand, authors usually define through combinations of: one or more dictionary definitions, one or more connotative meanings, the etymology (origins), comparisons and/or contrasts with other terms, examples, and negation—telling what it doesn't mean.

Words that may signal definition include the following:

define as
is
known
the term means
is stated as
is used to mean

Topic sentences such as these alert you to watch for definitions:

The first definition of *communicate* in the dictionary states that it is "To make known, impart; transmit." Now, let us look at other possible definitions. (Adapted from Bittner, *Each Other*)

(*You would read for details that give additional definitions for communicate.*)

The word *diet* has many meanings.

(*You would read for details that give various meanings of the word* diet.)

Practice   Determine the main idea and how the details develop and support that idea.

[1]Sexual harassment is defined by federal regulations as "unwelcome sexual advances, requests for sexual favors, and other verbal and physical contact of a sexual nature." [2]However, there are as many different definitions of what constitutes sexual harassment in the workplace as there are workers. [3]To some, an offensive comment or joke is sexual harassment. [4]Some define it as sexually explicit pictures or written material, while others interpret sexual harassment to mean inappropriate physical contact.

_____

_____

Explanation   The main idea is "although there is an official definition, there are probably as many different definitions of what constitutes sexual harassment in the workplace as there are workers." The author then provides the official definition in sentence 1, and three additional definitions in sentences 2–4.

ORGANIZING USING CLASSIFICATION

When authors want to break a large subject into parts to examine how each part contributes to the whole, they often use classification. Additionally, when they need to bring order to a group of ideas, activities, or things, they will divide or classify them according to their characteristics. The main idea usually identifies what will be divided or classified and often tells how many divisions will be considered.

Words that may indicate division or classification include the following:

analyze
categories
classifications
groups
classes
ways

elements

features

methods

kinds

types

parts

factors

issues

reasons

sorts

Topic sentences such as the following alert you to division or classification of information:

Before you can create a healthy menu, you must understand the three essential elements of a healthy diet.

(*You would read to find out the three essential elements.*)

Mutual funds are broadly divided into three classes according to their investment objectives.

(*You would read to find out the three classes of investment objectives.*)

Practice   Determine the main idea and how I developed the details to support that idea.

[1]To write an effective mystery, you must first decide what type of mystery you really want to write. [2]This is because *mystery* is only an umbrella term for a type of fiction with several subcategories. [3]A mystery can be a detective story, a police procedural, or a romantic suspense. [4]It could also be a spy story like the fast-paced, sexually charged work of Ian Fleming who created the British secret service agent James Bond. [5]Another subcategory is the adventure novel, such as Clive Cussler's *Serpent*. [6]Still another type of mystery story is based on actual events never fully resolved by the authorities. (McGrath, *Magazine Article Writing Handbook*)

_____

_____

Explanation   The main idea is "to write an effective mystery, you must first decide what type of mystery you really want to write." To develop and support that idea, I divide the large category of *mysteries* into six subcategories: detective story, police procedural, romantic suspense, spy story, adventure novel, and unresolved actual events.

ORGANIZING USING CAUSE AND EFFECT

Cause and effect—reasons and results—explain why or how something happened and the result of the action. Using a cause-and-effect pattern of organization, an author can examine the reasons for events or situations and their consequences, or predict the possible consequences of a given situation.

An author can begin with the cause(s) and give the result(s), or can begin with the result(s) and give the cause(s). As this implies, there can be a single cause with a single effect, a single cause with multiple effects, multiple causes with a single effect, or multiple causes with multiple effects. Furthermore, cause and effect can be a causal chain—where, like falling dominoes, an action results in an effect, which causes something else, which causes something else, and so on.

Words that signal cause include the following:

because
for this reason
due to
cause
on account of
if [this] then [this]

Words that signal a result or effect include the following:

as a result
since
consequently
therefore
thereby
thus
in effect
resulting
the outcome is

Topic sentences such as the following alert you to look for a cause-and-effect relationship:

There are many reasons Americans are choosing to get less and less news from traditional newspapers and network television.

You would read for details that give the reasons (causes) why Americans are getting less news from newspapers and TV (effect).

Although it is difficult to predict all of the long-term effects of air pollution, a few are already known.

You would read for details that give the effects of air pollution (cause).

Three interrelated factors contributed to the demise of ragtime as a piano style. (Brooks, *American Black Musical Heritage*)

You would read for the details that give the three reasons (causes) why ragtime music lost popularity (effect).

Practice   Determine Nebel and Wright's main idea and how they use cause and effect to develop and support that idea.

[1]From the dawn of human history until the beginning of the 1800s, population increased slowly and variably with periodic setbacks. [2]The main reason for this slow and uncertain population growth was the often-deadly diseases, such as smallpox, diphtheria, measles, and scarlet fever. [3]These diseases hit infants and children particularly hard. [4]For example, it was not uncommon for a woman who had seven or eight live births to have only one or two children

reach adulthood. [5]In addition, epidemics of diseases such as the black plague of the fourteenth century, typhus, and cholera would kill large numbers of adults. Famines, severe shortages of food, also took their toll. (Adapted from Nebel and Wright, *Environmental Science*)

———————————————————————————————

———————————————————————————————

Explanation   The main idea—"from the dawn of human history until the beginning of the 1800s, population increased slowly and variably with periodic setbacks"—is the result (effect). Their details in sentences 2–5 give the reasons (causes) for the slow and erratic population growth: deadly diseases that killed infants and children, epidemics of diseases that killed adults, and famines.

ORGANIZING USING A COMBINATION OF PATTERNS

For the purpose of learning about the ways authors organize information, it's useful to practice on paragraphs that have one primary pattern. But good writing usually combines several patterns within a paragraph or chapter. This means that most of the paragraphs and multi-paragraph selections you read will use a combination of patterns such as examples of likenesses and differences, a definition that clarifies a cause or an effect, and a time sequence that helps you understand the classification of an issue. This is why it is important to remember that your goal is to use what you discover about the organization as a clue to understanding the ideas and details you need.

Practice   Determine DuBrin's main idea and how he develops and supports that idea.

[1]One of the major consequences of high self-esteem is good mental health. [2]People with high self-esteem feel good about themselves and have a positive outlook on life. [3]For example, a person with high self-esteem will probably shrug off a negative comment about his or her appearance as simply being the other person's point of view. [4]On the other hand, a person with low self-esteem might crumble if somebody insulted his or her appearance. [5]If faced with an everyday setback such as losing keys, the high self-esteem person might think, "I have so much going for me, why fall apart over this incident?" whereas the low self-esteem person would fall apart. (Adapted from DuBrin, *Human Relations*)

———————————————————————————————

———————————————————————————————

Explanation   The main idea—"one of the major consequences of high self-esteem is good mental health"—states a cause and effect. The cause, high self-esteem, results in good mental health. To develop and support the idea, he gives examples that compare how high self-esteem people and low self-esteem people would handle the same situation.

Practice   Identify Callwood's main idea and how she develops and supports that idea.

[1]We have many examples to support the view that the Canadians were much more law-abiding than the Americans during the Klondike gold rush. [2]For instance, the American town of Skagway in the Alaskan panhandle was run by a ruthless American gangster and miners were often robbed of their gold on Main Street in broad daylight. [3]Across the border in Canada, Yukon mining towns

were so law-abiding that a miner could leave his gold in an unlocked cabin. (Adapted from Callwood, "Portrait of Canada")

_____

_____

Explanation   The main idea is "the Canadians were much more law-abiding than the Americans during the Klondike gold rush." To develop and support that idea she gives an example that compares how a miner would be treated in both areas: He would be robbed of his gold by the lawless Americans; his gold would be safe with the law-abiding Canadians.

■ EXERCISE 4.3: IDENTIFYING THE MEANING OF SIGNAL WORDS AND PHRASES

Circle the letter of the term that best describes what the underlined word, phrase, or punctuation signals.

1. Both oral and written communication involve the creation and sending of messages. <u>However</u>, they differ in a number of ways. (Barker and Barker, *Communication*)
   a. continuation of thought
   b. change in direction of thought
   c. definition
   d. example

2. By law, a learning disability <u>is defined as</u> a significant gap between a person's intelligence and the skills the person has achieved at each age. (National Institute of Mental Health, *Learning Disabilities*)
   a. change in direction of thought
   b. summary
   c. definition
   d. effect

3. <u>In short</u>, the goal of this book is to develop a framework to help you motivate yourself to achieve your personal goals.... (Manz and Neck, *Mastering Self-Leadership*)
   a. cause
   b. summary
   c. continuation of thought
   d. example

4. The roots of rock and roll can be found in the basic popular forms of music in the United States<u>—</u>folk, jazz, and pop. (Brown, *The Art of Rock and Roll*)
   a. classification
   b. example
   c. process
   d. change in direction of thought

5. <u>Like</u> Lincoln, Johnson was an ambitious self-made man from southern yeoman stock. (Unger, *These United States*)
   a. comparison
   b. contrast
   c. definition
   d. effect

6. The self-concept, or the way a person thinks about himself or herself in an overall sense, is an important part of personality development. A successful person—one who is achieving his or her goals in work or personal life—usually has a positive self-concept. <u>In contrast</u>, an unsuccessful person often has a negative self-concept. (DuBrin, *Human Relations*)

    a. comparison

    b. contrast

    c. example

    d. process

■ **EXERCISE 4.4: IDENTIFYING SIGNAL WORDS AND PUNCTUATION AND WHAT THEY MEAN**

Identify the signal word, phrase, or punctuation the author uses and tell what it signals.

1. [1]With each passing year the political hold of the Civil War became a little weaker, especially among northern voters. [2]Yet party loyalty remained intense.... (Unger, *These United States*)

    The signal word in sentence 2 is _____

    It signals _____

2. We begin by studying a communication model and the three types of communication important to our study in this text: intrapersonal, interpersonal, and mass communication. (Bittner, *Each Other*)

    The signal punctuation is _____

    It signals _____

3. [1]Watching television is an especially significant popular custom for two reasons. [2]First, it is the most popular leisure activity in developed countries throughout the world. [3]Second, television is the most important way by which knowledge of popular customs, such as professional sports, is rapidly spread across Earth's surface. (Rubenstein, *Introduction to Human Geography*)

    The signal word in sentence 2 is _____

    It signals _____

    The signal word in sentence 3 is _____

    It signals _____

4. [1]Consumers are demanding more organic-friendly building materials and "green" woods (not endangered) and leading manufacturers and retailers are responding. [2]For example, Home Depot stores sell only woods from managed forests. (*Universal Press Syndicate*, "Consumer Buying Habits Are Changing")

    The signal phrase in sentence 2 is _____

    It signals _____

5.   [1]Downhill skiing and snowboarding, the flashiest winter sports, attract more than 11 million participants a year. [2]But other cold-weather activities are getting their fair share of enthusiasts, too. [3]For example, in 1998, 7.8 million Americans ice skated, and 2.6 million Americans went cross-country skiing. (Doheny, "Winter Sports," *LA Times*)

The signal word in sentence 2 is _____

It signals _____

The signal phrase in sentence 3 is _____

It signals _____

6.   [1]The number of violent crimes reported to the police do not reflect the actual amount of violent crime in society. [2]This is because many crimes are never reported to police. (Davis and Palladino, *Psychology*)

The signal phrase in sentence 2 is _____

It signals _____

■ EXERCISE 4.5: IDENTIFYING AN AUTHOR'S PATTERN OF ORGANIZATION

First, identify the main idea. Then, identify the primary pattern of organization. Finally, explain how the organization would help you be a more active reader.

Example

[1]Physical noise is concerned with sounds that may interrupt the communication process. [2]If a truck goes by when Sally and Jim are speaking and they do not hear each other, that would be an example of physical noise. [3]Perhaps it starts to rain and they need to interrupt the conversation to take cover. [4]That would also be physical noise. (Bittner, *Each Other*)

Explanation

- The main idea in this paragraph is "sounds that interfere with conversations are called physical noise."
- The author's primary pattern of organization is example.
- Considering the main idea and the organization, you would read to find examples to help clarify your understanding of physical noise and how it can interrupt the communication process.

1.   [1][Andrew] Johnson lacked Lincoln's winning personal qualities. [2]Lincoln was confident in his own abilities. [3]Johnson suffered from severe self-doubts, a weakness that made him open to flattery. [4]Lincoln was friendly and enjoyed people. [5]Johnson was a loner with few friends or close advisers. [6]Lincoln was flexible, a natural compromiser. [7]Johnson was a rigid man who could be sweet-talked out of a position, but when defied directly, refused to budge…. (Adapted from Unger, *These United States*)

a.   Main idea _____

b.   Primary organization _____

c.   Considering the main idea and the organization, what would you read to find out? _____

_____

2.   [1]Before 1860 most fresh meat came from local butchers. [2]Dressed carcasses spoiled too quickly to come from distant sources and shipping live animals created large losses in weight. [3]But in the generation following the Civil War, three developments helped transform the business of supplying the public with meat. [4]First, an increasing proportion of Americans came to live in cities, remote from the farms where meat animals were fattened. [5]Second, an expanding railroad network made the products of the prairies and plains of the West more accessible to city consumers. [6]Third, in the 1870s, the railroads introduced refrigerated cars, allowing chilled fresh beef and pork to be shipped long distances without spoilage. (Unger, *These United States*)

a.   Main idea _____

b.   Primary organization _____

c.   Considering the main idea and the organization, what would you read to find out? _____

_____

3.   [1]America has had many "Wests." [2]The colonial West was the forested region just beyond the settled Atlantic coastal plain. [3]On the eve of the American Revolution, the West was the great river valley across the Appalachian Mountains. [4]For the generation preceding the Civil War, it was the land between the Mississippi and the Missouri. [5]The "Last West" of 1865 to 1910 was the broad expanse of territory stretching from the Missouri River to the Pacific Ocean. (Unger, *These United States*)

a.   Main idea _____

b.   Primary organization _____

c.   Considering the main idea and the organization, what would you read to find out? _____

_____

4.   [1]The term vegetarian means different things to different people. [2]Strict vegetarians, or vegans, avoid all foods of animal origin, including dairy products and eggs. [3]The few people who fall into this category must work hard to ensure that they get all of the necessary nutrients. [4]Far more common are lacto-vegetarians, who eat dairy products but avoid flesh foods. [5]Their diet can be low in fat and cholesterol, but only if they consume skim milk and other lowfat or nonfat products. [6]Ovo-vegetarians add eggs to their diet, while lacto-ovo-vegetarians eat both dairy products and eggs. [7]Pesco-vegetarians eat fish, dairy products, and eggs, while semivegetarians eat chicken, fish, dairy products, and eggs. (Donatelle and Davis, *Access to Health*)

a.   Main idea _____

b. Primary organization _____

c. Considering the main idea and the organization, what would
you read to find out? _____

_____

5. [1]The drought of 1988 affected a large portion of the United
States and Canada and was one of North America's worst
droughts in this century. [2]In the United States alone, direct economic losses were estimated to be $40 billion. [3]In July, at the
height of the drought, 40 percent of the country experienced either severe or extreme drought conditions. [4]By October, over 70
percent of the United States had suffered some socioeconomic
losses. [5]In addition to widespread crop damage, fires raged in
parts of the Northwest, and reservoirs in many areas were dry
or critically low. [6]One of the most unexpected impacts of the
drought was the disruption of barge traffic on the Mississippi,
Missouri, and Ohio Rivers. [7]Heavy economic losses resulted because 45 percent of all grain, coal, and petroleum shipped in the
central United States moves by barge. (Lutgens and Tarbuck,
The Atmosphere)

a. Main idea _____

b. Primary organization _____

c. Considering the main idea and the organization, what would
you read to find out? _____

_____

6. [1]If you were to search through the library for books about the atmosphere, many of the titles would contain the term *weather*,
whereas others would have the word *climate*. [2]What is the difference between these two terms? [3]Weather is a word used to de-
note the state of the atmosphere at a particular place for *a short
period of time*. [4]Weather is constantly changing—hourly, daily,
and seasonally. [5]Climate, on the other hand, might best be described as an aggregate or composite of weather. [6]Stated another
way, the climate of a place or region is a generalization of the
weather conditions over *a long period of time*. (Lutgens and Tarbuck, *Foundations of Earth Science*)

a. Main idea _____

b. Primary organization _____

c. Considering the main idea and the organization, what would
you read to find out? _____

_____

7. [1]Instruments with keyboards have been popular for several hundred years, since they are relatively easy to learn and can play
both melody and harmony together. [2]For example, the harpsichord and clavichord were well known in the sixteenth century.... [3]Another keyboard instrument, the pipe organ, reached a
high point of development in the eighteenth century.... [4]The
piano was invented in the early eighteenth century and

gradually replaced the harpsichord as the most popular keyboard instrument. (Adapted from Politoske, *Music*)

a. Main idea _____

b. Primary organization _____

c. Considering the main idea and the organization, what would you read to find out? _____

_____

8. [1]The breakup of the Beatles was undoubtedly caused by some of the following: (1) the end of group creativity, (2) a need for individual creativity, (3) a personality conflict, (4) family pressures, (5) legal complications, and (6) financial necessity. [2]We can argue for any or all of these causes. (Brown, *The Art of Rock and Roll*).

a. Main idea _____

b. Primary organization _____

c. Considering the main idea and the organization, what would you read to find out? _____

_____

9. [1]The differences between Los Angeles and San Francisco are striking. [2]First, the climates are totally different. [3]San Francisco has hills and fog. [4]It rains a lot and the weather is colder. [5]Also, it is, relatively speaking, a much more sophisticated town. [6]Whereas Los Angeles is a relaxed community of sun worshipers, San Francisco is artistic, cultured, and just a bit snobbish. [7]Its history is no longer than that of Los Angeles but it is substantially more cosmopolitan. [8]While Los Angeles had quick increases in population, San Francisco stayed basically the same. (Adapted from McGrath and McGrath, *California Towns*)

a. Main idea _____

b. Primary organization _____

c. Considering the main idea and the organization, what would you read to find out? _____

_____

10. [1]In 1822 a French inventor named Joseph Nicéphore Niépce (1765–1833) succeeded in making the first permanent photographic image. [2]He then joined forces with a younger man, Louis-Jacques-Mandé Daguerre (1789–1851), who had devised an improved camera. [3]After ten more years of chemical and mechanical research, the daguerreotype, using positive exposures, was unveiled. [4]That announcement encouraged the Englishman William Henry Fox Talbot (1800–1877) to complete his own paper negative photograph process a short time later. (Adapted from Janson and Janson, *A Basic History of Art*)

a. Main idea _____

b. Primary organization _____

    c. Considering the main idea and the organization, what would you read to find out? _____

■ EXERCISE 4.6: IDENTIFYING RELATIONSHIPS AMONG IDEAS

First, identify the main idea. Then, use the author's organization to identify the relationships among ideas and sentences.

1.   [1]Two types of thought patterns that a person could adopt are what might be called opportunity thinking and obstacle thinking. [2]Opportunity thinking involves a pattern of thoughts that focus on the opportunities and possibilities that situations or challenges hold. [3]Creative, innovative individuals who contribute to the major breakthroughs and advances in our world most likely possess this sort of pattern of thinking. [4]Their beliefs, their imagined future experiences, and their self-talk probably spur them on to undertake new opportunities. [5]Obstacle thinking, on the other hand, involves a focus on the roadblocks and pitfalls of undertaking new ventures. [6]Such a mental pattern fosters avoidance of challenges in favor of more secure actions, often with substantially lesser potential payoffs. (Manz and Neck, *Mastering Self-Leadership*)

    a. Main idea _____

    b. What is the relationship of sentence 5 to sentence 2? (Underline the correct answer.)

       Sentence 5 continues the same thought as sentence 2.

       Sentence 5 presents a contrasting thought to sentence 2.

       Sentence 5 presents an effect of sentence 2.

       Sentence 5 presents examples of sentence 2.

2.   [1]The United States has a higher rate of violent crime than does any other industrialized nation. [2]For example, the risk of being murdered in the United States is now 7 to 10 times that in most European countries (Lore and Schultz, 1993). [3]Comparable differences exist between the United States and Europe for rape and robbery. (Alexander, *Adjustment and Human Relations*)

    a. Main idea _____

    b. What is the relationship of sentence 3 to sentence 2? (Underline the correct answer.)

       Sentence 3 continues the same thought as sentence 2.

       Sentence 3 gives a contrasting thought to sentence 2.

       Sentence 3 gives an effect of sentence 2.

       Sentence 3 gives an example of sentence 2.

3.   [1]Much of what we have learned about human memory has been inspired by the development of computers. [2]In what ways might a computer and the human memory be alike?

    [3]Like the computer, human memory has been characterized as an information-processing system that has three separate stages—an input or encoding stage, a storage stage, and a retrieval stage during which an already stored memory is called

into consciousness. ⁴Let's take a closer look at each of these stages.... (Davis and Palladino, *Psychology*)

a. Main idea _____

b. What is the relationship of sentence 3 to sentence 2? (Underline the correct answer.)

Sentence 3 gives a contrasting thought to sentence 2.

Sentence 3 gives an example of sentence 2.

Sentence 3 gives a definition for sentence 2.

Sentence 3 gives a cause for sentence 2.

4. ¹A quiet but powerful revolution is reshaping the United States. ²The number of elderly people—women and men aged 65 and over—is increasing more than twice as fast as the population as a whole. ³Between 1970 and 1996, while the overall U.S. population rose 31 percent, the number of seniors climbed by 69 percent, and the number over age 85 soared by 167 percent. ⁴This "graying" of the United States promises profound effects. (Macionis, *Sociology*)

a. Main idea _____

b. What is the relationship of sentence 2 to sentence 1? (Underline the correct answer.)

Sentence 2 continue the same thought as sentence 1.

Sentence 2 presents a contrasting thought to sentence 1.

Sentence 2 presents an effect of sentence 1.

Sentence 2 presents a cause for sentence 1.

5. ¹Understanding what someone is saying often involves much more than listening and speaking. ²It is often what is *not* actually said that may speak louder than any words. ³Rolling your eyes, looking at the floor or ceiling when speaking rather than maintaining eye contact, body movements, hand gestures— all these nonverbal clues influence the way we interpret messages. ⁴Researchers have found that only 7 percent of the meaning of a message comes from the words spoken. ⁵An astounding 93 percent of the meaning comes from nonverbal cues. (Donatelle and Davis, *Access to Health*)

a. Main idea _____

b. What is the relationship of sentence 3 to sentence 2? (Underline the correct answer.)

Sentence 3 presents a contrasting thought to sentence 2.

Sentence 3 provides a definition of terms in sentence 2.

Sentence 3 presents examples of sentence 2.

Sentence 3 presents an effect of sentence 2.

6. ¹Shy people tend to lack social skills. ²They avoid eye contact and are inclined to withdraw when spoken to. ³They show little interest or vitality, and they pause too long in conversations. ⁴Many have not learned how to meet others. ⁵For instance, they have not learned how to start a conversation and keep it going or how to end social encounters. ⁶Most shy people have social anxiety. ⁷For example, they fear being evaluated, embarrassed,

ridiculed, rejected, and found inadequate. (Alexander, *Adjustment and Human Relations*)

a.   Main idea _____

b.   What is the relationship of sentence 5 to sentence 1? (Underline the correct answer.)

Sentence 5 continues the same thought as sentence 1.

Sentence 5 presents a contrasting thought to sentence 1.

Sentence 5 presents an example of sentence 1.

Sentence 5 presents a cause for sentence 1.

7.   [1]Earth's crust is the source of a wide variety of minerals, many of which are useful and essential to people. [2]In fact, practically every manufactured product contains material obtained from minerals. [3]Most people are familiar with the common uses of basic metals, including aluminum in beverage cans, copper in electrical wiring, and gold in jewelry. [4]But fewer are aware that pencil "lead" does not contain lead metal but is really made of the soft black mineral called graphite. [5]Baby powder (talcum powder) is ground-up rock made of the mineral talc, with perfume added. [6]Drill bits impregnated with pieces of diamond (a mineral) are used by dentists to drill through tooth enamel. [7]The common mineral quartz is the main ingredient in ordinary glass and is the source of silicon for computer chips. [8]And on and on. [9]Thus, as the material demands of modern society grow, the need to locate additional supplies of useful minerals also grows, and becomes more challenging as the easily mined sources become depleted. (Lutgens and Tarbuck, *Foundations of Earth Science*)

a.   Main idea _____

b.   What is the relationship of sentence 2 to sentence 1? (Underline the correct answer.)

Sentence 2 continues the same thought as sentence 1.

Sentence 2 presents a contrasting thought to sentence 1.

Sentence 2 presents an example of sentence 1.

Sentence 2 presents a cause for sentence 1.

8.   [1]In recent years evidence has clearly shown that the dangers of smoking are not restricted to the smoker. [2]Tobacco smoke in the air is damaging to anyone who inhales it, not just the smoker. [3]For this reason, many states require restaurants to have smoking and nonsmoking sections. [4]And in many parts of the country, smoking in public places has been restricted, if not prohibited. (Miller and Levine, *Biology*)

a.   Main idea _____

b.   What is the relationship of sentences 3 and 4 to sentences 1 and 2? (Underline the correct answer.)

Sentences 3 and 4 present effects of sentences 1 and 2.

Sentences 3 and 4 present contrasting thoughts to sentences 1 and 2.

Sentences 3 and 4 present examples of sentences 1 and 2.

Sentences 3 and 4 present causes for sentences 1 and 2.

9. [1]Police frequently use wiretapping and other sophisticated means of "bugging." [2]In its first wiretapping case, in 1928, the Supreme Court held that intercepting telephone conversations without a warrant was not an unreasonable search or seizure. [3]In 1967 it reversed that decision, however. (McClenaghan, *Magruder's American Government*)

    a. Main idea _____

    b. What is the relationship of sentence 3 to sentence 2? (Underline the correct answer.)

        Sentence 3 continues the same thought as sentence 2.

        Sentence 3 presents a contrasting thought to sentence 2.

        Sentence 3 presents an example of sentence 2.

        Sentence 3 presents a cause for sentence 2.

10. [1]The development of sophisticated computer technology has made information on almost any topic widely available. [2]Yet new problems have surfaced in the Information Age. [3]For example, many computer databases show the health, employment, or credit history of individuals. [4]The unauthorized use of such personal information has become a widespread concern. [5]Breaking into computer systems to steal, alter, or destroy data is another problem of the Information Age. (Clayton, Perry, Reed, and Winkler, *America: Pathways to the Present*)

    a. Main idea _____

    b. What is the relationship of sentence 2 to sentence 1? (Underline the correct answer.)

        Sentence 2 continues the same thought as sentence 1.

        Sentence 2 presents a contrasting thought to sentence 1.

        Sentence 2 presents an example of sentence 1.

        Sentence 2 presents a cause for sentence 1.

    c. What is the relationship of sentence 5 to sentence 2? (Underline the correct answer.)

        Sentence 5 presents a definition for sentence 2.

        Sentence 5 presents a contrasting thought to sentence 2.

        Sentence 5 presents an example of sentence 2.

        Sentence 5 presents a cause for sentence 2.

CHAPTER REVIEW

SUMMARY OF KEY IDEAS

*   Figuring out how groups of words and sentences relate to one another is key to understanding what you read. Because a paragraph can have any number of sentences and any number of details, an important aspect of the relationships is how details relate to and support a main idea.

*   There are two general categories of details that support main ideas: major details and minor details. A major detail is a specific piece of information that directly supports and explains the main idea. A minor detail is a very specific piece of information that supports and explains a major detail.

- In addition to major and minor details, some paragraphs contain information that is interesting, and sometimes important, but does not support or develop the main idea. This type of information is called *irrelevant* to the paragraph.
- Six common ways, or patterns, textbook authors use to organize details that support and explain main ideas are: examples or listing, comparison and/or contrast, time order or steps in a sequence, definition, classification, and cause and effect. In addition, authors often combine two patterns.
- Authors sometimes use words or punctuation to signal particular types of information, changes in direction of thought, and shifts in viewpoint.

SELF CHECK

- I can distinguish among major details, minor details, and irrelevant details.
- I can identify the pattern(s) of organization an author uses to develop details.
- I can identify signal words and phrases.

PUTTING IT ALL TOGETHER

Complete the exercises following each paragraph:

1. [1]Americans generally agreed that their new nation should be a <u>democracy</u>, or government by the people. [2]Specifically, they favored the creation of a <u>republic</u>, a government run by the people through their elected representatives. [3]Yet people held widely differing views on how much influence ordinary citizens should have in the governing of the republic. (Clayton, Perry, Reed, and Winkler, *America: Pathways to the Present*)

    a. a democracy is _____

    b. a republic is _____

    c. main idea: _____

    d. The signal word in sentence 3 is _____

    e. It signals (underline the correct answer):
        a change in direction of thought
        a continuation of the same thought
        an effect

2. [1]Not everyone who is convicted of a crime and sentenced ends up in prison. [2]Some offenders are ordered to prison only to have their sentences suspended and a probationary term imposed. [3]They may also be ordered to perform community service activities as a condition of their probation. [4]During the term of probation these offenders are required to submit to supervision by a probation officer and to meet other conditions set by the court. [5]Failure to do so results in <u>revocation</u> of probation and <u>imposition</u> of the original prison sentence. [6]Other offenders, who have served a portion of their sentences, may be freed on parole.

[7]They will be supervised by a parole officer and assisted in their readjustment to society. [8]As in the case of probation, failure to meet the conditions of parole may result in parole revocation and a return to prison. (Schmalleger, *Criminal Justice*)

    a.   revocation means _____

    b.   imposition means _____

    c.   main idea: _____

    d.   The relationship of sentences 2 and 6 to sentence 1 is (underline the correct answer):

        Sentences 2 and 6 give major details to support sentence 1.

        Sentences 2 and 6 give minor details to support sentence 1.

        Sentences 2 and 6 are irrelevant to sentence 1.

3.   [1]Humans use birds for many purposes. [2]People in cold climates discovered long ago that in addition to being soft and comfortable, down feathers are good <u>insulators</u>. [3]Therefore, down feathers are frequently used in making comforters and jackets. [4]Many birds are favorite foods the world over, and raising them is part of the economy in many countries. [5]With its low fat content, bird meat is a healthful source of protein in a balanced human diet. [6]Birds such as chickens and turkeys have been specially bred for their meat. [7]Because <u>domestic</u> strains of chickens and turkeys do not fly, their chest muscles are seldom used, making this part of the bird juicy and tender "white meat." [8]The leg and thigh muscles of these birds, used constantly for walking and running, are the "dark meat." (Miller and Levine, *Biology*)

    a.   insulators are _____

    b.   domestic means _____

    c.   main idea: _____

    d.   The signal word in sentence 3 is _____

    e.   It signals (underline the correct answer):

        continuation of thought

        cause

        definition

        effect

    f.   The relationship of sentences 2 and 4 to sentence 1 is (underline the correct answer):

        Sentences 2 and 4 give major details to support sentence 1.

        Sentences 2 and 4 give minor details to support sentence 1.

        Sentences 2 and 4 are irrelevant to sentence 1.

4.   [1]Drag boat racing, which has been taking place across the United States since the 1950s, was once known as a high speed, high thrill, but highly dangerous sport. [2]After eight driver <u>fatalities</u> in 1986, many predicted the end of organized drag boat racing. [3]But drag boat racers aren't the kind of folks to give up. [4]They analyzed the situation and, with the support of the International Hot Boat Association (IHBA), developed a variety of safety measures including the now-<u>mandated</u> driver safety capsules for the high-danger pro classes. [5]Today, drag boat racing is back stronger and safer than ever. [6]It's kept its high speed—racers

routinely eclipse numbers in the 240 mph range—and high excitement edge. [7]It's drawing ever-increasing numbers of racers and spectators and ESPN coverage of IHBA races is now common. (McGrath and McGrath, *Performance Racing Industry*)

a. fatalities means _____

b. mandated means _____

c. main idea: _____

d. the signal word in sentence 3 is _____

e. it signals (underline the correct answer):
   continuation of thought
   change in direction of thought
   definition
   effect

5. [1]Of the various elements of weather and climate, changes in air pressure are the least noticeable. [2]In listening to a weather report, generally, we are interested in moisture conditions (humidity and precipitation), temperature, and perhaps wind. [3]It is the rare person, however, who wonders about air pressure. [4]Although the hour-to-hour and day-to-day <u>variations</u> in air pressure are not <u>perceptible</u> to human beings, they are very important in producing changes in our weather. [5]For example, it is variations in air pressure from place to place that generate winds that in turn can bring changes in temperature and humidity. [6]Air pressure is one of the basic weather elements and a significant factor in weather forecasting. (Lutgens and Tarbuck, *The Atmosphere*)

a. variations means _____

b. perceptible means _____

c. main idea _____

d. How does sentence 5 relate to sentence 4? (Underline the correct answer.)
   Sentence 5 gives a definition of 4.
   Sentence 5 gives an example of 4.
   Sentence 5 gives a contrast to 4.

e. The signal phrase that points out the relationship is _____

   _____

6. [1]When rap music first appeared on the scene, music critics said it wouldn't last, record companies felt it was too harsh and black-oriented to cross over, and parents dismissed it as the latest fad. [2]By January 1992, rappers were found as high as #3 on *Billboard*'s top 200 album list. [3]Within ten years, rap had become a powerful and <u>controversial</u> force in American popular culture. [4]Rap music grew from its <u>humble</u> street beginnings in Harlem and the South Bronx to a <u>dominant</u> media through traditional music vehicles like cassettes and CDs, as well as television coverage in videos and talk shows, rappers as actors, film themes, concerts, advertising, and other promotional components. [5]Now, groups such as Hammer, Public Enemy, Ice Cube,

Ghetto Boyz, Salt 'N Pepa, 2 Live Crew, NWA, Tone Loc, and Queen Latifah have reached mainstream popularity. (Adapted from Berry, "Redeeming the Rap Music Experience")

a. controversial means _____

b. humble means _____

c. dominant means _____

d. main idea: _____

7. [1]The presence of the ozone layer in our atmosphere is of <u>vital</u> importance to those of us on earth. [2]The reason lies in the capability of ozone to absorb damaging ultraviolet radiation from the sun. [3]Ultraviolet rays are the "burning" rays of the sun, those that allow some people to acquire a tan and many others to suffer a sunburn. [4]If ozone did not act to filter out a great deal of the ultraviolet radiation and these rays were allowed to reach the surface of the earth, our planet would likely be <u>uninhabitable</u> for most life as we know it. (Lutgens and Tarbuck, *The Atmosphere*)

a. vital means _____

b. uninhabitable means _____

c. main idea: _____

d. How does sentence 2 relate to sentence 1? (Underline the correct answer.)

    Sentence 2 gives an example of 1.

    Sentence 2 gives the cause of 1.

    Sentence 2 gives an effect of 1.

8. [1]The life of a student can be stressful. [2]Among the <u>stressors</u> to cope with are exams in subjects you do not understand well, having to write papers on subjects unfamiliar to you, working your way through the complexities of registration, or having to deal with instructors who do not see things your way. [3]Another source of severe stress for some students is having too many <u>competing</u> demands on their time. [4]On most campuses you will find someone who works full-time, goes to school full-time, and has a family. (Adapted from DuBrin, *Human Relations*)

a. stressors are _____

b. competing means _____

c. main idea: _____

d. How does DuBruin develop and support the main idea? (Underline the correct answer.)

    with examples

    with definitions

    with effects

e. How does sentence 3 relate to sentence 2? (Underline the correct answer.)

    Sentence 3 continues the thought with another example.

    Sentence 3 changes the direction of thought with a contrasting example.

    Sentence 3 gives the cause.

9. [1]In the 1800s Louis Pasteur and others made the major discovery that diseases were caused by infectious agents (now identified as bacteria, viruses, and parasites) and that they were <u>transmitted</u> via water and food, insects, and other vermin. [2]These discoveries caused major improvements in sanitation and <u>personal hygiene</u>. [3]Then techniques of providing protection by means of vaccinations were discovered. [4]With the discovery of antibiotics such as penicillin in the 1930s, often-fatal diseases such as pneumonia could be cured. [5]Improvements in nutrition began to be significant as well. [6]In short, better sanitation, medicine, and nutrition brought about spectacular reductions in death rates, especially among children and infants. (Adapted from Nebel and Wright, *Environmental Science*)

    a. transmitted means _____

    b. personal hygiene means _____

    c. main idea: _____

    d. How does sentence 2 relate to sentence 1? (Underline the correct answer.)
        Sentence 2 continues the thought with another example.
        Sentence 2 changes the direction of thought with a contrasting example.
        Sentence 2 gives the cause.
        Sentence 2 gives the effect.

    e. The signal phrase that points out the relationship is _____

    _____

10. [1]As adults, we're often tempted to skip breakfast and start the day with a cup of coffee on the run. [2]But the old <u>adage</u> that "breakfast is the most important meal of the day" is absolutely right; and it's even more important for our kids than it is for us. [3]It has been shown that children who eat a healthy breakfast do better in school. [4]They concentrate more intently, and have more energy and <u>stamina</u>. [5]They even score higher on tests. [6]In fact, students who participated in one school breakfast program had significantly higher math grades than those who didn't. (Kraft Foods, *Family Roundtable*)

    a. adage means _____

    b. stamina means _____

    c. main idea: _____

    d. How does sentence 3 relate to sentence 2? (Underline the correct answer.)
        Sentence 3 gives an example of 2.
        Sentence 3 gives a cause of 2.
        Sentence 3 gives an effect of 2.

    e. How does sentence 4 relate to sentence 3? (Underline the correct answer.)
        Sentence 4 gives an example of 3.
        Sentence 4 gives a cause of 3.
        Sentence 4 gives an effect of 3.

CROSSWORD PUZZLE

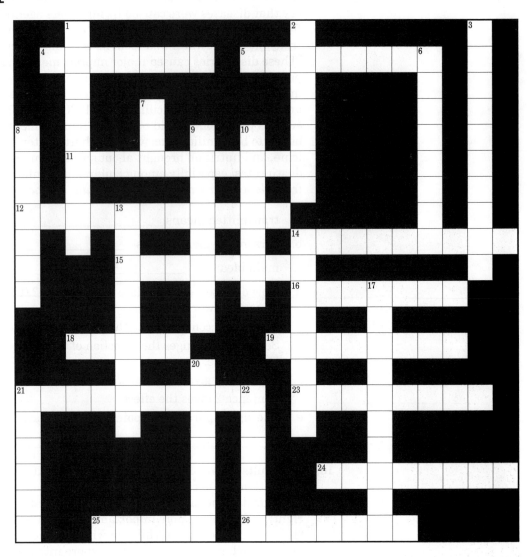

ACROSS

4 time period without rain
5 required
11 deaths
12 apparent or observable
14 coming before
15 order of events
16 revolutionary
18 necessary
19 give differences
21 similar or equivalent
23 likely to
24 excessive compliments
25 handles
26 results of

DOWN

1 change, make different
2 strong
3 changes
6 used up
7 by way of
8 give similarities
9 to make fun of
10 brutal and vicious
13 necessary
14 happening occasionally
17 unrelated
20 clearly evident
21 reasons why
22 take part in

WORD LIST (NOT ALL USED)

causes	fatalities	predictable
comparable	flattery	radical
compare	inclined	ridicule
contrast	insignificant	sequence
copes	intense	transform
depleted	irrelevant	variations
drought	mandated	via
effects	obvious	violent
engage	perceptible	vital
essential	periodic	
extemporaneous	preceding	

LOG ON TO THE WEB

Practice good reading skills as you check out what a reviewer thinks about the latest books. Log on to one of these sites, one of the online bookstores, or use a search directory/engine to locate a review of a book that sounds interesting.

http://www.cnn.com/books/reviews

http://www.usatoday.com/life/enter/books/leb1.htm

Print out the review. Write: (1) the name of the person who wrote the review and what you know about him or her; (2) the main idea of the review; (3) how the writer primarily developed and supported that main idea, such as with examples; and (4) why you would or would not read the book.

IDEAS FOR WRITING AND DISCUSSION

A. Compare and contrast what going to school is like for you now with the last time you were in school. Some of the factors you might want to consider are your attitude and the attitudes of your classmates, the amount of reading and study required, and the teachers.

B. Recall a teacher who stands out in your memory. Decide what makes the teacher memorable, such as personality, teaching style, or mannerisms. Describe him or her, using specific examples.

C. Being "successful" means different things to different people—writers, movie stars, professional athletes, friends, family. Find at least five definitions of success. Describe how you define success.

INTERPRETING WHAT YOU READ

CHAPTER PREVIEW

Objectives
- Distinguish between facts and opinions.
- Make valid inferences.

Sections

CHAPTER FOCUS

In Chapter 2 you discovered that understanding individual words is important. In Chapters 3 and 4, you found that understanding sentences and paragraphs is also important. Sometimes, however, authors do not clearly or directly state all you need to know to fully understand their message. Often you must go beyond what is written. You must interpret what the author means by what and how he or she says it.

SECTION 5.1   DISTINGUISHING BETWEEN FACTS AND OPINIONS

Not everything that is written is factual, nor does it need to be. The problem is that authors don't always say which statements are fact and which statements are opinion. Therefore, part of your job as a reader is to distinguish between the facts and the opinions.

Statements of *fact* tell about people, places, things, and events objectively, without value judgments or personal interpretations. A fact can be verified. By verified I mean that you can check the accuracy of the information and that no matter where you look or whom you ask, the information is the same. Examples of facts include the following:

Five candidates are running for the school board in next week's election.

As people age, physical changes occur in the body.

Facts, when verified, are reliable support for main ideas and good sources of information.

Statements of *opinion* tell about people, places, things, and events subjectively from the author's point of view. Opinions express the author's thoughts, feelings, beliefs, and attitudes. Opinions cannot be verified; the information can change depending on where you look or whom you ask. Examples of opinions include the following:

> The candidates in next week's school board election are the best we've ever had running for the office.

> Loss of hearing is the most difficult effect of aging.

An opinion is not right or wrong, or good or bad. However, depending on the amount and type of information the author considered before forming the opinion, it can be valid or invalid. You should be skeptical of invalid opinions.

On the other hand, valid opinions can be helpful. Actually, it's often the author's insight, wisdom, and conclusions that help us understand ideas. I call these thoughtful, coherent evaluations an author makes from the available evidence *reasoned judgments*.

Words and phrases like these examples can signal that an author is stating an opinion.

JUDGMENTAL WORDS LIKE THESE OFTEN SIGNAL AN OPINION:

good

bad

nice

wonderful

important

insignificant

the worst

the best

ugly

pretty

smart

dumb

safe

dangerous

CONDITIONAL WORDS LIKE THESE OFTEN SIGNAL AN OPINION:

possibly

probably

perhaps

apparently

likely

often

seemingly

maybe

PHRASES LIKE THESE SIGNAL AN OPINION:

I believe
it is believed
one explanation is
I feel
I suspect
in my view
it is likely that
this suggests
it is usually the case that
in all likelihood

■ EXERCISE 5.1: DISTINGUISHING BETWEEN FACTS AND OPINIONS

Read each sentence. Decide if it is a statement of fact or an opinion. Remember, a fact is an objective statement that can be proved true or false and an opinion is a subjective statement that cannot be proved true or false. Mark it *F* if it is a fact or *O* if it is an opinion.

Example

_____   The typical kitchen in 2010 will probably be more like a living room with comfortable seating, furniture-like cabinets, and lavish entertainment centers.

Explanation   Even though many predictions are based on reliable information and made by informed individuals, they are still opinions about what might happen in the future. Since they cannot be proved true or false at this time, statements like this one should be marked *O* for opinion.

_____ 1. There's no question that word-processing programs streamline the writing process.
_____ 2. Phoenix is the sixth-largest rental car market in the nation.
_____ 3. A typical 20-year-old house with adequate attic insulation loses more energy to air leaks than from any other source.
_____ 4. The book includes complete step-by-step instructions for seven patterns for beginning woodworkers.
_____ 5. Nothing makes you feel right at home like a good book, a purring cat, and a cup of tea.
_____ 6. Every rock contains clues about the environment in which it formed.
_____ 7. By 2005, e-books will be more popular than paperback books.
_____ 8. Some high-tech companies actually have more personal computers than telephones.
_____ 9. Adobe is an ancient building material.
_____ 10. The simplest things provide the most pleasure.

■ **EXERCISE 5.2: DISTINGUISHING BETWEEN FACTS AND OPINIONS**

Read each sentence. Decide if it is a statement of fact or an opinion. Remember, a fact is an objective statement that can be proved true or false and an opinion is a subjective statement that cannot be proved true or false. Mark it *F* if it is a fact or *O* if it is an opinion.

_____ 1. NBC's Sydney Olympics coverage drew the lowest national ratings for a Summer or Winter Games since 1968.

_____ 2. Job Corps is the nation's largest residential training program for men and women ages 16 to 24.

_____ 3. Nothing compares to the grand sights and sounds one can experience in Africa.

_____ 4. Wal-Mart Stores, Inc., is the world's largest retailer.

_____ 5. Seventy percent of all automobile crashes happen at low speed and close to home.

_____ 6. In any recipe, fresh ingredients are always superior to frozen ingredients.

_____ 7. The Denver Broncos fans made it into the *Guinness Book of World Records* for the loudest cheer—128.7 decibels.

_____ 8. Attending a job fair is the best way to find a new job.

_____ 9. Willie Morris's autobiographical novel, *My Dog Skip*, is a perfect piece of bedtime reading for kids and their parents.

_____ 10. In 1900, the average age of death was 46. Today, the average age is 78.

Of course real writing is rarely this obvious. Authors, even textbook authors, often use a combination of facts, opinions, and reasoned judgments to support and explain their ideas. You may even find facts and opinions in the same sentence.

■ **EXERCISE 5.3: DISTINGUISHING BETWEEN FACTS AND OPINIONS**

Answer the questions following each paragraph.

1. ¹In Salzburg, Austria, you can visit the places that were used in the movie version of *The Sound of Music*. ²Made in 1964, starring Julie Andrews and Christopher Plummer, it is one of the best movies of all time. ³You can walk through the Mirabell Gardens where Maria and the children danced around the statue of Pegasus, the winged horse, as they sang the "Do-Re-Mi" song. ⁴You can visit the Leopoldskron Castle, which was used as the setting for the von Trapp family home. ⁵You can also see the Mondsee Cathedral where scenes of the marriage of Maria to the Baron were shot.

   a. Is sentence 1 fact, opinion, or combination of fact and opinion? _____

      If it includes both, list which information is fact and which is opinion. _____

      _____

b. Is sentence 2 fact, opinion, or combination of fact and opinion? _____

If it includes both, list which information is fact and which is opinion. _____

_____

2. [1]Downhill skiing and snowboarding, the flashiest winter sports, attract more than 11 million participants a year. [2]But other cold-weather activities are getting their fair share of enthusiasts, too. [3]For example, in 1998, 7.8 million Americans ice skated, and 2.6 million Americans went cross-country skiing. (Doheny, "Winter Sports," *LA Times*)

a. Is sentence 1 fact, opinion, or combination of fact and opinion? _____

If it includes both, list which information is fact and which is opinion. _____

_____

b. Is sentence 3 fact, opinion, or combination of fact and opinion? _____

If it includes both, list which information is fact and which is opinion. _____

_____

3. [1]The earliest device created to measure the passage of time was the sundial. [2]It measured the sun's shadow. [3]The water clock was an improvement over the sundial since it didn't depend on the sun. [4]Once the art of glass making was perfected, the hourglass was created to mark the passage of time with sand. [5]However, none of these devices were as creative as the modern clock.

a. Is sentence 1 fact, opinion, or combination of fact and opinion? _____

If it includes both, list which information is fact and which is opinion. _____

_____

b. Is sentence 5 fact, opinion, or combination of fact and opinion? _____

If it includes both, list which information is fact and which is opinion. _____

_____

4. [1]The salt cedar, or tamarisk tree, is a serious threat to native plants and wildlife across much of the Southwest. [2]One way it forces out other plants and animals is by using large amounts of water. [3]For example, one salt cedar alone can use 200 gallons of water a day, more than the amount used by a small family. [4]It also adds large amounts of salt to the soil and rivers. [5]The trees now cover more than 1 million acres.

a. Is sentence 3 fact, opinion, or combination of fact and opinion? _____

If it includes both, list which information is fact and which is opinion. _____

_____

    b. Is sentence 5 fact, opinion, or combination of fact and opinion? _____

       If it includes both, list which information is fact and which is opinion. _____

       _____

5. ¹Science-fiction movies are fascinating. ²If they are well produced, they succeed in transporting us into unfamiliar worlds and making us feel quite comfortable in them. ³Often, after the initial wonderment at where we are "taken," we settle in to follow the plot much as we would with an old-fashioned "western" or situation comedy. ⁴The unfamiliar quickly becomes commonplace. ⁵We begin to believe in the characters, even those who are rather different from us humans. (Rose, Glazer, and Glazer, *Sociology*)

    a. Is sentence 1 fact, opinion, or combination of fact and opinion? _____

       If it includes both, list which information is fact and which is opinion. _____

       _____

    b. Is sentence 5 fact, opinion, or combination of fact and opinion? _____

       If it includes both, list which information is fact and which is opinion. _____

       _____

6. ¹While there will always be exceptions, most good-paying jobs now require specialized education. ²The earnings gap between college graduates and those without specialized skills continues to widen. ³Family income for high school dropouts fell 10 percent. ⁴For college graduates, it has soared up 28 percent, says Cleveland-based economist John Burke. ⁵Clearly, workers with the best earning potential have specific marketable skills—skills learned and honed through a college education. (Adapted from Harris-Tuck, Price, and Robertson, *Career Patterns*)

    a. Is sentence 2 fact, opinion, or combination of fact and opinion? _____

       If it includes both, list which information is fact and which is opinion. _____

       _____

    b. Is sentence 5 fact, opinion, or combination of fact and opinion? _____

       If it includes both, list which information is fact and which is opinion. _____

       _____

■ EXERCISE 5.4: DISTINGUISHING BETWEEN FACTS AND OPINIONS

Answer the questions following each paragraph.

1. ¹We first acquire the use of symbols and begin uttering sounds in infancy. ²Gradually we acquire our first words, and from

approximately two to six years of age, we increase our vocabularies from a few words to about 8000. [3]As we continue to increase our vocabularies and build sentences, we gain the ability to handle complex language skills. [4]Our opportunity and ability to interact with other people are very important to this stage of language growth. (Bittner, *Each Other*)

a. Is sentence 2 fact, opinion, or combination of fact and opinion? _____

   If it includes both, list which information is fact and which is opinion. _____

   _____

b. Is sentence 4 fact, opinion, or combination of fact and opinion? _____

   If it includes both, list which information is fact and which is opinion. _____

   _____

2. [1]Human beings need some daily exercise or physical activity, not just for weight control but for optimal health. [2]The type and the amount of exercise that have been shown beneficial to health involve about half an hour a day of moderate exertion. [3]Many pleasant activities such as walking, bicycling, dancing, tennis, gardening, and even lovemaking are sufficient to satisfy this daily requirement. [4]Thus many experts agree that we do not need to push ourselves to the limit of endurance in order to benefit from exercise. (Adapted from Alexander, *Adjustment and Human Relations*)

a. Is sentence 1 fact, opinion, or combination of fact and opinion? _____

   If it includes both, list which information is fact and which is opinion. _____

   _____

b. Is sentence 4 fact, opinion, or combination of fact and opinion? _____

   If it includes both, list which information is fact and which is opinion. _____

   _____

3. [1]As adults, we're often tempted to skip breakfast and start the day with a cup of coffee on the run. [2]But the old adage that "breakfast is the most important meal of the day" is absolutely right; and it's even more important for our kids than it is for us. [3]It has been shown that children who eat a healthy breakfast do better in school. [4]They concentrate more intently, and have more energy and stamina. [5]They even score higher on tests. [6]In fact, students who participated in one school breakfast program had significantly higher math grades than those who didn't. (Kraft Foods, *Family Roundtable*)

a. Is sentence 3 fact, opinion, or combination of fact and opinion? _____

   If it includes both, list which information is fact and which is opinion. _____

   _____

4. [1]Ronald Reagan's second-term problems were aggravated by the president's age and health. [2]Reagan was already seventy when he became president, the oldest man to hold the presidential office. [3]In addition, he had survived an assassination attempt in 1981, and by 1987 he had undergone surgery for colon cancer and an enlarged prostate. [4]At times in his second term he seemed to be tired, distracted, and forgetful. [5]He still read prepared speeches magnificently, but did poorly at extemporaneous press conferences where he had to think on his feet, and so avoided them. [6]Some Americans believed he had lost his grip. (Unger, *These United States*)

   a. Is sentence 2 fact, opinion, or combination of fact and opinion? _____

      If it includes both, list which information is fact and which is opinion. _____

      _____

   b. Is sentence 5 fact, opinion, or combination of fact and opinion? _____

      If it includes both, list which information is fact and which is opinion. _____

      _____

5. [1]Generally speaking, supervisors create one of three climates, or working environments, for employees. [2]Some supervisors are very controlling and strict. [3]The direct opposite of a strict, structured climate is a permissive atmosphere with few controls or restrictions. [4]The third type, a democratic climate, is one in which the supervisor maintains a leadership role but creates a team feeling by keeping all employees involved. [5]A permissive climate will always reduce productivity while a democratic climate will always increase productivity.

   a. Is sentence 1 fact, opinion, or combination of fact and opinion? _____

      If it includes both, list which information is fact and which is opinion. _____

      _____

   b. Is sentence 5 fact, opinion, or combination of fact and opinion? _____

      If it includes both, list which information is fact and which is opinion. _____

      _____

6. [1]Legal immigration to the United States has reached the highest level since the early twentieth century, yet the number of people who wish to migrate to the United States is much higher than the quotas permit. [2]Many people who cannot legally enter the United States are now immigrating illegally. [3]Those who do so are called undocumented immigrants. (Rubenstein, *Introduction to Human Geography*)

   a. Is sentence 1 fact, opinion, or combination of fact and opinion? _____

If it includes both, list which information is fact and which is opinion. _____

_____

b. Is sentence 2 fact, opinion, or combination of fact and opinion? _____

If it includes both, list which information is fact and which is opinion. _____

_____

SECTION 5.2   MAKING VALID INFERENCES

We're walking down our street and we see smoke. We infer there is a fire.

As we head into the movie theater, we notice that all the people coming out of the movie are smiling and happy. We infer they enjoyed the movie.

We're driving in heavy traffic when all of a sudden we see all the cars in the right lane are trying to merge over into the left lane. We infer there is something blocking the right lane.

In each situation we've made an inference—a sensible, reasoned conclusion about what we do not know based on the information we do know. Some people call them *educated guesses*.

MAKING INFERENCES WHEN READING

We also make inferences when we read. Although we don't have clues like smoke or smiles, we do have the word and punctuation clues the author gives us.

For example, as you discovered in Chapter 2, we often infer the meaning of unfamiliar words. In this sentence from *Environmental Science*, Nebel and Wright do not state the meaning of "treks," but they do give you information to help figure out its meaning:

> In Tanzania, women and girls in rural villages may have to walk miles to collect the water—often polluted—that they will use for drinking, cooking, and washing. Similar <u>treks</u> of increasing length must be taken to collect the firewood for cooking.

Based on the information in the previous sentence—"may have to walk miles to collect the water," we can infer that in this sentence "treks" means long walks.

We also infer how the author views his or her subject. In this paragraph from his text *The Art of Rock and Roll*, we can infer how Brown feels about Elton John and his music even though he doesn't state it.

> Although John was most significant in the early 1970s, that is up to 1975, he has remained active and is not yet nostalgic. He is still progressing. Like all rock stars who pass the age of thirty, he has become old by commercial standards. He is no longer the new sensation, but he remains a genius in the context of his time. Although some critics have suggested that his singing is mechanical and nonexpressive, I believe this charge to be false. Elton John expresses his words in the context of the melodic and musical line, and within the appropriate context, his singing is both expressive and musical.

Based on the words and phrases Brown uses to describe Elton John's ability and music—"he has remained active and is not yet nostalgic"; "he is still progressing; he remains a genius in the context of his time"; "his singing is both expressive and musical"—we can infer that Brown feels Elton John is still a great musician.

BUT BE CAREFUL

Inferences are, however, only *reasonable* conclusions—a best guess. Therefore, we can make a mistake. We can make an invalid inference. To increase your chances of making valid, appropriate inferences, use the following guidelines:

1. Be sure you understand what is stated. It's almost impossible to make a statement about what is not known if you are unclear about what is known.
2. Make certain your inferences are based on and supported by the information the author does give.
3. Check that your inferences are not contradicted by any of the author's stated information.

■ EXERCISE 5.5: MAKING VALID INFERENCES

Circle the inference you can reasonably make based on the information given.
Example

Although parents tend to think that peer pressure is the primary influence on drinking by teenagers, youngsters say otherwise. Therefore parents must set a good example by using alcohol in moderation, preferably with meals, and never suggesting it as a solution for stress or other emotional problems.

a. Parents have at least some influence on whether or not teens drink.
b. Parents are the primary influence on whether or not teens drink.
c. Peers are the primary influence on whether or not teens drink.

Explanation You should have circled *a*.

a. Valid inference. The author states that peers are not the only influence and that parents need to set a good example. Therefore we can infer that parents have some influence.
b. Invalid inference. The author does not give us enough information to infer that parents are the *primary* influence.
c. Invalid inference. The author contradicts this statement with "youngsters say otherwise."

1. Blood is something special. It can't be manufactured, and it can't be replaced with animal blood. This year over 4 million Americans will need a blood transfusion to survive illness or injury.
   a. The accident rate is increasing.
   b. There is a need for people to become blood donors.
   c. Human blood can be manufactured.
2. There are more than 300 kinds of hummingbirds, but amazingly, only the ruby-throated hummingbird is found east of the Mississippi River. The western United States is home to about eighteen types. Most of the other varieties live in Central and South America. None are found outside the Western Hemisphere.
   a. People who live in Arizona have more chance of seeing several different kinds of hummingbirds than those who live in New York.

b.   The ruby-throated hummingbird is only found east of the Mississippi.

c.   You can see many hummingbirds in New Zealand, Australia, and other countries in the Southern Hemisphere.

3.   For a healthy person, aerobic exercise strengthens the heart, and enhances general muscle tone, strength, and elasticity. It burns calories, increases weight loss, and increases the likelihood that weight loss will be maintained. It also decreases the risk of coronary artery disease, diabetes, and high blood pressure. It is also associated with decreased anxiety and depression and an enhanced sense of well-being.

a.   Everyone can benefit from aerobic exercise.

b.   For those who can exercise, aerobic exercise has several beneficial effects.

c.   You cannot improve general muscle tone with aerobic exercise.

4.   Play brings joy and laughter to childhood. It is also the way children learn about themselves, their environment, and the people around them. As they play, children learn to solve problems, get along with other people, and control their bodies. Playing helps children express their creativity and develop leadership skills.

a.   Playing takes valuable time away from more useful activities.

b.   Play is most valuable to babies.

c.   Play is a valuable activity for children.

5.   The age-old belief that you need at least eight hours of sleep per night has been proved incorrect. Some people need nine hours of sleep; others get by nicely on six. The average for most people is about seven-and-a-half hours.

a.   The amount of sleep a person needs varies with each individual.

b.   The older you are, the more sleep you need.

c.   Everyone should get at least eight hours of sleep each night.

6.   Inactivity and overeating are the two leading causes of being overweight among both children and adults. Early eating patterns, the number of fat cells acquired early in life, metabolism, age, and environmental and genetic factors also play a significant role.

a.   If people would stop overeating, no one would be overweight.

b.   A number of factors contribute to being overweight.

c.   Children and adults gain weight for different reasons.

■   **EXERCISE 5.6: MAKING VALID INFERENCES**

Circle all of the inferences you can reasonably make based on the information given.

Example

Before they bought a recreational vehicle (RV), Jack and Sally's annual summer vacation with their children was like trying to herd cattle. They were always trying to force their kids into some kind of line: at the airport, the hotel, and even restaurants. Everybody was always cranky.

a.   Jack and Sally travel a lot on business.

b.   Jack and Sally enjoy traveling with their family in the RV more than when they used to fly and stay in hotels.

c. Jack and Sally have more than one child.

d. Jack and Sally take their yearly vacation in the winter.

Explanation   You should have circled *b* and *c*.

a. Invalid inference. The author does not give us any information about whether Jack and Sally travel on business.

b. Valid inference. The author states that Jack and Sally remember that the unpleasant aspects of travel, like forcing the kids into lines and everybody being cranky, took place before they bought the RV.

c. Valid inference. The author states "children."

d. Invalid inference. This contradicts the author's information: "annual summer vacation."

1. Once-in-a-lifetime opportunities and get-rich-quick pitches have been around for years. These "sure deals" are pitched to us in late-night TV infomercials, anonymous Web sites, dinner-hour phone calls, and our morning newspaper. The pitchmen make them sound so good, it's easy to get our hopes up. But no matter where we find them, one thing is certain: Only the pitchmen will get richer.

    a. It's easy for pitchmen to make these sure deals sound good because they always make people rich.

    b. Only opportunities that will definitely make investors money can be advertised on television and newspapers.

    c. If a once-in-a-lifetime opportunity seems too good to be true, it probably is too good to be true.

    d. In most get-rich-quick schemes, only the person selling them will get rich.

2. Resting on the eastern edge of the Cascade Range, the town of Bend boasts an exciting mix of high desert, volcanoes, forests, rivers, and mountains. Visitors and residents enjoy a variety of recreational opportunities from white-water rafting to hiking to fishing. In addition, this Oregon outdoor paradise offers first-class downhill skiing and miles of untamed wilderness for mountain bikers.

    a. You can only enjoy outdoor activities in Bend during the summer.

    b. There is at least one mountain close to Bend.

    c. People who enjoy being outdoors would have a lot of activities to choose from in Bend.

    d. There is an active volcano in Bend.

3. The number of Americans age 65 or older is increasing as more people survive heart attacks, cancer, strokes, and other ailments that often used to be fatal. This means more people will have to figure out a way to deal with the financial burden of long-term care. For example, the average cost for care in a nursing home in the United States is currently $50,000–$60,000 a year, but experts expect the cost to double over the next ten years.

    a. Medical science is making it possible for Americans to live longer.

    b. Americans need to develop a sound money strategy to make sure they can pay for long-term care.

    c. The cost for nursing home care is expected to decrease over the next ten years.

    d. Most people have enough money in their savings account to pay for long-term care.

4. Twenty percent of all new businesses disappear in the first year, and 50 percent are gone after the first seven years, according to Price Waterhouse, the Big Eight accounting firm. And, the smaller your business, the more likely it will fall to the damaging effects of a single problem or error.

    a. More than half of all new businesses have problems with employees during the first year.

    b. Small business owners must be careful, knowledgeable, skillful, and lucky for their business to survive.

    c. Small businesses have a better chance of success than big businesses.

    d. Starting a business is risky.

5. The FBI estimates that as many as 2,300 children are reported missing to the police each day. Some become lost; some run away. Some are abducted, and others are thrown away. Some fall prey to crime, are abused, exploited, murdered. Therefore, teaching children about dangerous situations has become as necessary as teaching them the ABCs. Fortunately, with the right information and techniques, parents can raise happy, outgoing children while teaching them to use their eyes, ears, and knowledge to make appropriate judgments about situations, and to turn to a trusted adult for help if a problem does arise.

    a. Teaching children to be aware and alert doesn't mean teaching them to be fearful and afraid.

    b. Teaching children to stay away from strangers will keep them safe.

    c. Children face a variety of dangerous and scary situations.

    d. Children should be protected from information about scary people and situations.

6. Having a personal purpose or goal for reading is how you focus your attention on specific aspects of a selection. If you don't set a specific purpose, you are saying that everything in the selection is of equal value and that you want to learn it all in complete detail. Although this total-mastery approach may be necessary in a few reading assignments each term, other times it will just lead to frustration and information overload.

    a. It's important to remember everything you read in every assignment.

    b. Setting a purpose for reading an assignment is a good idea.

    c. When you set a purpose for reading, you are more likely to find the information you need.

    d. Teachers expect you to read every assignment the same.

■ EXERCISE 5.7: MAKING VALID INFERENCES

Complete the exercises following each selection.

SELECTION A

Most books about what's wrong with baseball and how to fix it make you feel as if you've been cornered by a drunk at a noisy party. Bob Costas's "Fair Ball: A

Fan's Case for Baseball" puts you more in mind of a good conversation during a rainout that makes you forget the game is on hold.

Mr. Costas, who says he is "a 'Bull Durham' guy, not a 'Field of Dreams' guy," makes his points with neat, forceful prose. In arguing persuasively against the current set-up of a divisional winners race plus wild-card race, he writes that "baseball doesn't offer slam-bam moment-to-moment action. It isn't easily enhanced by hype. It draws drama from context." Which is a better way of saying that more playoffs—á la hockey and basketball—detract from the primary appeal of baseball: the long season and the pennant race…. (Book review by Allen Barra)

1. We can infer that Barra:
   a. dislikes Costas's book.
   b. likes Costas's book.
   Please explain what Barra said that led you to infer your answer. _____

   _____

2. We can infer that Barra:
   a. thinks Costas is a good writer.
   b. thinks Costas is a poor writer.
   Please explain what Barra said that led you to infer your answer. _____

   _____

SELECTION B

When you annotate a reading selection, you do things such as circle unfamiliar words and define them in the margin, bracket significant sentences or paragraphs and paraphrase them in the margin, and restate the thesis and main ideas in your own words. Rephrasing an idea into your own words makes you think the idea through and process its meaning. Using your own words to annotate is an active notetaking process that requires thinking.

On the other hand, using colored pens to highlight text is a passive notetaking activity. Often, students don't even understand the material they highlight. Whenever they think something may be important, they mark it and promise to go back and read it later. In essence, they just postpone the reading assignment. (Adapted from McGrath, *Understanding Diverse Viewpoints*)

1. We can infer that I recommend:
   a. annotating more than highlighting.
   b. highlighting more than annotating.
   Please explain what I said that led you to infer your answer.

   _____

   _____

2. We can infer that I believe:
   a. students learn the same from rephrasing ideas as from highlighting sentences.
   b. students learn more from rephrasing ideas in their own words than from highlighting a sentence.
   Please explain what I said that led you to infer your answer.

   _____

   _____

■ **EXERCISE 5.8: MAKING VALID INFERENCES**

Complete the exercises following each selection.

SELECTION **A**

There are three forms of communication between people. One is the written form—letters, memos, faxes, e-mails, etc. The second is the verbal form—face-to-face conversations, telephone conversations, voice mail, intercom discussions, video conferencing, etc. The third involves the transmission of attitudes.

   The first two forms of communication are so important to the profitable operation of an organization that we tend to think they are the only ones. We forget that we also communicate our attitudes through facial expressions, hand gestures, and other more subtle forms of body language. Sometimes people will greet others with a positive voice, but their body language (negative facial expression) sends a contrasting signal. As the expression claims, sometimes your attitude speaks so loudly that others cannot hear what you say. (Chapman and O'Neil, *Your Attitude Is Showing*)

   1. We can infer that Chapman and O'Neil think:
       a. of the three forms of communication, only written and verbal are important.
       b. all three forms of communication are very important.

       Please explain what Chapman and O'Neil said that led you to infer your answer. _____

       _____

   2. We can infer that Chapman and O'Neil think:
       a. educating people about how we communicate our attitudes through facial expressions, hand gestures, and other forms of body language would improve interpersonal communication.
       b. the traditional emphasis on written and verbal skills is all that's needed for good interpersonal communication.

       Please explain what Chapman and O'Neil said that led you to infer your answer. _____

       _____

SELECTION **B**

Spend a few minutes on the road and you'll realize that many beginning drivers lack basic knowledge of driving courtesy, safe driving practices, and crash-avoidance techniques. The amount of training most teens receive before they drive is not sufficient considering the dense and intense driving environment many of them will face.

   Most teens think "driver's ed" is a joke. In some respects, they're right. Teaching young drivers when to use turn signals and how to parallel park is simply not enough.

   Now there is a growing clamor for graduated driver-licensing programs. The concept is to gradually phase in driving privileges for new licensees as they "demonstrate growth in driving skills and responsible operation of motor vehicles." The misguided premise for graduated licensing is that time is a substitute for training…. (Adapted from Franklin, "Point of View," *USA Today*)

   1. We can infer Franklin believes that America's driver's education system:
       a. is working fine.
       b. needs changing.

Please explain what Franklin said that led you to infer your answer. _____

_____

2. We can infer Franklin believes that a graduated driver-licensing program:
   a. is not a good way to improve the skills of beginning drivers.
   b. is a good way to improve the skills of beginning drivers.
   Please explain what Franklin said that led you to infer your answer. _____

_____

_____

CHAPTER REVIEW

SUMMARY OF KEY IDEAS

- Statements of fact tell about people, places, things, and events objectively, without value judgements or personal interpretations. Facts, when verified, are reliable support for main ideas and good sources of information.
- Statements of opinion tell about people, places, things, and events subjectively from the author's point of view. Opinions express the author's thoughts, feelings, beliefs, and attitudes. An opinion is not right or wrong, or good or bad. However, depending on the amount and type of evidence the author considered before forming the opinion, it can be valid or invalid.
- Most authors use a combination of facts and opinions to support and explain their ideas.
- You should be skeptical of invalid opinions. However, opinions based on a thoughtful, coherent evaluation of the available evidence can be helpful. In fact, it's often an author's insight, wisdom, and conclusions—his or her reasoned judgments—that help us understand ideas.
- An inference is a sensible, reasoned conclusion about what we do not know based on the information we do know. Some people call them *educated guesses*.
- Because authors don't directly state everything they want us to know, we must make inferences when we read.
- An inference is only a *reasonable* conclusion—a best guess. Therefore, an inference can be wrong.
- To increase your chances of making valid, appropriate inferences, use the following guidelines:

  Be sure you understand what is stated. It's almost impossible to make a statement about what *is not known*, if you are unclear about what *is known*.

  Make certain your inferences are based on and supported by the information the author does give.

  Check that your inferences are not contradicted by any of the author's stated information.

SELF CHECK

- I can distinguish between facts and opinions.
- I can make good inferences.

PUTTING IT ALL TOGETHER

Complete the exercises following each paragraph.

1. [1]Because two of every three deaths and one of every three hospitalizations in the United States today are linked to largely <u>preventable</u> behaviors—tobacco use, alcohol abuse, sedentary activities, and overeating, for example—primary and secondary prevention are essential to reducing the incidence (number of new cases) and prevalence (number of existing cases) of diseases and disabilities. (Donatelle and Davis, *Access to Health*)

    a. preventable means _____

    b. Main idea _____

        _____

    c. Is this sentence fact, opinion, or combination of fact and opinion? _____

        If it includes both, list which information is fact and which is opinion. _____

        _____

    d. Circle the statement that is a valid inference:
        Most deaths are sudden and unexpected.
        Adopting healthier behaviors could prevent some illnesses.
        It's very difficult to prevent getting sick.

2. [1]Throughout history, sports have been oriented primarily toward males. [2]The first modern Olympic Games held in 1896, for example, excluded women from competition; in the United States, until recently, even Little League teams in most parts of the country <u>barred</u> girls from the playing field. [3]Such exclusion has often been defended by unfounded notions that girls and women lack the strength or the stamina to play sports or that women risk losing their femininity if they do. (Macionis, *Sociology*)

    a. barred means _____

    b. Main idea _____

        _____

    c. Is sentence 2 fact, opinion, or combination of fact and opinion? _____

        If it includes both, list which information is fact and which is opinion. _____

        _____

    d. Is sentence 3 fact, opinion, or combination of fact and opinion? _____

If it includes both, list which information is fact and which is opinion. _____

_____

e. Circle the statement that is a valid inference:

Some Little League teams now allow girls to play on their teams.

Men are stronger than women.

Several women won gold medals in the 1896 Olympics.

3. [1]Not getting enough sleep can make a child <u>distracted</u>, easily frustrated and, in some cases, hyperactive. [2]This last behavior might seem <u>counterintuitive</u>: When most of us get tired, we wind down, our emotions get quieter. [3]But fatigue makes some adults and children more active, more intense. [4]In kids, this behavior sometimes gets treated with drugs like Ritalin when trying to help them stay rested would be a better first step. (Wilkoff, *Getting Serious about Sleep*)

a. distracted means _____

b. counterintuitive means _____

c. Main idea _____

_____

d. Is sentence 4 fact, opinion, or combination of fact and opinion? _____

If it includes both, list which information is fact and which is opinion. _____

_____

e. Circle the statement that is a valid inference:

Dr. Wilkoff will sometimes work with patients to improve their sleep patterns before he prescribes drugs.

Dr. Wilkoff believes that only adults can suffer the effects of too little sleep.

Dr. Wilkoff doesn't believe in drugs such as Ritalin for children.

4. [1]Americans today expend much less energy than did previous generations, perhaps as much as a few hundred calories per day less. [2]All the "advances" that make our life easier—like e-commerce, drive-up teller machines and automatic doors—contribute to the current <u>epidemic</u> of obesity and related diseases. (Krucoff and Krucoff, *Healing Moves*)

a. an epidemic is _____

b. Main idea _____

c. Is sentence 1 fact, opinion, or combination of fact and opinion? _____

If it includes both, list which information is fact and which is opinion. _____

_____

d. Circle the statement that is a valid inference:

Technology makes life in America more difficult.

Americans eat less today than past generations did.

If Americans exercised more, they would probably be healthier.

5. [1]Safeguarding the world's diversity of species is <u>integral</u> to a sustainable future. [2]Yet, as humans dominate and alter increasing portions of the planet, increasing numbers of species are threatened with extinction for various reasons, one of which is simple monetary gain. [3]Illegal trade in wildlife is an estimated $2–3 billion-a-year business, with profits comparable to the drug trade. (Nebel and Wright, *Environmental Science*)

    a. integral means _____

    b. Main idea _____

        _____

    c. Is sentence 2 fact, opinion, or combination of fact and opinion? _____

        If it includes both, list which information is fact and which is opinion. _____

        _____

    d. Circle the statement that is a valid inference:

        The world doesn't really need very many species of wildlife.

        There is only one reason species are dying out.

        Although it's not legal, people sell endangered wildlife for big profits.

6. [1]When a university I was associated with faced hiring a new president, it hired an <u>interim</u> president to run the university during the search process. [2]The person hired in the interim did not bring to the job the traditional credentials of a Ph.D. and academic experience. [3]The individual had spent his career in business, not education. [4]But during the time he spent as interim president, *he listened.* [5]He listened to every level of the university from janitor to dean. [6]He listened to every <u>constituent</u> of the university from alumni to student. [7]He listened to every friend of the university from business executive to local civic leader. [8]A quiet person who dressed casually and undertalked every conversation, the interim president kept the university running smoothly. [9]During his tenure, the university experienced a tremendous "calming" effect that was talked about long after he left. (Adapted from Bittner, "Listening," *Each Other*)

    a. interim means _____

    b. a constituent is a _____

    c. Main idea _____

        _____

    d. Is sentence 9 fact, opinion, or combination of fact and opinion? _____

        If it includes both, list which information is fact and which is opinion. _____

    e. Circle the statements that are valid inferences:

        The interim president was talked about after he left because people liked him and thought he did a good job.

Bittner thinks the interim president's ability to listen to people was an important factor in his success.

The interim president was successful because he didn't have a Ph.D.

7.   [1]A type of stereotyping that is <u>subtle</u> and rarely mentioned is physical attractiveness. [2]Psychological research shows that many people in our society equate character with looks. [3]According to the attractiveness stereotype, we view people who are attractive as "more sensitive, kind, interesting, strong, poised, modest, sociable, outgoing, exciting, and sexually warm." [4]Furthermore, we tend to assume that they will "hold better jobs, have more successful marriages, and lead happier and more fulfilling lives." (Adapted from Bucher, *Diversity Consciousness*)

a.   subtle means _____

b.   Main idea _____

_____

c.   How do sentences 3 and 4 relate to sentence 2? (Circle the correct answer.)

Sentences 3 and 4 give an explanation and examples of sentence 2.

Sentences 3 and 4 give the cause of sentence 2.

Sentences 3 and 4 give the definition of a term in sentence 2.

d.   Is sentence 2 fact, opinion, or combination of fact and opinion? _____

If it includes both, list which information is fact and which is opinion. _____

_____

e.   Circle the statement that is a valid inference:

People who are attractive are more sociable and exciting.

Stereotyping is rarely accurate or useful.

We hardly ever stereotype people any more.

8.   [1]The Civil War cut off the Texas cattle industry from its major markets. [2]During these <u>fallow</u> years, the cattle ran wild on the Texas grasslands, and by 1866 there were an estimated 5 million head. [3]Meanwhile, the rest of the country, having <u>depleted</u> its cattle stock to meet the Union army's needs, was starved for beef. [4]In Texas, cattle were selling for $4 a head, while in the eastern cities they were worth as much as $40 and $50 a head. (Unger, *These United States*)

a.   fallow means _____

b.   depleted means _____

c.   Main idea _____

_____

d.   Is sentence 3 fact, opinion, or combination of fact and opinion? _____

If it includes both, list which information is fact and which is opinion. _____

_____

e. Circle the statements that are valid inferences:

The eastern cities were a major market for the Texas cattle industry.

During the Civil War, Texas had more cattle than it could use.

Texas didn't supply much, if any, of the Union army's beef.

9. [1]Word processing is the perfect example of how automation can be used to increase productivity and <u>foster</u> creativity. [2]It reduces the effort you must devote to the routine aspects of writing so you can focus your attention on its creative aspects. [3]As a result, most word processing users will agree that their writing styles have improved. [4]The finished product is less <u>verbose</u>, better organized, without spelling errors, and, of course, more visually appealing. (Long and Long, *Computers*)

a. foster means _____

b. verbose means _____

c. Main idea _____

_____

d. Is sentence 1 fact, opinion, or combination of fact and opinion? _____

If it includes both, list which information is fact and which is opinion. _____

e. Circle the statements that are valid inferences:

Long and Long believe that using word processing usually improves a person's writing.

Long and Long believe that using word processing usually makes a person more productive.

Long and Long believe that all good writers use word processing.

10. [1]"No higher-level job can be <u>obtained</u> without a good command of the language," says Steven Harwood, chief of nuclear medicine at the Veterans Administration Hospital in Bay Pines, Florida. [2]"Writing skills are the most important skills you can develop—especially for obtaining higher-management-level jobs. [3]You must be able to clearly communicate your ideas to others." (Carter and Troyka, *Majoring in the Rest of Your Life*)

a. obtained means _____

b. Main idea _____

_____

c. Is sentence 2 fact, opinion, or combination of fact and opinion? _____

If it includes both, list which information is fact and which is opinion. _____

d. Circle the statements that are valid inferences:

Dr. Harwood believes people who want good jobs should have good writing skills.

Dr. Harwood believes good writing skills are more important for people in medicine than in other occupations.

Dr. Harwood would be more likely to promote a person with a good command of the language than one with poor communication skills.

CROSSWORD PUZZLE

ACROSS

3 characteristic, normal
7 ancient building material
8 reasoned conclusion
11 essential, important
12 statement that can be verified
15 illness, disease
17 best
19 wordy
21 statement that cannot be verified
23 encourage
25 interesting, engaging
27 passive, inactive

DOWN

1 make worse
2 financial, relating to money
4 forecast of what might happen
5 sharpened
6 sound, logical
8 first, beginning
9 deviation, difference
10 widespread outbreak
13 personal story, memoir
14 dormant
16 extravagant
18 used up
20 prohibited, excluded
22 achieved
24 clear, apparent
26 change, modify

WORD LIST (NOT ALL USED)

adage	fact	obtained
adobe	fallow	obvious
aggravate	fascinating	opinion
ailment	foster	optimal
alter	honed	prediction
autobiography	inference	sedentary
barred	initial	typical
depleted	integral	valid
epidemic	lavish	verbose
exception	monetary	

LOG ON TO THE WEB

The purpose of a newspaper editorial is to influence readers to adopt a particular viewpoint. To accomplish that, skillful editorial writers use a combination of facts and opinions. Log on to one of these newspaper's opinion page or use a search directory/engine to locate a newspaper editorial that interests you.

> News-Press in Santa Barbara, California, at
> http://www.newspress.com/np_home/fedits.html
>
> Washington Post in Washington D.C. at
> http://www.washingtonpost.com/wp-dyn/opinion
>
> Las Vegas Sun in Las Vegas, Nevada, at
> http://www.lasvegassun.com/opinion/editorials
>
> Journal Sentinel in Milwaukee, Wisconsin at
> http://www.jsonline.com/news/editorials
>
> Denver Post in Denver, Colorado, at
> http://www.denverpost.com/opinion/opinion.htm

Print out the editorial and write the following:

1. One fact the writer used
2. One opinion the writer stated
3. What you believe the editorial writer wants you to do or believe

IDEAS FOR WRITING AND DISCUSSION

A. Think about an item you would like to buy in the next few months, such as a computer, a refrigerator, or a guitar. Make a list of sources you could use for factual information about the different brands of the item. What makes you trust these sources? Next, list sources you believe would provide opinions you could trust about the different brands of the item. Why do you believe they would provide useful opinions? Finally, list sources you think might try to unfairly influence your decision. Why or how do you think they would try to influence you?

B. In 1999, three professors at the University of Miami conducted a study to examine college students' attitudes about reading. They found that students who were having difficulty in their courses described reading as a passive activity—"reading is looking at the pages and seeing words." On the other hand, academically successful readers viewed reading as an active process—"reading is when you understand what the author is saying."

What inferences can you make about the relationship between the way the students view reading and their academic success? Although this information is only from one study, what can you infer you should do to be a more successful reader?

CHAPTER 6

READING MULTI-PARAGRAPH SELECTIONS

CHAPTER PREVIEW

Objectives

- Set a purpose for reading.
- Preview chapters and articles.
- Identify the thesis of a multi-paragraph selection.

Sections

6.1   Preparing to Read Multi-Paragraph Selections

6.2   Identifying the Thesis

CHAPTER FOCUS

You read many different types of material for many different reasons. Today, for example, you might locate a specific piece of information in a ten-page report for your boss, catch up on the day's events in the newspaper, surf the Internet, read a text assignment for class, make a casserole from a new cookbook, and spend some time with your favorite author's new novel. In each of these situations, your purpose for reading, your knowledge of the subject, the author's writing style, the length of the reading, and the medium (the type and form of the publication) are different.

Even among school assignments when your general purpose is reading for learning, your specific purpose, knowledge of the subject, the author's writing style, the length of the reading, and the medium vary. For example, consider these two assignments:

Assignment 1   For your Introduction to Computers class, you are to read the first chapter—35 pages—in the text to prepare for tomorrow's lecture. You use computers all the time and know quite a bit about them. The textbook was written by your professor in easy-to-read language for beginning students. It includes several photographs and illustrations to help explain the information.

Assignment 2   For your Introduction to Art History class, you are to read a three-page magazine article on Michelangelo so you can participate in a small group discussion about Italian Renaissance art. You've never taken an art class before and rarely read anything about art or artists. The article was written by an art historian for people who work in museums. The article is only available on microfiche.

These sample assignments reinforce the concepts that (1) the demands of reading assignments vary a great deal, (2) the length of the assignment—the number of pages you have to read—is not always a major consideration, and (3) how you read always depends on your purpose, your knowledge of the subject, the author's writing style, and the medium. Therefore, it's important to know *why you're reading* and *what you're reading* before you begin.

SECTION 6.1   PREPARING TO READ MULTI-PARAGRAPH SELECTIONS

Reading individual paragraphs accurately and efficiently is critical to academic success. However, a paragraph is usually part of a longer multi-paragraph work such as a chapter or article. This is because authors need more than one paragraph to fully explain and support their overall idea.

So even though a paragraph is an important unit of thought, it is equally important to understand how a paragraph relates to the paragraphs before it and after it, and how the group of paragraphs support and explain the author's overall idea. It is also important to know what parts of the information you need to know when you finish reading the selection.

SETTING A PURPOSE FOR READING

Sometimes as I walk through the library, I stop and ask students, "Why are you reading that text chapter or article?" Unfortunately, their answer is usually "because it was assigned." I say unfortunately because if your only purpose for reading an assignment is "it was assigned," when you finish reading you have fulfilled your purpose—whether or not you understand the information. Successful college readers always go beyond the "it was assigned" purpose. They develop specific reasons for reading based on what they need to know when they finish reading.

When you are reading for learning, your purpose will almost always include understanding the selection's overall idea called the thesis. In addition, you will usually have other reasons for reading—information in addition to the thesis that you need to understand.

Without a clear understanding of why you are reading a selection and what you need to know when you finish reading, you must read everything in the selection with equal emphasis and try to learn it all in complete detail. Although this total-mastery approach may be necessary in a few reading assignments each term, most of the time it leads to frustration and information overload. However, when you clearly identify your reasons for reading, you can focus your attention on specific aspects of a selection.

For example, if you were preparing to take a quiz over key vocabulary in the second chapter of your psychology text, you wouldn't need to read the chapter with the same emphasis on the thesis and main ideas that you would need if you were preparing for a discussion group. If you were going to give an oral report on that chapter, you would read it with more attention to major details than if you were preparing to listen to a lecture about it.

Deciding what kind of information you need to know before you begin to read will make you a more effective and efficient reader.

PREVIEWING

Previewing a multi-paragraph reading assignment—examining it in an orderly way before you begin to read—takes only a few minutes and can help you clarify your reasons for reading and improve your comprehension. When you preview, you read key structural organizers, like titles and subtitles, to get an overview of how the selection is organized and its core ideas. Although the organizing features vary among different kinds of reading materials, such features emphasize important content and are key to improving your comprehension.

PREVIEWING A TEXT CHAPTER

Textbooks almost always have chapter titles, headings, subheadings, bold or italicized type, and summaries. They may also include an introduction, learning objectives, unit summaries, and practice or review questions.

To preview a chapter, read elements such as the following:

- titles, headings, and subheadings
- introduction or introductory paragraphs
- chapter objectives
- margin notes and annotations
- bold, underlined, and italic words
- pictures, charts, and diagrams
- summary or concluding paragraph
- end-of-chapter questions and exercises

Once you are in the habit of previewing, you should be able to preview a thirty-page text chapter with clear structural elements in about ten minutes. Of course, if a selection lacks organizing features or is particularly complex, you may need to spend a little more time previewing.

■ EXERCISE 6.1: PREVIEWING A TEXT CHAPTER

To complete Exercises 6.1 and 6.2 you will need to read the following:

- title
- introduction/chapter focus
- chapter objectives
- key terms

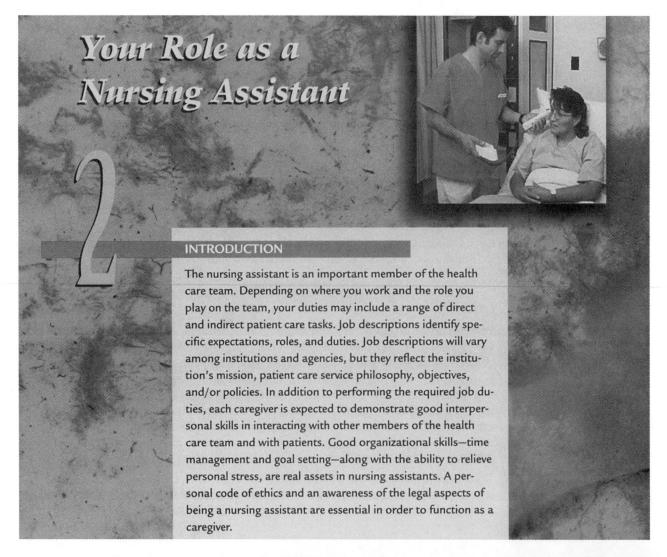

Your Role as a Nursing Assistant

2

INTRODUCTION

The nursing assistant is an important member of the health care team. Depending on where you work and the role you play on the team, your duties may include a range of direct and indirect patient care tasks. Job descriptions identify specific expectations, roles, and duties. Job descriptions will vary among institutions and agencies, but they reflect the institution's mission, patient care service philosophy, objectives, and/or policies. In addition to performing the required job duties, each caregiver is expected to demonstrate good interpersonal skills in interacting with other members of the health care team and with patients. Good organizational skills—time management and goal setting—along with the ability to relieve personal stress, are real assets in nursing assistants. A personal code of ethics and an awareness of the legal aspects of being a nursing assistant are essential in order to function as a caregiver.

OBJECTIVES

When you have completed this chapter, you will be able to:

- Display qualities that are desirable in a good patient/nursing assistant.
- Identify duties and role functions of nursing assistants.
- Practice good personal hygiene.
- Behave ethically.
- Keep confidences to yourself.
- Work accurately.
- Be dependable.
- Follow rules and instructions.
- Develop cooperative staff relationships.
- Show respect for patients' rights.
- Explain how laws affect you and the patients you care for.
- Report incidents.

KEY TERMS

accountable

accuracy

competency

cooperation

dependability

ethical behavior

hazard

hygiene

incident

informed consent

interpersonal skills

malpractice

negligence

stress

Use the excerpt at the bottom of page 128 and the excerpt above, both from *Being a Nursing Assistant*, eighth edition, by Francie Wolgin, to answer the following questions:

1. What is the title of this chapter?

   _____

2. What are two important ideas in the Introduction?

   _____

   _____

3. According to Wolgin, what are two things a reader will be able to do when they complete this chapter?

   _____

   _____

4. How many key terms are listed for this chapter?

   _____

■ EXERCISE 6.2: PREVIEWING A TEXT CHAPTER

Use Chapter 6 in *this* textbook to answer these questions:

1. What is the title of this chapter?

   _____

2. What are two important ideas in the Chapter Focus?

   _____

   _____

3. How many objectives are listed for this chapter? List them:

   _____

   _____

   _____

■ **EXERCISE 6.3: PREVIEWING A TEXT CHAPTER**

To complete Exercises 6.3 and 6.4 you will need to read the following:

- headings and subheadings
- margin notes and annotations
- bold, underlined, and italic words

THE NURSING ASSISTANT: AN IMPORTANT CAREGIVER

accountable To be answerable for one's behavior; legally or ethically responsible for the care of another

competency A demonstrable skill or ability

Being a nursing assistant is not just another job—it is a serious occupation. There are many new things to learn and so many things to do as a caregiver. The fundamental patient care tasks and procedures for which you will be **accountable** can be found on the health care institution's or agency's job description. Your instructor can review any state licensing or certification **competency** requirements that apply to you.

 KEY IDEA

Remain sensitive to what you would want if you or one of your loved ones were the patient. *Empathy* and *understanding* from those caring for a patient are part of the treatment. Frequently, they are as important as medicine or therapy in helping the patient to get well.

■ Role of the Nursing Assistant

Whether you are called nursing assistant, patient care assistant, patient care associate, certified nurse assistant, or some other title to reflect these roles, you will be working under the supervision of the nurse manager or team leader. We will use the terms *nursing assistant* and *immediate supervisor* to refer to you and the person who supervises you. Your immediate supervisor usually makes your assignments, provides feedback on how well you are doing, and keeps track of your overall performance. Ask your immediate supervisor for help when you do not know how to do an assigned procedure or when you are unsure of yourself. It is better to get help than to do something wrong.

If you think you are being asked to do more than you were taught to do, remember that everything you do as a nursing assistant will be supervised by a registered professional nurse. That professional nurse can either provide any additional instruction you may need or will direct you to the proper person or department for such education. Everyone in health care is expected to be continually learning new and updated information on how to best care for patients and their loved ones.

■ Duties and Functions of the Nursing Assistant

A general summary of a job description will state that the nursing assistant works under the direct or general supervision of a registered nurse, contributing to the delivery of patient care through performance of selected day-to-day activities; maintenance of a functional and aesthetic environment conducive to patient well-being; demonstration of unit/area designated competencies; and interaction with patients considering their developmental, age-specific, cultural, and spiritual preferences. Refer to Table 2–1 to review an example of the specific duties and functions expected of three different levels of nonlicensed caregivers. Special education is provided for each level.

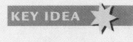 **KEY IDEA**

Caregivers are expected to have good interpersonal skills that enable them to get along well with others, approach and resolve conflicts constructively, problem solve, and maintain confidentiality of information acquired in their role as caregivers.

Use the excerpt at the bottom of page 130, from Wolgin's *Being a Nursing Assistant*, to answer these questions:

1. List the excerpt's main heading and subheadings. (Let the different sizes and styles of type used in the main heading and subheadings help you indent specific subheads under their more general head.)

   _____

   _____

   _____

2. What do you predict the paragraphs under the subheading "Role of the Nursing Assistant" contain?

   _____

   _____

3. How does Wolgin define *accountable*?

   _____

4. What is the purpose of the margin note Key Idea?

   _____

■ **EXERCISE 6.4: PREVIEWING A TEXT CHAPTER**

Use Chapter 6 in *this* textbook to answer these questions:

1. List the chapter's title, headings, and subheadings.

   _____

   _____

   _____

   _____

   _____

2. What do you predict the paragraphs under the subheading "Section 6.2   Identifying the Thesis" (on page 136) will contain?

   _____

   _____

   _____

   _____

3. What words are italicized in the last paragraph of "Chapter Focus" (on page 126)?

   _____

   _____

   _____

   Why do you think they are italicized?

   _____

■ EXERCISE 6.5: PREVIEWING A TEXT CHAPTER

To complete Exercises 6.5 and 6.6 you will need to read the following:

- summary
- end-of-chapter questions

SUMMARY

The nursing assistant is an important member of the health care team. In your role as caregiver, you will be ensuring that patients do not suffer any extra pain and will be making a patient's stay in the health care institution easier. Good interpersonal skills and hygiene are expected in a nursing assistant. Good organizational skills can help make the many duties and responsibilities of the job more manageable and less stressful. As a member of the nursing team, a nursing assistant will be expected to subscribe to the high standard that professional nurses and health care providers set for themselves. Always remember that patients are entitled to respect for their human rights. They must be kept safe and properly cared for at all times. Laws concerning patients and workers in health care institutions protect both the patients and the workers. Be aware of the legal aspects of your job and understand the importance of reporting incidents in your institution's overall safety program.

CHAPTER REVIEW

FILL IN THE BLANK

Read each sentence and fill in the blank line with a word that completes the sentence.

1. When you are legally or ethically responsible for the care of another, you are said to be _____.

2. Working or acting together for mutual benefit is called _____.

3. Good _____ includes good personal cleanliness and appearance.

4. You demonstrate good _____ when you plan, prioritize, and organize your work in order to get it done in a given time period.

5. _____ behavior includes keeping promises, doing what you should do, and acting in accordance with the rules and standards for right conduct and practice.

MULTIPLE CHOICE

Choose the best answer for each question or statement.

1. Caregivers are expected to have good communication skills to allow them to understand their patients and to work as a team.

   a. True.

   b. False.

2. Positive traits in a nurse assistant are all of the following except

   a. being trustworthy.

   b. enjoying working with others.

   c. liking things only a certain way.

   d. liking to learn new things.

3. The code of ethics includes following all of these standards except

   a. carrying out faithfully the instructions you are given.

   b. respecting the right of all patients to beliefs that are different from yours.

   c. letting the patient know it is your pleasure to do your job.

   d. All of the above.

4. Do not discuss patient information with

   a. other patients.

   b. relatives and friends of the patient.

   c. your family.

   d. All of the above.

5. Negligence is doing something or not doing something when a reasonably prudent nursing assistant would have done it under the same conditions.

   a. True

   b. False

6. Whenever an incident happens, remember that it is an unforeseen event that occurs without intent and so does not need to be reported.

   a. True

   b. False

Use the excerpts at the bottom of page 132, from Wolgin's *Being a Nursing Assistant*, to answer these questions:

1. What are two important ideas in the Summary that were in the Introduction?

   _____

   _____

2. What is one important idea in the Summary that was not in the Introduction?

   _____

3. What is the answer to the Chapter Review's Fill in the Blank question 1?

   _____

   Where did you find the answer?

   _____

■ **EXERCISE 6.6: PREVIEWING A TEXT CHAPTER**

Use Chapter 6 in *this* textbook to answer these questions:

1. What are two important ideas in the Summary of Key Ideas (on page 143) that were in the Chapter Focus?

   _____

   _____

2. What is one important idea in the Summary of Key Ideas that was not in the Chapter Focus?

   _____

■ **EXERCISE 6.7: PREVIEWING A TEXT CHAPTER**

Preview a chapter in a textbook for one of your other classes and answer these questions:

1. List the chapter's title, headings, and subheadings. (Indent appropriately.)

   _____

   _____

   _____

   _____

   _____

2. What information do you predict the paragraphs under the first heading will contain?

   _____

   _____

3. List one key idea from the Introduction or introductory paragraphs.

   _____

4. Are objectives listed?

_____

5. Are key terms identified in any way, such as a list or bold type?

_____

6. If there is a Summary, list one key idea.

_____

7. Are there end-of-chapter questions or exercises?

_____

PREVIEWING AN ARTICLE

Magazine and journal articles use different structures than textbooks, but they can also be useful. An article almost always has a title and author. Often, it has information about the author, headings, and sometimes even subheadings. In addition, important words may be in bold or italic type and there may be an introduction or summary.

Taking a few minutes to preview an article gives you a head start on good comprehension.

■ EXERCISE 6.8: PREVIEWING AN ARTICLE

Previewing a multi-paragraph selection takes only a few minutes and can significantly improve your comprehension, reduce your frustration and help you clarify your purpose for reading.

Preview the following article, "Social Security: Your Number." In other words, read the title, author, headings, introduction, and information in and just before the parentheses. As you preview the article, answer the questions that are listed after the article.

SOCIAL SECURITY: YOUR NUMBER

from *Social Security Administration Publication No. 05-10002*

Introduction

Many of us got our Social Security number about the time we got our first job. It was a symbol of our right to work and our responsibility to pay taxes. And, like getting a driver's license, it was symbolic of becoming an adult. Today, many parents apply for a number for their newborns even before they leave the hospital!

Just as having a Social Security number is no longer a symbol of adulthood, the number's use is no longer confined to working and paying taxes. In ever increasing numbers, government agencies, schools, and businesses rely on Social Security numbers to identify people in their computer systems. Everyone seems to want your Social Security number.

Use of the Number

The Social Security Administration (SSA) is aware of concerns about the increasing uses of the Social Security number for client identification and record keeping purposes. You should not use your Social Security card as an identification card. However, several other government agencies are permitted by law to use Social Security numbers, but there is no law either authorizing or prohibiting their use. Banks and other financial institutions use the numbers to report interest earned on accounts to the Internal Revenue Service (IRS). Other government agencies use Social Security numbers in computer matching operations to stop fraud and abuse. For example, using Social Security numbers, some state death records are matched to Medicare records to uncover Medicare and Social Security fraud.

Privacy of Records

Although we can't prevent others from asking for your number, you should know that giving it to them does NOT give them access to your Social Security records. The privacy of your records is guaranteed unless (1) disclosure to another government agency is required by law or (2) the information is needed to conduct Social Security or other government health or welfare programs.

If a business or other enterprise asks you for your Social Security number, you can refuse to give it to them. However, that may mean doing without the purchase or service for which your number was requested.

Our primary message is this: Be careful with your Social Security number and your card and protect their privacy whenever possible.

The Original Purpose of the Social Security Number

When Social Security began in 1935, a system was needed to keep track of the earnings, and eventually the benefits, of people who worked in jobs covered under the new program. Because many people use more than one name over a lifetime or share the same name, a numerical identifier was selected.

What the Numbers Mean

The nine-digit Social Security number is divided into three parts. The first three numbers generally indicate the state of residence at the time a person applies for his or her first card. Originally, the lowest numbers were assigned to the New England states, and the numbers grew progressively higher in the South and West. However, in recent years, this geographical relationship has been disrupted somewhat by the need to allocate numbers out of sequence as state populations change.

The middle two digits of a Social Security number have no special significance, but merely serve to break the numbers into blocks of convenient size. The last four characters represent a straight numerical progression of assigned numbers.

SSA has issued more than 383 million Social Security numbers, and about 6 million new numbers are assigned each year. But even at this rate, there will be no need to reissue the same numbers, revise the present system, or devise a new numbering system for several generations. For this reason, SSA plans to continue using the nine-digit number.

Types of Social Security Cards

SSA issues three types of Social Security cards. The first type of card is the card most people have, and has been issued since 1935. It shows the person's name and Social Security number, and it lets the person work without restriction. SSA issues it to U.S. citizens and permanent resident aliens.

The second type of card bears the legend "Not Valid for Employment." SSA issues it to people from other countries who are lawfully admitted to the United States without INS work authorization, but who need a number because of a federal, state, or local law requiring a Social Security number to get a benefit or service.

SSA began issuing the third type of card in 1992. It bears the legend "Valid for Work Only with INS Authorization." It is issued to people who are admitted to the United States on a temporary basis with Immigration and Naturalization Service (INS) authorization to work.

Applying for a New or Replacement Card

If you need to get a Social Security number or want to replace your lost or stolen card, or get a card showing your new name, call or visit Social Security. These services are free. You will need to complete an application and furnish one or more documents as identification.

You can also download Form SS-5 for a new or replacement card. To get a Social Security number, you will need to provide documents that show your identity, age, and citizenship or lawful alien status. To replace your lost or stolen card, you usually need one identifying document. To change the name on your card, you need to show one or more documents that identify you by your old name and your new name. If you were born outside the United States, generally you also must show proof of U.S. citizenship or lawful alien status. Your replacement card will have the same number as your old card.

1. From the title, what do you predict the article is about (i.e., what is the topic)?

   _____

2. Based on the author of the article, do you predict it will be primarily fact or primarily opinion?

   _____

   Please explain your reasoning.

   _____

3. Which section would you read if you wanted information about the different types of Social Security cards?

   _____

4. What is the SSA?

   _____

   What is the IRS?

   _____

5. What information do you predict will be included in the section "What the Numbers Mean"?

   _____

SECTION 6.2   IDENTIFYING THE THESIS

Just as a main idea is the unifying idea that holds a paragraph together, the thesis is the unifying idea that holds the many paragraphs of the essay or chapter together. When you know the thesis of a selection, you have the idea that helps you connect, understand, and remember all the other ideas.

The thesis sentence is often stated in the first paragraph of a selection to prepare the reader for the rest of the paragraphs. However, the thesis can appear anywhere in the selection.

In addition, the thesis can be implied. This means that in many selections you must put all of the author's ideas together and infer the thesis. Like other inferences, inferring the thesis requires your best reasoned conclusion based on the information you are given.

No matter where the thesis is located, your strategy for identifying and understanding the thesis is the same:

1. Identify the topic by answering "who or what is the entire selection about?"
2. Clarify the controlling thought by answering "what does the author want me to know or understand about the topic?"
3. Combine the topic and controlling thought to form the thesis.
4. State the thesis in your own words.

Example 1   Your purpose for reading the following selection, "Getting Organized," is to identify the thesis.

GETTING ORGANIZED

excerpted from *Adjustment and Human Relations* by Tricia Alexander

---

[1]Sometimes we are so busy that we feel we don't have time to plan, but in fact, no matter how busy we are, we should find it worthwhile to take time to plan our activities. Perhaps we don't have time to plan *and* do absolutely everything else we would like to get done. Yet, by neglecting to plan, we will free very little time; and by failing to plan, we shall probably not discriminate among the essential and nonessential activities. If we spend only ten minutes at the beginning or end of the day planning, our efforts will be repaid many times over. The less time we feel we have to spare, the more important it is to plan our time carefully.

[2]Planning and making choices involve careful thinking and decision making. In the process, we learn to recognize what criteria we use in setting priorities. In all types of planning, we makes lists and set priorities. A most useful planning strategy is to make a daily "To Do" list. Not all of the items on the list are of equal value. Once we have made a list, we need to set priorities on the basis of what is important to us on this particular day.

[3]To make this task easier, we can use an ABC Priority System. Write a capital letter *A* next to those items on the list that have a high value, a *B* for those with medium value, and a *C* for those with a low value. As we do this,

we'll be using our subjective opinion as to the relative value of each item. By comparing the items with one another, we'll help ourselves come up with the ABC priority choices for each entry on the list. If it seems necessary, the activities can be broken down further so that A-items become A-1, A-2, and A-3.

[4]Our ABC priorities may change over time. Today's C may become tomorrow's A. For instance, grocery shopping may be a C activity for awhile, but eventually the cupboards become bare. Our priorities can be adjusted continually, according to the best use of our time right now. If we start with our A activities and always do them first, we can rest assured that we'll always be making the best use of our time. Our C activities may *never* get done if they do not become more urgent with the passage of time. That's okay! If we chronically have more activities on our list than we can manage to get done, we may eventually discard some C items, realizing that we are simply too busy to get to them.

[5]"To Do" lists are most effective when made each day, when the items are prioritized in an ABC fashion, and when items are crossed off as each task is completed. The list should be kept in sight, so that we can look at it several

times a day. We can make a game out of trying to plan just the right amount of activities for each day so that we can score a "bingo" at the end of each day. The bingo means that all of the items for the day get crossed off. It's a good idea to get started on top priority items right away before any unexpected events of the day crop up and interfere with our plan. Toward the end of the day, we can initiate whatever actions are necessary to finish up our "bingo card" for a perfect score [Lakein, *How to Get Control of Your Time and Your Life*, 1973].

[6]One of the most important strategies to keep in mind is that getting panicky is never productive. It's amazing how much can be accomplished when one keeps plugging away, making little bits of progress toward the finish line. Be calm, and be relentless in your efforts.

1. Who or what is Alexander writing about? (the topic)

    _____

2. What does Alexander want you to understand about the topic? (controlling thought)

    _____

3. Therefore, the thesis of this selection is

    _____

Explanation   Who or what is Alexander writing about? *Planning.* What does Alexander want you to understand about planning? *It saves time and helps you be more efficient.* Therefore, the thesis is: *Taking a few minutes to plan will actually save you time and make you more efficient.*

Example 2   Your purpose for reading the following selection, "Causes of Cultural Change," is to identify the thesis.

CAUSES OF CULTURAL CHANGE

excerpted from *Sociology* by John J. Macionis

[1]Cultural changes are set in motion in three ways. The first is *invention*, the process of creating new cultural elements. Invention has given us the telephone (1876), the airplane (1903), and the aerosol spray can (1941), each of which has had a tremendous impact on our way of life. Invention goes on constantly, as indicated by the thousands of applications submitted annually to the U.S. Patent Office.

[2]*Discovery*, a second cause of cultural change, involves recognizing and better understanding something already existing—from a distant star to the athletic prowess of U.S. women. Many discoveries result from scientific research. Yet discovery can also happen quite by accident, as when Marie Curie left a rock on a piece of photographic paper in 1898 and thus discovered radium.

[3]The third cause of cultural change is *diffusion*, the spread of cultural traits from one society to another. The technological ability to send information around the globe in seconds—by means of radio, television, facsimile (fax), and computer—means that the level of cultural diffusion has never been greater than it is today.

1. Who or what is Macionis writing about? (the topic)

    _____

2. What does Macionis want you to understand about the topic? (controlling thought)

    _____

3. Therefore, the thesis of this selection is

    _____

Explanation   Who or what is Macionis writing about? *Cultural changes.* What does Macionis want you to understand about cultural changes? *That there are three causes.* Therefore, the thesis is: *Three factors can cause changes in our culture.*

■ **EXERCISE 6.9: READING A MULTI-PARAGRAPH SELECTION**

FEATURED SELECTION: "WHEN X-COLD STRIKES"

BEFORE YOU READ

About the Author   Robert McGrath is a freelance writer. His work appears in numerous national publications. This selection is from *Young Americans*.

Words to Know

> *affecting* (¶1): happening to, impacting
> *seasonal clothing* (¶9): clothing appropriate to the season/temperature

An Idea to Think About   Have you ever gotten caught out in a storm and gotten wet? Did you get cold? How did you get warm? *As you read,* find out why getting cold can be dangerous and what you can do about it.

WHEN X-COLD STRIKES

Robert L. McGrath

---

¹X-cold is hypothermia—body temperature lowered too rapidly by chilling from wet, wind, and cold. It brings quick collapse of mental and physical functions, affecting anyone, young or old.

²It's exception-cold, extensive-cold. X-cold happens when unexpected winter wind, rain, or snow arrives. Your clothes get wet and lose up to 90 percent of their insulating value. Water is held against your body with a chilling effect, even though outside temperatures can be as high as 50°F.

³Your body temperature, normally 98.6°F, drops to 94°F or below. If it cools further, it's a danger point—X-cold—because cooling to 80°F can produce death.

⁴If you know how to prevent it, X-cold won't spoil your outdoor fun. Watch for these signals:

Chattering teeth and shivering.
Slow, hard-to-understand speech.
Forgetfulness, confusion.
Fumbling hands.
Stumbling, difficulty in walking.
Sleepiness (the person going to sleep may never wake up).

Exhaustion (if the person can't get up after a brief rest, X-cold has taken over).

⁵X-cold reduces reasoning power and judgment because of lack of oxygen to the brain. The affected person usually denies that anything is wrong.

⁶What can you do? Find shelter. Build a fire. Get the victim out of wind, rain, snow. Strip off wet clothing and put on dry clothes or wrap up in a sleeping bag. Give warm drinks. Avoid medicines—they may slow down body processes even more.

⁷Body heat trapped by insulating clothing is the best protection against cold. Wear loose-fitting, lightweight clothing in several layers. Put on a knit cap—more than half the body's heat can be lost through the head. That extra warmth will send added blood to your feet, making them feel more comfortable.

⁸Remember, weather may pull surprises. Unexpected changes can bring sharp wind, driving rain, snow—conditions producing X-cold.

⁹Use your head. Wear seasonal clothing. Don't let X-cold—hypothermia—keep you from enjoying our great outdoors the year round.

EXERCISE 6.9 QUESTIONS

Vocabulary

Circle the letter of the best definition for the underlined word.

1. "It brings quick <u>collapse</u> of mental and physical functions, affecting anyone, young or old." (¶1)
   a. rise
   b. increase
   c. breakdown
   d. growth

2. "Your clothes get wet and lose up to 90 percent of their <u>insulating</u> value." (¶2)
    a. heavy
    b. protection
    c. fashionable
    d. knit

Comprehension

Determine whether the statements in sentences 3–5 are true or false, and write your answer. Also, if the statement is false, rewrite it to make it true.

3. Hypothermia can affect anyone of any age.

    _____

    _____

4. A person affected by hypothermia usually asks for help immediately.

    _____

    _____

5. It's important to wear gloves because more than half the body's heat can be lost through the hands.

    _____

    _____

6. Circle the letter of the sentence that best expresses the thesis:
    a. Insulating clothing is the best protection against cold.
    b. Hypothermia reduces reasoning power and judgment.
    c. X-cold can be deadly so take immediate steps to reverse it or better yet, prevent it.
    d. The weather is unpredictable.

7. What are four warning signs of hypothermia?

    _____

    _____

    _____

    _____

8. What are four positive actions you can take to counteract hypothermia?

    _____

    _____

    _____

    _____

9. In paragraph 5, what does the word "because" signal? (Circle the letter of the correct answer.)
    a. continuation of thought
    b. change in direction of thought
    c. cause
    d. effect

10. Write the main idea of paragraph 5.

    _____

    _____

■ **EXERCISE 6.10: READING A MULTI-PARAGRAPH SELECTION**

FEATURED SELECTION: "HEALTHY AGING: A LIFELONG PROCESS"

BEFORE YOU READ

About the Authors   Rebecca J. Donatelle, Ph.D., CHES, is an associate professor and Coordinator of Graduate Studies in the Department of Public Health at Oregon State University. Lorraine Davis, Ph.D., CHES, is a professor of health education and Vice Provost for Academic Personnel at the University of Oregon. This selection is from Chapter 21 of their text *Access to Health.*

Words to Know

> *prolong* (¶1): lengthen, extend
> *inevitable* (¶3): certain, cannot be avoided
> *chronological age* (¶3): calendar age, number of years lived
> *predispositions* (¶4): tendencies toward
> *vulnerabilities* (¶4): susceptibility for, sensitivity to
> *ostracism* (¶6): exclusion from, segregation

Ideas to Think About   How do you describe an "old" person? At what age do you think someone is "old"? Do all people act "old" when they reach that age? Do some people act "old" before they reach that age? *As you read,* find out what experts say about the aging process and if "older" always means a decline in physical and mental health.

HEALTHY AGING: A LIFELONG PROCESS

Rebecca Donatelle and Lorraine Davis

---

[1]In a society that seems to worship youth, researchers have finally begun to offer some good—even revolutionary—news about the aging process: Growing old doesn't have to mean a slow slide to disability, loneliness, and declining physical and mental health. Health promotion, disease prevention, and wellness-oriented activities can prolong vigor and productivity, even among those who haven't always had model lifestyles or given healthful habits priority. In fact, getting older may actually mean getting better in many ways—particularly socially, psychologically, and intellectually.

Growing Old: Life Passages

[2]Every moment of every day, we are involved in a steady aging process. Everything in the universe—animals, plants, mountain peaks, rivers, planets, even atoms—changes over time. This process is commonly referred to as aging. Aging is something that cannot be avoided, despite the perennial human quest for a fountain of youth. Since you can't stop the process, why not resolve to have a positive aging experience by improving your understanding of the various aspects of aging, taking steps toward maximizing your potential, and learning to adapt and develop strengths you can draw upon over a lifetime?

[3]Who you are as you age and the manner in which you view aging (either as a natural part of living or as an inevitable move toward disease and death) are important factors in how successfully you will adapt to life's transitions.

If you view these transitions as periods of growth, as changes that will lead to improved mental, emotional, spiritual, and physical phases in your development as a human being, your journey through even the most difficult times may be easier. No doubt you have encountered active, vigorous, positive 80-year-olds who wake up every morning looking forward to whatever challenges the day may bring. Such persons are socially active and have a zest for life. Many of them seem much younger than their chronological age, even though their physical casing may be weathered and gray. In contrast, you have probably met 50-year-olds who lack energy and enthusiasm, who seem resigned to tread water for the rest of their lives. These people often appear much older than their chronological age.

[4]From the moment of conception, we have genetic predispositions that influence our vulnerabilities to many diseases, our physical characteristics, and many other traits that make us unique. Maternal nutrition and health habits influence our health while we are in the womb and during the early months after birth. From the time we are born, we begin to take on characteristics that distinguish us from everyone else. We grow, we change, and we pass through many physical and psychological phases. Aging has traditionally been described as the patterns of life changes that occur in members of all species as they grow older. Some believe that it begins at the moment of conception. Others contend that it starts at birth. Still others believe that true aging does not begin until we reach our 40s.

[5]Typically, experts and laypersons alike have used chronological age to assign a person to a particular lifecycle stage. However, people of different chronological ages view age very differently. To the 4-year-old, a college freshman seems quite old. To the 20-year-old, parents in their 40s are over the hill. Have you ever heard your 65-year-old grandparents talking about "those old people down the street"? Views of aging are also colored by occupation. For example, a professional linebacker may find himself too old to play football in his mid-30s. Although some baseball players have continued to demonstrate high levels of skills into their 40s, most players are considering other careers by the time they reach 40. Airline pilots and policemen are often retired in their 50s, while college professors, U.S. senators, and even U.S. presidents may work well into their 70s. Perhaps our traditional definitions of aging need careful reexamination.

Redefining Aging

[6]Discrimination against people based on age is known as ageism. When directed against the elderly, this type of discrimination carries with it social ostracism and negative portrayals of older people. A developmental task approach to life-span changes tends to reduce the potential for ageist or negatively biased perceptions about what occurs as a person ages chronologically.

[7]As people pass through critical periods in their lives, they are either successful or unsuccessful in their attempts to achieve specified goals. Those who are successful usually develop positive coping skills that carry over into other areas of their lives. They tend to think confidently and independently and are more prepared to "experience" life. Those who fail in these rites of passage either develop a sense of learned helplessness and lose confidence in their ability to succeed or learn to cope by compensating for their failures in productive ways.

[8]The study of individual and collective aging processes, known as gerontology, explores the reasons for aging and the ways in which people cope with and adapt to this process. Gerontologists have identified several types of age-related characteristics that should be used to determine where a person is in terms of biological, psychological, social, legal, and functional life-stage development:

[9]• *Biological age* refers to the relative age or condition of the person's organs and body systems. Does the person who is 70 years old have the level of physiological functioning that might be expected of someone in that age group? You have heard of the 70-year-old runner who has the cardiovascular system of a 40-year-old. In contrast, a 20-year-old suffering from progeria (symptoms resembling accelerated aging) may be physiologically closer to a 60-year-old. Arthritis and other chronic conditions often accelerate the aging process.

[10]• *Psychological age* refers to a person's adaptive capacities, such as coping abilities and intelligence, and to the person's awareness of his or her individual capabilities, self-efficacy, and general ability to adapt to a given situation. Although chronic illness may render someone physically handicapped, that person may possess tremendous psychological reserves and remain alert and fully capable of making decisions. Psychological age is typically assessed on the basis of everyday behavior, personal interviews, or tests.

[11]• *Social age* refers to a person's habits and roles relative to society's expectations. People in a particular life stage usually share similar tastes in music, television shows, and politics. Whereas rap music and/or heavy metal often appeal to teenagers and people in their 20s, they may repel middle-aged and older people. Cartoons and children's shows probably don't offer the same attraction for you in college that they did when you were a child.

[12]• *Legal age* is probably the most common definition of age in the United States. Legal age is based on chronological years and is used to determine such things as voting rights, driving privileges, drinking age, eligibility for Social Security payments, and a host of other rights and obligations.

[13]• *Functional age* refers to the ways in which people compare to others of a similar age. Heart rate, skin thickness, hearing, and other individual characteristics are analyzed and compared. A person's ability to perform a given job-related task is also part of this assessment. It is difficult to separate functional aging from many of the other types of aging, particularly chronological and biological aging.

What Is Normal Aging?

[14]Contemporary gerontologists have begun to analyze the vast majority of people who continue to live full and productive lives throughout their later years. In the past, our youth-oriented society has viewed the onset of the physiological changes that occur with aging as something to be dreaded. The aging process was seen primarily from a pathological (disease) perspective, and therefore as a time of decline; the focus was not on the gains and positive aspects of normal adult development throughout the life span. Many of these positive developments occur in the areas of emotional and social life as older adults learn to cope with and adapt to the many changes and crises that life may hold in store for them.

[15]Gerontologists have devised several categories for specific age-related characteristics. For example, people who reach the age of 65 are considered to fit the general category of old age. They receive special consideration in the form of government assistance programs such as Social Security and Medicare. People aged 65 to 74 are viewed as the young-old; those aged 75 to 84 are the middle-old group; those 85 and over are classified as the old-old.

[16]You should note that chronological age is not the only component to be considered when objectively defining aging. The question is not how many years a person has lived, but how much life the person has packed into those years. This quality-of-life index, combined with the inevitable chronological process, appears to be the best indicator of the "aging gracefully" phenomenon. The eternal question then becomes "How can I age gracefully?" Most experts today agree that the best way to experience a productive, full, and satisfying old age is to take appropriate action to lead a productive, full, and satisfying life prior to old age. Essentially, older people are the product of their lifelong experiences, molded over years of happiness, heartbreak, and day-to-day existence.

EXERCISE 6.10 QUESTIONS

Vocabulary

Match each word in the left column with the best definition in the right column.

1. perennial (¶2) _____   a. disgust
2. quest (¶2) _____   b. constant
3. laypersons (¶5) _____   c. nonexperts
4. render (¶10) _____   d. make
5. repel (¶11) _____   e. search

Comprehension

Determine whether the statements in sentences 6 and 7 are true or false, and write your answer. Also, if the statement is false, rewrite it to make it true.

6. Discrimination against people based on age is known as ageism.

   _____

   _____

7. Chronological age is the only component that should be considered when objectively defining aging.

   _____

   _____

8. Circle the letter of the sentence that best expresses Donatelle and Davis's thesis:
   a. Everything in the universe ages.
   b. We can and should try to lead happy and productive lives no matter what our chronological age.
   c. Gerontology explores the reasons for aging and the ways in which people cope with and adapt to this process.
   d. Some people seem much younger than their chronological age.

9. Gerontologists have identified five types of "age." List and explain them.

   _____

   _____

   _____

   _____

   _____

10. What do Donatelle and Davis say appears to be the best indicator of the "aging gracefully" phenomenon?

    _____

11. Circle the letter of the sentence that best expresses the main idea of paragraph 3.
    a. If you have a positive outlook about getting older, your journey through even the most difficult times may be easier.

    b. Who you are as you age and the manner in which you view aging are important factors in how successfully you will adapt to life's transitions.

    c. Fifty-year-olds can appear much older than their chronological age and eighty-year-olds can appear much younger than their chronological age.

    d. If you have a negative outlook about getting older, your journey may be more difficult.

12. What is the relationship of paragraphs 9–13 to paragraph 8? Which of the following do they provide?

    a. examples

    b. steps in a process

    c. causes

    d. effects

CHAPTER REVIEW

SUMMARY OF KEY IDEAS

- Each time you read, your purpose, your knowledge of the subject, the author's writing style, and the medium (the type and form of the publication) are different. Therefore, it's important to know *why you're reading* and *what you're reading* before you begin.

- Without a clear understanding of why you are reading a selection and what you want to know when you finish reading, you must read everything in the selection with equal emphasis and try to learn it all in complete detail. This is why having a personal purpose for reading will make you a more effective and efficient reader.

- When you preview, you read key structural organizers, like titles and subtitles, that give you a view of the content. Previewing takes only a few minutes and can significantly improve your comprehension, reduce your frustration, and help you clarify your purpose for reading.

- Although the organizing features vary among reading materials, such features emphasize important content and are key to good comprehension.

- A multi-paragraph selection, like an article or text chapter, is a group of related paragraphs that support and explain one overall main idea called the thesis.

- Just as a main idea is the unifying idea that holds a paragraph together, the thesis is the unifying idea that holds the many paragraphs of the essay or chapter together. When you know the thesis of a selection, you have the idea that helps you connect, understand, and remember all the other ideas.

- The thesis can appear anywhere in a chapter or essay or it can be implied. Your strategy for identifying and understanding the thesis is as follows:

  Identify the topic by answering "Who or what is the entire selection about?"

  Clarify the controlling thought by answering "What does the author want me to know or understand about the topic?"

  Combine the topic and controlling thought to form the thesis.

  State the thesis in your own words.

SELF CHECK

- I can set a specific purpose for a reading assignment.
- I can preview multi-paragraph reading assignments.
- I can identify the thesis of a multi-paragraph selection.

PUTTING IT ALL TOGETHER

FEATURED SELECTION 1: "CHANGE YOUR BAD HABITS TO GOOD"

BEFORE YOU READ

About the Author   Robert Epstein, Ph.D., is a professor at United States International University in San Diego and an editor for *Psychology Today*. His recent books include *Self-Help without the Hype* and *Pure Fitness: Body Meets Mind*. This article is from *Treatment Today*.

Words to Know

proposed (¶1) suggested
distinctly (¶2) clearly
regimens (¶3) regular patterns of exercise
exaggeration (¶6) overstatement
strides (¶7) steps forward, progress
gizmos (¶11) gadgets
spurred (¶13) urged

An Idea to Think About   How do you change a habit? Say, for example, you are in the habit of nibbling on junk food every evening as you watch television. If you want to stop snacking, how can you do it? *As you read*, find out what researchers think are the three best ways to change a habit.

CHANGE YOUR BAD HABITS TO GOOD:
TO GET YOURSELF STARTED IN A NEW DIRECTION, TRY THE THREE M'S

Robert Epstein

[1]At the University of California, my students and I surveyed more than 2000 years of self-change techniques—perhaps most of the major self-change methods that have ever been proposed by religious leaders, philosophers, psychologists, and psychiatrists. We also reviewed the scientific research literature on self-change, a topic that behavioral scientists began to explore in earnest in the 1960s.

[2]Here is what we found: Of the hundreds of self-change techniques that have been suggested over the centuries, perhaps only a dozen are distinctly different. Many have now been subjected to scientific study, meaning that researchers have tried to see which ones work best.

[3]Three deserve special mention: they're powerful, simple, and easy to learn. What's more, individuals who have made successful changes in their lives—changes in eating habits, exercise regimens, career paths, coping strategies, and so on—often relied on one or more of these methods.

[4]To get yourself started in a new direction, try the Three M's.

Modify Your Environment

[5]People who have never tried this are astounded by the enormous effect it often has. One of my students got herself bicycling every day simply by putting her bicycle in her doorway before she left for school. When she returned home that was the first thing she saw, and that's all she needed to start pedaling away. I've known several people who have overcome nail-biting simply by buying 50 nail files and distributing them everywhere: in their pockets, their desks, and their bedrooms. With a nail file always within reach, they tended to groom rather than bite.

[6]My children have used this simple technique many times. Justin, my 17-year-old, often places small fluorescent reminder notes at eye level on the inside of the frame of his bedroom door. A recent one read "Remember to

shampoo the dog on Saturday or Dad will kill you." (Here he was using exaggeration to good effect.)

[7]The power of rearranging one's space has been well demonstrated in studies since it was first reported in the 1960s. Psychologist Israel Goldiamond of the University of Chicago taught this technique to patients with a variety of personal problems. For example, a young woman who had difficulty studying made dramatic strides when she got a better desk lamp and moved her desk away from her bed.

[8]Psychologist Richard Stuart, who ultimately became a director at Weight Watchers International, showed in the 1960s that overweight women could lose pounds by modifying both their eating behavior and "stimulus environment"—for example, eating from smaller plates and confining all food to the kitchen. To change your *self*, change your world.

Monitor Your Behavior

[9]I've been reading research studies on self-monitoring for 20 years, and I've conducted some myself. To be honest, I still don't fully understand why this technique works, but it does, and remarkably well for most people. The fact is, if you monitor what you do, you'll probably do better.

[10]Weigh yourself regularly and you may well start to lose weight. Keep a record of what you eat and you'll probably start eating more wisely.

[11]Use gizmos. If you say "you know" too much, wear a golf counter on your wrist, and press the count button whenever you catch yourself saying "you know." I'll bet you say it less frequently in just a few days. If a wrist counter is embarrassing, then make a small tear in a piece of paper in your pocket each time you say "you know." The result is the same: You become more aware of what you're doing, and that makes you perform better.

[12]If techniques like this sound silly, keep in mind that the power of self-monitoring has been demonstrated by a variety of research conducted over the past four decades. In a study I published in 1978 with Claire Goss, for example, we taught a disruptive fifth-grade boy to rate his own classroom behavior twice a day. He simply checked off a score for himself, indicating how well-behaved he had been in the morning or afternoon. With his awareness increased, he stayed in his seat more than usual, completed more assignments, and rarely got in trouble.

[13]A similar study by Canadian researchers Thomas McKenzie and Brent Rushall showed that teenagers arrived more promptly at a swim practice when they were given an attendance sheet to record their arrival times. Working with emotionally disturbed children, Sonya Carr of Southeastern Louisiana University and Rebecca Punzo, a New Orleans teacher, reported that self-monitoring improves academic performance in reading, mathematics, and spelling. Recent research even demonstrated that students will compose better stories given a simple checklist that includes elements of good writing. Dozens of studies have similar results, all spurred by heightening our awareness of our behavior.

Make Commitments

[14]When you make a commitment to another person, you establish what psychologists call a contingency of reinforcement; you've automatically arranged for a reward if you comply and a punishment if you don't. It puts some pressure on you, and that's often just what you need.

[15]For instance, if you want to exercise more, arrange to do it with a friend. If you don't show up, your friend will get angry, and that may be just the ticket to keeping you punctual. Decades of research have demonstrated the power of this strategy. For example, in 1994 Dana Putnam and other researchers at the Virginia Polytechnic Institute and State University showed that patients who made written commitments were far more likely to take prescribed medicine than patients who hadn't. Mary Lou Kau and Joel Fischer of the University of Hawaii reported a case of a woman who got herself to jog regularly by setting up a simple arrangement with her husband: He paid her quarters and took her out on weekends whenever she met her jogging goals.

[16]There's good news here for all of us. We can meet many of the demands and overcome many of the challenges of life with simple skills—straightforward practices that anyone can master and that don't require willpower—in other words, with skill, not will.

SELECTION 1 QUESTIONS

Vocabulary

Circle the letter of the best definition for the underlined word.

1. "... behavioral scientists began to explore in earnest in the 1960s." (¶1)
   a. seriously
   b. honestly
   c. in laboratories
   d. in teams

2. "People who have never tried this are <u>astounded</u> by the enormous effect it often has." (¶5)
   a. angered
   b. confused
   c. amazed
   d. insulted

Comprehension

Determine whether the statements in sentences 3–5 are true or false, and write your answer. Also, if the statement is false, rewrite it to make it true.

3. Modifying your environment often involves rearranging your living space.

   _____

   _____

4. If you monitor what you do, you'll probably do better.

   _____

   _____

5. Making a commitment to another person often helps us do better.

   _____

   _____

6. Circle the letter of the sentence that best expresses the thesis:
   a. Using three simple self-change skills can help us meet and overcome many of life's demands and challenges.
   b. Of the hundreds of self-change techniques suggested over the centuries, perhaps only a dozen are distinctly different.
   c. The power of rearranging one's space has been well demonstrated in studies since it was first reported in the 1960s.
   d. If you want to exercise more, arrange to do it with a friend.

7. List the "Three M's."

   _____

   _____

   _____

8. Epstein says "individuals who have made successful changes in their lives—changes in eating habits, exercise regimens, career paths, coping strategies, and so on—often relied on one or more of these methods." Is this a statement of fact or opinion? Please explain your answer.

   _____

   _____

9. What is the relationship of paragraph 10 to paragraph 9? Which of the following does it provide?
   a. examples
   b. definitions
   c. causes
   d. effects

10. What is the relationship of paragraph 15 to paragraph 14? Which of the following does it provide?

    a. examples

    b. definitions

    c. causes

    d. effects

FEATURED SELECTION 2: "HOW TO WRITE CLEARLY"

BEFORE YOU READ

About the Author   When Edward T. Thompson was Editor-in-Chief of *Reader's Digest*, International Paper asked him to share some of what he had learned in his more than twenty years with the magazine famous for making complicated subjects understandable to millions of readers.

Words to Know

clarity (¶9): clearness, precision

detract (¶10): take away from, lessen

ironically (¶14): appears to be contradictory

endeavoring (¶22): attempting, trying

belabor (¶31): to discuss for an unreasonably long period of time

An Idea to Think About   Are you one of the thousands of students who don't like to write? If so, what about writing discourages you? *As you read,* find out seven basic guidelines that might make writing easier for you.

How to Write Clearly

Edward T. Thompson

[1]If you are afraid to write, don't be.

[2]If you think you've got to string together big fancy words and highflying phrases, forget it.

[3]To write well, unless you aspire to be a professional poet or novelist, you only need to get your ideas across simply and clearly.

[4]It's not easy. But it is easier than you might imagine.

[5]There are only three basic requirements:

[6]First, you must *want* to write clearly. And I believe you really do, if you've stayed with me this far.

[7]Second, you must be willing to *work hard*. Thinking means work—and that's what it takes to do anything well.

[8]Third, you must know and follow some *basic guidelines*.

[9]If, while you're writing for clarity, some lovely, dramatic, or inspired phrases or sentences come to you, fine. Put them in.

[10]But then with cold, objective eyes and mind ask yourself: "Do they detract from clarity?" If they do, grit your teeth and cut the frills.

Follow Some Basic Guidelines

[11]I can't give you a complete list of "dos and don'ts" for every writing problem you'll ever face.

[12]But I can give you some fundamental guidelines that cover the most common problems.

1. Outline What You Want to Say

[13]I know that sounds grade-schoolish. But you can't write clearly until, *before you start*, you know where you will stop.

[14]Ironically, that's even a problem in writing an outline (i.e., knowing the ending before you begin).

[15]So try this method:

- On 3" x 5" cards, write—one point to a card—all the points you need to make.
- Divide the cards into piles—one pile for each group of points *closely related* to each other. (If you were describing an automobile, you'd put all the points about mileage in one pile, all the points about safety in another, and so on.)

- Arrange your piles of points in a sequence. Which are most important and should be given first or saved for last? Which must you present before others in order to make the others understandable?
- Now, *within* each pile, do the same thing—arrange the points in logical, understandable order.

[16]There you have your outline, needing only an introduction and conclusion.

[17]This is a practical way to outline. It's also flexible. You can add, delete, or change the location of points easily.

2. Start Where Your Readers Are

[18]How much do they know about the subject? Don't write to a level higher than your readers' knowledge of it.

[19]Caution: Forget that old—and wrong—advice about writing to a 12-year-old mentality. That's insulting. But do remember that your prime purpose is to *explain* something, not prove that you're smarter than your readers.

3. Avoid Jargon

[20]Don't use words, expressions, phrases known only to people with specific knowledge or interests.

[21]Example: A scientist, using scientific jargon, wrote, "The biota exhibited a one hundred percent mortality response." He could have written "All the fish died."

4. Use Familiar Combinations of Words

[22]A speech writer for President Franklin D. Roosevelt wrote, "We are endeavoring to construct a more inclusive society." F. D. R. changed it to, "We're going to make a country in which no one is left out."

[23]Caution: By familiar combinations of words, I do *not* mean incorrect grammar. *That* can be *un*clear. Example: John's father says he can't go out Friday. (Who can't go out? John or his father?)

5. Use "First-Degree" Words

[24]These words immediately bring an image to your mind. Other words must be "translated" through the first-degree word before you see the image. Those are second/third-degree words.

First-degree words	Second/third-degree words
face	visage, countenance
stay	abide, remain, reside
book	volume, tome, publication

[25]First-degree words are usually the most precise words, too.

6. Stick to the Point

[26]Your outline—which was more work in the beginning—now saves you work. Because now you can ask about any sentence you write: "Does it relate to a point in the outline? If it doesn't, should I add it to the outline? If not, I'm getting off the track." Then, full steam ahead on the main line.

7. Be as Brief as Possible

[27]Whatever you write, shortening—*condensing*—almost always makes it tighter, straighter, easier to read and understand.

[28]Condensing, as *Reader's Digest* does it, is in large part artistry. But it involves techniques that anyone can learn and use.

- *Present your points in logical ABC order:* Here again, your outline should save you work because, if you did it right, your points already stand in logical ABC order—*A* makes *B* understandable, *B* makes *C* understandable and so on. To write in a straight line is to say something clearly in the fewest possible words.

- Don't waste words telling people what they already know: Notice how we edited this "Have you ever wondered how banks rate you as a credit risk? ~~You know of course, that it's some combination of facts about your income, your job, and so on But actually, m~~ Many banks have a scoring system...."

- *Cut out excess evidence and unnecessary anecdotes:* Usually, one fact or example (at most, two) will support a point. More just belabor it. And while writing about something may remind you of a good story, ask yourself: "Does it really help to tell the story or does it slow me down?"

  [32](Many people think *Reader's Digest* articles are filled with anecdotes. Actually, we use them sparingly and usually for one of two reasons: Either the subject is so dry it needs some "humanity" to give it life; or the subject is so hard to grasp, it needs anecdotes to help readers understand. If the subject is both lively and easy to grasp, we move right along.)

- Look for the most common word wasters: windy phrases.

Windy phrases	Cut to ...
at the present time	now
in the event of	if
in the majority of instances	usually

- *Look for passive verbs you can make active:* Invariably, this produces a shorter sentence. "The cherry tree was chopped down by George Washington." (Passive verb and nine words.) "George Washington *chopped* down the cherry tree." (Active verb and seven words.)

- *Look for positive/negative sections from which you can cut the negative:* See how we did it here: "The answer ~~does not rest with carelessness or in competence. It lies largely in~~ is having enough people to do the job."

- Finally, to write more clearly by saying it in fewer words: When you've finished, stop.

SELECTION 2 QUESTIONS

Vocabulary

Match each word in the left column with the best definition in the right column.

1.	aspire (¶3) ____	a.	basic
2.	fundamental (¶12) ____	b.	shortening
3.	prime (¶19) ____	c.	desire
4.	precise (¶25) ____	d.	stories
5.	condensing (¶27) ____	e.	primary
6.	anecdotes (¶31) ____	f.	accurate

Comprehension

Determine whether the statements in sentences 7–9 are true or false, and write your answer. Also, if the statement is false, rewrite it to make it true.

7. According to Thompson, you must know where you want your writing to stop before you begin.

   _____

   _____

8. You need a large vocabulary with big fancy words to write well.

   _____

   _____

9. Using active verbs instead of passive verbs usually makes writing shorter and clearer.

   _____

   _____

10. Circle the letter of the sentence that best expresses Thompson's thesis.
    a. You must want to write clearly.
    b. You can't write clearly without an outline.
    c. To write well you need to get your ideas across simply and clearly.
    d. Whenever you write, be as brief as possible.

11. Thompson says there are three basic requirements for getting your ideas across simply and clearly. List them.

    _____

    _____

    _____

12. List the three signal words Thompson used to alert you to the three basic requirements.

    _____

    _____

    _____

13. List Thompson's *fundamental guidelines* that cover most common writing problems.

_____

_____

_____

_____

_____

_____

_____

14. What is the relationship of paragraphs 29–35 to paragraph 28? Which of the following do they provide?

a. examples

b. steps in a process

c. causes

d. effects

FEATURED SELECTION 3: "THINK QUICK"

BEFORE YOU READ

About the Author   R. Daniel Foster was a writer and contributing editor for *Choices for Living* magazine when he wrote this article in 1997.

Words to Know

lapses (¶2): small errors or slips

linear (¶3): in a straight line

snippets (¶3): small segments

virtually limitless (¶4): almost without limit

vexes (¶6): irritates, annoys

minutiae (¶6): details, trivia

deluge (¶17): flood, overflow

An Idea to Think About   When was the last time you forgot something such as the name of someone, a birthday, or an important appointment? Why do you think you forgot it? *As you read*, find out how your memory works and some techniques experts recommend for sharpening your memory skills.

THINK QUICK!

R. Daniel Foster

[1]Lost your car keys again? Can't remember the name of the person you just called on the phone? Forget to buy milk when you went to the store?

[2]Relax—stress, lack of sleep, overwork, and just plain overload of information can cause momentary memory lapses. But if you understand how memory works, you can also understand how to remember things better.

[3]Storing and retrieving memories is far from a linear, predictable process. "Memory is nearly always reconstructive—we don't go around imprinting a true and accurate version of everything we see," says Dr. Patricia Tun, director of the Memory and Cognition Laboratory at Brandeis University in Waltham, Massachusetts. "We constantly receive and store snippets of information. When

we try to remember an event, we reconstruct from the bits and pieces."

⁴Besides those snippets of information, long-term memory also contains your mental dictionary and encyclopedia, a permanent store of knowledge about your world—who was the first U.S. president, what is the sum of two plus two. Your storage capacity for such facts is virtually limitless, and it's well-preserved even into late age, barring disease.

⁵But short-term memory is not nearly as complex—or dependable. The information held there lasts for a matter of seconds, about the time it takes to dial a telephone number you've just heard. By the time you begin talking, the numbers have vanished. Short-term or working memory is what you have at the top of your mind in any given moment. It might be the last few minutes of conversation or a glance at the clock for the time.

⁶What most vexes people is the chore of transferring information from short- to long-term memory. People's names, of course, are high on the list of easily forgettable minutiae, as are everyday tasks such as watering plants and taking the car in for service.

⁷"To get memory to become permanent, pay attention to how you process it," says Dr. James St. James, associate professor of psychology at Millikin University in Decatur, Illinois. "Look for patterns, associations, or visual cues. To remember a telephone number, try looking at the number pattern on the telephone pad. Some companies spell out the numbers with letters. We call these retrieval cues. The more of them you have, the more you'll remember things."

⁸Retrieval cues are often based on the senses. Smell some chalk, and you're transported back to second grade. Taste a White Castle hamburger, and you're back in your hometown haunt. Hear a certain song, and you're driving country roads outside of Dublin. Anything you can do to associate an event or name with looks, smells, sounds, touches, or tastes will help you retrieve that memory later.

⁹To help remember a name, for instance, St. James suggests gathering concrete pieces of information you can associate with the name. What color is the person's hair? How tall are they? What town are they from? "These are all cues that will help your brain group their name in with all the other information," says St. James. Also try repeating the name out loud, or rhyme it with an aspect of the person. Ted has red hair, so you remember Red-Ted.

Memory Boosters

¹⁰Here are some techniques experts recommend for sharpening your memory skills:

¹¹• Pay attention. Many people can't remember names, locations, or other details because they were not focusing on the information. "If you don't pay attention to something in the first place, you're not going to remember it well later," says Tun. "It helps to slow down. Set priorities, decide what's important, and focus on it. Turn off the radio or TV and do one thing at a time.

¹²• Use aids such as to-do lists and calendars. Just the act of writing things down will help you remember them, plus you'll have the written reminder if you need it. Another kind of aid is a designated spot for everyday items—always put your keys on the keyrack and your glasses next to the bed. You can also place objects where they are visual reminders of tasks to be done. Put library books next to the door, along with an umbrella if rain is expected.

¹³• Cluster information in some way that's relevant for you. For instance, the number 149220011957 may seem difficult to memorize, but break it into component parts—1492, 2001, 1957—and the task is achievable.

¹⁴• Other helpful memory tricks include rhymes ("Thirty days hath September") or acronyms (to remember the five great lakes, think of HOMES: Huron, Ontario, Michigan, Erie, Superior).

¹⁵• Visualize. Images are easy to remember because they're concrete. Parking structures use such devices as a blue giraffe and purple elephant to help shoppers locate their cars. But if you're parked on level A with no animal in sight, try associating the letter with a friend—Alison, for example. See her clearly in your mind, and you'll be more likely to remember level A when searching for your car later.

¹⁶• Get creative. If you need to remember to buy laundry detergent, carrots, spinach, mushrooms, and oatmeal at the store, try visualizing this: A washing machine spinning with salad ingredients inside and a giant box of oatmeal on top. The washer will jog your memory to buy detergent, the spinning salad will lead you to the carrots, spinach, and mushrooms, and the giant box of oatmeal will stick out in your mind. The more vivid, and sometimes odd, images are, the more they work, experts say.

Will Memory Fade?

¹⁷Measurable changes in memory often start in a person's 40s and 50s, say experts. "But most people shouldn't worry," says Tun. "They're usually just spread too thin and have a deluge of information coming at them. Not remembering names and forgetting where things are placed is experienced by the young and old." It's time to see a doctor, she says, when problems with language occur, or when things that are familiar are forgotten, like the route to the store.

¹⁸As you age, there are plenty of ways to keep your memory sharp. Work on getting enough sleep, eating a balanced diet, and reducing stress, since lack of sleep, poor nutrition, and anxiety can all impair memory.

¹⁹Exercising your brain—either through purely mental activities such as reading or crossword puzzles, or physical activity such as learning a new dance step—can increase the number of neuron connections and help delay age-related memory loss. "One of the best predictors of how long memory lasts is vocabulary," says Tun. "Those who read a lot and keep learning tend to hold onto memory." Regular physical exercise, she notes, keeps arteries clear and blood and oxygen pumping to the brain.

²⁰Just getting out and experiencing new things can help. "New activity creates memory landmarks," says Dan Mikels, president of the California-based Memory School, which teaches employees and students how to improve their memory. "We need to keep creating these landmarks as we age. Learn a new language, try different foods, listen to new music, travel to new places. In regard to memory, there's much truth to the 'use it or lose it' theory."

SELECTION 3 QUESTIONS

Vocabulary

Match each word in the left column with the best definition in the right column.

1. momentary (¶2) ____	a.	recovering, reclaiming
2. retrieving (¶3) ____	b.	excepting, excluding
3. reconstruct (¶3) ____	c.	temporary, brief
4. barring (¶4) ____	d.	group together
5. cluster (¶13) ____	e.	hurt, worsen
6. vivid (¶16) ____	f.	lifelike, graphic
7. impair (¶18) ____	g.	rebuild, put together

Comprehension

Determine whether the statements in sentences 8–10 are true or false, and write your answer. Also, if the statement is false, rewrite it to make it true.

8. Most memory problems are caused by the aging process.

    _____

    _____

9. Your long-term memory storage capacity is virtually limitless.

    _____

    _____

10. Many people can't remember details because they don't focus on the information.

    _____

    _____

11. Circle the letter of the sentence that best expresses Foster's thesis:
    a. One of the best predictors of how long memory lasts is vocabulary.
    b. To remember a name, associate it with concrete pieces of information you already know.
    c. Understanding how your memory works can help you understand how to remember things better.
    d. Stress and lack of sleep can cause temporary memory lapses.

12. Compare and contrast long- and short-term memory. Include details such as the kinds of information they hold, the general storage capacities, and the length of time information is stored.

    _____

    _____

13. State the main idea of paragraph 11.

    _____

    _____

14. Is paragraph 5 primarily fact, opinion, or combination of fact and opinion? If it includes both, list which information is fact and which is opinion.

_____

_____

_____

15. What is the relationship of paragraphs 19 and 20 to paragraph 18? Which of the following do they provide?
    a. give additional definitions
    b. give additional examples of effects
    c. continue the thought with examples
    d. change direction of thought with examples

FEATURED SELECTION 4: "SEVEN STEPS TO SAFER SUNNING"

BEFORE YOU READ

About the Author   Paula Kurtzweil is a member of the Food and Drug Administration's (FDA) public affairs staff. This selection is adapted from an *FDA Consumer* article that originally appeared in June 1996, and was revised in February 1997. The Sunscreen Regulations were finalized in May 1999.

Words to Know

verge (¶2): edge, threshold, brink

emit (¶4): give off

prevalent (¶5): common

opaque (¶22): not transparent

derived (¶38): obtained from

An Idea to Think About   A sunburn can be painful and dangerous. What steps do you take to make sure you don't get sunburned? *As you read*, find out why sunburns are dangerous and what you can do to prevent a sunburn.

SEVEN STEPS TO SAFER SUNNING

Paula Kurtzweil

¹Put away the baby oil. Toss out that old metal sun reflector. Cancel your next appointment to the local tanning salon.

²These are new days with new ways of sunning, and the practices that traditionally have gone into obtaining the so-called "healthy tanned" look are on the verge of fading into history.

³In their place: safer sun practices that preserve people's natural skin color and condition.

⁴That's what health experts are hoping for as the evidence against exposure to the sun and sunlamps continues to mount. Both emit harmful ultraviolet (UV) radiation that in the short term can cause painful sunburn and in the long term may lead to unsightly skin blemishes, premature aging of the skin, cataracts and other eye problems, skin cancer, and a weakened immune system.

⁵ᵃThe problems may become more prevalent, too, if, as some scientists predict, the Earth's ozone layer continues to be depleted. ᵇAccording to the Environmental Protection Agency, scientists began accumulating evidence in the 1980s that the ozone layer—a thin shield in the stratosphere that protects life from UV radiation—is being depleted by certain chemicals used on Earth. ᶜAccording to the most recent estimates from the National Aeronautics and Space Administration, the ozone layer is being depleted at a rate of 4 to 6 percent each decade. ᵈThis means additional UV radiation reaching Earth's surface—and our bodies.

[6]Although people with light skin are more suscepti- ble to sun damage, darker skinned people, including African Americans and Hispanic Americans, also can be affected.

[7]You may have already started to take precautions. But are you doing all you can?

[8]The following recommendations come from various ex- pert organizations, including the American Academy of Dermatology, American Cancer Society, American Acade- my of Ophthalmology, Skin Cancer Foundation, American Academy of Pediatrics, National Cancer Institute, National Weather Service, and Food and Drug Administration. FDA regulates many items related to sun safety, including sun- screens and sunblocks, sunglasses, and sun-protective clothing that makes medical claims. The agency also sets performance standards for sunlamps.

[9]Here are seven steps to safer sunning:

1. Avoid the Sun

[10]This is especially important between 10 A.M. and 3 P.M., when the sun's rays are strongest. Also avoid the sun when the UV Index is high in your area.

[11]The UV Index is a number from 0 to 10+ that indicates the amount of UV radiation reaching the Earth's surface dur- ing the hour around noon. The higher the number, the greater your exposure to UV radiation if you go outdoors. The Na- tional Weather Service forecasts the UV Index daily in 58 U.S. cities, based on local predicted conditions (see Figure 1).

Figure 1

NOAA/EPA Ultraviolet Index/UVI/Forecast

1:58 P.M. EDT Tue September 19, 2000
Valid Sep 20, 2000 at Solar Noon/Approximately Noon Local Standard Time or 1:00 P.M. Local Daylight Time
The UV Index is categorized by EPA as follows

UVI	Exposure Level
0 1 2	Minimal
3 4	Low
5 6	Moderate
7 8 9	High
10 And Greater	Very High

City	State	UVI	City	State	UVI
Albuquerque	NM	7	Little Rock	AR	6
Anchorage	AK	1	Los Angeles	CA	6
Atlantic City	NJ	6	Louisville	KY	5
Atlanta	GA	6	Memphis	TN	6
Baltimore	MD	6	Miami	FL	8
Billings	MT	3	Milwaukee	WI	2
Bismarck	ND	2	Minneapolis	MN	2
Boise	ID	5	Mobile	AL	6
Boston	MA	5	New Orleans	LA	6
Buffalo	NY	5	New York	NY	6
Burlington	VT	4	Norfolk	VA	7
Charleston	WV	6	Oklahoma City	OK	4
Charleston	SC	6	Omaha	NE	3
Cheyenne	WY	4	Philadelphia	PA	6
Chicago	IL	2	Phoenix	AZ	7
Cleveland	OH	4	Pittsburgh	PA	5
Concord	NH	5	Portland	ME	4
Dallas	TX	6	Portland	OR	4
Denver	CO	5	Providence	RI	5
Des Moines	IA	2	Raleigh	NC	7
Detroit	MI	3	Salt Lake City	UT	6
Dover	DE	6	San Francisco	CA	6
Hartford	CT	5	San Juan	PU	12
Honolulu	HI	11	Seattle	WA	3
Houston	TX	6	Sioux Falls	SD	2
Indianapolis	IN	4	St. Louis	MO	3
Jackson	MS	6	Tampa	FL	7
Jacksonville	FL	6	Washington	D.C.	6
Las Vegas	NV	6	Wichita	KS	4

Source: Climate Prediction Center, National Weather Service, Washington, D.C.

The index covers about a 30-mile radius from each city. Check the local newspaper or TV and radio news broadcasts to learn the UV Index in your area. It also may be available through your local phone company and is available on the Internet at the National Weather Service Climate Prediction Center's home page.

[12]Don't be fooled by cloudy skies. Clouds block only as much as 20 percent of UV radiation. UV radiation also can pass through water, so don't assume you're safe from UV radiation if you're in the water and feeling cool. Also, be especially careful on the beach and in the snow because sand and snow reflect sunlight and increase the amount of UV radiation you receive.

[13]People with darker skin will resist the sun's rays by tanning, which is actually an indication that the skin has been injured. Tanning occurs when ultraviolet radiation is absorbed by the skin, causing an increase in the activity and number of melanocytes, the cells that produce the pigment melanin. Melanin helps to block out damaging rays up to a point.

[14]Those with lighter skin are more likely to burn. Too much sun exposure in a short period results in sunburn. A sunburn causes skin redness, tenderness, pain, swelling, and blistering. Although there is no quick cure, the American Academy of Dermatology recommends using wet compresses, cool baths, bland moisturizers, and over-the-counter hydrocortisone creams.

[15]Sunburn becomes a more serious problem with fever, chills, upset stomach, and confusion. If these symptoms develop, see a doctor.

2. Use Sunscreen

[16]With labels stating "sunscreen" or "sunblock," these lotions, creams, ointments, gels, or wax sticks, when applied to the skin, absorb, reflect, or scatter some or all of the sun's rays.

[17]Some sunscreen products, labeled "broad-spectrum," protect against two types of radiation: UVA and UVB. Scientists now believe that both UVA and UVB can damage the skin and lead to skin cancer.

[18]Other products protect only against UVB, previously thought to be the only damaging type.

[19]Some cosmetics, such as some lipsticks, also are considered sunscreen products if they contain sunscreen and their labels state they do.

[20]Sunblock products block a large percentage of UV radiation.

[21]FDA requires the labels of all sunscreen and sunblock products to state the product's sun protection factor, or "SPF," from 2 on up. The higher the number, the longer a person can stay in the sun before burning. Beginning in 1993, FDA suggested 30 as the upper SPF limit because it was felt that anything above this offers little additional benefit and might expose people to dangerous levels of chemicals.

[22]FDA also advised manufacturers that "water-resistant" or "sweat-resistant" products must list an SPF for both before and after being exposed to water or sweat. FDA also proposed that products claiming to be sunblocks have an SPF of at least 12 and contain titanium dioxide, the only opaque agent that blocks light. Also, any tanning product that doesn't contain a sunscreen would have to state on the label that the product does not contain a sunscreen.

[23]Experts recommend broad-spectrum products with SPFs of at least 15. They also suggest applying the product liberally—about 30 milliliters (1 ounce) per application for the average-size person, according to The Skin Cancer Foundation—15 to 30 minutes every time before going outdoors. It should be applied evenly on all exposed skin, including lips, nose, ears, neck, scalp (if hair is thinning), hands, feet, and eyelids, although care should be taken not to get it in the eyes because it can irritate them. If contact occurs, rinse eyes thoroughly with water.

[24]Sunscreens should not be used on babies younger than 6 months because their bodies may not be developed enough to handle sunscreen chemicals. Instead, use hats, clothing, and shading to protect babies from the sun. If you think your baby may need a sunscreen, check with your pediatrician.

[25]For children 6 months to 2 years, use a sunscreen with at least an SPF of 4, although 15 or higher is best.

3. Wear a Hat

[26]A hat with at least a 3-inch brim all around is ideal because it can protect areas often exposed to the sun, such as the neck, ears, eyes, and scalp. A shade cap (which looks like a baseball cap with about 7 inches of material draping down the sides and back) also is good. These are often sold in sports and outdoor clothing and supply stores.

[27]A baseball cap or visor provides only limited protection but is better than nothing.

4. Wear Sunglasses

[28]Sunglasses can help protect your eyes from sun damage.

[29a]The ideal sunglasses don't have to be expensive, but they should block 99 to 100 percent of UVA and UVB radiation. [b]Check the label to see that they do. [c]If there's no label, don't buy the glasses.

[30]And, don't go by how dark the glasses are because UV protection comes from an invisible chemical applied to the lenses, not from the color or darkness of the lenses.

[31]Large-framed wraparound sunglasses are best because they can protect your eyes from all angles.

[32]Children should wear sunglasses, too, starting as young as 1, advises Gerhard Cibis, a pediatric ophthalmologist in Kansas City, Missouri. They need smaller versions of real, protective adult sunglasses—not toy sunglasses. Kids' sunglasses are available at many optical stores, Cibis says.

[33]Ideally, says the American Academy of Ophthalmology, all types of eyewear, including prescription glasses, contact lenses, and intraocular lens implants used in cataract surgery, should absorb the entire UV spectrum.

5. Cover Up

[34]Wear lightweight, loose-fitting, long-sleeved shirts, pants, or long skirts as much as possible when in the sun. Most materials and colors absorb or reflect UV rays. Tightly weaved cloth is best.

[35]Avoid wearing wet clothes, such as a wet T-shirt, because when clothes get wet, the sun's rays can more easily pass through. If you see light through a fabric, UV rays can get through, too.

6. Avoid Artificial Tanning

[36]Many people believe that the UV rays of tanning beds are harmless because sunlamps in tanning beds emit primarily

UVA and little, if any, UVB, the rays once thought to be the most hazardous. However, UVA can cause serious skin damage, too. According to some scientists, UVA may be linked to the most serious form of skin cancer, melanoma. A 1996 unpublished risk analysis by FDA scientists Sharon Miller, Scott Hamilton, and Howard Cyr, Ph.D., concluded that people who use sunlamps about 100 times a year may be increasing their exposure to "melanoma-inducing" radiation by up to 24 times compared with the amount they would receive from the sun.

[36] [sic]

[37]Because of sunlamps' dangers, health experts advise people to avoid them for tanning.

[38]Several products that claim to give a tan without UV radiation carry safety risks, too. These include so-called "tanning pills" containing carotenoid color additives derived from substances similar to beta-carotene, which gives carrots their orange color. The additives are distributed throughout the body, especially in skin, making it orange. Although FDA has approved some of these additives for coloring food, it has not approved them for use in tanning agents. And, at the high levels that are consumed in tanning pills, they may be harmful. According to John Bailey, Ph.D., acting director of FDA's Office of Cosmetics and Colors, the main ingredient in tanning pills, canthaxanthin, can deposit in the eyes as crystals, which may cause injury and impaired vision.

[39]Tanning accelerators, such as those formulated with the amino acid tyrosine or tyrosine derivatives, are ineffective and also may be dangerous. Marketers promote these products as substances that stimulate the body's own tanning process, although the evidence suggests they don't work, Bailey says. FDA considers them unapproved new drugs that have not been proved safe and effective.

[40]Two other tanning products, bronzers and extenders, are considered cosmetics for external use. Bronzers, made from color additives approved by FDA for cosmetic use, stain the skin when applied and can be washed off with soap and water. Extenders, when applied to the skin, interact with protein on the surface of the skin to produce color. The color tends to wear off after a few days. The only color additive approved for extenders is dihydroxyacetone.

[41]Although they give skin a golden color, these products do not offer sunscreen protection. Also, the chemicals in bronzers may react differently on various areas of your body, producing a tan of many shades.

7. Check Skin Regularly

[42]You can improve your chances of finding precancerous skin conditions, such as actinic keratosis—a dry, scaly, reddish, and slightly raised lesion—and skin cancer by performing simple skin self-exams regularly. The earlier you identify signs and see a doctor, the greater the chances for successful treatment.

[43]The best time to do skin exams is after a shower or bath. Get used to your birthmarks, moles, and blemishes so that you know what they usually look like and then can easily identify any changes they undergo. Signs to look for are changes in size, texture, shape, and color of blemishes or a sore that does not heal.

[44]If you find any changes, see your doctor. Also, during regular checkups, ask your doctor to check your skin.

[45]The more of these practices you can incorporate into your life, the greater your chances of reducing the damage sun can cause. And by teaching these same practices to children, you can help them get off to a lifetime of safer sun practices.

SELECTION 4 QUESTIONS

Vocabulary

Circle the letter of the best definition for the underlined word.

1. "… safer sun practices that <u>preserve</u> people's natural skin color and condition." (¶3)
    a. waste
    b. highlight
    c. destroy
    d. maintain

2. "… <u>premature</u> aging of the skin, cataracts and other eye problems…." (¶4)
    a. too early
    b. too late
    c. heavy
    d. light

3. "… if, as some scientists predict, the Earth's ozone layer continues to be <u>depleted</u>." (¶5)
    a. unused
    b. untouched
    c. out of danger
    d. used up

4. "Although people with light skin are more <u>susceptible</u> to sun damage...." (¶6)
    a. sore
    b. sensitive
    c. insensitive
    d. rough
5. "They also suggest applying the product <u>liberally</u>...." (¶23)
    a. conservatively
    b. generously
    c. carefully
    d. sparingly

Comprehension

Determine whether the statements in sentences 6–8 are true or false, and write your answer. Also, if the statement is false, rewrite it to make it true.

6. Only the expensive dark-colored sunglasses do a good job of protecting your eyes from the sun.

    _____

    _____

7. Both UVA and UVB can damage the skin and lead to skin cancer.

    _____

    _____

8. The lower the "SPF" number on a sunscreen or sunblock product, the longer a person can stay in the sun before burning.

    _____

    _____

9. Circle the letter of the sentence that best expresses Kurtzweil's thesis.
    a. If, as some scientists predict, the Earth's ozone layer continues to be depleted, we will have even more sun-related problems.
    b. The best time to do skin exams is after a shower or bath.
    c. Although we should stay out of the sun, the UV rays of tanning beds are harmless because they emit primarily UVA and little, if any, UVB.
    d. Because of the harmful effects of exposure to the sun and sunlamps, health experts hope we'll use safer sun practices to preserve our natural skin color and condition.
10. List three of the organizations that contributed to Kurtzweil's recommendations for safer sunning.

    _____

    _____

    _____

11. List the source of the Ultraviolet Index Forecast in Figure 1.

    _____

12. List Kurtzweil's seven steps to safer sunning.

    _____

    _____

    _____

    _____

    _____

    _____

    _____

13. In paragraph 5, what is the relationship of sentence d to sentence c?
    a. Sentence d gives an example of sentence c.
    b. Sentence d gives a definition for sentence c.
    c. Sentence d gives a cause for sentence c.
    d. Sentence d gives an effect of sentence c.

14. Is sentence 29a primarily fact, opinion, or combination of fact and opinion? If it includes both, list which information is fact and which is opinion.

    _____

    _____

    Is sentence 29c primarily fact, opinion, or combination of fact and opinion? If it includes both, list which information is fact and which is opinion.

    _____

    _____

15. According to Figure 1, which city was predicted to have the highest UVI Exposure Level? What is the predicted level?

    _____

    _____

16. According to Figure 1, what UVI Exposure Level was predicted for the city closest to your home?

    _____

Vocabulary Extra

Each of these words has a prefix and/or a suffix added to the root word. (1) Break the word into its component parts (root, prefix, and/or suffix), (2) define each word part, and (3) define the whole word. For help, use the Roots, Prefixes, Suffixes table on pages 17–18 or refer to your dictionary.

1. harmful (¶4)

    root word _____

    definition _____

    prefix _____

    definition _____

suffix _____

definition _____

harmful means _____

2. precautions (¶7)
   root word _____

   definition _____

   prefix _____

   definition _____

   suffix _____

   definition _____

   precautions means _____

3. invisible (¶30)
   root word _____

   definition _____

   prefix _____

   definition _____

   suffix _____

   definition _____

   invisible means _____

4. harmless (¶36)
   root word _____

   definition _____

   prefix _____

   definition _____

   suffix _____

   definition _____

   harmless means _____

5. unpublished (¶36)
   root word _____

   definition _____

   prefix _____

   definition _____

   suffix _____

   definition _____

   unpublished means _____

6. ineffective (¶39)
   root word _____

   definition _____

prefix _____

definition _____

suffix _____

definition _____

ineffective means _____

7. unapproved (¶39)
    root word _____

    definition _____

    prefix _____

    definition _____

    suffix _____

    definition _____

    unapproved means _____

8. precancerous (¶42)
    root word _____

    definition _____

    prefix _____

    definition _____

    suffix _____

    definition _____

    precancerous means _____

FEATURED SELECTION 5: "THE NEW FRONTIER"

BEFORE YOU READ

About the Authors   Dr. Cayton is Professor of History at Miami University in Oxford, Ohio. Dr. Perry is Research Professor of History at Vanderbilt University in Nashville, Tennessee. Dr. Reed directs the African American Studies Program at the University of Houston. Dr. Winkler is Professor of History at Miami University in Oxford, Ohio.

This selection is excerpted from Chapter 28, "The Kennedy and Johnson Years: 1960–1968," of their text *America: Pathways to the Present*.

An Idea to Think About   From what you've read and heard about President John F. Kennedy how would you describe him, his 1960 election, and his time in office? *As you read*, find out about the programs he proposed to improve the economy and to address the issues of poverty and civil rights.

1960
John F. Kennedy
elected President

1961
Alan Shepard
becomes first
American to
travel in space

1962
John Glenn
becomes first
American to
orbit Earth

1962
Michael Harrington
publishes The
Other America

1963
President Kennedy
assassinated

1960　　　　**1962**　　　　**1964**

1 The New Frontier

SECTION PREVIEW

Objectives

1　Describe the election of 1960 and its outcome.
2　Summarize Kennedy's domestic programs.
3　Explain Americans' reaction to President Kennedy's assassination.
4　*Key Terms* Define: mandate; New Frontier; Warren Commission.

Main Idea

Before his assassination in 1963, President John F. Kennedy proposed a number of domestic programs to improve the economy and to address issues of inequality, including poverty and civil rights. Most of Kennedy's proposals were defeated in Congress.

Reading Strategy

Reinforcing Main Ideas As you read the section, create a list of the programs that Kennedy proposed.

On September 26, 1960, millions of Americans turned on their televisions to watch as two presidential candidates squared off in the country's first televised debate. The two candidates were Republican Richard Nixon (Eisenhower's Vice President) and Democrat John F. Kennedy. With studio lights glaring, Nixon appeared tired and hot. Kennedy, in contrast, looked polished and relaxed. He had hired consultants to help him with makeup and clothes. This debate and the three that followed had a major impact on the outcome of the election. The debates also changed forever the role that television would play in American politics.

The Election of 1960

Kennedy, a Massachusetts Democrat who had served in the United States House of Representatives and Senate, faced serious obstacles in his quest for the presidency. He was only forty-three years old, and many questioned whether he had the experience needed for the nation's highest office. In addition, Kennedy was a Roman Catholic, and no Catholic had ever been elected President. Kennedy put an end to the

religion issue when he won the primary in the largely Protestant state of West Virginia. With that hurdle behind him, he campaigned hard, with promises to spur the sluggish economy.

During the last years of the Eisenhower administration, the Gross National Product (GNP) had grown very slowly. In addition, the economy had suffered several recessions. During the campaign, Kennedy proclaimed that it was time to "get America moving again."

In the election, Kennedy won by an extraordinarily close margin.[†] Though the electoral vote was 303 to 219, Kennedy won by only 120,000 popular votes out of more than 34 million cast. If but a few thousand voters in Illinois or Texas had cast ballots for Nixon, the Republicans would have won. As a result of

Presidential candidates Richard Nixon and John F. Kennedy squared off in a series of televised debates in 1960.

[†] Although the youngest person ever to be elected President, Kennedy was not the youngest ever to hold the office. Theodore Roosevelt, who became President when McKinley was assassinated, was the youngest to hold the office.

Jacqueline and John F. Kennedy dazzled the nation with their beauty, youth, and glamour. *Government Why was Kennedy's administration later nicknamed Camelot?*

this razor-thin victory, Kennedy entered office without a strong **mandate.** A mandate is a set of wishes expressed to a candidate by his or her voters. Without such a mandate, Kennedy would have difficulty pushing his more controversial measures through Congress.

No matter how slim his margin of victory, Kennedy was now President. In ringing phrases he declared in his Inaugural Address:

> **KEY DOCUMENTS** ❝Let the word go forth from this time and place, to friend and foe alike, that the torch has been passed to a new generation of Americans, born in this century, tempered by war, disciplined by a hard and bitter peace. . . . And so, my fellow Americans, ask not what your country can do for you; ask what you can do for your country.❞
>
> —*John F. Kennedy,* Inaugural Address

The new administration was buoyant, energetic, and full of optimism. Jacqueline Kennedy, the President's wife, charmed the country with her grace. Nobel Prize winners visited the White House. The Kennedys and their friends loved to play touch football on the lawn or take long hikes.

The administration, which seemed full of idealism and youth, later earned the nickname

"Camelot" after a 1960 Broadway musical. The musical portrayed the legendary kingdom of the British King Arthur. Arthur dreamed of transforming medieval Britain from a country in which "might makes right," or the strong always get their way, into one where power would be used to achieve right.

Kennedy's Domestic Programs

In a speech early in his administration, Kennedy said that the nation was poised at the edge of a **New Frontier.** The name stuck and was used to describe Kennedy's proposals to improve the economy, give aid to the poor, and breathe new life into the space program.

The Economy Concerned about the continuing recession, Kennedy hoped to work with the business community to restore prosperity to the nation. Often, however, he faced resistance from executives who were suspicious of his plans. The worst fears of business leaders were realized in the spring of 1962. When the U.S. Steel Company announced that it was raising the price of steel by $6 a ton, other firms did the same. Worried about inflation, Kennedy called the price increase unjustifiable and charged that it showed "utter contempt for the public interest." He ordered a federal investigation into the possibility of price-fixing. Under that pressure, U.S. Steel and the other companies backed down. Business leaders remained angry, and the stock market fell in the steepest drop since the Great Crash of 1929.

On the larger issue of ending the economic slump, Kennedy proposed cutting taxes. In 1963 the President called for a $13.5 billion cut in taxes over three years. The measure would reduce government income and create a budget deficit at first. Kennedy believed, however, that the extra cash in taxpayers' wallets would stimulate the economy and bring added tax revenues in the end. The tax-cut proposal was soon bottled up in a congressional committee and stood little chance of passage.

Combating Poverty and Inequality Kennedy also was eager to take action against poverty and inequality. In his first two years in office, Kennedy hoped that he could help the poor simply by stimulating the economy. In 1962 author Michael Harrington described the situation of the poor in his book, *The Other America.* Harrington's book revealed that while many Americans were enjoying the prosperity of the

1950s, a shocking one fifth of the population was living below the poverty line. Kennedy began to believe that direct aid to the poor was necessary.

Despite his concern, Kennedy rarely succeeded in pushing legislation through Congress. Kennedy's ambitious plans for federal aid for education and medical care for the aged both failed. Kennedy did succeed, however, in raising the minimum wage and passing the Housing Act of 1961. This act provided $4.9 billion for urban renewal. Congress also approved the Twenty-Fourth Amendment to go to the states for ratification. This amendment outlawed the poll tax, which was still being used in five southern states to keep poor African Americans from voting.

The Space Program Kennedy was more successful in his effort to breathe life into the space program. Following the Soviet Union's launch of *Sputnik* in 1957, numerous government agencies and industries had been working furiously with NASA, the National Aeronautics and Space Agency, to place a manned spacecraft in orbit around Earth. As part of the Mercury program, seven test pilots were chosen to train as astronauts in 1959. Government spending and the future of NASA seemed uncertain, however, when a task force appointed by Kennedy recommended that NASA concentrate on exploratory space missions without human crews.

All of this changed in April 1961. The Soviet Union announced that Yuri Gagarin had become the first human to travel in space and had circled Earth on board the Soviet spacecraft *Vostok*. Gagarin's flight rekindled Americans' fears that the United States was falling behind the Soviet Union.

Twenty-three days later, on May 5, 1961, the United States made its own first attempt to send a person into space. Astronaut Alan Shepard made a 15-minute suborbital flight that reached an altitude of 115 miles. Though this flight did not match the orbital flight of the Soviets, its success did convince Kennedy to move forward. On May 25, Kennedy issued a bold challenge to the nation. He said the United States "should commit itself to achieving the goal, before this decade is out, of landing a man on the moon."†

Both the nation and the government accepted the challenge, and funding for NASA

---

† For the remainder of the decade, succeeding NASA flights brought the country closer and closer to its goal. On July 20, 1969, United States astronaut Neil Armstrong became the first person to set foot on the moon.

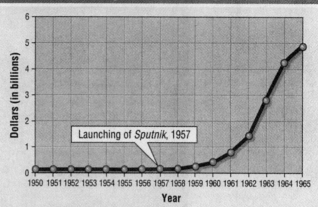

Federal Funding of NASA, 1950–1965

Y-axis: Dollars (in billions); X-axis: Year

Launching of *Sputnik*, 1957

*National Aeronautics and Space Administration
Source: Historical Statistics of the United States, Colonial Times to 1970

Interpreting Graphs NASA grew out of the National Advisory Committee for Aeronautics, which was established in 1915. Alarmed by the launching of *Sputnik*, in 1958 Congress authorized the new federal agency to promote the research and development of air and space. *Economics How does the graph illustrate the influence of the Soviet Union's* Sputnik *on United States policy?*

was increased. Less than a year later, on February 20, 1962, John Glenn successfully completed three orbits around Earth and landed in the Atlantic Ocean near the Bahamas. Later that year Kennedy spoke at Rice University in Houston, Texas:

**Main Idea
CONNECTIONS**

Why did Kennedy's space program succeed while most of his other domestic programs did not?

AMERICAN VOICES ❝We set sail on this new sea because there is new knowledge to be gained, and new rights to be won, and they must be won and used for the progress of all people. . . . [O]nly if the United States occupies a position of preeminence can we help decide whether this new ocean will be a sea of peace or a new, terrifying theater of war.❞

—*John F. Kennedy*

Kennedy Is Assassinated

On November 22, 1963, as Kennedy looked ahead to reelection the following year, he traveled to Texas to mobilize support. Texas Governor John Connally and his wife Nelly met Kennedy and his wife at the airport in Dallas. Together they rode through the streets of Dallas in an open limousine. Thousands of supporters lined the route of the motorcade. Suddenly shots rang and bullets struck both Connally and the President. While Connally

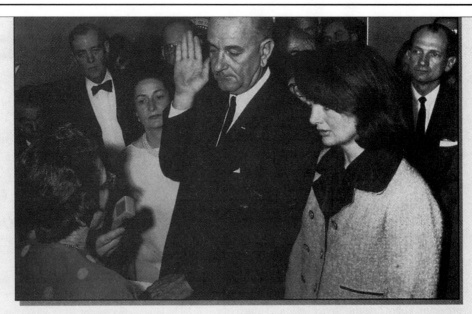

A sad and solemn-looking Lyndon Johnson is sworn in as President aboard Air Force One shortly after President Kennedy's assassination. A grief-stricken Jacqueline Kennedy (right) looks on. *Culture What was the nation's reaction to Kennedy's death?*

was only wounded, President Kennedy was pronounced dead soon after his arrival at a nearby hospital. The country was shattered. Millions of Americans remained glued to their television sets for the next four days as the impact of the tragedy sank in.

Shortly after Kennedy's death, a commission headed by Chief Justice Earl Warren was formed to investigate the crime. The prime suspect in Kennedy's assassination was Lee Harvey Oswald, a former marine and supporter of Cuba's Fidel Castro. Two days after Kennedy's assassination, Oswald was transferred from one jail to another. While the nation watched on television, Dallas nightclub owner Jack Ruby stepped through the crowd of reporters and

fatally shot Oswald. After months of investigation, the **Warren Commission** declared that Oswald had worked alone in shooting the President. Since then, however, some people have argued that Oswald was involved in a larger conspiracy, and that he was killed in order to protect others who had helped plan Kennedy's murder.

Lyndon Johnson, who had also traveled to Dallas with Kennedy, took the presidential oath of office on board Air Force One just ninety minutes after Kennedy's death. Johnson went on to make good use of the spirit of hope and the desire for change that Kennedy had inspired. He saw enacted much of the legislation that his predecessor had tried to push through Congress.

SECTION 1 REVIEW

Comprehension

1. *Key Terms* Define: (a) mandate; (b) New Frontier; (c) Warren Commission.

2. *Summarizing the Main Idea* What were some of the successes and failures of Kennedy's domestic policies?

3. *Organizing Information* Create a time line of the major events in the space program between 1959 and 1962.

Critical Thinking

4. *Analyzing Time Lines* Review the time line at the start of the section. How did President Kennedy respond to Michael Harrington's book, *The Other America*?

5. *Drawing Inferences* Why was the Kennedy administration nicknamed "Camelot"? How did the dream of Camelot end?

Writing Activity

6. *Writing an Expository Essay* Write an essay describing the role of television in the election of 1960 and its role today.

CROSSWORD PUZZLE

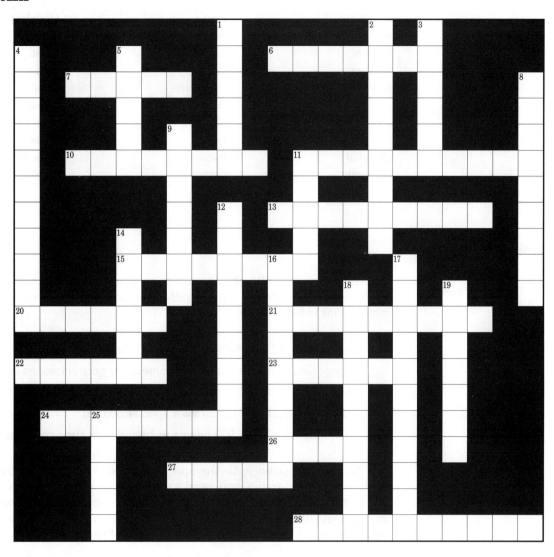

ACROSS

6   excessive, exceptional
7   search
10   breakdown
11   defenseless, unprotected
13   common
15   details, trivia
20   in a straight line
21   seriously
22   desire
23   flood, overflow
24   used up
26   give off
27   irritates, annoys
28   shortening

DOWN

1   small errors or slips
2   constant, ongoing
3   make
4   basic
5   disgust
8   generously
9   excepting, excluding
11   on the edge of
12   amazed
14   lessen, worsen
16   stories
17   sensitive
18   protection
19   clearness
25   primary

WORD LIST

anecdotes	emit	prevalent
aspire	extreme	prime
astounded	fundamental	quest
barring	impair	render
clarity	insulation	repel
collapse	lapses	susceptible
condensing	liberally	verge
deluge	linear	vexes
depleted	minutiae	vulnerable
earnestly	perennial	

LOG ON TO THE WEB

The Web offers a wealth of information on almost any topic you can imagine. Log on to one of these sites or use a search directory/engine to locate a site with information that interests you.

> The Food and Drug Administration's site at http://www.fda.gov
>
> Classic Crime Stories http://va.crimelibrary.com/classicstories.htm
>
> The Great Outdoor Recreation pages at http://www.gorp.com
>
> CBS's SportsLine at http://www.sportsline.com
>
> *Time* magazine's top 100 people at http://www.time.com/time100

Read a selection with the specific purpose of understanding the thesis. Print out the selection you read and write down: (1) the complete address (http://www. ...), (2) the name of the person or company who sponsors and maintains the site, (3) the name of the person who wrote information you read, (4) what you know about the writer, and (5) the thesis of the selection.

IDEAS FOR WRITING AND DISCUSSION

A. It is estimated that people entering the workforce today will change careers about six times during their lifetime. Visit your college's career center and gather information on three potential careers for yourself. Compare and contrast the skills and attitudes needed among the three careers.

B. Each time you read, your purpose for reading, your knowledge of the subject, the author's writing style, the length of the reading, and the medium (the type and form of the publication) are different. Which of these factors make reading most difficult for you? What positive actions do you take to reduce the problems? What advice would you give to other readers on how to improve their comprehension?

C. Today you can choose to take many of your college courses in college classrooms or over the Internet. What do you see as some of the positive effects and some of the negative effects of each alternative?

It's All about Attitude

Some people are always grumbling because roses have thorns;
I am thankful that thorns have roses.

—Alphonse Karr

When you look at this glass, do you see it as half full or half empty?

How you answer may tell a lot about your view of the world and your chances for happiness and success.

This is because people who are optimistic—those who see the glass as half full—expect great things, work hard for those things, and are likely to achieve them. People with a positive attitude always look for the "can do" side of every situation. On the other hand, pessimists—those who see the glass as half empty—seem to search for the "can not do" side of a situation.

"You're given a certain amount of skill, talent, and good looks in life," says Richard Carlson, author of *Don't Sweat the Small Stuff* (Hyperion 1997). "The rest is attitude." In fact, research by University of Pennsylvania psychologist Martin Seligman confirms that optimistic people are happier, healthier, and more successful than those with a negative attitude toward life.

In addition, a positive attitude is contagious. When your attitude is sincere, the people around you relate to you and your activities with an energy and positive attitude that creates a winning, successful environment.

But a positive attitude does not pop into your mind by itself. How you feel and react are decisions you make every day. The authors in this theme provide insight and advice for making those decisions. Each of the readings is by a different author, of a different length, and requires different tasks.

Dr. Charles Swindoll opens the theme with "Attitudes," a short essay on why he believes a person's attitude is important. Next, Dr. Barbara K. Bruce and Ms. Denise Foley ask, "Is It Time for an Attitude Adjustment?"

In *Choosing a Positive Attitude: Your Survival Strategy for Balancing Work and Personal Life*, Dr. Reneé Magid provides specific advice on ways to begin choosing a positive attitude that will help both you and those around you.

Then, in an excerpt from their classic text *Your Attitude Is Showing: A Primer of Human Relations*, professors Elwood N. Chapman and Sharon Lund O'Neil discuss how to "Hold on to Your Positive Attitude."

And finally, Ana Veciana-Suarez reminds us how the "'Little Engine' Holds a Valuable Life Lesson."

FEATURED SELECTION 1: "ATTITUDES"

BEFORE YOU READ

About the Author   Dr. Charles Swindoll is president of Dallas Theological Seminary, senior pastor of the Stonebriar Community Church in Frisco, Texas, and the main speaker on the world-wide radio broadcast *Insight for Living*.

Words to Know

> *convey* (¶1): communicate, tell
> *incredible*: (¶1) unbelievable

An Idea to Think About   What do you think is the most important decision you make every day? *As you read*, find out what Dr. Swindoll thinks is his most important decision.

ATTITUDES

Charles Swindoll

[1a]Words can never adequately convey the incredible impact of our attitude toward life. [1b]The longer I live, the more convinced I become that life is 10 percent what happens to us and 90 percent how we respond to it.

[2a]I believe the single most significant decision I can make on a day-to-day basis is my choice of attitude. [2b]It is more important than my past, my education, my bankroll, my successes or failures, fame or pain, what other people think of me or say about me, my circumstances, or my position. [2c]Attitude keeps me going or cripples my progress. [2d]It alone fuels my fire or assaults my hope. [2e]When my attitudes are right, there's no barrier too high, no valley too deep, no dream too extreme, no challenge too great for me.

SELECTION 1 QUESTIONS

Vocabulary

Circle the letter of the best definition for the underlined word.

1. "The longer I live the more convinced I become that life is 10 percent what happens to us and 90 percent how we <u>respond</u> to it." (¶1)
   a. question
   b. react
   c. disagree
   d. agree

2. "I believe the single most <u>significant</u> decision I can make on a day-to-day basis is my choice of attitude." (¶2)
   a. important
   b. unimportant
   c. minor
   d. timely

Comprehension

3. Circle the letter of the sentence that best expresses the thesis:
   a. Attitude keeps us going.
   b. Words can't describe the impact of our attitude.

    c. Choosing to have a positive attitude every day makes our life better.

    d. Our happiness depends on how much education, money, fame, and success we achieve.

4. What does Swindoll think is the most important decision he can make every day?

_____

5. According to Swindoll, "life is _____ what happens to us and _____ how we respond to it."

6. What does Swindoll think can happen when his "attitudes are right?"

_____

_____

7. The relationship of sentences 2c and 2d to sentence 2b is:

    a. They continue the same thought.

    b. They define terms.

    c. They tell the cause.

    d. They change the direction of thought.

8. What does the word "it" refer to in sentences 2b and 2d?

    a. I

    b. amount of money

    c. day-to-day living

    d. choice of attitude

FEATURED SELECTION 2: "IS IT TIME FOR AN ATTITUDE ADJUSTMENT?"

BEFORE YOU READ

About the Authors Dr. Barbara K. Bruce, a psychologist at the Mayo Clinic, Rochester, Minnesota, is on the editorial board of Mayo Clinic *Women's Health-Source*. Ms. Denise Foley, a contributing writer for Mayo Clinic *Women's Health-Source*, is co-author of *The Women's Encyclopedia of Health*. This article is from *USA Today Magazine*, September 1998.

Words to Know

> *inherit* (¶1): to receive certain characteristics from ancestors
>
> *provocatively suggests* (¶2): implies information that excites
>
> *stature* (¶3): height, build
>
> *susceptibility for* (¶3): capacity or sensitivity for
>
> *chronic* (¶4): constant, continuous
>
> *invariably* (¶5): always, without fail
>
> *Pollyanna-like attitude* (¶7): excessively and persistently optimistic
>
> *Chicken Little [attitude]* (¶8): excessively and persistently pessimistic
>
> *berate* (¶15): yell at, belittle
>
> *plausible* (¶16): possible, probable
>
> *salvage* (¶17): recover, retrieve

An Idea to Think About Is your general attitude—optimistic or pessimistic—the same today as it was when you were a baby? *As you read*, find out if Bruce and Foley think people can change their attitude.

Is It Time for an Attitude Adjustment?

Barbara K. Bruce and Denise Foley

[1]You got your blue eyes from Dad and your strawberry blond hair from Mom. The tiny bump on the bridge of your nose definitely is from Grandpa William. However, did you also inherit your pessimistic attitude or your sunny outlook? Are you genetically programmed to see the glass as half empty or half full?

[2]Recent research suggests that some personality traits and attitudes indeed may be part of your genetic blueprint. In 1996, scientists announced they had located genes linked to anxiety, addiction, happiness, and pessimism. Their studies provocatively suggest that you may have been born to be grumpy, hostile, a worrier, outgoing, or cheerful. You even may be one of those people who is born to be wild because you carry a thrill-seeking gene.

[3a]If you have struggled all your life with chronic worry, dark moods, or a short fuse, does this research mean you are a born loser in a biological game of chance? [3b]The answer is "no." [3c]Biology is not destiny, nor is your attitude entirely a matter of luck. [3d]Part of your personality is inherited, but, at most, only half is. [3e]That leaves a lot of room for self-improvement. [3f]Even more encouraging, the genes for personality aren't like those for eye color and height. [3g]Your blue eyes and short stature are determined by your DNA. [3h]You merely inherit a susceptibility for doom and gloom—and, conversely, cheerfulness. [3i]Whether you see the glass as half empty or half full is largely up to you.

[4]Chronic worrying, flying into a rage at the slightest provocation, or always expecting the worst are traits worth changing, but there are other reasons to adjust your attitude. Studies show that being positive pays off. Research has found that individuals with positive outlooks do better in school, their careers, and personal lives than pessimists. In one study, for instance, insurance salespeople who had positive outlooks sold 56 percent more insurance than less-optimistic co-workers. That result convinced one of the nation's largest insurance companies to start hiring people based on their optimism, not just their salesmanship.

[5]Optimists invariably are physically and mentally healthier. Studies have found that they rarely get depressed and anxious. Optimists are more likely to take better care of themselves by eating right, exercising, and getting checkups. One study found that young women who considered themselves "positive" knew more about cancer and did more to prevent it than those who were more pessimistic.

[6]When optimists do get sick, they recover quicker. Heart bypass patients who were more upbeat recovered faster from surgery and felt better at a five-year follow-up than pessimists who had the same operation. In another study, pregnant women who were upbeat during their third trimester were less likely to have postpartum depression.

[7]Being positive isn't a Pollyanna-like attitude that somehow things will work out for the best. Optimists believe they can make things succeed. They look at setbacks as temporary and failures as learning experiences. Like the "Little Engine That Could," they think they can, which gives them the energy and motivation to make it happen. Their positive attitude buffers them against stress because they react to adversity by planning and taking action. That makes them feel in control. When things do go wrong, they make the best of it. They face life's slings and arrows with a sense of hope.

[8]On the other hand, if you have a gloomy outlook on life, are hostile, or, like Chicken Little, are fretting constantly that the sky is falling, studies show you are at high risk for developing depression and anxiety. That's because, when you predict the future—and you do—it always looks bleak. You are more likely to do poorly in school and work largely because you have so little confidence in your abilities. Even your health may suffer. Research has found that pessimism can shorten your life, and hostility—specifically having an aggressive and cynical view of people and the world around you—predisposes you to heart disease. You are more likely to feel helpless, not hopeful, when adversity strikes.

[9]In small doses, some of these negative attitudes can be constructive. There are times when anger is appropriate—if you are snubbed by a good friend or feel you have been passed over for a promotion, for example. If you are worried that your marketing presentation won't go over or that you haven't prepared well enough for your meeting, anxiety can prod you to work even harder. Even a little caution is healthy—ask any safety engineer, CEO, or mother.

[10]If you are consumed by worry, though, you won't have the energy to put into your preparation. If you are too cautious, you may not take calculated risks that could be beneficial to you. If you don't believe anything you can do will make a difference, you are likely to quit too soon, perhaps within reach of your goal.

[11]There is no way to know whether your personality traits are the result of nature or nurture. Nevertheless, whether your negativity is inborn or just an entrenched habit, you can learn to be more upbeat.

[12]Your first obstacle will be your automatic thoughts. You may not even be aware of what you are thinking when, for instance, someone cuts you off in traffic or your best friend doesn't return your call. You may know that you react with anger when the car swerves in front of you or automatically assume that your friend either hates you or is deathly ill, but you may not know why. Recognizing your automatic thoughts will be the first step toward changing them.

[13]*Keep a daily log.* Carry a notebook and pen with you and jot down what you are thinking and feeling when faced with a problem. Look for patterns, especially of blame, guilt, anger, and despair. Note how often you use the words "always" and "never," as in "I always mess up" and "My friends never come through for me." Note all-or-nothing statements such as "If I don't get this promotion, I'm no good." Rate the intensity of your thoughts and feelings, from mild to extreme.

[14]*Challenge your thoughts.* Put your automatic thoughts to the test. Ask yourself these questions:

- How true and reasonable are my thoughts?
- What proof do I have to support my thinking?
- Is there another possible explanation or conclusion I can draw? If so, what?
- Do I think worrying about something is necessary to my success?
- Is there someone else I can ask to test the reality of my thinking?
- Does it help—or hurt—me to think this way?
- Even if I am right, is it something I can deal with?

[15]*Be nice to yourself.* Don't beat yourself up when things go wrong. Don't call yourself names. If your best friend was having a bad day, you wouldn't berate her for everything she did wrong. You would treat her like a friend—which is how you should treat yourself.

[16]*Look for the silver lining.* Psychologists call this "reframing." You need to learn a new way to look at things. Instead of being discouraged by criticism or a setback, consider these things feedback that will help you find new and better ways to accomplish what you want. For example, if your boss suggests that you may have missed an important market in your report, use the information to make the report better. Look for other plausible explanations for events that make you angry or upset. Maybe your best friend hasn't returned your phone call because he's busy or his answering machine is broken, not because he is angry with you, inconsiderate, or dead. Moreover, the driver who cut you off could be rushing to the hospital.

[17]*Use bad experiences to your advantage.* Researchers at the University of California at Davis asked 2,000 people about the worst times in their lives—ranging from divorce to job loss to combat. They were surprised to find that most individuals were able to salvage something positive from their most traumatic experiences. Some learned how strong they were; others, what wonderful friends and resources they had. Some found a renewed faith in God. Most thought their experiences made them better able to cope with other problems that came along.

[18]*Distract yourself.* To calm angry feelings or lift a bad mood, do something positive and engrossing. Rent a funny movie. Do a 3-D puzzle. Plan a dream vacation. Plant some flower bulbs. Take a brisk walk outdoors. Count your blessings. One of the best coping skills optimists have is their ability to remember all the good things in their lives when bad times come along. Make a list of your blessings. Pick something from every realm of your life—family, work, and community. When things go wrong, pull out your list and remind yourself of what is going right.

[19]*Create a success.* When you feel down, tackle a moderately challenging chore you have been putting off, like inserting family photos in an album or painting your bathroom. Afterwards, you'll feel a sense of accomplishment.

[20]*Try a dose of good humor.* The act of laughing, even if it is forced, tends to improve your mood and enhance your ability to come up with creative solutions to your problems. One way to get a quick laugh—especially when there is nothing funny about what is happening to you—is to do the "tee-hee" exercise developed by psychotherapist Annette Goodheart. Simply add the words, "tee-hee" to the end of a sentence describing your gloom, as in "I'm going to be downsized, tee-hee" or "I just burned a $40 standing rib roast and my in-laws are coming, tee-hee." It sounds so silly, you just have to laugh.

What Words Do You Live By?

Many of us share automatic thoughts—platitudes we heard from our parents when we were growing up. Unconsciously, these may be the words we live by. Take the following test to learn if you face life with a positive or negative outlook. Put a check mark next to the phrases that best describe your feelings.

1. Every dark cloud has a silver lining.
2. It's better to be safe than sorry.
3. Seize the day.
4. Look before you leap.
5. Treat everyone the way you would like to be treated.
6. When it rains, it pours.
7. The best things in life are free.
8. There's no such thing as a free lunch.
9. Love is the answer.
10. Every person for himself/herself.

Scoring: Count up the odd-numbered and even-numbered phrases you picked. The more odd-numbered platitudes you chose are an indication that you do indeed look for the silver lining in every dark cloud. If you chose more even-numbered phrases, you are more focused on the dark cloud.

SELECTION 2 QUESTIONS

Vocabulary

Match each word in the left column with the best definition in the right column.

1. chronic (¶3) ___   a. makes susceptible
2. destiny (¶3) ___   b. constant, habitual
3. provocation (¶4) ___   c. credible, believable
4. buffers (¶7) ___   d. securely established
5. predisposes (¶8) ___   e. fate, inevitable future
6. entrenched (¶11) ___   f. reason, cause
7. plausible (¶16) ___   g. shields, protects

Complete sentences 8–11 below with the most appropriate form of the following words:

pessimist (n)   pessimistic (adj)
optimist (n)   optimistic (adj)

8. People with a positive outlook on life are more likely to succeed than those with a _____ attitude.

9. A _____ is often depressed and anxious.

10. A person with a positive outlook on life is called an _____.

11. _____ people believe they can succeed.

Comprehension

Determine whether the statements in sentences 12–14 are true or false, and write your answer. Also, if the statement is false, rewrite it to make it true.

12. Whether you see the glass as half empty or half full is largely up to you.

   _____

   _____

13. People with a gloomy outlook are just as healthy as optimists.

   _____

   _____

14. All of our personality traits and attitudes are inherited.

   _____

   _____

15. Circle the letter of the sentence that best expresses the thesis:
   a. Research suggests our personality is inherited.
   b. Even though we may inherit a susceptibility for some personality traits, we can choose and control our attitude.
   c. Most individuals are able to salvage something positive from even their most frightening experiences.
   d. Pessimists are not as healthy as optimists.

16. According to Bruce and Foley, being an optimist pays off. List two examples of the payoff.

   _____

   _____

17. Why are pessimists more likely to do poorly in school and work?

   _____

   _____

18. In paragraph 3, sentence h, what does the word "conversely" signal?
   a. continuation of thought
   b. change in direction of thought
   c. definition
   d. effect

19. Circle the letter of the sentence that best expresses the main idea of paragraphs 5 and 6.

    a. Optimists get more exercise than pessimists.

    b. Pessimists don't recover from surgery as fast as optimists.

    c. Women who have a positive outlook know more about cancer and do more to prevent it.

    d. Optimists are physically and mentally healthier than pessimists.

20. What signal/transition phrase do Bruce and Foley use to begin paragraph 8?

    _____

    That phrase signals:

    a. a continuation of the same thought

    b. a change in direction of thought (contrast)

    c. an effect

21. In paragraph 16, Bruce and Foley say people should "look for the silver lining." What does that mean? Why is it a good thing to do?

    _____

    _____

22. What is the relationship of paragraphs 13–20 to paragraph 12? Which of the following do they provide?

    a. examples

    b. definitions

    c. causes

    d. effects

FEATURED SELECTION 3: "CHOOSING A POSITIVE ATTITUDE"

BEFORE YOU READ

About the Author   Psychologist Dr. Reneé Magid has written a number of articles for working adults. This is one of a series of *Lifelets* from the "All about Feelings" category of the Life Station by Initiatives, Inc.

Words to Know

spawn (¶2): cause, produce

colleagues (¶6): co-workers, associates

whiner (¶10): a person who complains all the time

aptitude (¶13): ability

waver (¶18): become less sure, reduce

charismatic (¶22): a personality that has a special charm, energy, and power that captures people's attention

morale (¶25): a person or group's spirit, confidence, or enthusiasm

devise (¶38): create, develop

insurmountable (¶38): impossible, overwhelming

manifest (¶42): to appear, show

As you preview, complete this outline of the article

Where Does Attitude Come From?

_____

_____

The Case for Maintaining a Positive Attitude
Your Attitude at Work
Keeping an Attitude Journal

_____

Getting Help When You Need It
Three Steps to Using a Positive Attitude to Face Challenges

                    _____

                    _____

                    _____

Sharing Your Positive Attitude

_____

Learn More about Choosing a Positive Attitude

An Idea to Think About   When you are faced with a big problem or having a difficult time with feelings of stress, anger, or self-doubt, what do you typically do? *As
you read*, look for other positive things Magid suggests you can do.

Choosing a Positive Attitude: Your Survival Strategy for Balancing Work and Personal Life

Reneé Magid

---

[1]Janice is a very upbeat person. Just seeing her makes us smile. She tells the funniest stories about herself as she juggles work with caring for two small boys. But no matter how busy she is, she remembers that your mom was scheduled for surgery or that your daughter had a big gymnastics meet over the weekend. She takes time to ask about what's going on in your life.

[2]Rob, on the other hand, seems to walk around with a cloud over his head. He moans and groans about every little thing. A change in office procedures is sure to spawn a week's worth of gripes from Rob about why it won't work and how they should have left things the way they were.

[3]We all know of people who are naturally cheerful like Janice and seem to be enjoying life. When we pass them in the hallway at work or in a supermarket aisle, we automatically smile and stop to chat.

[4]Then there are people who are the opposite, like Rob, always complaining and focusing on their own problems. We duck out of the way to avoid them so we don't have to listen to their gripes.

[5]The difference between Janice and Rob is not the number of problems they face, but the way they face them. Janice maintains a positive attitude about life, no matter what it holds in store. Rob has a negative attitude. Most of us are somewhere in between these personalities. Some days we are "up" and things are going our way. Other days we are "down" and nothing seems to turn out right. Research demonstrates that most of us feel down about three days out of ten, so in general people have a good attitude toward life.

[6]What about your attitude? Do your colleagues and family members see you as an upbeat person, one they want to be around? If not, it may be helpful to know that

there are ways to begin choosing a positive attitude that will help both you and those around you.

Where Does Attitude Come From?

[7]Your attitude is based on past memories and learned judgments about people, events, and circumstances, as well as personal thoughts and more recent experiences, all of which contribute to the way you view life. Attitude represents both the way you view things internally and how you project yourself to others. It influences how you react to circumstances and how you share your feelings and ideas with those around you.

[8]A positive attitude means cultivating a mindset tipped in favor of positive thinking, hope, and joy. Having a negative attitude means you tend to focus on the downside of life, always assuming the worst about others or events.

[9]Parents have a strong influence on whether their children will view life with a positive or negative attitude. Remember Janice and Rob: Janice's parents, for example, cheered her efforts at school and elsewhere. They taught her to pick herself up when things went wrong, learn from her mistakes, and get on with life. Learning to focus on the positive aspects of life rather than the negative ones was a special gift that Janice's parents gave her and it continues to serve her well.

[10]Rob's mother, on the other hand, was a whiner. She distrusted anything new and was constantly on the lookout for flaws in everything, whether it was an object, an idea, or new neighbors. Even when things were going her way, she was sure bad luck was just around the corner. Rob learned from his mother that life is full of pitfalls and disappointments.

[11]Think for a moment about your own upbringing. What did you learn as a child? Does your outlook on life today mirror the way your parents viewed life? Because attitudes are learned, not inborn, you can work on developing a positive attitude no matter how you were raised. No one needs to remain trapped inside a negative attitude that often triggers self-defeating behavior patterns.

[12]Keep in mind that the choice is yours to view things in a positive or negative way. You can allow negative thinking to be a shadow in your life or direct your thoughts toward the positive side of events and circumstances. There are many good reasons for choosing a positive attitude.

A Positive Attitude Leads to Success More Often

[13]Experts estimate that meeting challenges successfully is 80 percent attitude and 20 percent aptitude. Those who choose a positive mental outlook on problems and life in general seem to meet with success more often. Therefore, choosing a positive attitude will give you an advantage at home and at work over those who have a negative attitude.

[14]While we may not be able to alter the amount of intelligence or talent we were born with or the problems we face, we can all benefit from improving the way in which we approach obstacles. Developing a positive mental outlook can help achieve success in both your personal life and professional life.

[15]Successful, mentally healthy people are not automatically positive, but have learned how to create that state of mind. Having a positive attitude is your choice and the responsibility for changing a negative attitude is yours.

Ways to Overcome a General Negative Attitude

[16]While most people have an occasional bad day, some have difficulty with their attitude *every* day. If you suspect a general negative attitude is holding you back from success at work and at home, consider the following steps to foster positive thinking:

[17]When you get up in the morning, you have two choices. You can say, "Today is going to be a lousy day" or "Today is going to be a wonderful day." Remember, the choice is yours. Your outlook has a definite effect on how you will feel. As you dress, keep your "self-talk" positive and visualize yourself having a great day.

[18]As the day progresses, your positive attitude may begin to waver. Someone has pushed your wrong button. Feelings of anger, stress, and self-doubt begin creeping into your mind. Once again, you have two choices in how you react. You can say, "Why does this always happen to me? I just knew this would happen!" or "Why am I so upset? What is really going on?"

[19]When something happens that triggers your negative thoughts, sit quietly at your desk for a few minutes and mentally review what is frustrating you. Try to identify whether it is fear, insecurity, regret, or guilt. Then deal with the individual or the problem honestly and get back on track.

[20]If you make a mistake, check your internal vision for negative responses that can prevent you from correcting your mistakes and moving on. What kind of dialogue plays in your head? Do you chastise yourself with self-defeating criticism, such as "I can't do anything right!" and "I can't believe I said something that stupid!"

[21]Or does making a mistake prompt constructive criticism that helps you learn from mistakes and improve yourself, such as "I'm going to take my time and try to do a better job next time," and "I need to stop and think a moment before I speak to make sure I say what I mean to say." A positive attitude is easiest to achieve when your internal vision and "self-talk" are positive.

The Case for Maintaining a Positive Attitude

- [22]A positive attitude can lead to higher energy levels, greater creativity, and an improved personality.
- A positive attitude is the most powerful and priceless personality characteristic a person can possess.

- You can easily make the most of other physical and mental characteristics by communicating them through a positive attitude.
- Charismatic personalities always have one very important thing in common: a positive attitude.
- A cheerful, positive outlook can convince others that you are "beautiful," even if, in fact, your looks are average.
- Successful people learn how to build and maintain positive working relationships that, in turn, create a human support system for everyone involved. This is true in the office or at home.
- Leaders who follow certain attitude-building principles, such as, "attitudes are caught—not taught," are measurably more successful.
- A positive attitude is the key to success in any problem-solving effort or major lifestyle change, such as giving up smoking or retirement. Without it, things look darker, take longer, and failure is more likely to occur because of a "doom and gloom" approach.
- Research suggests that as much as 80 percent of all disease may originate from stress. A negative attitude can intensify stress in your life.

Your Attitude at Work

[23]Nowhere is a positive attitude more appreciated than at the workplace. Given a choice, many people would prefer to be somewhere else enjoying themselves rather than at work. We all have assignments we have to do or particular tasks we hate.

[24]Approaching a job with a positive attitude, however, can make the time fly, while negative thoughts make the day seem endless. Working alongside an upbeat person makes any task much more pleasant, while working with a grouch can spoil a perfectly good day.

[25]Similarly, the workplace itself may foster a particular attitude among individuals. Morale may be high or low, depending on different circumstances. Both positive and negative attitudes travel quickly and set the tone in the workplace.

[26]Supervisors depend upon the positive attitudes of individuals to establish a "team spirit." They know that attitudes are contagious. Projecting a positive outlook can help make everyone's job a little easier and more enjoyable. Putting positive ideas, words, and actions into practice helps you feel more upbeat yourself, and transmits this to others, as well.

[27]Career success depends on two very important factors: good work skills and good human relations. Displaying a positive attitude helps build cooperation, trust, and loyalty. We all may have varying contributions to make at work, in terms of talent or brain power, but those who contribute to overall feelings of goodwill are appreciated. In fact, in some professions, such as sales and customer relations, a positive attitude can be valued more than talent.

[28]Since approximately half your waking hours are spent in the workplace and success is related to attitude, it's important to maintain a positive attitude. Here are some practical advantages to developing a positive attitude in yourself and those around you.

- [29]Analyze the quality of your conversations with others. Do you talk constantly about yourself and your problems? You may need to train yourself to become an active listener by asking others about themselves and then really paying attention to what they are saying.
- Think in terms of "I can," whether you are tackling a big project or learning a new skill.
- Be direct with individuals who constantly complain or give negative messages. Tell them, "I am working on creating a more positive attitude in our department and I would appreciate your support."
- Facing a difficult problem at work or at home can create a drain on a co-worker's energy. Be supportive and optimistic about their ability to overcome challenges rather than contributing to their problems by adding your own doubts or sharing bad experiences you had.
- At the end of the day, focus on the positive aspects of your day and don't let yourself dwell on small mistakes or what went wrong.

[30]Keep in mind that your attitude affects not only you, but those around you. It is easy to note those people with positive and negative attitudes when vacation times roll around. The positive workers are genuinely missed and cheerfully welcomed back. Negative individuals give their co-workers a much needed vacation—from them! How do you want others to view you?

Keeping an Attitude Journal

[31]If you suspect a negative attitude is holding you back at work, it may help to keep a journal of your negative feelings and analyze what you have written to learn why you feel like you do. Use a chart like the one that follows for at least two weeks. Then go back and analyze patterns of your behavior. Check the situations that affect your attitude positively and negatively.

Attitude Journal

I experienced the following:

feelings/responses

When/What prompted this?

What was my reaction?

Attitude Adjustments

[32]No one escapes the daily pressures of life. Negative influences turn up when you least expect them or need them, and it's up to you how you handle them when they do. Change is a constant in our lives, at work, and at

home, and therefore attitude adjustments are necessary. Think about keeping your attitude in top condition with the following suggestions.

- [33]A daily and weekly "attitude check" is a vital part of maintaining your positive attitude. And despite our best efforts, sometimes a major attitude renewal becomes necessary.
- Whether you discover you need a light overhaul or a major tune-up in the attitude department, plan intelligently to get yourself strongly motivated again.
- Positive attitude reinforcement is never more necessary than immediately following a defeat or failure.
- No matter how difficult or trying the circumstance or situation, there is always the possibility of finding one positive element if you look long enough.
- A positive attitude does not mean ignoring troubles, but rather accepting them and making the best of them. It means reacting to a crisis with a plan, not a "why me?" attitude.
- By choosing a positive attitude over a negative one, you choose to make life pleasant for yourself, your family, and your co-workers. They will respond with appreciation and by demonstrating how much they enjoy being around you. Your positive attitude will go a long way toward contributing to your success at work and in life.

Get Help When You Need It

[34]However you try to maintain a positive attitude, problems can arise that may weigh you down. When personal or work-related crises occur, no one expects you to keep smiling when you want to cry. It is neither healthy nor honest to pretend nothing is wrong while facing a significant lifestyle change, the loss of someone close to you, a serious illness, or a major setback at work. While thinking positively can alter your response to a situation, it will not erase a problem such as an alcoholic spouse or a terminally ill parent, and these issues need to be addressed with the help of a professional counselor.

[35]If you are struggling with a severe negative attitude, you may need to seek out professional help to discover the underlying causes. People who are suffering from depression, for example, cannot just "snap out of it," no matter how much they wish they could. Deep-seated resentment about a situation at work or at home will not just go away if ignored.

Three Steps to Using a Positive Attitude to Face Challenges

[36]There are some situations, however, when taking a positive approach will lead to your success in overcoming challenges. The next time you are experiencing a really difficult time, try the following course of action.

Step 1: Slow Down until You Gain a Positive Perspective

[37]Whenever faced with a big problem, there are several positive things you can do:

- It often helps to make simple physical and mental adjustments. If you begin responding negatively to a problem, pause and take a few slow deep breaths, forcing yourself to think before you react. Monitor your internal dialogue tape and notice if it's playing "negative scripts" that sound a lot like your parents, a teacher, an older sibling, or a critical colleague, blaming or shaming you for past mistakes. Replace those "negative scripts" with positive talk, telling yourself that it's okay, you can do it, etc. Praise yourself for being willing to examine the problem and work on resolving the situation.
- Take time to assess your position. You may not be able to focus properly on your work when a crisis arises. Rather than hide your problem behind a cheery face, you may need to confide in your supervisor or someone else that things are not going well.
- Be willing to accept help. If you've always been the upbeat person at work, it may be hard to admit you need help yourself. Keep in mind that you have most likely been there for others. They probably would welcome the opportunity to repay your kindness by extending you the same sympathy or helping you share your work load.
- Get away from the situation for a few hours; or if possible, take a personal day to sort things out.
- Seek the advice of someone you respect and consider knowledgeable about a problem of this nature. Find a professional counselor, doctor, or clergyman to help you work things out.
- "Sleep on it." Sometimes solutions seem to present themselves to us in dreams, or we may wake up with a surprising "Aha!"

Step 2: Identify the Best Possible Solution

[38]Although it's never an easy process, using the scientific method to analyze problems and devise possible solutions is more helpful than just guessing what needs to be done. Engage yourself in the accepted, traditional, scientific decision-making process with the following three procedures. If your problem still seems insurmountable or you feel unsure which solution is the wisest choice, contact a professional for guidance.

- Gather all the facts. Try to examine the situation from as many different perspectives as you can.
- Outline all the possible alternatives. Don't hesitate to try a new way of handling the situation.
- Weigh all the factors of each alternative to arrive at the best decision. Listing your choices on paper will help you evaluate them and remind you that there are many options to choose from.

Step 3: Live with the Solution Gradually

[39]Spinning your wheels or rehashing mistakes can bring you down. Move forward once you've gathered all the information about how to tackle a problem.

- Make a decision. Don't go back and forth, endlessly weighing all the pros and cons involved. Reach a conscious decision and get moving. It may not be the ideal solution, but it's the best one you've found.

- Remember to let go. Once a decision is made, it's counter-productive to reprocess the problem over and over or try to place blame for what went wrong.

- Restore your positive attitude. Give yourself credit for your maturity in taking the necessary steps, and devote your time and energy to reestablishing a positive approach.

Sharing Your Positive Attitude

[40]In both personal life and work life, sharing a positive attitude can be beneficial to yourself and to those around you. Below are different ways people share their positive attitudes. Think about which of these you can incorporate into your behavior.

- Being more positive around those with whom you have daily contact.

- Going out of your way to visit, or talk with, friends who may be having trouble with *their* attitudes.

- Sharing your positive attitude by sending token items such as cards or flowers to those you care about.

- Being more sensitive as a listener instead of focusing on your problems.

- Sharing humor through cartoons, funny articles, or jokes.

- Communicating your attitude through upbeat phone conversations, paying compliments to others, etc.

[41]As you implement your choices, remind yourself that the more you give your attitude away, the more positive it will remain.

Conclusion

[42]It's been said that nothing is either good or bad, but thinking makes it so. If you want good things to manifest in your life, think positive. Other people will appreciate your "up" attitude. Knowing how to interact harmoniously, while working together and solving differences in a positive way, gives you a distinct career advantage and contributes to your family's ability to tackle problems.

[43]To win at the "Game of Life" requires a consistently positive attitude, which results in personal satisfaction, strong relationships, and success in a meaningful career. It helps to remember that no one remains totally positive at all times, but that it's always possible to return to it again and again. The more you do this, the easier it becomes to establish this practical and pleasurable pattern in your life.

"Most people are about as happy as they want to be."
Abraham Lincoln

Learn More about Choosing a Positive Attitude

Chapman, Elwood N. *Your Attitude Is Showing: A Primer of Human Relations*. New York: Macmillan, 1991.

Hill, Napoleon and W. Clement Stone. *Success through a Positive Mental Attitude*. New York: Simon & Schuster, 1987.

Hopson, Barrie and Mike Scally. *Transition: Positive Change in Your Life and Work*. San Diego: Pfeiffer & Company, 1993.

Stautberg, Susan S. and Marcia L. Worthing. *Balancing Acts!: Juggling Love, Work, Family, and Recreation*. New York: Master Media Limited, 1992.

SELECTION 3 QUESTIONS

Vocabulary

Circle the letter of the best definition for the underlined word.

1. "A positive attitude means <u>cultivating</u> a mindset tipped in favor of positive thinking, hope, and joy." (¶8)
   a. reducing, shortening
   b. plowing
   c. showing, displaying
   d. encouraging, promoting

2. "Do you <u>chastise</u> yourself with self-defeating criticism, such as 'I can't do anything right!' and 'I can't believe I said something that stupid!'" (¶20)
   a. reward
   b. scold, yell at
   c. write
   d. forgive

3. "Supervisors depend upon the positive attitudes of individuals to establish a 'team spirit.' They know that attitudes are <u>contagious</u>." (¶26)
   a. catching
   b. difficult
   c. make people ill
   d. important

4. "Knowing how to interact <u>harmoniously</u>, while working together and solving differences in a positive way...." (¶42)
   a. pleasantly
   b. rudely
   c. loudly
   d. harshly

Match each word in the left column with the best definition in the right column.

5. *flaws* (¶10) ___   a. picture, imagine
6. *alter* (¶14) ___   b. faults, problems
7. *visualize* (¶17) ___   c. critical, important
8. *foster* (¶25) ___   d. change
9. *vital* (¶33) ___   e. encourage, help

Comprehension

Determine whether the statements in sentences 10 and 11 are true or false, and write your answer. Also, if the statement is false, rewrite it to make it true.

10. Those who choose a positive mental outlook on problems and life don't seem to be any more successful than those with a negative outlook.

_____

_____

_____

11. Career success depends on two very important factors: good work skills and good human relations.

_____

_____

_____

12. Circle the letter of the sentence that best expresses the thesis:
    a. The difference between Janice and Rob is not the number of problems they face, but the way they face them.
    b. When we approach a job with a positive attitude, we make the time go faster and the work seem more pleasant.
    c. When we consistently choose to have a positive attitude, we're healthier, happier, and more successful.
    d. The more you share a positive attitude, the more positive it will remain.

13. Circle the letter of the sentence that best expresses the main idea of paragraphs 9 and 10.
    a. Janice received a special gift from her parents.
    b. Parents have a significant influence on their children's attitude toward life.
    c. Rob's mother distrusted anything new and was constantly on the lookout for flaws in everything.

14. What signal/transition phrase does Magid use in the first sentence of paragraph 10?

    _____

    That phrase signals:
    a. a continuation of the same thought
    b. a change in direction of thought (contrast)
    c. an effect

15. Write a sentence that expresses the main idea of paragraph 12.

    _____

    _____

16. What is the relationship of paragraphs 17–21 to paragraph 16?
    a. They list the effects.
    b. They define terms.
    c. They continue the thought with examples.

17. What signal/transition word does Magid use to begin paragraph 25?

    _____

    That phrase signals:
    a. a continuation of the same thought
    b. a change in direction of thought (contrast)
    c. an effect

18. Magid lists several positive things you can do when you're faced with a big problem or having a difficult time with feelings of stress, anger, or self-doubt. List two examples.

    _____

    _____

Vocabulary Extra

Each of these words has a prefix and/or a suffix added to the root word. (1) Break the word into its component parts (root, prefix, and/or suffix), (2) define each word part, and (3) define the whole word. For help, use the Roots, Prefixes, Suffixes table on pages 17–18 or refer to your dictionary.

1. distrusted (¶10)

    root word _____

    definition _____

    prefix _____

    definition _____

    suffix _____

    definition _____

    distrusted means _____

2. successful (¶15)

    root word _____

    definition _____

    prefix _____

    definition _____

    suffix _____

    definition _____

    successful means _____

3. insecure (¶19)

    root word _____

    definition _____

    prefix _____

    definition _____

    suffix _____

    definition _____

    insecure means _____

4. priceless (¶22)
    root word _____

    definition _____

    prefix _____

    definition _____

    suffix _____

    definition _____

    priceless means _____

5. enjoyable (¶26)
    root word _____

    definition _____

    prefix _____

    definition _____

    suffix _____

    definition _____

    enjoyable means _____

6. renew (¶33)
    root word _____

    definition _____

    prefix _____

    definition _____

    suffix _____

    definition _____

    renew means _____

7. unsure (¶38)
    root word _____

    definition _____

    prefix _____

    definition _____

suffix _____

definition _____

unsure means _____

8. reestablish (¶39)
    root word _____

    definition _____

    prefix _____

    definition _____

    suffix _____

    definition _____

    reestablish means _____

FEATURED SELECTION 4: "HOLD ON TO YOUR POSITIVE ATTITUDE"

BEFORE YOU READ

About the Authors   Elwood N. Chapman was a professor at Chaffey College and a nationally-known speaker and consultant until his death in 1995. Sharon Lund O'Neil is a professor and associate vice provost at the University of Houston. She has received many teaching awards and is widely published in human relations. This is Chapter 3, from their text *Your Attitude is Showing: A Primer of Human Relations*, ninth edition.

Words to Know

> *attribute* (¶1): characteristic
> *subtle* (¶4): indirect
> *stimulus* (¶6): anything that causes action
> *preceding* (¶22): coming before, previous
> *complement* (¶26): add to, completes
> *complimentary* (¶27): making a positive, flattering statement
> *passive* (¶29): submissive, offering no opposition
> *insolvency* (¶31): cannot pay debts, bankrupt
> *clique* (¶34): small, often snobbish group of people
> *frivolous* (¶43): silly, not serious

An Idea to Think About   Think about your job—the work you do for a business or at home. What are the first five words that pop into your mind? Are the words mostly positive or mostly negative? *As you read*, look for how much influence Chapman and O'Neil think those words—your attitude—have on your success.

Chapter 3

HOLD ON TO
YOUR POSITIVE ATTITUDE

"It's hard to stay positive under pressure."

[1]*Attitude* is a common word. You hear it almost every day. Professors use it on campus. Managers discuss it at work. Employment counselors look for it among applicants. You hear people say: "He's got an attitude" (indicating a possible problem), while others say "I wish I had her consistently positive attitude." No other attribute will have more influence upon your future. A positive attitude can be your most priceless possession.

[2]If you can create and keep a positive attitude toward your job, your company, and life in general, you should not only move up the ladder of success quickly and gracefully, you should also be a happier person. If you are unable to be positive, you may find many career mobility doors closed to you, and your personal life less than exciting.

Three Faces of Communication

[3]There are three forms of communication between people. One is the written form—letters, memos, faxes, e-mails, etc. The second is the verbal form—face-to-face conversations, telephone conversations, voice mail, intercom discussions, video conferencing, etc. The third involves the transmission of attitudes.

[4]The first two forms of communication are so important to the profitable operation of an organization that we tend to think they are the only ones. We forget that we also communicate our attitudes through facial expressions, hand gestures, and other more subtle forms of body language. Sometimes people will greet

18

19

HOLD ON TO YOUR POSITIVE ATTITUDE

others with a positive voice, but their body language (negative facial expression) sends a contrasting signal. As the expression claims, sometimes your attitude speaks so loudly that others cannot hear what you say.

Your Attitude Is Showing

[5]Every time you report for work, every time you attend a staff meeting, every time you go through a formal appraisal, every time you take a coffee break, and every time you go out socially, be aware that *your attitude is showing.*

[6]Because attitude can play such an important role in your future, let's take a closer look at the meaning of the word itself. *Attitude* is defined by most psychologists as a mental set that causes a person to respond in a characteristic manner to a given stimulus. You have many attitudes, or mental sets. You have attitudes toward certain makes of automobiles, toward certain social institutions (schools, churches, and the like), toward certain careers, lifestyles, and people.

[7]You also have a wide variety of job attitudes. You build attitudes toward your supervisor and the people with whom you work, toward the job you do, toward company policies, toward the amount of money you are being paid. In addition to these specific attitudes, you have a basic, or total, attitude toward your job and toward life itself. Strictly speaking, then, attitude is the *way you look at your whole environment.*

[8a]You can look at your job in any way you wish. [8b]On the one hand, you can focus your attention on all its negative aspects (odd hours, close supervision, poor location). [8c]On the other hand, you can focus your attention on the more positive factors of the job (harmonious work environment, good learning opportunities, good benefits). [8d]All jobs have both positive and negative factors. [8e]How you choose to perceive yours is an important decision.

[9]Attitude is the way you view and interpret your environment. Some people can push unpleasant things out of sight and dwell largely on positive factors. Others seem to enjoy the unpleasant and dwell on these negative factors.

What You See in Life Influences Your Attitude

[10]If you go around looking for what is wrong with things, wondering why things are not better, and complaining about them, then you will be a negative person in the minds of most people. If you do the opposite—look for what is good and don't focus on

20
CHAPTER 3

unpleasant things—you will be a positive person in the minds of most people.

[11]Some people (through imaging) keep their positive attitudes by viewing life as a circle with both positive and negative factors competing to gain as much "mind time" as possible. Negative factors constantly try to command attention, pushing positive factors to the side.

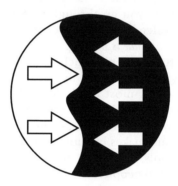

[12]To offset a negative drift, positive people discipline their minds to concentrate primarily upon positive factors, thus pushing the negative to the outer perimeter of their thinking.

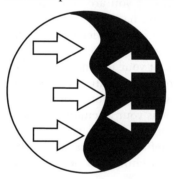

[13]There is no perfect job or position. One job may have more favorable aspects than another, but all jobs have some unpleasant ones. The employee who dwells on the unfavorable factors has a negative attitude. The employee who is determined to look for factors that are favorable will slowly become a more positive person.

[14]Therefore, even if you start a new job or assignment with a positive attitude, you must make sure that it remains positive. It is possible that you will meet a few people with negative attitudes who will attempt to persuade you to think as they do. These fac-

tors could influence you and destroy what otherwise would have been an excellent start.

[15]To be a positive person, you need not think your company is perfect. That would be foolish. You would eventually become disillusioned. On the other hand, unless you feel that the majority of factors are favorable, you will eventually become negative, and you will show it.

The Moment You Can No Longer Be Positive about Your Career with Your Company, Your Chances for Success Diminish

[16]No one can be positive all the time. You will naturally have periods of doubt. These temporary periods will not hurt you seriously. But a consistently negative attitude that persists for weeks or months will destroy your future with the organization. If you find your negative attitude cannot be improved in your present setting, and you honestly feel such an attitude is justified, you should resign.

[17]A positive attitude is essential to career success for many reasons:

[18]1. When you are positive you are usually more energetic, motivated, productive, and alert. Thinking about negative things too much has a way of draining your energy. Put another way, a positive attitude opens a gate and lets your inner enthusiasm spill out. A negative attitude, on the other hand, will keep the gate closed.

[19]2. First impressions are important on the job because they often have a lasting effect. Co-workers you meet for the first time appear to have little radar sets tuned in to your attitude. If your attitude is positive, they receive a friendly, warm signal, and they are attracted to you. If your attitude is negative, they receive an unfriendly signal, and they try to avoid you.

[20]3. A positive employee contributes to the productivity of others. A negative employee does not. Attitudes are caught more than they are taught. Both negative and positive attitudes are transmitted on the job. They are picked up by others. A persistently negative attitude, like the rotten apple in the barrel, can spoil the positive attitudes of others. It is very difficult to maintain a high level of productivity while working next to a person with a negative attitude.

[21]4. Co-workers like you when you are positive. They like to be around you because you are fun. Your job is more interesting and

22

CHAPTER 3

exciting because you are in the middle of things and not on the outside complaining. When you are negative, people prefer to stay clear of you. A negative person may build good relationships with a few other people (who are perhaps negative themselves), but such a person cannot build good relationships with the majority of employees.

[22]5. The kind of attitude you transmit to management will have a considerable influence on your future success. Management constantly reads your mental attitude, even though you may feel you are successful in covering it up. Supervisors can determine your attitude by how you approach your job, react to directives, handle problems, and work with others. If you are positive, you will be given greater consideration when special assignments and promotion opportunities arise.

If your job involves customer, client, or patient contacts, you should place additional emphasis on everything stated in the preceding list. Your attitude is significant in all relationships, but it is crucial when you are in a service position.

[23]It is important to realize that a positive attitude involves far more than a smile. A smile, of course, is helpful in transmitting a positive attitude. However, some people transmit a positive attitude even when they seldom smile. They convey positiveness by the way they treat others, the way they look at their responsibilities, and the perspective they take when faced with a problem.

[24]Attitude is a highly personal thing. It is closely tied to your self-concept, or the way you look at yourself. Because attitude is so personal, talking about it is not easy. People often freeze when the word is mentioned. As a result, management may never talk to you about your attitude. They may never say, for example, "Let's be honest. Your attitude is negative. What are you going to do about it?" *But everyone will know when your attitude is showing.*

[25]How, then, do you make sure you keep your positive attitude when things get tough? How do you keep a good grip on it when you are discouraged? How do you keep it in good repair on a day-to-day basis over the years? Here are a few simple suggestions.

Build a More Positive Attitude in One Environment and You Will Be More Successful in Another

[26]Your positive or negative attitude is not something that you can hang on a hook. It follows you wherever you go. It is reasonable to assume, then, that if you make a greater effort to be a more

positive person in your social and personal lives, your effort will automatically spill over and help you on the job. By the same token, if you make a greater effort to develop a more positive attitude at work, your effort will make a contribution to your social and personal lives. One effort will complement the other.

Talk about Positive Things

[27]Negative comments are seldom welcomed by fellow workers on the job; nor are they welcomed by those you meet in the social scene. The best way to be positive is to be complimentary. Constant gripers and complainers seldom build healthy and exciting relationships with others.

Look For the Good Things in the People with Whom You Work, Especially Your Supervisors

[28]Nobody is perfect, but almost everybody has a few worthwhile qualities. If you dwell on people's good features, it will be easier for you to like them and easier for them to like you. Make no mistake about one thing: People usually know how you react to them even if you don't communicate verbally.

Look For the Good Things in Your Organization

[29]What are the factors that make it a good place to work? Do you like the hours, the physical environment, the people, the actual work you are doing? What about opportunities for promotion? Do you have chances for self-improvement? What about your wage and benefit package? Do you have the freedom you seek? No job is perfect, but, if you concentrate on the good things, the negative factors may seem less important. Seeing the positive side of things does not mean that you should ignore negative elements that should be changed. Far from it! A positive person is not a weak person. A positive person is usually confident, assertive (within limits), and an agent of change within an organization. Management is not seeking passive people who meekly conform. They want spirited, positive people who will make constructive and thoughtful improvements.

[30]If you decide to stay with an organization for a long time, you would be wise to concentrate on its good features. Staying positive may take a considerable amount of personal fortitude, but it is the best way to keep your career on an upward track. If you think positively, you will act positively and you will succeed.

24
CHAPTER 3

Avoid Financial Problems through Planning and Discipline

[31]On-campus surveys indicate that students frequently fail academically and drop out because of financial problems. It also appears that career employees troubled with financial worries often turn negative and lose the promotions that would provide the extra money that could help them pay off their bills. Unfortunately, few of these individuals realize that their positive attitudes are being sacrificed along with their credit ratings. Instead of seeking and accepting family or professional financial counseling, they permit their insolvency to lead them into attitudinal bankruptcy. When attitudinal bankruptcy happens, they pay a double penalty.

Don't Permit a Fellow Worker—Even a Supervisor—Who Has a Negative Attitude to Trap You into His (or Her) Way of Thinking

[32]You may not be able to change a negative person's attitude, but at least you can protect your own positive attitude from becoming negative. The story of Sandy will emphasize this point.

> **Sandy.** Sandy was a little uneasy about her new job. It was a fine opportunity, and she knew the standards were very high. Would she have the skills needed? Could she learn fast enough to please her supervisor? Would the older employees like her? Although Sandy's concern was understandable, it was not justified. In addition to being highly qualified for the job, she had a happy, positive attitude that wouldn't stop. She was seldom depressed.
>
> Everything went very well for Sandy for a while. Her positive attitude was appreciated by all. Slowly, however, her fellow workers and supervisor noticed a change. Sandy became more critical of her colleagues, her job, and the company. Her usual friendly greetings and helpful ideas were gradually replaced by complaints. What had happened? Without realizing it, Sandy was showing the effects of the friendships she had made on the job. Needing acceptance in a strange environment, she had welcomed the attention of a clique of employees who had a negative attitude—a group that management already viewed critically.
>
> Sandy was not able to confine her negative attitude to her job. Soon, again without realizing it, she let her negative attitude spill over into her social life. In fact, it troubled her boyfriend so much that he had it out with her one night. His words were a little rough. "Look, Sandy. When you are happy, you are very attractive and fun to be around. But frankly, when you are negative you are a real bore, and I never have a good time with you. I think those so-called friends you hang round with on the job are killing what was once a beautiful personality."

25
HOLD ON TO YOUR POSITIVE ATTITUDE

It wasn't a happy evening, but Sandy got the message. She made a vow to recapture and hang on to the positive attitude she had previously enjoyed. Not only was she successful in recapturing her positive attitude, but she also converted a few of her previously negative friends to her way of thinking. Her action saved her career.

Make Frequent Self-Assessments

[33]When friends casually ask me "How are you doing?" I often jokingly reply: "I'm not sure but I intend to sit under a tree tomorrow and ask myself some questions to find out." Most employees make the mistake of waiting around for their organizations to complete an annual formal appraisal instead of frequently sitting under a shady tree somewhere and asking themselves questions similar to these.

Am I currently transmitting a positive or negative attitude?

Is my attitude influencing the quality and quantity of my personal productivity in a positive way?

Am I sufficiently positive to be considered a fun and comfortable co-worker?

Am I communicating to superiors through my attitude that I seek career advancements?

Are my customers, clients, or co-workers responding to my attitude in an upbeat manner?

[34]Whatever form your self-assessment takes (attitude is a most personal matter), *use it frequently*. Check your attitude as you would the amount of gasoline in your car. Talk to yourself about the progress you are making. Don't sit around expecting someone else to do it for you.

John. John's boss is a believer in formal appraisal programs. Instead of annual evaluations, he would prefer going through the process twice each year. In discussing the good showing John made on his current appraisal, his boss said: "John, I have noticed that your attitude and productivity always improves shortly before appraisal time and then settles back a few weeks afterward. I think it would be smart for you to appraise yourself every few weeks during the year. By periodic appraisal checks you would keep a more positive attitude and deserve a higher rating than I can give you now. Consistency is a big factor and I recommend frequent self-appraisals."

26
CHAPTER 3

Serendipity

[35]Holding on to your positive attitude will never be easy. There are many techniques, however, that can help. Some will be discussed later in this book. One that will help you get started, especially when an irritating problem surfaces, is saying the word *serendipity*.

[36]The word *serendipity* was coined by Horace Walpole in 1754 when he put the fairy tale *The Three Princes of Serendip* to paper. A modern version by Elizabeth Jamison Hodges was published in 1964. It is a delightful story of three princes who travel from kingdom to kingdom in a lighthearted, compassionate manner. In helping others solve their problems, they are led to the solution of a problem in their own kingdom.

[37]Serendipity lends itself to many interpretations. To some, it is a gift to help them find agreeable things not sought. To everyone it is a "happiness" word. The magic comes into play when we realize that a "lighter approach" can often not only solve a problem but cause something good to happen in our lives.

[38]In short, serendipity is an attitude—an apparently frivolous mental set that can help us view our work environment in a more humorous and forgiving manner. It is an attitude that temporarily moves responsibility aside and encourages one to rise above any negative situation. A serendipitous attitude is within the reach of everyone and, when achieved, fortuitous things may happen. For example, when you have a lighthearted, mischievous, festive way of looking at things, others are intrigued and may invite you to share beautiful experiences with them that, in turn, can enhance your life. Serendipity is a state of mind that is symbolized by the clowns on the cover of this book. It is a wonderful attitude to take to a party. There are also times when it can be a lifesaver in the workplace.

> Like plants, your attitude needs
> nurturing in order to grow.

SELECTION 4 QUESTIONS

Vocabulary

Circle the letter of the best definition for the underlined word.

1. "If your job involves customer, client, or patient contacts, you should place additional <u>emphasis</u> on everything...." (¶22)
   a. work
   b. people, workers
   c. importance
   d. time

2. "Management is not seeking passive people who <u>meekly</u> conform." (¶29)
   a. mildly
   b. boldly
   c. happily
   d. impatiently

3. "Am I currently <u>transmitting</u> a positive or negative attitude?" (¶37)
   a. writing
   b. communicating
   c. keeping
   d. holding

Rephrase the underlined passages using your own words.

4. "If you are unable to be positive, <u>you may find many career mobility doors closed to you</u>...." (¶2)
   _____

5. "Staying positive may take a considerable amount of <u>personal fortitude</u>...." (¶30)
   _____

6. "Instead of seeking ... financial counseling, they permit their insolvency to lead them into <u>attitudinal bankruptcy</u>." (¶31)
   _____

7. "John's boss is a believer in formal <u>appraisal programs</u>." (¶39)
   _____

8. "A serendipitous attitude is within the reach of everyone and, when achieved, <u>fortuitous things may happen</u>." (¶43)
   _____

Comprehension

Determine whether the statements in sentences 9 and 10 are true or false, and write your answer. Also, if the statement is false, rewrite it to make it true.

9. All jobs have both positive and negative factors.
   _____
   _____

10. A positive attitude isn't really essential to career success.

    _____

    _____

11. Circle the letter of the sentence that best expresses the thesis.
    a. Keeping a positive attitude about your job, the company you work for, and life in general will help you be a happier and more successful person.
    b. There are three forms of communication between people.
    c. Attitude is the way you view and interpret your surroundings.
    d. If you spend your time looking for what is wrong with things and complaining about them, you will be viewed as a negative person.

12. Complete this outline map of paragraph 3. Label each entry as a main idea, major detail, or minor detail.

    There are three forms of communication between people (_____)

        Written forms (Major detail)

          _____   (_____)

          _____   (_____)

          _____   (_____)

          e-mails   (_____)

        Verbal forms (_____)

          _____   (_____)

          _____   (_____)

          voice mail   (_____)

          _____   (_____)

          video conferencing   (_____)

        _____ (_____)

13. How do Chapman and O'Neil define "attitude"?

    _____

14. In paragraph 8, what is the relationship of sentence c to sentence b?
    a. a continuation of the same thought
    b. a change in direction of thought (contrast)
    c. an effect

    The phrase that signals it is:

    _____

15. Chapman and O'Neil quote the expression, "sometimes your attitude speaks so loudly that others cannot hear what you say." List two specific examples of body language that we use to communicate our attitudes.

    _____

16. Write the main idea of paragraph 13.

    _____

17. How much influence do Chapman and O'Neil think your attitude
    has on your success in the workplace? Circle your answer.

    a. significant influence

    b. some influence

    c. very little influence

    d. no influence

FEATURED SELECTION 5: "'LITTLE ENGINE' HOLDS A VALUABLE LIFE LESSON"

BEFORE YOU READ

About the Author   Ana Veciana-Suarez is a family columnist for *The Miami Herald*.

Words to Know

embodies (¶1) incorporates, brings together

mantra (¶2) personal inspirational chant

classic morality tale (¶2) traditional story with a moral

stymied (¶3) frustrated, unable to explain

analogy (¶3) comparison

traits (¶4) characteristics

laments (¶6) whining, complaining

shroud ourselves (¶9) wrap ourselves

catastrophic (¶12) disastrous, terribly harmful

laud (¶17) praise

An Idea to Think About   When you are faced with a difficult task, do you most often
tell yourself "I think I can," or "I don't think I can"? How often are you right? *As
you read,* find out why Veciana-Suarez believes such self-talk is important.

'LITTLE ENGINE' HOLDS A VALUABLE LIFE LESSON

Ana Veciana-Suarez

---

[1]"The Little Engine That Could" is one of my favorite children's stories. Chugging, struggling, forcing itself to do what it fears most, the little engine embodies much of what I try to teach my children.

[2]I think I can … I think I can … I think I can. Consider it a personal mantra. To be able to do anything, you must first "believe" you can. And to believe you can, you must possess a certain sense of confidence and hope. "The Little Engine That Could" is the classic morality tale of someone who chooses to see the glass half-full.

[3]I thought of this long-forgotten story during a conversation with a friend the other day when, stymied for an explanation about a mutual acquaintance's behavior, I cited the little engine. It struck her as incredibly funny, but she agreed the analogy fit.

[4]Our mutual acquaintance shares few traits with the little engine, which is really too bad. Her glass is always half-empty. Maybe too many of us see it that way, and then wonder why we're so unhappy and frustrated.

[5a]Our acquaintance has managed, in small ways and by large acts, to isolate herself. [5b]Ask her to break routine, to try something new, to give a stranger a chance, to open her heart, and she won't because she believes she can't. [5c]The world she sees is a threatening, conspiring one.

[6a]Her laments are legendary. [6b]They have become a joke among those who know her. [6c]Nothing escapes the pallor of her unfounded gloom. [6d]Not the weather—which is always too cold or too hot. [6e]Not a party—too many people or not enough of the right ones. [6f]Not even an unexpected windfall—it could have come sooner or could have been better.

[7]She is defeated before she begins. There's never any "I think I can … I think I can …" only "I won't … I won't … I won't."

[8]"She's so negative," my friend said.

[9]All of us shroud ourselves in that negativism at one time or another. And we should—occasionally. We need to wallow in misery every once in a while. It's only when we stay too long in the mire or make it a lifelong personal statement that it repels.

[10]Pessimism is like a bad smell. You can't get away from it fast enough; you want to flush it out of your life.

[11]I would much rather spend my time with someone who will remark about the spectacular spring morning instead of worry about the predicted afternoon thunderstorm.

[12]What always has fascinated me are stories of people who overcome great odds to recover from tragedies: the woman with a terrible childhood who becomes an exemplary mother; the rich man who, after losing it all, wins it back and devotes his life to the poor; the athlete who comes back from a catastrophic injury. They are the real-life examples of little engines that could.

[13]About five years ago, I interviewed a teen-age boy, a defensive lineman on his football team, who had been hit by an 18-wheeler while riding his bike down a rural road in Palm Beach County, Fla. The impact crushed not only his body but also his dreams of playing college football.

[14]But the kid refused to wallow in what unquestionably was a miserable situation. He got over his initial despair and put all his efforts first into moving his toes, then his feet, then his legs. He worked so hard at rehabilitating himself that he sobbed while relearning to walk. He finally did, more than two years later. He never played college ball—that happens only in movies—but he could play tag in his back yard.

[15]"I could have been dead," he said.

[16]Thousands of interviews later, I still remember his words.

[17]There's a lot to be said about the philosophy of "it could be worse." There's plenty more to laud about "making the best of a bad situation." I have told my children just that so, so many times.

[18]I truly believe you can teach optimism, nourish hopefulness, bestow enthusiasm. It all starts with the belief: I think I can ... I think I can ... I think I can.

SELECTION 5 QUESTIONS

Vocabulary

Circle the letter of the best definition for the underlined word.

1. "And to believe you can, you must <u>possess</u> a certain sense of confidence and hope." (¶2)
   a. forfeit
   b. give up
   c. have
   d. pretend

2. "... I <u>cited</u> the little engine." (¶3)
   a. ignored
   b. referred to
   c. explained
   d. neglected

3. "... becomes an <u>exemplary</u> mother ..." (¶12)
   a. well-known
   b. popular
   c. poor
   d. excellent

Rephrase these sentences using your own words.

4. "Her glass is always half-empty." (¶4)

   _____

5. "Our acquaintance has managed, in small ways and by large acts, to isolate herself." (¶5)

   _____

   _____

6. "Nothing escapes the pallor of her unfounded gloom." (¶6)

   _____

Comprehension

Determine whether the statements in sentences 7–9 are true or false, and write your answer. Also, if the statement is false, rewrite it to make it true.

7. To be able to do anything, you must first "believe" you can.

   _____

   _____

8. "The Little Engine That Could" is a children's story.

   _____

   _____

9. Most of us prefer to spend time with people who are pessimistic rather than optimistic.

   _____

   _____

10. Circle the letter of the sentence that best expresses the thesis.
    a. You should read classic stories with a moral to children.
    b. The world is a threatening and conspiring place.
    c. You'll have a better chance of accomplishing what you want if you think you can.
    d. People can recover from devastating accidents.

11. What is the relationship of sentence 5b to sentence 5a? Which of the following does it provide?
    a. an example
    b. a change in direction of thought (contrast)
    c. a definition

12. What is the relationship of sentences 6d, 6e, and 6f to sentence 6c? Which of the following do they provide?
    a. examples
    b. causes
    c. definitions of terms

13. In paragraph 14, Veciana-Suarez says "…—that happens only in movies—…." Explain what she means?

    _____

    _____

14. Veciana-Suarez mentions several people she believes are real-life examples of little engines that could. Name one person you know or have read about who you believe is an example of a little engine that could.

    _____

CROSSWORD PUZZLE

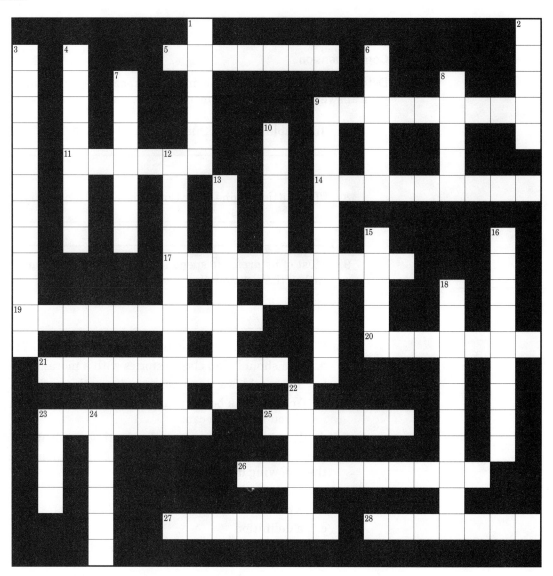

ACROSS

5 react
9 possible, believable
11 create, develop
14 picture, imagine
17 always, without fail
19 unbelievable
20 frustrated, unable to explain
21 coworkers, associates
23 whining, complaining
25 communicate, tell
26 securely established
27 shields, protects
28 fate, inevitable future

DOWN

1 yell at, belittle
2 change
3 disastrous, terribly harmful
4 incorporates, brings together
6 characteristics
7 recover, retrieve
8 critical, important
9 reason, cause
10 height, build
12 important
13 silly, not serious
15 faults, problems
16 coming before, previous
18 adds to, completes
22 encourage, help
23 praise
24 mildly

WORD LIST (NOT ALL USED)

alter	entrenched	predisposes
berate	flaws	provocation
buffers	foster	respond
catastrophic	frivolous	salvage
chronic	incredible	significant
colleagues	insurmountable	stature
complement	invariably	stymied
contagious	laments	traits
convey	laud	visualize
destiny	meekly	vital
devise	plausible	
embodies	preceding	

LOG ON TO THE WEB

You can find dozens of sites on the Web that have information about "how to keep a positive attitude." For example, pages like these reprint magazine articles:

"It's all in your head!" from *BizSuccess*, by Gary Lockwood at <http://www.bizsuccess.com/head.htm>.

"Essential Skills and Competencies for Personal Mastery in Learning Organizations" from *Technology*, by Dr. Jim Penrod at <http://www.memphis.edu/is/technology/spr99/mastery.htm>.

Sites like these have stories, quotes, and research on attitude:

http://www.y-knot.com/attitude.htm

http://www.winningattitude.com

Log on to one of these sites or use a search directory/engine to locate another site with information about "how to keep a positive attitude."

Read one article or story. Write down: (1) the complete address (http://www. ...), (2) the name of the person or company who sponsors and maintains the site, (3) the name of the person who wrote the information, (4) what you know about the writer, and (5) one important thing you learned from the information on "how to keep a positive attitude."

IDEAS FOR WRITING AND DISCUSSION

A. The authors in this theme share a common viewpoint about the importance of our attitude. Describe their viewpoint. Also describe two of their supporting ideas that mean the most to you.

B. Describe a person you know who is almost always upbeat. What does he or she say and do to communicate his or her positive attitude? How do you think he or she maintains a positive attitude?

C. We all know negative individuals—those who see every glass as half empty. Which of their words and actions are most annoying or troublesome? What techniques can you use to counteract their negative influence?

D. Self-assessment, talking to yourself about your progress, can be done in many ways. What techniques do you recommend for: work, school, personal growth? What cautions do you have for a person doing a self-assessment?

OUR FIRST AMENDMENT FREEDOMS

Congress shall make no law respecting an establishment of religion, or prohibiting the free exercise thereof; or abridging the freedom of speech, or of the press, or the right of the people peaceably to assemble, and to petition the Government for a redress of grievances.

—First Amendment to the Constitution

The First Amendment to the Constitution was proposed by Congress on September 25, 1789, and ratified by the necessary three-fourths of the States on December 15, 1791. The power of the First Amendment and the protection it provides Americans confront us daily.

Most Americans celebrate the freedoms guaranteed by the First Amendment. However, many also feel that the freedoms are sometimes dangerous. For example: Can teachers and students say anything they want in a classroom? Can newspapers print anything they want about anyone? Can librarians have any books they want in a school or other public library? Can employees email any type of jokes and pictures? But, if they can not do these things, who decides what can be said or printed or shelved or e-mailed?

Many Americans believe that people in the public eye, such as professional athletes, movie stars, rap musicians, and politicians, should be free to express personal opinions without the threat of punishment. However, others believe that people in positions of influence should be held to a higher standard—although who defines and sets the higher standard is often unclear.

Some Americans combine "freedom of speech, or of the press" into "freedom of expression." They then call anything that is said, printed, projected, or performed, "expression" and therefore feel it is covered under the First Amendment. Others, however, feel that when "freedom of expression" is stretched to protect things such as gossip, racial slurs, obscenity, and pornography, the concept is questionable.

Perhaps, as Oliver Wendell Holmes said, "The only useful test of whether someone believes in the First Amendment is whether he or she would vigorously protect the views of the people they hate."

How we react to the situations and controversies created by our freedoms helps define who we are and how we want our society to behave. Paul McMasters, ombudsman with the First Amendment Center says it is possible that "without the First Amendment, our society—and our lives—might be calmer, safer, even more civil." However, he adds, there is "little doubt that we would be considerably less free."

Authors in this theme provide a historical perspective, current information, and personal insight on the First Amendment. Each of the readings is by a different author, of a different length, and requires different tasks.

To provide an overview of the topic, "Civil Liberties: First Amendment Freedoms," Chapter 19 in *Magruder's American Government* text by William A. McClenaghan opens the theme.

Next, we get a snapshot of American's current views on our First Amendment freedoms in the *State of the First Amendment 2000*, by Kenneth A. Paulson, executive director of the First Amendment Center.

Newspaper columnist Bill Thompson asks, "Well, Would You Rather Have an Unfree Press?" And finally, in "You Be the Judge," Chip Rowe asks us to see how closely we agree with the courts about what is and is not "free speech."

FEATURED SELECTION 1: "CIVIL LIBERTIES: FIRST AMENDMENT FREEDOMS"

BEFORE YOU READ

About the Author   *Magruder's American Government* was first published in 1917 and is revised annually. It was conceived and written by Frank Abbott Magruder (1882–1949), and the author of the current edition is William A. McClenaghan, professor of political science at Oregon State University in Corvallis, Oregon.

Words to Know

Look for the *Key Terms* at the beginning of each section.

An Idea to Think About   How would your life be different if you lived in a country with a dictatorial government rather than a democratic government? *As you read*, find out what individual rights we enjoy in the United States.

484

CHAPTER

Civil Liberties: First Amendment Freedoms

Chapter Preview

How much violence—how many murders and how many other criminal acts—have you seen on television? Quite a few, probably. Indeed, one advocacy group, Americans for Responsible Television (ART), says that the typical high school senior today, to this point in his or her life, has seen an astonishing 33,000 murders and some 200,000 other acts of violence on television. Whatever the accuracy of that claim, ART and several other groups insist that government must act to curb the portrayal of violence on television and elsewhere in the entertainment field—in the movies and on compact discs, for example.

What do you think? What, if anything, should government do about violence on television, in the movies, on recordings, and so on? As you compose your answer to that question you must contemplate the central topic of this chapter: freedom of expression.

★ Participation Activities ★

- Conduct a debate about the voicing of unpopular views.
- Perform a skit about what might occur if no limits on free speech existed.

As you read, focus on the main objective for each section. Understand:

1. The relationship between liberty and government.
2. The importance of religious freedom in the United States.
3. The scope of and limits on free speech and free press.
4. The relationship between individual liberties and national security.
5. The limits on the freedoms of assembly and petition.

▲ **Freedom of Religion** Among other rights, every citizen of the United States has the right to worship according to his or her beliefs, without fear of interference from the government.

1 The Unalienable Rights

Find Out:

- For what reasons were individual rights included in the Constitution?
- What factors limit individual rights?
- For what reasons is the Due Process Clause of the 14th Amendment so important?

Key Terms:

Bill of Rights, civil liberties, civil rights, alien, Due Process Clause

Have you ever heard of Walter Barnette? Probably not. How about Toyosaburo Korematsu? Dollree Mapp? Clarence Earl Gideon? Almost certainly, the same answer: No.

Walter Barnette was a Jehovah's Witness who told his children not to salute the flag or recite the Pledge of Allegiance. Toyosaburo Korematsu was a citizen of the United States interned by the Federal Government during World War II. Dollree Mapp was fined $25 for possessing "lewd and lascivious books." And Clarence Earl Gideon was sentenced to prison for breaking into and entering a poolroom.

You will encounter their names again over the next few pages, for each of them played an important part in the building and protecting of the rights that all Americans hold.

Rights and Liberties in American Political Thought

A commitment to personal freedom is deeply rooted in America's colonial past. Over centuries, the English people had waged a continuing struggle for individual rights, and the early colonists brought a dedication to that cause with them to America.

Their commitment took root here, and it flourished. The Revolutionary War was fought to preserve and expand the rights of the individual against government. In proclaiming the independence of the new United States, the founders of this country declared:

❝We hold these truths to be self-evident, that all men are created equal, that they are endowed by their Creator with certain unalienable Rights, that among these are Life, Liberty and the pursuit of Happiness. . . . to secure these rights, Governments are instituted among Men.❞

The Framers of the Constitution repeated that justification for the existence of government in the Preamble to the Constitution.

The Constitution, as it was written at Philadelphia, contained a number of important guarantees—notably in Article I, Sections 9 and 10 and in Article III. Unlike many of the first State constitutions, however, it did not include a general listing of the rights of the people.

The outcry that that omission raised was so strong that several States ratified the Constitution only with the understanding that such a listing be immediately added. The first session of the new Congress met that demand with a series of proposed amendments. Ten of them, the **Bill of Rights**, were ratified by the States and became a part of the Constitution on December 15, 1791. Later amendments, especially the 13th and the 14th, have added to the Constitution's guarantees of personal freedom.

The Constitution guarantees many rights and liberties to the American people. However, there are several points you must understand about the overall shape of those guarantees.

Civil Rights and Civil Liberties   The distinction between civil rights and civil liberties is at best murky. Legal scholars often disagree on the matter, and the two terms are quite often used interchangeably. In general, however, **civil liberties** are protections against government. They are guarantees of the safety of persons, opinions, and property from the arbitrary acts of government. Examples of civil liberties include freedom of religion, freedom of speech and press, and the guarantees of fair trial.

The term **civil rights** is sometimes reserved for those positive acts of government that seek to make constitutional guarantees a reality for all people. From this perspective, examples of civil rights would include the prohibitions of discrimination on the basis of race or sex set out in the Civil Rights Act of 1964.

Individual Rights and the Principle of Limited Government

As you know, government in the United States is limited government. It can do only those things the sovereign people have given it the power to do. The Constitution is filled with examples of this fact. Chief among them are its many guarantees of personal freedom. Each one of those guarantees is either an outright prohibition or a restriction on the power of government to do something.

All governments have and use authority over individuals. The all-important difference between a democratic government and a dictatorial one lies in the extent of that authority. In a dictatorial regime, the government's powers are practically unlimited. The government regularly suppresses dissent, often harshly. In the United States, however, governmental authority is closely limited. As Justice Robert H. Jackson once wrote:

❝If there is any fixed star in our constitutional constellation, it is that no official, high or petty, can prescribe what shall be orthodox in politics, nationalism, religion, or any other matter of opinion or force citizens to confess by word or act their faith therein.❞[1]

Relativity of Individual Rights

The Constitution guarantees a number of rights. But no one has the right to do as he or she pleases. Rather, all persons have the right to do as they please as long as they do not infringe on the rights of others. Each person's rights are relative to the rights of every other person.

To illustrate the point, everyone in the United States has a right of free speech, but no one enjoys absolute freedom of speech. A person

---

[1]In *West Virginia Board of Education* v. *Barnette*, 1943; see page 497.

can be punished for using obscene language, or for using words in a way that causes another person to commit a crime—for example, to riot or to desert from the military. The Supreme Court dealt with the point in *ApolloMedia Corporation* v. *United States,* 1999. There, it unanimously upheld a federal law that makes it illegal for anyone to send obscene and intentionally annoying e-mail via the Internet.

Justice Oliver Wendell Holmes once put the relative nature of each person's rights this way:

❝The most stringent protection of free speech would not protect a man in falsely shouting fire in a theatre and causing a panic.❞[2]

When Rights Conflict

Sometimes different guarantees of rights come into conflict with one another. As a not uncommon example: freedom of the press versus the right to a fair trial.

In a widely noted case, Dr. Samuel Sheppard of Cleveland, Ohio, had been convicted of murdering his wife. His lengthy trial was widely covered in the national media. On appeal, Sheppard claimed that the highly sensational coverage had denied him a fair trial. The Supreme Court agreed. It rejected the free press argument, overturned his conviction, and ordered a new trial, *Sheppard* v. *Maxwell,* 1966.

Persons to Whom Rights Are Guaranteed

Most constitutional rights are extended to all persons. The Supreme Court has often held that "persons" covers **aliens**—foreign-born residents, noncitizens—as well as citizens.

Not all rights are given to aliens, however. Thus, the right to travel freely throughout the country is guaranteed to all citizens by the Constitution's two Privileges and Immunities clauses.[3] But aliens can be restricted in this regard.

▲ **Free Press Versus Fair Trial**   Dr. Samuel Sheppard (right) sought a new trial following his conviction in 1954 for the murder of his wife. Extensive media coverage of the case highlighted the conflict between the right to a fair trial and freedom of the press.

Early in World War II, all persons of Japanese descent living on the Pacific Coast were evacuated—forcibly moved—inland. Some 120,000 persons, two-thirds of them native-born American citizens, were detained in "war relocation camps." Many suffered economic and other hardships. In 1944 the Supreme Court reluctantly upheld the forced evacuation as a reasonable wartime emergency measure.[4] The relocation program has been strongly criticized over the years.

In 1988, the Federal Government admitted that the wartime relocation was unnecessary and unjust. Congress voted to pay $20,000 to each of the internees still alive. It also declared: "On behalf of the nation, the Congress apologizes."

---

[2]In *Schenck* v. *United States,* 1919; see page 506.

[3]Article IV, Section 2, Clause 1 and the 14th Amendment; see page 91. The guarantee does not extend to citizens in jail, on bail, committed to a mental institution, etc.

[4]*Korematsu* v. *United States,* 1944; however, on the same day the Court held in *Ex parte Endo* that once the loyalty of any citizen internee had been established, no restriction could be placed on that person's freedom to travel that was not legally imposed on all other citizens.

Federalism and Individual Rights

Federalism produces this complex pattern of individual rights guarantees:

1. Some rights are guaranteed against the National Government only.
2. Some rights are guaranteed against the States and their local governments only.
3. A great many rights are guaranteed against both the National Government and the States and their local governments.
4. Some rights guaranteed against a State and its local governments arise from the National Constitution while others arise from that State's own constitution.

Over time, the Supreme Court has modified (lessened) some of the impact of federalism here, especially in a long series of decisions involving the 14th Amendment's Due Process Clause. Before you can understand that complicated matter, however, you must grasp this point: The provisions of the Bill of Rights apply against the National Government only—not the States.

The Scope of the Bill of Rights   Remember, the first 10 amendments were originally intended as restrictions on the new National Government, not on the already existing States. And that is the fact of the matter today.[5]

Internment Camps   "They say: 'We did it for your protection.' When you protect somebody, you don't aim a gun at the guy you're protecting": the words of a Japanese internee.

Take the 2nd Amendment to make the point here. It reads:

> ❝A well-regulated militia being necessary to the security of a free state, the right of the people to keep and bear arms shall not be infringed.❞

As a provision in the Bill of Rights, this restriction applies only to the National Government. The States can and do limit the right to keep and bear arms. They can require the registration of all or of certain guns, forbid the carrying of concealed weapons, and so on.

The Modifying Effect of the 14th Amendment   Again, the provisions of the Bill of Rights apply against the National Government only. This does *not* mean, however, that the States can deny basic rights to the people.

In part, the States cannot do that because each of their own constitutions contains a bill of rights. Also, they cannot because of the 14th Amendment's **Due Process Clause**. It says:

> ❝No State shall . . . deprive any person of life, liberty, or property, without due process of law. . . .❞

The Supreme Court has often held that this provision means that no State can deny to any person any right that is "basic or essential to the American concept of ordered liberty."

But what rights are "basic or essential"? In a long series of cases, the Court has ruled that most of the protections set out in the Bill of Rights are also within the meaning of the 14th Amendment, and so apply against the States.

In effect, the Supreme Court has "nationalized" the Bill of Rights—by holding that most of its protections apply against the States, as a part of the meaning of the 14th Amendment's Due Process Clause.

The Court began this historic process in *Gitlow* v. *New York*, in 1925. That landmark case involved Benjamin Gitlow, a communist, who had been convicted in the State courts of criminal anarchy. On appeal, the Supreme Court

---

[5]The Supreme Court first held that the provisions of the Bill of Rights restrict only the National Government in *Barron* v. *Baltimore*, 1833.

upheld Gitlow's conviction and the State law under which he had been tried. In deciding the case, however, the Court made this crucial point: Freedom of speech and press, which the 1st Amendment says cannot be denied by the National Government, are also "among the fundamental personal rights and liberties protected by the Due Process Clause of the 14th Amendment from impairment by the States."

Soon after *Gitlow*, the Court held each of the 1st Amendment's guarantees to be covered by the 14th Amendment. It struck down State laws involving speech (*Fiske* v. *Kansas*, 1927; *Stromberg* v. *California*, 1931), the press (*Near* v. *Minnesota*, 1931), assembly and petition (*DeJonge* v. *Oregon*, 1937), and religion (*Cantwell* v. *Connecticut*, 1940). In each of those cases, the Court declared a State law unconstitutional as a violation of the 14th Amendment's Due Process Clause.

The Court extended the scope of the 14th Amendment's Due Process Clause even further in several cases in the 1960s—to the point where, today, it covers nearly all of the guarantees set out in the Bill of Rights.

Thus, in *Mapp* v. *Ohio*, 1961, the Court held that the 14th Amendment's Due Process Clause prohibits unreasonable searches and seizures by State and local authorities, and also forbids them the use of any evidence gained by such illegal actions—just as the 4th Amendment restricts the actions of federal law enforcement officers.

In later cases, the Court gave the same 14th Amendment coverage to:

—the 8th Amendment's ban on cruel and unusual punishment, in *Robinson* v. *California*, 1962;

—the 6th Amendment's right to counsel, in *Gideon* v. *Wainwright*, 1963;

—the 5th Amendment's ban on self-incrimination, in *Malloy* v. *Hogan*, 1964;

—the 6th Amendment's right of persons accused of crime to confront the witnesses against them, in *Pointer* v. *Texas*, 1965;

—the 6th Amendment's right of persons accused of crime to compel witnesses to testify in their behalf, in *Washington* v. *Texas*, 1967;

—the 6th Amendment's guarantee of a speedy trial, in *Klopfer* v. *North Carolina*, 1967;

—the 6th Amendment's guarantee of trial by jury, in *Duncan* v. *Louisiana*, 1968; and

—the 5th Amendment's ban of double jeopardy, in *Benton* v. *Maryland*, 1969.

The Role of the 9th Amendment

As you know, the Constitution contains many guarantees of individual rights. But nowhere in the Constitution—and, indeed, nowhere else—will you find a complete catalog of all of the rights held by the American people.

The little-noted 9th Amendment declares that there are rights beyond those set out in so many words in the Constitution:

“The enumeration in the Constitution of certain rights shall not be construed to deny or disparage others retained by the people.”

Over the years, the Supreme Court has found that there are, in fact, a number of other rights "retained by the people." For example: The guarantee that an accused person will not be tried on the basis of evidence unlawfully gained; and the right of a woman to have an abortion without undue interference by government.

Section 1 Review

1. Define: Bill of Rights, civil liberties, civil rights, alien, Due Process Clause

2. According to the Declaration of Independence, governments exist for what reason?

3. How do individual rights guarantees illustrate the principle of limited government?

4. In what sense are individual rights relative to each other?

5. In what sense has the Supreme Court "nationalized" most of the protections set out in the Bill of Rights?

6. For what reason is it impossible to list all of the rights guaranteed by the Constitution?

Critical Thinking

7. Identifying Assumptions (p. 19) For what reason do you think the Supreme Court found that the right to a fair trial outweighed freedom of the press in *Sheppard*? Do you agree with this decision?

★

2 Freedom of Religion

Find Out:

■ For what reason is freedom of expression vital to democracy?

■ To what extent does the Constitution prohibit government establishment of religion?

■ To what extent do Americans enjoy free exercise of religion?

Key Terms:

Establishment Clause, Free Exercise Clause

A century and a half ago, Alexis de Tocqueville came to the United States from France to observe life in the young nation. He later wrote that he had searched for the key to the greatness of America in many places: in its large harbors and deep rivers; in its fertile fields and boundless forests; in its rich mines and vast world commerce; in its public schools and institutions of learning, its democratic legislature, and matchless Constitution. Yet, not until he went into the churches of America, Tocqueville said, did he understand the genius and power of this country.

In this section, you will read about the important—and often controversial—guarantees of religious freedom found in the Constitution.

Religion and the Bill of Rights

A free society cannot possibly exist without the rights of free expression—without what has been called a "free trade in ideas."

Freedom of expression is protected in the 1st Amendment:

❝Congress shall make no law respecting an establishment of religion, or prohibiting the free exercise thereof; or abridging the freedom of speech or of the press; or the right of the people peaceably to assemble, and to petition the government for a redress of grievances.❞

And, as you know, the 14th Amendment's Due Process Clause protects these freedoms from the arbitrary acts of States or their local governments.

It is not surprising that the Bill of Rights provides first for the protection of religious liberty.

Religion has always played a large and important role in American life. Many of the early colonists, and many later immigrants, came here to escape persecution for their religious beliefs.

The 1st and 14th amendments set out two guarantees of religious freedom. They prohibit (1) an "establishment of religion" (the Establishment Clause) and (2) any arbitrary interference by government in "the free exercise" of religion (the Free Exercise Clause).[6]

Separation of Church and State

The **Establishment Clause** sets up, in Thomas Jefferson's words, "a wall of separation between church and state." But just how high is that wall? That question remains a matter of continuing and often heated controversy.

Government has done much to encourage churches and religion in this country. Thus, nearly all property of and contributions to churches and religious sects are free from federal, State, and local taxes. Most public officials take an oath of office in the name of God. Sessions of Congress and of most State legislatures and many city councils open with prayer. The nation's anthem and its coins and currency make reference to God. Clearly, the limits of the Establishment Clause cannot be described in precise terms.

The Supreme Court did not hear its first Establishment Clause case until 1947. A few earlier cases did involve government and religion, but none of them involved a direct consideration of the "wall of separation."

The most important of those earlier cases was *Pierce* v. *Society of Sisters*, 1925. There, the Court held an Oregon compulsory school attendance law unconstitutional. That law required parents to send their children to *public* schools. It was purposely intended to eliminate private, and especially parochial (church-related) schools. In destroying the law, the Court did not reach the Establishment Clause question. Instead, it found

---

[6]Also, Article VI, Section 3 provides that ". . . no religious test shall ever be required as a qualification to any office or public trust under the United States." In *Torcaso* v. *Watkins*, 1961, the Supreme Court held that the 14th Amendment puts the same restriction on the States.

the law to be an unreasonable interference with the liberty of parents to direct the upbringing of their children, and, so, in conflict with the Due Process Clause of the 14th Amendment.

The first direct ruling on the Establishment Clause came in *Everson* v. *Board of Education*, a 1947 case often called the *New Jersey School Bus Case*. There the Court upheld a State law that provided for the public, tax-supported busing of students attending any school in the State, including parochial schools. Critics attacked the law as a support of religion in that it relieved parochial schools of the need to pay for busing and so freed their money for other, including religious, purposes. The Court disagreed; it found the law to be a safety measure intended to benefit children, no matter what schools they might attend.

Since that decision, the largest number of the Court's Establishment Clause cases have involved, in one way or another, religion and education.

Released Time   "Released time" programs allow public schools to release students from school time to attend religious classes.

In *McCollum* v. *Board of Education*, 1948, the Court struck down the released time program in Champaign, Illinois, because the program used public facilities for religious purposes. In *Zorach* v. *Clauson*, 1952, however, the Court upheld New York City's released time program because that program required that the religious classes be held in private places.

Prayers and the Bible   The Court has now decided six major cases involving the recitation of prayers and the reading of the Bible in public schools.

In *Engel* v. *Vitale*, 1962, the Court outlawed the use, even on a voluntary basis, of a prayer written by the New York State Board of Regents. The "Regents' prayer" read:

66 Almighty God, we acknowledge our dependence upon Thee, and we beg Thy blessings upon us, our parents, our teachers, and our country. 99

The Supreme Court held that

66 The constitutional prohibition against laws respecting an establishment of religion must at least mean that in this country it is no part of the business of government

to compose official prayers for any group of the American people to recite as part of a religious program carried on by government. 99

The Supreme Court extended that holding in two 1963 cases. In *Abington School District* v. *Schempp*, it struck down a Pennsylvania law that required that each school day begin with readings from the Bible and a recitation of the Lord's Prayer. In *Murray* v. *Curlett*, the Court erased a similar rule in the city of Baltimore. In both cases the Court found violations of

66 the command of the 1st Amendment that the government maintain strict neutrality, neither aiding nor opposing religion. 99

Since then, the Supreme Court has found these practices to be unconstitutional:

—a Kentucky law that required that copies of the Ten Commandments be posted in all public school classrooms, *Stone* v. *Graham*, 1980.

—Alabama's "moment of silence" law, *Wallace* v. *Jaffree*, 1985. That law provided for a one-minute period of silence, for "meditation or voluntary prayer," at the beginning of each school day.

—the offering of prayer as part of a public school graduation ceremony, in a Rhode Island case, *Lee* v. *Weisman*, 1992.

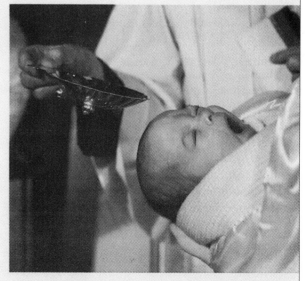

▲ **Freedom of Expression**   Which specific 1st Amendment right is being exercised by the participants in this Catholic baptismal ceremony?

▲ **Bar Mitzvah**   The right of Americans to practice religion in their own way is being exercised in this ceremony, which initiates boys into the Jewish religion.

To sum up these rulings, the Court has held that public schools cannot sponsor religious exercises. But it has not held that individuals cannot pray, when and as they choose, in schools, or in any other place. Nor has it held that students cannot study the Bible in a literary or historic frame in the schools.

These rulings have stirred strong criticism. Many individuals and groups have long proposed that the Constitution be amended to allow voluntary prayer in the public schools.

Despite the several decisions here, both organized prayer and Bible readings are found in a great many public school classrooms today.

Student Religious Groups   Congress has dealt with the matter of prayer in public schools in only one law, the Equal Access Act of 1984. That statute declares that any public high school that receives federal funds—nearly all do—must allow student religious groups to meet in the school on the same terms that it sets for other student organizations.

The Supreme Court upheld the law in *Westside Community Schools* v. *Mergens* in 1990. The case arose at Westside High School in Omaha, Nebraska, in 1985. Several students asked school officials for permission to form a Christian Club at Westside High. They said that membership in their group would be voluntary and open to all students. The Christian Club's purposes were to permit students to read and discuss the Bible, have fellowship, and pray together.

School officials denied the students' request, mainly on Establishment Clause grounds. The students then took their case to the federal courts, where they finally won their point.

In *Rosenberger* v. *University of Virginia*, 1995, the Court ruled that the university, a public school, had trampled on the free-speech rights of those students who belonged to a campus Christian group. It found that the school had violated those rights when it refused to pay for the printing of the Christian group's newspaper—even though it did pay for the printing of the publications of a wide range of other (nonreligious) student organizations.

Evolution   In *Epperson* v. *Arkansas*, 1968, the Court struck down a State law forbidding the teaching of the scientific theory of evolution. The Court held that the Constitution

❝forbids alike the preference of a religious doctrine or the prohibition of theory which is deemed antagonistic to a particular dogma. . . . The State has no legitimate interest in protecting any or all religions from views distasteful to them.❞

The Court found a similar law to be unconstitutional in 1987. In *Edwards* v. *Aguillard*, it voided a 1981 Louisiana law that provided that whenever teachers taught the theory of evolution, they also had to offer instruction in "creation science." The Court held that the law violated the Establishment Clause because its "primary purpose [was] to endorse a particular religious doctrine."

Seasonal Displays   Many public bodies sponsor celebrations of the holiday season with street

Civil Liberties: First Amendment Freedoms   **493**

How to Express Your Opinion

1. Decide what you think and why. Your opinion should be clearly thought out and supported by evidence. This may involve doing some research, both to help you form an opinion and to help support that opinion with facts.

2. Know your constitutional rights. It is important for you to know that you have a right to express your opinion on public policy matters to public officials. You should also research the rights you have with regard to the particular issue about which you are concerned; this information will help you support your opinion with facts.

3. Choose a form of expression. You can express your opinion in many ways. You must decide which form would be most effective, and how much time you can commit to the issue. Some forms of expression include: forming a group, writing letters to or calling

public officials, testifying at a school board hearing, and preparing an editorial for local newspaper, television, or radio.

4. Offer constructive suggestions. When expressing your opinion, be careful not to criticize others; show sympathy for their position and offer alternative proposals for dealing with a situation. End with a summary of your position.

5. Determine which public official can do something about the issue. For the best response to your concerns, aim your efforts at the most appropriate targets—those officials who are directly responsible for dealing with your concerns.

▲ **Interpreting Charts**   Read the steps outlined in the chart. Then explain why it is important to a democratic society for all people to express their opinions effectively.

decorations, programs in public schools, and the like. Can these publicly sponsored observances properly include expressions of religious belief?

In *Lynch* v. *Donnelly*, 1984, the Court held that the city of Pawtucket, Rhode Island, could include the Christian nativity scene in its seasonal display, which also featured nonreligious objects such as candy canes and Santa's sleigh and reindeer. But that ruling left open this question: What about a public display made up *only* of a religious symbol?

The Court faced that question in 1989. In *County of Allegheny* v. *ACLU* it held that the county's seasonal display "endorsed Christian doctrine," and so violated the 1st and 14th amendments. The county had placed a large display celebrating the birth of Jesus on the grand stairway in the county courthouse, with a banner proclaiming "Glory to God in the Highest."

At the same time, however, the Court upheld another holiday display in *Pittsburgh* v. *ACLU*. The city's display consisted of a large Christmas tree, an 18-foot menorah, and a sign declaring the city's dedication to freedom.

Chaplains in Congress and the State Legislatures   Daily sessions of both houses of Congress and most of the State legislatures begin with prayer. In Congress, and in many States, a chaplain paid with public funds offers the opening prayer.

The Supreme Court has ruled that this practice, unlike prayers in the public schools, is constitutionally permissible—in a case involving Nebraska's one-house legislature, *Marsh* v. *Chambers*, 1983. The Court rested its distinction between school prayers and legislative prayers on two points. First, prayers have been offered in the nation's legislative bodies "from colonial times through the founding of the Republic and ever since." Second, legislators, unlike schoolchildren, are not "susceptible to religious indoctrination or peer pressure."

Tax Exemptions   Every State exempts property of religious organizations used for religious purposes from State and local taxation. The Supreme Court has upheld this practice, *Walz* v. *New York City Tax Commission*, 1970.

▲ **Separation of Church and State**   Parochial, or religion-affiliated, schools are entitled to federal aid for only secular, or nonreligious, purposes.

A citizen named Walz had challenged the exemption of houses of worship from local property taxes. He argued that these exemptions made property tax bills higher than they would otherwise be, and that the exemptions amounted to a public support of religion.

The Court turned down Walz's plea. It found that those exemptions are evidence only of a State's "benevolent neutrality" toward religion, not support of it. Said the Court, the exemptions "create only a minimal and remote," and therefore permissible, "involvement between church and state."

But the Court has ruled that church-related schools that discriminate on the basis of race can be denied a tax-exempt status under federal law, *Bob Jones University* v. *United States* and *Goldsboro Christian Schools* v. *United States,* 1983. The schools involved in these 1983 cases argued that their racial policies reflected their sincerely held religious beliefs. The Supreme Court granted that point. It said, nevertheless, that the nation's interest in eradicating racial discrimination in education "substantially outweighs whatever burden denial of tax benefits places on [those schools in the] exercise of their religious beliefs."

State Aid to Parochial Schools   Most recent Establishment Clause cases have centered on this highly controversial question: What forms of State aid to parochial schools are constitutional?

Several States give help to private schools—including those related to church organizations—for transportation, textbooks, laboratory equipment, standardized testing, and much else.

Those who support that aid argue that parochial schools enroll large numbers of students who would otherwise have to be educated at public expense. They also point to the fact that the Supreme Court has held that parents have a legal right to send their children to those schools (*Pierce* v. *Society of Sisters*). To give that right real meaning, they say, the State must give some aid to parochial schools—to relieve parents of some of the double burden they carry because they must pay taxes to support the public schools their children do not attend. Many advocates also insist that schools run by religious organizations pose no real church-state problems, because, they say, those schools devote most of their time to secular (nonreligious) subjects rather than to sectarian (religious) ones.

Opponents of aid to parochial schools argue that those parents who choose to send children to parochial schools should accept the financial consequences of that choice. Many of them also insist that it is impossible to draw clear lines between secular and sectarian courses in parochial schools. They say that religious beliefs are bound to have an effect on the teaching of nonreligious subjects in church-run schools.

The *Lemon* Test   The Supreme Court has been picking its way through cases involving State aid laws for several years. In most of them, it now applies a three-pronged standard, the *Lemon* test: (1) The purpose of the aid must be clearly secular, not religious, (2) its primary effect must neither advance nor inhibit religion, and (3) it must avoid an "excessive entanglement of government with religion."

The test stems from *Lemon* v. *Kurtzman,* 1971. There, the Supreme Court held that the Establishment Clause is designed to prevent three main evils: "sponsorship, financial support, and active involvement of the sovereign in religious activity."

In *Lemon*, the Court struck down a Pennsylvania law that provided for reimbursements—financial payments—to private schools to cover their costs for teachers' salaries, textbooks, and other teaching materials in nonreligious courses.

The Court held that the State program was of direct benefit to the parochial schools, and so to the churches sponsoring them. It also found that the program required such close State supervision that it produced an excessive entanglement of government with religion.

A number of State aid programs have passed the *Lemon* test over the past 20 years, and others have failed it. Thus, for example, the Court has allowed the use of public funds to loan textbooks to students in parochial schools, in a case from Pennsylvania, *Meek* v. *Pittinger*, 1975. And it has held that a State can pay church-related schools what it costs them to administer the State's standardized tests, in a New York case, *Committee for Public Education and Religious Liberty* v. *Regan*, 1980. Both textbooks and standardized tests can be evaluated to be sure that they do not promote religion.

But public funds cannot be used to pay for such things as field trips for students at parochial schools, *Wolman* v. *Walter*, 1977. In that Ohio case, the Court said that field trips managed by parochial school teachers present "an unacceptable risk of fostering of religion." Nor can tax monies be used to pay any part of the salaries of parochial school teachers, including those who teach only secular courses, *Grand Rapids School District* v. *Ball*, 1985. The Court said in that Michigan case that while the contents of a book can be checked easily, the way a teacher handles a course cannot.[7]

The Supreme Court struck down a New York law that provided for direct cash payments to parents to reimburse them for the tuition they paid to schools operated by religious organizations, *Committee for Public Education* v. *Nyquist*, 1973. But the Court has upheld a Minnesota tax law that accomplishes the same end, *Mueller* v. *Allen*, 1983. That law gives parents a State income tax deduction for the costs of tuition, textbooks, and transportation. Parents can claim the tax break no matter what schools their children attend. Most public school parents pay little or nothing for these items. Hence, the law is of particular benefit to parents with children in private, mostly parochial, schools. The Court found that the law meets the *Lemon* test, and it also leaned on this point: The deduction is available to all parents with children in school, and they are free to decide which type of school their children attend.

In *Bowen* v. *Kendrick*, 1988, the Court took a more tolerant view of government aid to religion than it has in most recent cases. There, it upheld a controversial federal statute, the Adolescent Family Life Act of 1981. That law provides for grants to both public and private agencies dealing with the problems of adolescent sex and pregnancy. Some of the grants were made to religious groups that oppose abortion, prompting the argument that those groups use federal money to teach religious doctrine. However, the Supreme Court found the law's purpose—curbing "the social and economic problems caused by teenage sexuality, pregnancy, and parenthood"—to be a legitimate one. That some grants pay for counseling that "happens to coincide with the religious views" of some groups does not by itself mean that the federal funds are being used with "a primary effect of advancing religion."

And in a 1993 case from Arizona, *Zobrest* v. *Catalina Foothills School District,* the Court said that the use of public money to provide an interpreter for a deaf student who attends a Catholic high school does not violate the Establishment Clause. The Constitution, said the Court, does not lay down an absolute barrier to the placing of a public employee in a religious school.

But in *Board of Education of Kiryas Joel* v. *Grumet*, 1994, the Court struck down a New York law creating a school district purposely designed to benefit handicapped children in a tight-knit community of Hasidic Jews.

---

[7]The Court has taken a markedly different view toward public aid to church-related colleges and universities. Thus, in *Tilton* v. *Richardson*, 1971, it upheld federal grants for the construction of academic buildings to be used for nonreligious purposes at such institutions. The Court could find no excessive entanglement in these "one-shot" grants.

▲ **Free Exercise**   This clause protects religious freedom, but the law can require Hare Krishnas to limit distribution of their literature.

The Free Exercise of Religion

The second part of the constitutional guarantee of religious freedom is set out in the Constitution's **Free Exercise Clause**. That clause guarantees to each person the right to believe whatever that person chooses to believe in matters of religion. That right is protected by the 1st and the 14th amendments.

No person has an absolute right to act as he or she chooses, however. The Free Exercise Clause does *not* give one the right to violate the criminal laws, offend public morals, or otherwise threaten the health, welfare, or safety of the community.

The Supreme Court laid down the basic shape of the Free Exercise Clause in the first case it heard on the point, *Reynolds* v. *United States*, 1879. Reynolds, a Mormon, had two wives. That practice—polygamy—was allowed by the teachings of his church; but it was prohibited by a federal law banning the practice in any territory of the United States.

Reynolds was tried and convicted under the law. On appeal, he argued that the law violated his constitutional right to the free exercise of his religious beliefs. The Supreme Court disagreed, however. It held that the 1st Amendment does not forbid Congress the power to punish those actions that are "violations of social duties or subversive of good order." To hold otherwise, said the Court

❝ would be to make the professed doctrines of religious belief superior to the law of the land, and in effect permit every citizen to become a law unto himself. ❞

Over the years, the Court has approved many regulations of human conduct in the face of free exercise challenges. For example, it has upheld laws that require the vaccination of school children, *Jacobson* v. *Massachusetts*, 1905; that forbid the use of poisonous snakes in religious rites, *Bunn* v. *North Carolina*, 1949; and so-called blue laws that require businesses to be closed on Sundays, *McGowan* v. *Maryland*, 1961.

A State can require religious groups to have a permit to hold a parade on the public streets, *Cox* v. *New Hampshire*, 1941; and organizations that enlist children to sell religious literature must obey child labor laws, *Prince* v. *Massachusetts*, 1944. The Federal Government can draft those who have religious objections to military service, *Welsh* v. *United States*, 1970.[8] The Air Force can forbid an Orthodox Jew the right to wear his yarmulke—skull cap—while on active duty, *Goldman* v. *Weinberger*, 1986. The U.S. Forest Service can allow private companies to build roads and cut timber in national forests that Native Americans have traditionally used for religious purposes, *Lyng* v. *Northwest Indian Cemetery Protective Association*, 1988. And a State can deny unemployment benefits to a man fired by a private drug counseling group because he used peyote in violation of the State's drug laws—even though he ingested the hallucinogenic drug as part of a ceremony of his Native American Church, *Oregon* v. *Smith*, 1990.

But, over time, the Court has also found many actions by governments to be contrary to

---

[8]The Court has made this ruling many times. *Welsh* is the leading case from the Vietnam War period. There, the Court held that the only persons who could not be drafted were those "whose consciences . . . would give them no rest if they allowed themselves to become part of an instrument of war."

the Free Exercise guarantee. The Court did so for the first time in one of the landmark Due Process cases cited earlier in this chapter, *Cantwell* v. *Connecticut*, 1940. There, the Court struck down a law requiring a license before any person could solicit money for a religious cause.

There are many other cases in that line. Thus, Amish children cannot be forced to attend school beyond the 8th grade, because that sect's centuries-old "self-sufficient agrarian lifestyle essential to their religious faith is threatened by modern education," *Wisconsin* v. *Yoder*, 1972. But the Amish, who take care of their own people, must pay social security taxes, as all other employers do, *United States* v. *Lee*, 1982.

A State cannot forbid ministers to hold elected public offices, *McDaniel* v. *Paty*, 1978. Nor can it deny unemployment compensation benefits to a worker who quit a job because it involved some conflict with his or her religious beliefs, *Sherbert* v. *Verner*, 1963; *Thomas* v. *Indiana*, 1981; *Hobbie* v. *Florida*, 1987; *Frazee* v. *Illinois*, 1989.[9]

The Court has often held that "only those beliefs rooted in religion are protected by the Free Exercise Clause" (*Sherbert* v. *Verner*, 1963). But what beliefs are those "rooted in religion"? Clearly, religions that seem strange or even bizarre to most Americans are as entitled to constitutional protection as are the more traditional ones. To that point, the High Court recently struck down a Florida city's ordinance that outlawed animal sacrifices as part of any church services, *Lukumi Babalu Aye* v. *City of Hialeah*, 1993.

---

[9]Typically, State unemployment compensation laws bar such benefits to those who leave jobs voluntarily and "without good cause in connection with the work." Some bar benefits to those who are fired. In *Sherbert*, to take one example of these cases, a Seventh Day Adventist lost her job in a South Carolina textile mill when she refused to work on Saturdays, her Sabbath. In *Thomas*, a Jehovah's Witness who worked for a machinery company quit after he was transferred from one section of the company that was being closed down to another where gun turrets for tanks were made. He left because, he said, his religious beliefs would not allow him to work on war materials. Note this distinction between these two cases and *Oregon* v. *Smith*, 1990: Smith's conduct involved the violation of a State law.

The Jehovah's Witnesses have carried several important religious freedom cases to the Supreme Court. Perhaps the stormiest of the controversies that sect has stirred arose out of the Witnesses' refusal to salute the flag.

The Witnesses refuse to salute the flag because they see such conduct as a violation of the Bible's commandment against idolatry. In *Minersville School District* v. *Gobitis*, 1940, the Court upheld a Pennsylvania school board regulation requiring students to salute the flag at the beginning of each school day. Gobitis instructed his children not to do so, and the school expelled them. He went to court, basing his case on the constitutional guarantee. He finally lost in the Supreme Court, however. The Court declared that the board's rule was not an infringement of religious liberty. Rather, the Court held that the rule was a lawful attempt to promote patriotism and national unity.

Three years later, the Court reversed that decision. In *West Virginia Board of Education* v. *Barnette*, 1943, it held a compulsory flag-salute law unconstitutional. Justice Robert H. Jackson's words on page 486 are from the Court's powerful opinion in that case. So are these:

> ❝To believe that patriotism will not flourish if patriotic ceremonies are voluntary and spontaneous instead of a compulsory routine is to make an unflattering estimate of the appeal of our institutions to free minds.❞

Section 2 Review

1. **Define:** Establishment Clause, Free Exercise Clause
2. What does it mean to say that it is unclear how high the wall between church and state is?
3. Over what subjects have most Establishment Clause cases been fought?
4. What is the basic shape of the rights guaranteed by the Free Exercise Clause?

Critical Thinking

5. **Identifying Central Issues** (p. 19) Some observers feel that Supreme Court decisions such as *Engel* v. *Vitale* and *Murray* v. *Curlett* limit people's free exercise of religion. Do you agree or disagree?

★

Close Up on Key Issues

Can Public Schools Ban Political Protests?

Tinker v. *Des Moines Independent School District,* 1969

In December of 1965, a group of adults and students in Des Moines, Iowa, met to express their opposition to American involvement in the war in Vietnam. They decided to publicize their views in two ways: (1) by wearing black armbands during the holiday season, and (2) by fasting on two days, December 16 and December 31.

The principals of the Des Moines schools soon became aware of the protesters' plans. They met on December 14 and announced this policy: Any student wearing an armband to school would be asked to remove it. If the student refused, he or she would be suspended. Any student suspended for wearing an armband could not return to school until he or she appeared without that symbol.

On December 16, Mary Beth and Christopher Tinker wore black armbands to school. The next day their brother John and some other students did so, too. All were suspended and sent home. They did not return to school until after New Year's Day—that is, until after the end of the period for which they had planned their protest.

The Tinkers and several other students, acting through their parents, went to court. They asked the federal district court in Iowa to issue an injunction—a court order to prevent enforcement of the school district's ban on the wearing of armbands.

The federal district court refused to issue that order, and the federal court of appeals affirmed that decision. The Tinkers, supported by the American Civil Liberties Union, then took their case to the United States Supreme Court.

Review the following evidence and arguments presented to the Supreme Court:

Arguments for Des Moines School District

1. No one has an absolute right to freedom of expression. Reasonable limits may be placed on that right.
2. The ban on armbands was put in place to avoid disruption of school discipline.
3. The orderly atmosphere of the classroom, not the right to wear an armband, is entitled to constitutional protection.
4. School is not the appropriate place for a political demonstration. Controversies should be dealt with in classroom discussions, not by distracting protests.

Arguments for Tinker

1. The school district did not ban all political symbols, only black armbands. Such a selective ban is unconstitutional.
2. The students who wore armbands did not in fact disrupt school discipline.
3. The armbands were worn as symbols of the students' views and so were entitled to constitutional protection.
4. Students are as entitled to respect for their rights in school as in any other place.

Getting Involved

1. **Identify** the constitutional grounds upon which each side based its arguments.
2. **Debate** the opposing viewpoints presented in this case.
3. **Predict** how you think the Supreme Court ruled in this case and why. Then refer to page 769 of the Supreme Court Glossary to read about the decision. What do you think of the Court's decision?

3 Freedom of Speech and Press

Find Out:
- What is the breadth of the guarantees of free speech and free press?
- What are the limits on the guarantees of free speech and free press?

Key Terms:
libel, slander, shield law, symbolic speech, picketing

Think about this children's verse for a moment: "Sticks and stones may break my bones, but names will never hurt me." That rhyme says, in effect, that acts and words are separate things and that acts can do harm but words cannot.

Is that really true? Certainly not. You know that words can and do have consequences—sometimes powerful consequences. Words, spoken or written, can make you happy, sad, bored, informed, or entertained. They can also expose you to danger, deny you a job, or lead to other serious consequences.

In this section you will read about the Constitution's protection of the vitally important freedom of expression and how the meaning of those freedoms has developed over the course of American history.

Democracy and Freedom of Expression

The 1st and 14th amendments' protections of free speech and a free press serve two fundamentally important purposes:

1. To guarantee to each person a right of free expression—in the spoken and the written word, and by all other means of communication, as well.
2. To ensure to all persons a full, wide-ranging discussion of public affairs.

That is, the 1st and 14th amendments give to all people the right to have their say and to hear what others have to say. Most often, people think of these great freedoms in terms of that first purpose. The second one is just as important, however.

The American system of government depends on the ability of the people to make sound, reasoned judgments on matters of public concern. Clearly, people can best make such judgments when they know all of the facts in a given matter, *and* can hear all the available interpretations of those facts.

Justice Oliver Wendell Holmes once underscored the importance of that second purpose in these words:

    " Persecution for the expression of opinions seems to me perfectly logical. If you have no doubt of your premises and want a certain result with all your heart, you naturally express your wishes in law and sweep away all opposition. . . . But when men have realized that time has upset many fighting faiths, they may come to believe even more than they believe the very foundations of their own conduct that the ultimate good desired is better reached by free trade in ideas—that the best test of truth is the power of the thought to get itself accepted in the competition of the market. . . . That at any rate is the theory of our Constitution."[10]

As you examine the Constitution's 1st and 14th amendments here, keep two other key points in mind:

First, the guarantees of free speech and press are intended to protect the expression of unpopular views. That is because the opinions of the majority need, after all, little or no constitutional protection.

Second, some forms of expression are not protected by the Constitution. No person has an unbridled right of free speech or free press. Many reasonable restrictions can be placed on those rights.

You will see a number of illustrations of this point over the next several pages. For now, recall Justice Holmes's comment about the right to shout "Fire!" in a crowded theater. Or, note this restriction: No person has the right to libel or slander another. **Libel** is the false and malicious use of printed words; **slander** is such use of spoken words. Similarly, the law prohibits the use of

---

[10]Dissenting in *Abrams* v. *United States*, 1919.

obscene words, the printing and distributing of obscene materials, and false advertising.[11]

Obscenity

The 1st and 14th amendments do not protect obscenity, but in recent years the Court has had to wrestle several times with these questions: What language in printed matter, films, and other materials are, in fact, obscene? What restrictions can be properly placed on such materials?[12]

Today, the leading case is *Miller* v. *California*, 1973. There the Court laid down a three-part test to determine what material is obscene and what is not.

A book, film, recording, or other piece of material is legally obscene if (1) "the average person applying contemporary [local] community standards" finds that the work, taken as a whole, "appeals to the prurient interest"—that is, tends to excite lust; (2) "the work depicts or describes, in a patently offensive way," a form of sexual conduct specifically dealt with in an antiobscenity law; and (3) "the work, taken as a whole, lacks serious literary, artistic, political, or scientific value."

▲ **Freedoms of Speech and Assembly**   The 1st and 14th amendments guarantee freedom of expression to everyone in this country.

A sampling of Supreme Court decisions involving local attempts to regulate so-called adult book stores and similar places shows how thorny the problem can be. Most of what those stores sell cannot be mailed, sent across State lines, or imported—at least not legally. Still, those shops are usually well-stocked.

The 1st and 14th amendments do not prevent a city from regulating the location of "adult entertainment establishments," *Young* v. *American Mini Theaters,* 1976. A city can decide to bar the location of such places within 1,000 feet of a residential zone, church, park, or school, *City of Renton* v. *Playtimes Theaters, Inc.,* 1986. But a city cannot prohibit live entertainment in any and all commercial establishments, *Schad* v. *Borough of Mount Ephraim,* 1981 (a case that involved nude dancing in adult book stores).

The Supreme Court has upheld a State law that makes it a crime to possess or view child pornography, including films. In *Osborne* v. *Ohio,* 1990, the Court ruled that the State has a compelling interest in protecting the physical and the psychological well-being of minors and in the destruction of the market in which they are exploited.

In *Sable Communications* v. *FCC,* 1989, the Court struck down a federal statute aimed at

---

[11]Libel and slander involve the use of words, maliciously—with vicious purpose—to injure a person's character or reputation or expose that person to public contempt, ridicule, or hatred. Truth is generally an absolute defense against a libel or slander claim. The law is less protective of public officials, however. In *New York Times* v. *Sullivan,* 1964, the Supreme Court held that public officials cannot recover damages for a published criticism, even if exaggerated or false, unless "the statement was made with actual malice—that is with knowledge that it was false or with reckless disregard of whether it was false or not." Several later decisions have extended that ruling to cover "public figures" and even private individuals who have become involved in newsworthy events. Those public figures cannot win damages even for an "intentional infliction of emotional distress," *Hustler Magazine* v. *Falwell,* 1988.

[12]Congress passed the first of a series of laws to keep obscene matter from the mails in 1872. The current law was upheld by the Court in *Roth* v. *United States,* 1957. The law excludes "every obscene, lewd, lascivious, or filthy" piece of material. The Court found the law a proper exercise of the postal power (Article I, Section 8, Clause 7), and so not prohibited by the 1st Amendment. *Roth* marked the Court's first attempt to find an adequate definition of obscenity.

"dial-a-porn" services. That law made it a crime to use a telephone to send any "obscene or indecent" message for commerical purpose. A unanimous Court held that Congress can properly outlaw "obscene" calls, but it cannot bar those calls that are "merely indecent."

The High Court's most recent case involving obscenity and the 1st Amendment was decided in 1998. In *National Endowment for the Arts* v. *Finley,* the Court found 8 to 1 that the 1st Amendment does not prevent the NEA from using standards of decency when it decides which artists should (or should not) receive federal grants to support their work.

Prior Restraint

The Constitution allows government to punish some utterances, *after* they are made. But, with almost no exceptions, government cannot place any prior restraint on spoken or written words. That is, except in the most extreme situations, government cannot curb ideas before they are expressed.

Near v. *Minnesota*, 1931, is a leading case in point. The Supreme Court struck down a State law that prohibited the publication of any "malicious, scandalous, and defamatory" periodical. Acting under that law, a local court had issued an order forbidding the publication of the *Saturday Press*. The Minneapolis paper had printed several articles charging public corruption and attacking "grafters" and "Jewish gangsters." The Court held that the guarantee of a free press does not allow a prior restraint on publication, except in such extreme cases as wartime, or when a publication is obscene or incites readers to violence. The Court said that even "miscreant purveyors of scandal" and anti-Semitism have a constitutional protection against prior restraint.

The Constitution does not forbid any and all forms of prior censorship, but "a prior restraint on expression comes to this Court with a 'heavy presumption' against its constitutionality," *Nebraska Press Association* v. *Stuart*, 1976.[15] The

Court has used that general rule several times— for example, in the famous Pentagon Papers Case, *New York Times* v. *United States*, 1971.

In that case, several newspapers had obtained copies of a set of classified documents. The documents, widely known as the Pentagon Papers, were officially titled *History of U.S. Decision-Making Process on Viet Nam Policy.* They had been stolen from the Defense Department and then leaked to the press. The government sought a court order to bar their publication, but the Court held that the government had not shown that printing the documents would endanger the nation's security, and so had not overcome the "heavy presumption" against prior censorship.

The few prior restraints the Court has approved include regulations prohibiting the distribution of political literature on military bases without the approval of military authorities, *Greer* v. *Spock*, 1976; a CIA rule that agents must agree never to publish anything about the agency without the CIA's permission, *Snepp* v. *United States*, 1980; a federal prison rule that allows officials to prevent an inmate from receiving publications considered "detrimental to the security, good order, or discipline" of the prison, *Thornburgh* v. *Abbott*, 1989.

The Court has recently said that public school officials have a broad power to censor school newspapers, plays, and other "school-sponsored expressive activities." In *Hazelwood School District* v. *Kuhlmeier*, 1988, it held that educators can exercise "editorial control over the style and content of student speech in school-sponsored expressive activities so long as their actions are reasonably related to legitimate pedagogical [teaching] concerns."

Confidentiality

Can news reporters be forced to testify before a grand jury, in court, or before a legislative committee, and there be required to name their sources and reveal other confidential information?

Many reporters and news organizations insist that they must have the right to refuse to testify, the right to protect their sources. They argue that without this right they cannot assure confidentiality to their sources. Unless they can

---

[15]In this case a judge had ordered the media not to report certain details of a murder trial. The Court held the judge's gag order to be unconstitutional.

▲   **Federally Regulated**   Television and radio are subject to more federal regulation than other media, on the grounds that the airwaves they use are public property.

do that, reporters say, many sources will not give them information they need to keep the public informed.

Both State and federal courts have generally rejected the news media argument. In recent years several reporters have refused to obey court orders directing them to give information. As a consequence, a number of reporters have gone to jail, testifying to the importance of these issues.

In the leading case, *Branzburg* v. *Hayes*, 1972, the Supreme Court held that reporters, "like other citizens, [must] respond to relevant questions put to them in the course of a valid grand jury investigation or criminal trial." If the media are to receive any special exemptions, said the Court, the exemptions must come from Congress and the State legislatures.

To date, Congress has not acted on the Court's suggestion. However, some 30 States have passed so-called **shield laws**. These laws

give reporters some protection against having to disclose their sources or reveal other confidential information in legal proceedings in those States.

Motion Pictures

The Supreme Court took its first look at motion pictures early in the history of the movie industry. In 1915, in *Mutual Film Corporation* v. *Ohio*, the Court upheld a State law that barred the showing of any film that was not of a "moral, educational, or harmless and amusing character." The Court declared that "the exhibition of moving pictures is a business, pure and simple," and "not . . . part of the press of the country." With that decision, nearly every State and thousands of communities set up movie review—really movie censorship—programs.

The Court reversed itself in 1952, however. In *Burstyn* v. *Wilson*, a New York censorship case, it found that "liberty of expression by means of motion pictures is guaranteed by the 1st and 14th amendments."

Movie censorship is not necessarily unconstitutional, however. A State or local government can ban an obscene film, but only under a law that provides for a prompt judicial hearing. At that hearing that government must show that the picture in question is in fact obscene, *Teitel Film Corporation* v. *Cusack*, 1968.

Very few of the once common local movie review boards still exist. Most movie-goers now depend on the film industry's own rating system and on the comments of movie critics on television and in newspapers and magazines.

Radio and Television

Both radio and television broadcasting are subject to extensive federal regulation. Most of this regulation is based on the often-amended Federal Communications Act of 1934, which is administered by the Federal Communications Commission. As the Supreme Court has described the situation: "Of all forms of communication, it is broadcasting that has received the most limited 1st Amendment protection," *Red Lion Broadcasting Co.* v. *FCC*, 1969.

The Court has several times upheld this wide-ranging federal regulation as a proper exercise of the commerce power. Unlike newspapers and other print media, radio and television use the public's property—the public airwaves—to broadcast their materials. They have no right to do so without the public's permission—that is, without a proper license, *National Broadcasting Co.* v. *United States*, 1943.

The Court has regularly rejected the argument that the 1st Amendment prohibits such regulations. Instead, it has taken the view that the regulation implements the constitutional guarantee. It has held that there is no "unabridgeable 1st Amendment right to broadcast comparable to the right of every individual to speak, write, or publish." However, "this is not to say that the 1st Amendment is irrelevant to broadcasting. But . . . it is the right of the viewers and the listeners, not the right of the broadcasters, which is paramount."[16]

Congress has forbidden the FCC to censor the content of programs before they are broadcast. But the FCC can prohibit the use of indecent language, and it can take violations of the ban into account when a station applies for the renewal of its operating license, *FCC* v. *Pacifica Foundation*, 1978. The FCC has refused applications for renewal of licenses due to past use of objectionable practices. And Congress itself cannot prohibit the broadcasting of editorials by public radio and television stations, *FCC* v. *League of Women Voters of California*, 1984.

In several recent decisions, the Supreme Court has given the growing cable television industry broader 1st Amendment freedoms than those enjoyed by traditional television. A 1987 case, *Wilkinson* v. *Jones*, is fairly typical. There, the Court held that the States cannot regulate "indecent" cable programming. It reached that

---

[16]*Red Lion Broadcasting Co.* v. *FCC*, 1969, in which the Court upheld the fairness doctrine, an FCC rule in effect until its repeal by the commission in 1987. The rule provided that broadcasters had to air opposing viewpoints, not just one side, on important issues.

The FCC still enforces the equal time doctrine, set out in the Communications Act. The law's equal time provision means that if, for example, a television network makes air time available to one candidate for a public office, it must offer equal time to all other candidates for that office. Most of those who have opposed the fairness doctrine also oppose this rule and urge Congress to repeal it.

VOICES *on Government*

To the Press, on Freedom of the Press

Mario M. Cuomo, governor of New York, 1983–1995

❝The press . . . has the power to inform, but that implies the power to distort. You have the power to instruct, but that implies the power to mislead. . . . You can lead our society toward a more mature and discriminating understanding of the process by which we choose our leaders, make our rules, and construct our values. Or you can encourage people to despise our systems and avoid participating in them. You can teach our children a taste for violence, encourage a fascination with perversity and inflicted pain. Or you can show them a beauty they have not known. . . . You can make us all wiser, fuller, surer, sweeter than we are. Or you can do less. And worse. And one of the miracles of this democracy is that you are free to make all the choices.❞

decision by striking down a Utah law that prohibited the cable broadcast of any sexually explicit or other "indecent material" between the hours of 7 A.M. and midnight.

Symbolic Speech

People also communicate ideas by conduct—by the way a person does some particular thing. Thus, a person can say something with a facial expression or a shrug of the shoulders, or by carrying a sign or wearing an arm band. This mode of expression—expression by conduct—is known as **symbolic speech**.

Clearly, not all conduct amounts to symbolic speech. If it did, murder or robbery or any other crime could be excused on grounds that the person who committed the act meant to say something by doing so.

But, just as clearly, some conduct does express opinion. Take picketing in a labor dispute as an example. **Picketing** involves patrolling of a business site by workers who are on strike. By their conduct, picketers attempt to inform the public of the controversy, and to persuade others not to deal with the firm involved. Picketing is, then, a form of expression. If peaceful, it is protected by the 1st and 14th amendments.[17]

Generally, the Supreme Court has been sympathetic to the symbolic speech argument. But it has not given blanket 1st Amendment protection to that means of expression. As a sampling, note these cases:

United States v. *O'Brien*, 1968, involved four young men who had burned their draft cards to protest the war in Vietnam. A court convicted them of violating a federal law that makes that act a crime. O'Brien appealed, arguing that the 1st Amendment protects "all modes of communication of ideas by conduct." The Supreme Court disagreed. Said the Court: "We cannot accept the view that an apparently limitless variety of conduct can be labeled 'speech' whenever the person engaging in the conduct intends thereby to express an idea."

The Court also held that acts of dissent by conduct can be punished if: (1) the object of the protest—here, the war and the draft—is within the constitutional powers of the government; (2) whatever restriction is placed on expression is no greater than necessary in the circumstances; and (3) the government's real interest in the matter is not to squelch dissent.

Using that test, the court has denied some claims of symbolic speech. Thus, for example, it

held that a policeman does not have a constitutional right to protest a department dress code by growing long hair—even if he believes that to be "a means of expressing his attitude and lifestyle"—because a government has a reasonable stake in requiring a "similarity of garb and appearance" among its police officers, *Kelley* v. *Johnson*, 1976. And the Court upheld a National Park Service regulation under which a group of protesters was not allowed to sleep overnight in Lafayette Park near the White House, *Clark* v. *Community for Creative Non-Violence*, 1984.

Tinker v. *Des Moines School District*, 1969, on the other hand, is one of several cases in which the Court has come down on the side of symbolic speech. A small group of students in the Des Moines public schools had worn black armbands to publicize their opposition to the war in Vietnam. The school suspended them for it. The Court ruled that school officials had overstepped their authority and violated the Constitution. Said the Court: "It can hardly be argued that either students or teachers shed their constitutional rights to freedom of speech or expression at the schoolhouse gate."[18]

Campaign contributions are "a symbolic expression of support" for candidates, so the making of those contributions is entitled to constitutional protection, *Buckley* v. *Valeo*, 1976. Both federal and State laws regulate campaign contributions, but the fact that in politics "money is speech" greatly complicates that whole matter of campaign finance regulation (see Chapter 7).

Burning the American flag as an act of political protest is expressive conduct protected by the 1st and 14th amendments—so a sharply divided Court has twice held. In *Texas* v. *Johnson*, 1989, a 5–4 majority ruled that State authorities had violated a protester's rights when they prosecuted him under a law that forbids the "desecration of a venerated object." Johnson had set fire to

---

[17]The leading case on the point is *Thornhill* v. *Alabama*, 1940. There, the Court struck down a State law that made it a crime for one to loiter about or picket a place of business in order to influence others not to trade or work there. But picketing that is "set in a background of violence" can be prevented. Even peaceful picketing can be restricted if it is conducted for some illegal purpose, for example, to force someone to do something that is itself illegal.

[18]Do not read too much into this, however, for the Court added, it "has repeatedly affirmed the comprehensive authority of the States and of school authorities, consistent with fundamental constitutional safeguards, to prescribe and control conduct in the schools." The fact that in *Tinker* the students' conduct did not produce any substantial disruption of normal school activities was an important factor in the Court's decision.

an American flag during an anti-Reagan demonstration at the Republican National Convention in Dallas in 1984. Said the Court:

> *If there is a bedrock principle underlying the 1st Amendment, it is that the government may not prohibit the expression of an idea simply because society finds the idea itself offensive. . . . We do not consecrate the flag by punishing its desecration, for in doing so we dilute the freedom that this cherished emblem represents.*

The Court's decision in *Johnson* set off a firestorm of criticism around the country and prompted Congress to pass the Flag Protection Act of 1989. It, too, was struck down by the Court, 5 to 4, in *United States* v. *Eichman* in 1990—on the same grounds as those set out a year earlier in *Johnson*.

Commercial Speech

Commercial speech is speech for business purposes—mostly, advertising. Until fairly recently, it was generally thought that the 1st and 14th amendments did not protect such speech. In *Bigelow* v. *Virginia*, 1975, however, the Supreme Court held unconstitutional a State law that prohibited the newspaper advertising of abortion services. And in 1976 it struck down another Virginia law forbidding the advertisement of prescription drug prices, *Virginia State Board of Pharmacy* v. *Virginia Citizens Consumer Council.*

Not all commercial speech is protected, however. Thus, government can and does prohibit false and misleading advertisements, and the advertising of illegal goods or services.

In fact, government can even forbid advertising that is neither false nor misleading. Thus, in 1970 Congress banned cigarette ads on radio and television, and in 1986 it extended the ban to include chewing tobacco and snuff. The tobacco industry did not challenge the constitutionality of either of those actions.

In most of its commercial speech cases the Court has struck down some arbitrary restriction on advertising. Thus, in *44 Liquormart, Inc.* v. *Rhode Island*, 1996, the Court voided a State law that prohibited ads in which liquor prices were listed. The Court's decision was unanimous—and it amounted to the High Court's strongest statement against the regulation

of commercial speech since its landmark ruling in *Bigelow* in 1975.

The most recent commercial speech case involved ads for casino gambling. In *Greater New Orleans Broadcasting Association* v. *United States,* 1999, the Court struck down a federal law that barred those places from advertising by radio or on television.

One of the Court's first commercial speech cases had a peculiar twist to it. In *Wooley* v. *Maynard*, 1977, the Court held that a State cannot force its citizens to act as "mobile billboards"— not, at least, when the words used conflict with their religious or moral beliefs. The Maynards, who were Jehovah's Witnesses, objected to the New Hampshire State motto on their automobile license plates. The words *Live Free or Die* clashed with their belief in everlasting life, and so they covered those words with tape. For this, Maynard was arrested three times. On appeal, the Supreme Court sided with Maynard.

Section 3 Review

1. **Define:** libel, slander, shield law, symbolic speech, picketing
2. For what reason does the Constitution guarantee freedom of expression?
3. The rights of free speech and press are especially intended to protect the expression of what views?
4. When can government impose a prior restraint on expression?
5. Does the Constitution protect obscenity?
6. What special protections of freedom of expression do many news reporters enjoy?
7. What is the extent of government regulation of movies, radio, and television?
8. What are the constitutional protections of (a) symbolic speech? (b) commercial speech?

Critical Thinking

9. **Identifying Central Issues** (p. 19) Is American society better or worse off for allowing even those who promote racist and sexist views to express their beliefs?

★

4 Freedom of Expression and National Security

Find Out:

■ How do protection of civil rights and the demands of national security conflict?

■ How has government tried to settle that conflict?

Key Terms:

espionage, sabotage, treason, sedition

For several years in the early 1950s, Senator Joseph McCarthy waged an intense battle to rid the United States Government of what he claimed was communist infiltration. McCarthy found no real evidence of subversion. However, his smear tactics and wild accusations did manage to destroy the reputations and lives of dozens of innocent people.

Eventually, McCarthy was exposed and denounced for his actions. His story, however, touches on an important dilemma facing the American political system: Government has a right to protect itself against domestic threats to the nation's security. But how far can government go when it tries to accomplish that goal? In this section, you will focus on that dilemma.

Punishable Acts

Clearly, government can punish espionage, sabotage, and treason. These are forms of conduct. **Espionage** is the practice of spying for a foreign power. **Sabotage** involves an act of destruction intended to hinder a nation's war or defense effort. **Treason** is defined in the Constitution in Article III, Section 3. It can consist only in levying war against the nation or supporting its enemies.

Sedition presents a much more delicate problem, for it involves the use of spoken or written words. **Sedition** is the incitement of resistance to lawful authority. It does not necessarily involve acts of violence or betrayal.

The Alien and Sedition Acts

Congress first acted to curb opposition to government in the Alien and Sedition Acts of 1798.[19] Those laws gave the President power to deport undesirable aliens and made "any false, scandalous, and malicious" criticism of the government a crime. The acts were intended to stifle the opponents of John Adams and the Federalists.

The Alien and Sedition Acts were undoubtedly unconstitutional, but they were never tested in the courts. Some 25 persons paid fines or went to jail for violating them. The acts expired before President Jefferson took office and, in 1801, he pardoned those sentenced under the acts.

Seditious Acts in Wartime

Congress passed another sedition law during World War I, as part of the Espionage Act of 1917. That law made it a crime to encourage disloyalty, interfere with the draft, obstruct recruiting, incite insubordination in the armed forces, or hinder the sale of government bonds. The act also made it a crime to "willfully utter, print, write, or publish any disloyal, profane, scurrilous, or abusive language about the form of government of the United States."

More than 2,000 persons were convicted for violating the Espionage Act. The constitutionality of the law was tested and upheld several times. The most important of those tests came in *Schenck* v. *United States*, 1919.

Charles Schenck, an officer of the Socialist party, had been found guilty of obstructing the war effort. He had sent fiery leaflets to some 15,000 men who had been drafted, urging them to resist the call to military service.

The Supreme Court upheld Schenck's conviction. The case is particularly noteworthy because the Court's opinion, written by Justice

---

[19]This is the collective title given to a number of different laws passed by Congress at the time. Violations were punishable by a maximum fine of $2,000 and two years in prison. The first person convicted under the acts was Matthew Lyon, a member of Congress from Vermont. He had accused President Adams of "a continual grasp for power—an unbounded thirst for ridiculous pomp, foolish adulation and selfish avarice."

Oliver Wendell Holmes, established the "clear and present danger" rule.

66Words can be weapons. . . . The question in every case is whether the words used are used in such circumstances and are of such nature as to create a clear and present danger that they will bring about the substantive evils that Congress has a right to prevent.**99**

In short, the rule says that words can be outlawed, and those who utter them can be punished when the words they use trigger an immediate danger that criminal acts will follow.

Sedition in Peacetime

In 1940, however, Congress passed a new sedition law, the Smith Act, and made it applicable in peacetime. Congress later passed two other such statutes: the Internal Security (McCarran) Act of 1950 and the Communist Control Act of 1954.

The Smith Act makes it unlawful for any person to teach or advocate the violent overthrow of government in the United States or to organize or knowingly be a member of any group with such an aim. It also forbids conspiring with others to commit any of those acts.

The Court first upheld the Smith Act in *Dennis* v. *United States* in 1951. Eleven leaders of the Communist party had been convicted of advocating the overthrow of the Federal Government. On appeal, they argued that the law violated the 1st Amendment's guarantees of freedom of speech and press. They also claimed that no act of theirs constituted a clear and present danger to this country. The Court disagreed, and modified Justice Holmes's doctrine as it did so:

66An attempt to overthrow the government by force, even though doomed from the outset because of inadequate numbers or power of the revolutionists, is a sufficient evil for Congress to prevent. . . .**99**

The Court modified that holding in several later cases, however. In *Yates* v. *United States*, 1957, for example, the Court overturned the Smith Act convictions of several party leaders. It held: Merely to urge someone to *believe* something, in contrast to urging that person to *do* something, cannot be made illegal.

The result of *Yates* and other Smith Act cases was this: The Court upheld the constitutionality

▲ **Trial by Accusation**   In the 1950s Senator Joseph McCarthy's unjust accusations of "un-American" beliefs or activities created a climate of fear across the country.

of the law, but construed its provisions so that enforcement was practically impossible.

The McCarran Act proved to be an even less effective sedition law. It required every "communist-front" and "communist-action" organization to register with the attorney general. The act also created the Subversive Activities Control Board to decide which groups were subject to the law.

The Board first ordered the Communist party to register in 1953, and the Supreme Court held that it could be forced to do so, *Communist Party* v. *SACB*, 1961. It never actually did, however, largely because any person who came forward to register the party could then be charged as a "knowing member" under the Smith Act. In 1965 the Court held that to force someone into this position would contradict the 5th Amendment's guarantee against self-incrimination, *Albertson* v. *SACB*, 1965.[20]

The Court further limited the effectiveness of the McCarran Act by holding other parts of it to be unconstitutional. The net effect of the Court's response was to leave it a hollow shell.

---

[20]The decision left the SACB with no real functions to perform. It finally passed out of existence when Congress stopped funding it in 1973.

The Communist Control Act declares the Communist party in this country to be "a conspiracy to overthrow the Government of the United States." The act's goal was to outlaw the party and keep its candidates off the ballot in any election. The law was never enforced.

Two factors have made the matter of internal subversion much less prominent today than it was a few years ago. One is the overall ineffectiveness of the sedition laws. The other is that U.S.-Soviet relations are today remarkably different from what they were in the cold war period.

Not all applications of the clear and present danger rule have centered on members of the Communist party. Take *Brandenburg* v. *Ohio*, 1969, as a leading case in point.

Clarence Brandenburg, a Ku Klux Klan leader in Ohio, had been punished for violating the State's criminal syndicalism law. He had organized a rally where, standing in front of a burning cross, he had addressed a group of men, most of them hooded and some of them armed. Brandenburg shouted: "We are not a revengent organization, but if our President, our Congress, our Supreme Court continues to suppress the white, Caucasian race, it's possible that there might have to be some revengence taken." For those remarks an Ohio court sentenced Brandenburg to ten years in prison.

The Supreme Court reversed that conviction. It held that although Brandenburg had urged others to break the law, his remarks had produced no likelihood of "imminent lawless action."

Section 4 Review

1. **Define:** espionage, sabotage, treason, sedition
2. What were the Alien and Sedition Acts, and what became of them?
3. What is the clear and present danger rule?
4. What became of the Smith Act, McCarran Act, and the Communist Control Act?

Critical Thinking

5. **Checking Consistency** (p. 19) Should American society limit those who seek revolution, given the revolutionary history of this country?

★

5 Freedom of Assembly and Petition

Find Out:

■ For what reasons are there limits on the freedoms of assembly and of petition?

A noisy street demonstration by gay rights activists, or by neo-Nazis, or by any number of other groups; a candlelight vigil of opponents of the death penalty; the prolife faithful singing hymns as they picket an abortion clinic; prochoice partisans gathered on the steps of the State capitol . . . These are commonplace events today, and they are also everyday manifestations of freedom of assembly and petition.

In this section, you will examine the shape of that freedom and its importance to you and to all Americans.

The Constitution's Guarantees

The 1st Amendment guarantees

> ". . . the right of the people peaceably to assemble, and to petition government for a redress of grievances."

The 14th Amendment's Due Process Clause also protects those rights of assembly and petition against actions by the States or their local governments. The Supreme Court first made that holding in *DeJonge* v. *Oregon*, 1937.

A court in Oregon had found Dirk DeJonge guilty of violating Oregon's criminal syndicalism law. The statute prohibited "any unlawful acts" that were intended to bring about "industrial or political change or revolution." DeJonge had helped organize and had spoken at a meeting of the Communist party. For that behavior, a State court sentenced him to seven years in prison.[21]

The Supreme Court reversed DeJonge's conviction, declaring: "Peaceable assembly for lawful discussion cannot be made a crime."

---

[21]Note the close similarities between *DeJonge* and *Brandenburg* v. *Ohio*.

The Constitution protects the right of the people to assemble—to gather with one another—to express their views on public matters. It protects their right to organize—in political parties, pressure groups, and other organizations—to influence public policy. It also protects the people's right to bring their views to the attention of public officials by such varied means as written petitions, letters, or advertisements; lobbying; or parades, marches, or other demonstrations.

But, notice, the 1st and 14th amendments protect the rights of peaceable assembly and petition. The Constitution does not give people the right to incite others to violence, to block a public street, close a school, or otherwise to endanger life, property, or public order.

Time–Place–Manner Regulations

Government can make and enforce reasonable rules covering the time, place, and manner of assemblies. Thus, the Supreme Court has upheld a city ordinance that prohibits making a noise or causing any other diversion near a school if that action disrupts school activities, *Grayned* v. *City of Rockford*, 1972. It has also upheld a State law that forbids parades near a courthouse when they are intended to influence court proceedings, *Cox* v. *Louisiana*, 1965.

But rules for keeping the public peace must be more than reasonable. They must also be precisely drawn and fairly administered. In *Coates* v. *Cincinnati*, 1971, the Court struck down a city ordinance that made it a crime for "three or more persons to assemble" on a sidewalk or street corner "and there conduct themselves in a manner annoying to persons passing by, or to occupants of adjacent buildings." The Court found the ordinance too vague. It was so loosely drawn that it contained "an obvious invitation to discriminatory enforcement against those whose association together is 'annoying' because their ideas, their lifestyle, or their physical appearance is resented by the majority."

Government's rules must be content neutral. That is, while government can regulate assemblies on the basis of time, place, and manner, it cannot regulate them on the basis of what might be said there. Thus, in *Forsyth County* v. *Nationalist Movement*, 1992, the Court threw out a Georgia county's ordinance that levied a fee of up to $1,000 for public demonstrations. The law was contested by a white supremacist group seeking to protest the creation of a holiday to honor Martin Luther King, Jr. The Court found the ordinance not to be content neutral, particularly because county officials had unlimited power to set the exact fee to be paid by any group.

Notice that the power to control traffic or keep a protest rally from becoming a riot *can* be used as an excuse to prevent speech. The line between crowd control and thought control can be very thin, indeed.

Demonstrations on Public Property

Over the past several years, most of the Court's freedom of assembly cases have involved organized demonstrations. Demonstrations are, of course, assemblies.

▲ **Freedom of Petition**   When persons publicly solicit signatures or conduct opinion polls, they are exercising rights guaranteed under the 1st and 14th amendments.

Most demonstrations take place in public places—on streets and sidewalks, in parks or public buildings, and so on. Demonstrations take place in these locations because it is the public the demonstrators want to reach.

Demonstrations almost always involve some degree of conflict. Mostly, they are held to protest something, and so a clash of ideas is present. Many times there is also a conflict with the normal use of streets or other public facilities. It is hardly surprising, then, that the tension generated can sometimes rise to a serious level.

Given all this, the Supreme Court has often upheld laws that require advance notice and permits for demonstrations in public places. In an early leading case, *Cox* v. *New Hampshire*, 1941,[22] it unanimously approved such a law:

> The authority of a municipality to impose regulations in order to assure the safety and convenience of the people in the use of public highways has never been regarded as inconsistent with civil liberties but rather as one of the means of safeguarding the good order on which they ultimately depend. . . . The question in a particular case is whether the control is exercised so as to deny . . . the right of assembly and the opportunity for the communication of thought and the discussion of public questions.

Right-to-demonstrate cases raise many basic and thorny questions. How and to what extent can government regulate demonstrators and their demonstrations? Does the Constitution require that police officers allow an unpopular group to continue to demonstrate when its activities have excited others to violence? When, in the name of public peace and safety, can police properly order demonstrators to disband?

Among these cases, *Gregory* v. *Chicago*, 1969, remains typical. While under police protection, Dick Gregory and others had marched—singing, chanting, and carrying placards—from city hall to the mayor's home some five miles away. Marching in the streets around the mayor's house, they demanded the firing of the city's school superintendent and an end to de facto segregation in the city's schools.

---

[22]This is one of the several Jehovah's Witness cases referred to on page 497. Cox and several other Witnesses had violated a State law that required a license to hold a parade or procession on the public streets.

A crowd of several hundred people, including many residents of the all-white neighborhood quickly gathered. Soon, the bystanders began throwing insults and threats, rocks, eggs, and other objects. The police tried to keep order, but after about an hour, they decided that serious violence was about to break out. At that point, they ordered the demonstrators to leave the area. When Gregory and the others failed to do so, the police arrested them and charged them with disorderly conduct.

The convictions of the demonstrators were unanimously overturned by the High Court. The Court noted that the marchers had done no more than exercise their constitutional rights of assembly and petition. Neighborhood residents and others, not the demonstrators, had caused the disorder. So long as the demonstrators acted peacefully, they could not be punished for disorderly conduct.

Over recent years, the most controversial demonstrations have been those orchestrated by Operation Rescue and other anti-abortion groups. In the main, those groups' efforts have been aimed at discouraging women from seeking the services of abortion clinics; and those efforts have generated many lawsuits. In the most notable case to date, *Madsen* v. *Women's Health Services, Inc.*, 1994, the Supreme Court upheld a Florida judge's order directing protesters not to block access to an abortion clinic. The judge's order had drawn a 36-foot buffer zone around the clinic, and the High Court found that to be a reasonable limit on the demonstrators' activities.

Right of Assembly and Private Property

What of demonstrations on private property—for example, at shopping centers? The Court has heard only a few cases raising this question. However, at least this much can be said: The rights of assembly and petition do not give people a right to trespass on private property, even if they wish to express political views.

Privately owned shopping centers are not public streets, sidewalks, parks, and other "places of public assembly." Thus, no one has a constitutional right to do such things as hand out political leaflets or ask people to sign petitions in those places.

These comments are based on the leading case here, *Lloyd Corporation v. Tanner*, 1972. However, since that case the Court has held this: A State supreme court may interpret the provisions of that State's own constitution in such a way as to require the owners of shopping centers to allow the reasonable exercise of the right of petition on their private property. In that event, there is no violation of the property owners' rights under any provision in the federal Constitution, *PruneYard Shopping Center v. Robins*, 1980. In that case, several California high school students had set up a card table in the shopping center, passed out pro-Israeli pamphlets, and asked passersby to sign petitions to be sent to the President and Congress.

Freedom of Association

The guarantees of freedom of assembly and petition include a guarantee of association. That is, those guarantees include the right to associate with others to promote political, economic, and other social causes. That right is not set out in so many words in the Constitution, but the Supreme Court has said "it is beyond doubt that freedom to engage in association for the advancement of beliefs and ideas is an inseparable aspect" of the Constitution's guarantees of free expression, *National Association for the Advancement of Colored People v. Alabama*, 1958. Of course, there is no right to gather to pursue illegal ends.

The case just cited is one of the early right to associate cases. There, a State law required the Alabama branch of the NAACP to disclose the names of all its members in that State. When the organization refused a court's order that it do so, it was found in contempt of court and fined $100,000.

The Supreme Court overturned the contempt conviction. It said that it could find no legitimate reason why the State should have the NAACP's membership list.

You have seen some illustration of the guarantee of freedom of expression at work in earlier chapters. Recall, for example, *Tashjian v. Republican Party of Connecticut*, a 1986 case noted

"I DON'T WANT YOU PLAYING WITH THAT LITTLE JONES BOY... WHY, HIS FAMILY DOESN'T EVEN COMPOST!"

▲ **Interpreting Political Cartoons**
What bias is guiding this parent's decision to limit her son's freedom of association?

on page 162. In that case the Supreme Court held that a State's election laws cannot forbid a political party to allow independents to vote in that party's primary if the party wants to do so.

You will see other illustrations later on. Thus, in Chapter 21 you will consider such cases as *Roberts v. United States Jaycees*, 1984 and *Board of Directors of Rotary International v. Rotary Club of Duarte*, 1987. In both cases the Supreme Court rejected attempts by an all-male organization to invoke freedom of association as a shield against the admission of women to the club.

Section 5 Review

1. What does the guarantee of freedom of assembly and petition intend to protect?
2. On what basis can government regulate the rights of assembly and petition?
3. What factors make the right to demonstrate such a thorny issue?
4. For what reason is the right to associate protected by the Constitution?

Critical Thinking

5. **Identifying Alternatives** (p. 19) What might be an acceptable response to the announcement that a neo-Nazi group was planning a demonstration in your community?

★

Close Up on Primary Sources

Civil Liberties and the Constitution

*A*rthur Spitzer is the legal director of the Washington, D.C., chapter of the
American Civil Liberties Union (ACLU), a nonprofit, nonpartisan organization dedicated to protecting civil liberties and civil rights through litigation,
lobbying, and public education. Here, Spitzer explains how the Bill of Rights protects those who are not in the "majority."

Of all the sections of the Constitution, the Bill of Rights has the most direct impact on the everyday lives of all Americans. Most of the Constitution is a blueprint for the structure of the federal government—how officials are elected or appointed and what their duties are—but the Bill of Rights deals with the relationship of the government to its citizens.

Decisions in a democracy are made by majority rule, either directly, as in the election of the president and members of Congress, or indirectly, as when laws are passed by the legislature. But the purpose of the Bill of Rights is to put some matters outside the majority's rule: to say that there are some decisions the majority cannot be allowed to make.

But why shouldn't the majority always rule? The answer comes from the Declaration of Independence—that there are "certain inalienable rights" to which each of us is entitled as an individual. . . . The Bill of Rights protects those rights for each of us, individually, so that they cannot be taken away by a majority that may hate our particular race or religion or political activity.

People who are in the majority at any given moment often don't understand why they shouldn't be allowed to have their way. The simple answer is that by respecting the rights of others, they are protecting their own rights in the long run, because tomorrow, or next year, or ten years from now, they may be in the endangered minority.

History is replete with examples: when labor unions began organizing in the 1920s and 1930s, when civil rights workers began marching in the South, when people began demonstrating against the war in Vietnam, they were often called communists or traitors and local authorities often attempted to stop their activities. Yet ultimately, their causes prevailed. New religions—from Christianity 2,000 years ago, to the Christian Scientists and Mormons of the nineteenth century, to the Scientologists, Hare Krishnas, and "Moonies" of today—have almost always been despised and persecuted by the existing majority. Yet many religions that were once new and radical are well established and accepted by society today.

The lesson of history is that the only way to protect the rights of any of us is to protect the rights of all of us. . . . Because there will always be unpopular minorities, the fight to protect civil rights and civil liberties will never be completely won. But with the Bill of Rights to shield us from majority tyranny, the United States is likely to remain one of the freest societies that has ever existed on the face of the Earth.

Analyzing Primary Sources

1. Under what circumstances is majority rule not appropriate?
2. What does history teach us about the best way to protect our rights?

Chapter-in-Brief

Scan all headings, photographs, charts, and other visuals in the chapter before reading the section summaries below.

Section 1   The Unalienable Rights (pp. 485–489)
The Constitution, especially its Bill of Rights, guarantees many rights and liberties to the American people. These guarantees reflect the principle of limited government.

An individual's rights can be exercised only to the extent that they do not limit the rights of others. In cases where individual rights conflict, one right must take precedence.

The Bill of Rights restricts only the National Government. Each State constitution, however, contains its own bill of rights. Also, the 14th Amendment's Due Process Clause "nationalizes" most of the protections of the Bill of Rights.

Section 2   Freedom of Religion (pp. 490–497)
Freedom of expression is vital to democracy. One key component of this freedom is the freedom of religion.

Freedom of religion is guaranteed in part by the Establishment Clause. Still, the nature of the wall between church and state has been the subject of many court decisions.

Freedom of religion is also guaranteed by the Free Exercise Clause. This clause protects people's right to believe—though not necessarily to do—whatever they wish regarding religion.

Section 3   Freedom of Speech and Press (pp. 499–505)
The 1st and 14th amendments' guarantee of free speech and free press protect people's right to speak and their right to be heard.

There are limits to these rights. Obscene material is not protected, nor is slanderous and libelous speech. Freedom of the press does not allow reporters to withhold certain information from government. Movies and electronic media are also subject to regulation. In most cases, government cannot exercise prior restraint.

Symbolic and commercial speech also enjoy constitutional protection. Yet, government can limit both under certain circumstances.

Section 4   Freedom of Expression and National Security (pp. 506–508)
Government must protect itself from internal subversion. Therefore, government can regulate some expression in the interest of national security.

Historically, some government attempts to regulate opposition to the government have proven unworkable. For example, the Alien and Sedition Acts of 1798 and several anti-communist efforts of the cold war era were largely ineffective. However, the Supreme Court has held that government has a right to control speech that creates "a clear and present danger" of violence or harm to public order or national security.

Section 5   Freedom of Assembly and Petition (pp. 508–511)
The 1st Amendment guarantees the right to assemble peaceably and to petition for the redress of grievances. Government can reasonably regulate the time, place, and manner of such expression. Those regulations must, however, be "content neutral."

The Court has held that demonstrations targeted at specific private residences can be outlawed. Also, citizens do not generally enjoy the right to assemble on private property.

Freedom of assembly and petition includes a guarantee of association. This means that people are free to to associate with others in order to promote causes of mutual concern.

19 Chapter Review

Vocabulary and Key Terms

Bill of Rights (p. 486)
civil liberties (p. 486)
civil rights (p. 486)
aliens (p. 487)
Due Process Clause (p. 488)
Establishment Clause (p. 490)

Free Exercise Clause (p. 496)
libel (p. 499)
slander (p. 499)
shield laws (p. 502)
symbolic speech (p. 503)

picketing (p. 504)
espionage (p. 506)
sabotage (p. 506)
treason (p. 506)
sedition (p. 506)

Matching: *Review the key terms in the list above. If you are not sure of a term's meaning, look up the term and review its definition. Choose a term from the list above that best matches each description.*

1. the part of the Constitution that ensures that no State can deny any right that is "basic or essential to the American concept of ordered liberty"
2. designed to protect reporters in the media from having to reveal their confidential news sources
3. what striking workers do when they patrol outside a business
4. what the first 10 amendments to the Constitution are called
5. the crime of levying war against the United States or giving aid and comfort to the enemy

True or False: *Determine whether each statement is true or false. If it is true, write "true." If it is false, change the underlined word or words to make the statement true.*

1. <u>Symbolic speech</u> is the expression of beliefs or ideas by conduct.
2. An <u>alien</u> is one who is not a citizen of the state in which he or she lives.
3. When workers who are on strike patrol a business, they are engaged in a practice called <u>sabotage</u>.

4. That part of the Constitution in which many civil rights and liberties are spelled out is the <u>Free Exercise Clause</u>.

Word Relationships: *Distinguish between words in each pair.*

1. libel/slander
2. Free Exercise Clause/Establishment Clause
3. treason/sedition
4. espionage/sabotage
5. civil rights/civil liberties

Main Ideas

Section 1 (pp. 485–489)

1. What does it mean to say that the concept of individual freedom is rooted in American colonial history?
2. What does it mean to say that individual rights guaranteed in the Constitution are relative and not absolute?
3. What is the relationship between the 14th Amendment and the Bill of Rights?

Section 2 (pp. 490–497)

4. Summarize the meaning and impact of the Establishment Clause. How does this clause help guarantee "a free trade in ideas"?
5. Summarize the meaning and impact of the Free Exercise Clause. How does this clause help guarantee a "free trade in ideas"?

6. At what point can the government limit a person's exercise of religion?

Section 3 (pp. 499-505)

7. Why does the Constitution guarantee the right of people both to speak and to hear?

8. Give three examples of circumstances in which the freedom of speech is not protected under the Constitution.

9. What kinds of actions are protected as "speech"?

Section 4 (pp. 506–508)

10. Summarize the conflict between national security and individual rights.

11. What is the significance of the "clear and present danger" rule?

12. What has been the overall result of the United States' efforts to prevent internal subversion?

Section 5 (pp. 508–511)

13. At what point do people cease to enjoy the right to assemble and petition?

14. Briefly describe the nature of the limits a government can place upon assemblies.

15. (a) What is the freedom of association? (b) What is the limit on that freedom?

Critical Thinking

1. Checking Consistency (p. 19) The American government places the highest possible value on individual rights. Yet it also protects the rights of the many against the actions of the few. Are these statements consistent? If so, how?

2. Identifying Assumptions (p. 19) Consider the concept of "the free marketplace of ideas." What does this concept suggest about the role and responsibility of citizens in the American democratic society?

3. Predicting Consequences (p. 19) (a) Why is it so important that the Constitution guarantee the rights of people to assemble and associate. (b) What might happen if people could not enjoy this right?

–★Participation Activities ★–

1. Current Events Watch
Issues involving the 1st Amendment are regularly in the news. Select one current issue related to the 1st Amendment and write a dialogue between two people on opposite sides in the debate. Have both persons support their case by referring to the text of the Constitution and to historical examples.

2. Writing Activity
You are a Supreme Court justice hearing a case involving the free exercise of religion. Write an opinion in which you create a test for determining at what point a government can constitutionally restrict a person's free exercise of religion. Begin your opinion by stating the test you have established. Then, explain the reasoning on which you have based the test. Revise to correct any errors. Then make a final copy.

3. Internet Activity
Use the following URL:
http://www.freedomforum.org
to visit the Web site of the Freedom Forum First Amendment Center, part of a non-profit organization dedicated to study of 1st Amendment issues. Scan the portion of the site that summarizes recent 1st Amendment news, paying particular attention to stories concerning freedom of speech, press, and religion. Summarize three of these stories in one paragraph each.

FEATURED SELECTION 2: "STATE OF THE FIRST AMENDMENT 2000"

BEFORE YOU READ

About the Author   Kenneth A. Paulson is executive director of The First Amendment Center. The Center is an operating program of The Freedom Forum and is affiliated with the Newseum, The Freedom Forum's interactive museum of news. The Freedom Forum is a "nonpartisan, international foundation dedicated to free press, free speech, and free spirit for all people."

About the Survey   A State of the First Amendment survey is conducted annually by the First Amendment Center to examine public attitudes toward freedom of speech, press, religion and the rights of assembly and petition. These survey results are from telephone interviews conducted April 13–26, 2000, by The Center for Survey Research and Analysis at the University of Connecticut with 1,015 adults, ages 18 or older. The margin of sampling error is plus or minus 3 percentage points.

Words to Know

> *ratified* (¶1): approved
>
> *ambivalent* (¶2): uncertain, mixed feelings
>
> *perception* (¶7): viewpoint
>
> *curb* (¶16): control, restrict
>
> *attributable* (¶20): credited to
>
> *greater latitude* (¶22): more freedom
>
> *convening* (¶32): calling together
>
> *abated* (¶32): decreased, lessened

An Idea to Think About   How would you describe "the state of the First Amendment"? For example, do you think the press has too much freedom? *As you read*, find out how the American people feel about our First Amendment freedoms.

STATE OF THE FIRST AMENDMENT 2000

Kenneth A. Paulson

[1]The First Amendment, written and ratified at the close of the 18th century, may face its greatest test as we enter the 21st.

[2]While the 45 words of the First Amendment have gone unchanged since their adoption, unchanged does not mean unchallenged. Responses to the "State of the First Amendment 2000" survey suggest that Americans respect the First Amendment as an ideal but are ambivalent when it protects offensive ideas or troubling speech.

[3]In fact, most survey respondents were highly selective in their appreciation of the rights guaranteed by the First Amendment. While they applauded freedom of speech, they were concerned about freedom of the press and knew little about the rights of petition and assembly. Candidates looking for public consensus on First Amendment issues in this election year won't find one.

[4]But First Amendment issues will play a major role in campaigns nationwide. Debates over campaign finance reform, prayers in public schools, vouchers for religious schools, regulation of the Internet, and even the burning of the American flag—all will come into play this political season.

[5]Here are some key findings from the "State of the First Amendment 2000" survey:

[6]• *A majority of respondents favored government-imposed restrictions on the amount of money that can be contributed to a candidate's election campaign, even though a majority also agreed that "contributing money to a political candidate is an expression of free speech that should be protected by the Constitution." At the same time, a majority indicated that government should be more involved in religion, with teacher-led prayer allowed in public schools and government-funded vouchers for students attending private religious schools.*

[7] • *Almost three-quarters of all respondents believed that violence in the media contributes to violence in real life.* Violence on television, in video games, and in music was seen as a factor contributing to violence in society—a perception that may explain increasing calls for limitations on certain kinds of expression.

[8] • *Freedom of the press was far less popular with respondents than freedom of speech or religion,* with 51 percent of those surveyed saying the press in America has too much freedom to do what it wants.

[9] • Even as survey respondents were concerned over the traditional press' exercise of its First Amendment rights, *there was significant support for free speech on the Internet.* Seventy-four percent of respondents agreed that "material on the Internet should have the same First Amendment protections as printed material such as books and newspapers."

[10]Among emerging issues:

Campaign Finance Reform

[11]Our survey indicates that a majority of those polled believe the act of contributing money to a political candidate is an expression of free speech and should be protected by the First Amendment.

[12]Despite appreciating the connection between free speech and the funding of campaigns, most survey respondents also favored restrictions on contributions:

[13] • Fifty-three percent agreed that "the government should be able to place restrictions on the amount of money a political candidate can contribute to his or her own election campaign."

[14] • Fifty-seven percent agreed that "the government should be able to place restrictions on the amount of money a private individual can contribute to someone else's election campaign."

[15] • Sixty-eight percent agreed that "the government should be able to place restrictions on the amount of money a private corporation or a union can contribute to an election campaign."

[16]While most respondents were supportive of legislation that would curb campaign finance spending, only 38 percent would be in favor of amending the Constitution to give government a right to restrict campaign spending. Clearly, this is a significant societal concern, but most respondents were not willing to change the Constitution to address it.

Freedom of Religion

[17]Freedom of religion may have been the single most important freedom to the Founding Fathers.

[18]Today a majority of Americans clearly are comfortable with this freedom, with 63 percent of survey respondents saying they believe the amount of religious freedom in the United States is "about right."

[19]However, the number of Americans who believe there is too little religious freedom is increasing. In 1997, 21 percent of those surveyed said there was too little religious freedom. That grew to 26 percent in 1999. In the 2000 survey, 29 percent said there's inadequate religious freedom.

[20]This may be attributable to people who value their own freedom of religion but resent the establishment clause that prevents government-sponsored exercise of religion and prayer in public schools.

[21]We've also seen a steady increase in the number of survey respondents who strongly agree that public school officials should be allowed to lead prayer in schools. In 1997, that figure was 37 percent. By 2000, it had grown to 48 percent.

[22]In addition, a majority of those surveyed this year agreed that there should be greater latitude for other religious activities in public schools:

[23] • Sixty-one percent agreed that "local school officials should be allowed to post the Ten Commandments on the wall of a public school classroom."

[24] • Sixty-four percent agreed that "students should be allowed to lead prayers over the public address system at public school-sponsored events."

[25] • Finally, 64 percent of those polled agreed that "parents should have the option of sending their children to religious schools instead of public schools using vouchers or credits provided by the federal government."

[26]One surprise in the new survey was the level of support for using the Bible as a source of historical information. Fifty-six percent of respondents said "a public school teacher should be allowed to use the Bible as a factual text in a history or social studies class," a response that indicates support for classroom use of the Bible even as it suggests a blurred line between historic and religious belief.

Media Violence

[27]Most survey respondents saw a correlation between violent content in the news and entertainment media and violence in American society. To varying degrees, respondents blamed television, violent video games, and violent lyrics as culprits.

[28] • Eighty-three percent of respondents thought that television violence contributes to violence in real life.

[29] • Seventy-four percent said that violence in video games contributes to violence in real life.

[30] • Seventy-two percent said that violent lyrics in music contribute to violence in society.

Freedom of the Press

[31]The headline-grabbing finding of the "State of the First Amendment Survey 1999" was that 53 percent of Americans felt the press has too much freedom to do what it wants.

[32]The First Amendment Center followed up on the initial finding by convening focus groups, which suggested that the President Clinton/Monica Lewinsky scandal was the driving force behind the high level of dissatisfaction with America's news media. A follow-up survey in September 1999 indicated that the discontent had abated, leaving just 42 percent of Americans saying there was too much freedom of the press.

[33]The current survey was conducted in the spring of 2000, at a time when there was extensive coverage of the custody battle over Elian Gonzalez. Once again, the number of survey respondents who felt there was too much freedom in the press had risen, this time to 51 percent.

Freedom of Speech on the Internet

[34]As Americans increasingly make use of the Internet, their support for it as a vehicle for free speech grows.

[35] • Seventy-four percent of respondents agreed that "material on the Internet should have the same First Amendment protections as printed material such as books and newspapers." This was a substantial increase from 1999, when only 54 percent expressed that view.

[36] • The number of survey respondents with access to the Internet likewise increased significantly (from 56 percent to 68 percent) during the same time period. There appears to be a strong correlation between personal use of the Internet and respect for it as a medium of free expression.

[37]Even so, the kind of troubling speech that inclines Americans to support limits on free expression in the offline world leads them to support online limits as well.

[38] • Fifty-eight percent of survey respondents believed "the government should be able to restrict the posting of information on the Internet about how to make a bomb, even though such information is already available in books."

[39] • Fifty-eight percent believed that "the government should be able to restrict the posting of sexually explicit materials on the Internet, even though those same materials can be legally published in books and magazines."

[40]As for access to the Internet in public libraries—another developing area—Americans have conflicting views on that subject too.

[41]A very small percentage of the survey respondents—11 percent—believed that public libraries should give all visitors full access to the Internet.

[42]Fifty-three percent of those responding believed that public libraries should simply block children's access to potentially offensive sites.

[43]More than one-third of respondents, however, believed that public libraries should block access to potentially offensive Internet sites for all, whether adults or children.

State of the First Amendment

[44]Despite the title of this report, there clearly is no single "state of the First Amendment." While some freedoms have enthusiastic public support, others are at risk.

[45]Concern about society's challenges—stemming violence, protecting children, and addressing racial intolerance—can undercut support for freedom of expression.

[46]Free speech is widely supported in theory, but survey results suggest that a significant number of Americans are willing to sacrifice some freedom in order to curb ugly speech.

[47]Americans generally support freedom of the press, but are tempted to limit newsmedia rights when newscasts and newspapers offend or disappoint.

[48]The ambivalence Americans seem to feel toward their fundamental freedoms is somewhat disappointing, but not surprising. After all, the First Amendment was designed to protect minority viewpoints. By its nature, the American political process—and legislation that targets free expression—are driven by majority vote.

[49]Can we as a nation more fully embrace the First Amendment and not be tempted to chip away at it?

[50]The answer may lie in education. Many Americans acknowledge that they don't know as much about the First Amendment as they should.

[51]Most respondents to this Year 2000 survey were able to name only a single freedom contained in the First Amendment. Sixty-five percent of those polled said America's schools do only a fair or poor job of teaching students about First Amendment freedoms.

[52]In the end, embracing the First Amendment and all it protects may depend on knowing it more fully.

[53]With knowledge comes perspective, as well as respect and a greater appreciation for the Founding Fathers' greatest gift.

SELECTION 2 QUESTIONS

Vocabulary

Circle the letter of the best definition for the underlined word.

1. "Candidates looking for public <u>consensus</u> on First Amendment issues in this election year won't find one." (¶3)
   a. disagreement
   b. agreement
   c. differences
   d. points of view

2. "Most survey respondents saw a <u>correlation</u> between violent content in the news and entertainment media and violence in American society." (¶27)

   a. relationship

   b. division

   c. answer

   d. trouble

3. "To varying degrees, respondents blamed television, violent video games, and violent lyrics as <u>culprits</u>." (¶27)

   a. guilty causes

   b. confusing

   c. entertaining

   d. positive influences

4. "While some freedoms have <u>enthusiastic</u> public support, others are at risk." (¶44)

   a. pessimistic

   b. uncaring

   c. very negative

   d. highly positive

Comprehension

Determine whether the statements in sentences 5–7 are true or false, and write your answer. Also, if the statement is false, rewrite it to make it true.

5. More than half of the survey respondents felt the press has just about the right amount of freedom.

   _____

   _____

6. This survey suggests that Americans respect the First Amendment as an ideal but have mixed feelings when it protects offensive ideas or troubling speech.

   _____

   _____

7. Most respondents felt that violence on television, in video games, and in music contributes to violence in society.

   _____

   _____

8. Circle the letter of the sentence that best expresses the thesis:

   a. Many Americans don't know as much about the First Amendment as they should.

   b. Most Americans see a correlation between violent content in the news and entertainment media and violence in American society.

   c. There is no single "state of the First Amendment." While some freedoms have enthusiastic public support, others are at risk.

   d. Most people favor government-imposed restrictions on the amount of money that can be contributed to a candidate's election campaign.

9. What does Paulson think might have been the single most important freedom to the Founding Fathers?

    _____

10. What is the relationship of paragraphs 13, 14, and 15 to paragraph 12? Which of the following do they provide?
    a. examples
    b. steps in a process
    c. causes
    d. effects

11. Which of the survey results surprised you the most? Please explain.

    _____

    _____

    _____

    _____

12. What is "the Founding Fathers' greatest gift" that Paulson refers to in the last paragraph?

    _____

13. Is paragraph 1 primarily fact, opinion, or combination of fact and opinion? If it includes both, list which information is fact and which is opinion.

    _____

    _____

14. Is paragraph 3 primarily fact, opinion, or combination of fact and opinion? If it includes both, list which information is fact and which is opinion.

    _____

    _____

FEATURED SELECTION 3: "WELL, WOULD YOU RATHER HAVE AN UNFREE PRESS?"

BEFORE YOU READ

About the Author   Bill Thompson is a columnist for the *Fort Worth Star-Telegram*. This column appeared July 7, 1999.

Words to Know

> *abridge* (¶5): lessen, reduce, diminish
>
> *essence* (¶5): core, essential part
>
> *probe* (¶13): investigate

An Idea to Think About   Do you think the news media should be free to investigate and report all the "news"? If not, who do you think should set the limits? *As you read*, find out if Thompson thinks there should be limits on the press' freedom.

WELL, WOULD YOU RATHER HAVE AN UNFREE PRESS?

Bill Thompson

[1]Let's talk about the First Amendment.

[2a]You've heard about it. It's the first item in the Bill of Rights, which is the term we use to describe the first ten amendments to the Constitution of the United States. [2b]These amendments guarantee various fundamental rights and freedoms: the right to bear arms, the right to a fair trial, freedom from unreasonable search and seizure, freedom against self-incrimination....

[3]The founders of this country went out of their way to make sure there would be no confusion about the importance of such constitutional rights in the new American republic.

[4]Most constitutional scholars agree that the numerical order of the first ten amendments was not intended to prioritize them or rank their significance in any way. But there is no denying that the First Amendment set the tone for the Bill of Rights and helped set the direction that the new nation would take.

[5]The freedoms guaranteed by the First Amendment are crucial to the success of any democracy. To violate or abridge these rights is to undermine the essence of a democratic society.

[6]For those of us who have never committed the First Amendment to memory, here's what it says:

[7]"Congress shall make no law respecting an establishment of religion, or prohibiting the free exercise thereof; or abridging the freedom of speech, or of the press, or the right of the people peaceably to assemble, and to petition the Government for a redress of grievances."

[8]It's short and to the point. Freedom of religion. Free speech. Freedom of the press. The right to protest.

[9]Those guys had a way with words.

[10]I don't mean to ramble. But as the American people look toward a new century, there is reason to fear for the future of those rights.

[11]The First Amendment, especially, is under attack as never before. The results of a new poll reported in USA Today suggest that freedom of the press, in particular, has fallen into disfavor with the public. The poll was commissioned by the Freedom Forum, a pro-First Amendment foundation.

[12]According to the newspaper, 53 percent of those who responded to the poll said that the press in America has too much freedom—an increase of 15 percent from a similar poll conducted two years ago.

[13]Tony Mauro of USA Today reported that the poll indicated "nearly two-thirds of the public thinks the press should not be allowed to probe the private lives of public officials. And shrinking numbers of respondents think the news media should be allowed to endorse political candidates, report government secrets, or use hidden cameras."

[14]Mauro quoted a media lawyer/author named Bruce Sanford: "The public is so angry at the media these days that we are beginning to blind ourselves to the biggest threat, which is not the media but government regulation."

[15]Boy, is that the truth.

[16]It's understandable that the public gets disgusted with what seems to be the media's overemphasis on scandal, on violence, on "negative" news of every description. Even the media folks who serve up this stuff on a daily basis get disgusted with it.

[17]But the fact is, people are watching and reading all this news that they claim to hate. If they weren't, the media wouldn't be quite so eager to report it.

[18]But even if you happen to be one of those rare consumers who only reads the good news, who scrupulously avoids the bad and the ugly, you surely wouldn't want the government to decide what news can be printed and broadcast.

[19]Would you?

[20]The free press makes mistakes, just as any institution does, but the alternative is an unfree press. The sort of press, for example, that operates under the thumb of Yugoslav President Slobodan Milosevic. The sort of press that covers up Milosevic's crimes against humanity and refuses to tell the people of Yugoslavia why most of Western civilization has turned against their leaders and waged war against their country.

[21]We can't have it both ways. There is no such thing as a partly free press.

[22]We can accept the First Amendment and put up with occasional abuses of the freedom it guarantees. Or we can surrender this right that the founders considered so important that they placed it first on their list of most important rights.

[23]It's a clear-cut choice. There is nothing in between.

SELECTION 3 QUESTIONS

Vocabulary

Circle the letter of the best definition for the underlined word.

1. "These amendments guarantee various <u>fundamental</u> rights and freedoms...." (¶2)
   a. nonessential
   b. basic
   c. individual
   d. governmental

2. "Most constitutional scholars agree that the <u>numerical</u> order of the first ten amendments...." (¶4)
   a. number
   b. alphabetical
   c. special
   d. overall

3. "The freedoms guaranteed by the First Amendment are <u>crucial</u> to the success of any democracy." (¶5)
   a. fundamental
   b. unimportant
   c. insignificant
   d. scientific

Rephrase the underlined passages using your own words.

4. "... freedom of the press, in particular, <u>has fallen into disfavor with the public</u>." (¶11)

   _____

5. "... who <u>scrupulously avoids</u> the bad and the ugly...." (¶18)

   _____

Comprehension

Determine whether the statements in sentences 6–8 are true or false, and write your answer. Also, if the statement is false, rewrite it to make it true.

6. Recent polls indicate that an increasing number of Americans feel the press has too much freedom.

   _____

   _____

7. If people didn't watch and read all the bad and disgusting news they claim to hate, the media probably wouldn't be so eager to report it.

   _____

   _____

8. There is no such thing as a partly free press.

   _____

   _____

9. Circle the letter of the sentence that best expresses the thesis.
   a. Many people feel that the press in America has too much freedom.
   b. Yugoslavia doesn't have a free press.
   c. Although a free press makes mistakes, it is essential to preserving our democratic way of life.
   d. The First Amendment set the tone for the Bill of Rights and helped set the direction our new nation would take.

10. In paragraph 2, sentence b, the relationship of the second part of the sentence to the first part is:
    a. The second part gives examples of the "various fundamental rights and freedoms."
    b. The second part gives causes of the "various fundamental rights and freedoms."
    c. The second part gives effects of the "various fundamental rights and freedoms."

    The punctuation that signals it is:

    _____

11. Why is paragraph 7 in quotation marks?

    _____

12. What does media lawyer/author Bruce Sanford believe is our "biggest threat"? Explain what that means.

    _____

    _____

    _____

13. What is the relationship of paragraph 23 to paragraph 21? Which of the following does it provide?
    a. a continuation and restatement of the same thought
    b. a change in direction of thought
    c. an effect

FEATURED SELECTION 4: "YOU BE THE JUDGE"

BEFORE YOU READ

About the Author   Chip Rowe is an Associate Editor at *Playboy*. This article is from *Playboy*, August 1999.

Words to Know

> *compilation* (¶2): collection of
> *repetitiously* (¶3): over and over again
> *egregiously* (¶3): outrageously, excessively
> *conciliatory* (¶4): respectful, polite
> *latter-day* (¶7): recent, modern
> *abomination* (¶8): wickedness, immorality
> *disavow* (¶8): deny
> *imminent* (¶13): expected to happen soon
> *construe* (¶13): interpret, understand
> *scorned* (¶13): disliked, treated with disrespect

An Idea to Think About   Do you think "freedom of speech" guarantees us the right to say what we want whenever and wherever we want to say it? If not, what limitations do you think there should be? *As you read*, see how often you agree with the courts about the realities of free speech.

YOU BE THE JUDGE

Chip Rowe

[1]"Congress shall make no law respecting an establishment of religion, or prohibiting the free exercise thereof; or abridging the freedom of speech, or of the press, or the right of the people peaceably to assemble and to petition the government for a redress of grievances."

That's the First Amendment. Simple, right? Not always. Consider each of the following free speech cases. After you cast your vote, we'll tell you what the courts decided.

Classroom Profanity

[2]Cecilia Lacks instructed her 11th grade students in Berkeley, Missouri to write and videotape short plays. Many of the plays, which dealt with issues such as gang violence, included words such as fuck, shit, ass, bitch, and nigger. The 40-minute video compilation contained more than 150 of these words. The student-discipline code bans profanity, but Lacks said she believed the code applied only to behavior toward others. After the school board fired her, Lacks sued, arguing that she had been a facilitator for her students' creative expression and that her rights had been violated.

FREE SPEECH   ____
NOT FREE SPEECH ____

[3]VERDICT: Not free speech, according to the U.S. Supreme Court, which upheld an appeals court decision that said school employees should "promote generally acceptable social standards." The lower court had ruled that "a school district does not violate the First Amendment when it disciplines a teacher for allowing students to use profanity repetitiously and egregiously in their written work."

Do You Need a Lawyer?

[4a]In 1995, Allstate began a campaign to encourage accident victims to settle claims against its policyholders without hiring lawyers. [4b]The insurance giant sent a conciliatory letter ("we consider you our customer") and a flier titled "Do I Need an Attorney?" The answer, predictably, was "not necessarily." "Before you decide to see an attorney, you may wish to seek an offer with Allstate," the flier noted, pointing out that legal fees take up a good portion of any judgment. It cited an industry study that found people "generally settle their claims more quickly" if they don't hire counsel. It suggested that victims who hire counsel insist that the contingency fee apply only to the money that was more than Allstate's offer before the lawyer got involved. The campaign was a success. According to one report, it reduced by nearly 10 percent the number of Allstate settlements in which the claimant hired an attorney.

FREE SPEECH   ____
NOT FREE SPEECH ____

[5]VERDICT: Not free speech, according to several states. In West Virginia, the state bar association ruled that the flier violated a state statute against "unauthorized [legal] practice." In Connecticut, the insurance commissioner ordered Allstate to stop distributing the flier, citing a 1997 law that makes it illegal to "discourage the retention of an attorney" in cases involving injury or death. In Pennsylvania, the attorney general sued Allstate, saying the flier violated unfair-trade and consumer-protection laws. Under pressure from trial lawyers, the New York attorney general told Allstate to reword the flier, stop using the word "customer," and pay $15,000 in administrative costs. State officials in Indiana, New Jersey, North Carolina, and Texas also pressured the company to make changes.

Neo-Nazis on Parade

[6]Richard Barrett, head of the Mississippi-based Nationalist Movement, travels the country to warn against the "Mexicanization, Africanization, and homosexualization" of America. In 1994 he applied for a permit to parade down West Broadway in South Boston. He said he and 300 "pro-majority" supporters wanted to follow part of the route of the annual St. Patrick's Day parade, which organizers had canceled rather than allow gays and lesbians to participate. The city denied Barrett's request, citing concerns about traffic congestion and public safety during a busy Saturday afternoon shopping period. The city had approved Saturday afternoon marches by other groups, but the mayor later said he had feared violence.

FREE SPEECH   ____
NOT FREE SPEECH ____

[7]VERDICT: Free speech, according to a federal judge. He struck down the city's parade permit ordinance, saying it gives officials too much power to ban marches. After hearing testimony, the judge concluded that officials denied Barrett's permit not because of congestion or public safety but because they disagreed with the "nature and content of the Nationalist Movement's message." He added that Boston officials had "behaved like a latter-day Watch and Ward Society, guarding against offensive political opinion," but noted the irony that "much of the law that protects Barrett's rights developed as a result of the courage of the pioneers of the civil rights movement." The court ordered the city to pay Barrett $700 in damages and his attorneys $51,000 in fees.

Antigay Remarks

[8]In 1992, San Francisco mayor Frank Jordan appointed the Reverend Eugene Lumpkin (pastor of the Ebenezer Baptist Church) to the city's Human Rights Commission. The following year Lumpkin told a newspaper reporter, "It's sad that people have AIDS and what have you, but it says right here in scripture that the homosexual lifestyle is an abomination against God." Two weeks later,

on a television talk show, the pastor refused to disavow an Old Testament passage that says a man who has sex with another man should be stoned to death. That same day, the mayor fired Lumpkin, saying the pastor had "crossed the line from belief to behavior to advocacy" and "implied that he condoned physical harm." Lumpkin took his case to federal court, saying that the First Amendment gave him the right to express his religious beliefs.

FREE SPEECH   ＿＿＿

NOT FREE SPEECH ＿＿＿

[9]VERDICT: Not free speech, according to a federal court. While Lumpkin had the right to express his views, "the First Amendment does not assure him job security when he preaches homophobia" while serving as an ambassador for human rights. The U.S. Supreme Court agreed.

Anti-Abortion Ads

[10]Christ's Bride Ministries of McLean, Virginia purchased advertising space at public transit stations in Philadelphia, Baltimore, and Washington, D.C. Its posters claimed that "women who choose abortion suffer more and deadlier breast cancer" and included a toll-free phone number for a group called the American Rights Coalition. A federal health official complained to the D.C. transit authority that the ad was "misleading" and "unduly alarming" and "does not accurately reflect the weight of the scientific literature." After learning of the health official's comments, the Southeastern Pennsylvania Transportation Authority immediately removed the posters, expressing concerns about their accuracy. The ministry cried foul, saying it had a First Amendment right to display the ads.

FREE SPEECH   ＿＿＿

NOT FREE SPEECH ＿＿＿

[11]VERDICT: Free speech, according to a federal court. It ruled that advertising space within transit stations is a public forum, and that SEPTA had violated the ministry's rights because it had no consistent policy to regulate ad content and had allowed controversial campaigns in the past. The U.S. Supreme Court agreed.

Wanted Posters

[12]Pro-life activists distributed Wanted posters featuring photos of abortion providers. The posters offered a $5000 reward for "information leading to arrest, conviction, and revocation of license" of the doctors and provided their home addresses. Meanwhile, a Web site known as the Nuremberg Files called for the "baby butchers" to be put on trial for crimes against humanity and included personal information such as the doctors' addresses and the names of their children. The site also indicated which providers had been murdered by placing a line through their names.

FREE SPEECH   ＿＿＿

NOT FREE SPEECH ＿＿＿

[13]VERDICT: Not free speech, according to a federal jury in Portland, Oregon. The Supreme Court has held that speech that is likely to cause "imminent lawless action" can be restricted; the Portland jurors were asked to decide if a reasonable person would construe the posters and site as violating a 1994 law that prohibits the use of force or threats against abortion clinic employees and patients. The defense argued that abortion providers have been scorned for years and that the posters and site, while provocative, were not enough to make someone act violently. The jury awarded a group of doctors and the local chapter of Planned Parenthood $107 million in damages.

SELECTION 4 QUESTIONS

Vocabulary

Use the most appropriate form of the word in the sentence.

1. facilitate [verb]   facilitator [noun] (¶2)
    a. Doris worked as a group ＿＿＿＿＿＿＿＿ for the children staying at the domestic violence center.
    b. To ＿＿＿＿＿＿＿＿ the employment process, the application forms have been placed on the company's Web site.
2. predictably [adverb] (¶4) predict [verb]
    a. The August day in Phoenix was ＿＿＿＿＿＿＿＿ sunny and hot.
    b. Although he had studied, John couldn't ＿＿＿＿＿＿＿＿ his score on the exam.

Explain these passages in your own words.

3. "... insist that the contingency fee apply only to the money that
    was more than Allstate's offer before the lawyer got involved."
    (¶4)

    _____

    _____

4. "... crossed the line from belief to behavior to advocacy...." (¶8)

    _____

    _____

Comprehension

Determine whether the statements in sentences 5 and 6 are true or false, and
write your answer. Also, if the statement is false, rewrite it to make it true.

5. Understanding and enforcing the First Amendment is simple.

    _____

    _____

6. The First Amendment guarantees people the right to say any-
    thing anywhere.

    _____

    _____

7. Circle the letter of the sentence that best expresses the thesis.
    a. The U.S. Supreme Court rules on many freedom of speech
        cases.
    b. Although the First Amendment guarantees freedom of
        speech, there are limitations.
    c. The courts often award large settlements in First Amend-
        ment cases.
    d. There is no such thing as free speech.

8. In paragraph 4, sentence b, what is the relationship of the por-
    tion in parenthesis ("we consider you our customer") to the first
    portion of the sentence, "The insurance giant sent a conciliatory
    letter"? Which of the following does it provide?
    a. an example of the thought
    b. a definition
    c. a cause

9. In the case of Richard Barrett (Neo-Nazis on Parade, para-
    graphs 6 and 7), why did the court rule in his favor?

    _____

    _____

10. In the case of Reverend Eugene Lumpkin (Antigay Remarks,
    paragraphs 8 and 9), why did the court rule against him?

    _____

    _____

CROSSWORD PUZZLE

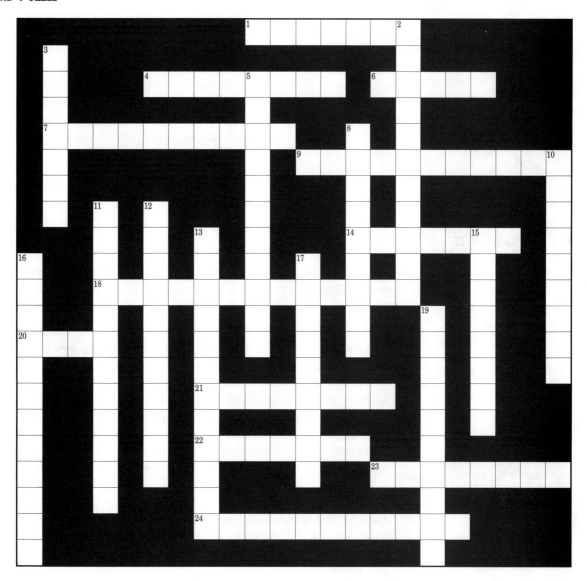

ACROSS

1 reduce, diminish
4 approved
6 investigate
7 uncertain, mixed feelings
9 wickedness, immorality
14 core, essential part
18 over and over again
20 control, restrict
21 expected to happen soon
22 treated with disrespect
23 freedom
24 relationship

DOWN

2 outrageously, excessively
3 deny
5 basic
8 agreement
10 number
11 credited to
12 collection of
13 highly positive
15 guilty causes
16 respectful, polite
17 calling together
19 viewpoint

WORD LIST (NOT ALL USED)

abated	correlation	latitude
abomination	culprits	numerical
abridge	curb	perception
ambivalent	disavow	probe
attributable	egregiously	ratified
compilation	enthusiastic	repetitiously
conciliatory	essence	scorned
consensus	fundamental	
convening	imminent	

LOG ON TO THE WEB

Our First Amendment freedoms impact us in many ways. Therefore, you can find information about the freedoms and their impact in many places on the Web. For example:

> The Freedom Forum at <http://www.freedomforum.org> is an excellent starting point for research into all first amendment rights. The site contains a comprehensive archive of news, legal materials, and links to speech, religion, press, and assembly sites.

> The Bonfire of the Liberties site at <http://www.humanities-interactive.org/exhibit1.html> is a fascinating look at censorship over the centuries. This site contains a large collection of graphic images that trace types of censorship, individuals affected by censorship, and much more.

> This site on workplace harassment at <http://www.law.ucla.edu/faculty/volokh/harass/protections> is maintained by Professor Eugene Volokh of the UCLA School of Law. It explores the free speech tensions that often happen when trying to protect against workplace harassment.

> This site, detailing one of the more controversial forms of expression, flag burning, <http://www.esquilax.com/flag> contains extensive coverage of the issue, including a history of flag burning and details on the legal activity currently underway.

> This Web site, <http://www.lib.siu.edu/cni/homepage.html> produced from the materials of Ralph E. McCoy, the Dean Emeritus of Library Affairs at Southern Illinois University, is an exhaustive reference guide to freedom of the press materials.

Log on to one of these sites or use a search directory/engine to locate another site with information about some aspect of our First Amendment freedoms.

Read one section or story about First Amendment freedoms. Write down: (1) the complete address (http://www. ...), (2) the name of the person or company who sponsors and maintains the site, (3) the name of the person who wrote the information, (4) what you know about the writer, and (5) one important thing you learned about First Amendment freedoms.

IDEAS FOR WRITING AND DISCUSSION

A. Based on your readings in this theme, which, if any, of the authors do you think would agree with Oliver Wendell Holmes that "The only useful test of whether someone believes in the First Amendment is whether he or she would vigorously protect the views of the people they hate." Which, if any, of the authors do you think would disagree with him? Please explain.

B. To protest the University of Colorado softening its policy on selling T-shirts produced in Third World sweatshops, a 20-year-old college student jumped onto the auditorium stage and shoved a blueberry pie into the face of CU Chancellor Richard Byyny. After the police charged the student with third-degree assault, newspaper columnist Clint Talbot wrote: "… her [the student's] act, though criminal, was a political statement. Like other forms of protest, it reflects the values of the First Amendment."

Do you share Talbot's feelings that such a protest "reflects the values of the First Amendment," or do you disagree with him? Please explain.

C. In Nevada, an angry parent got into a pushing and shoving match with his daughter's basketball coach. The parent was charged in the incident. The local newspaper ran an article when the parent pleaded guilty to a misdemeanor battery charge and agreed to undergo an anger-management evaluation. It ran a photograph of the parent with the article. The parent complained that the photograph "made him look like a criminal."

Now, a Nevada lawmaker has asked for legislation to be drafted that would "restrict use by newspapers of photographs of persons under certain circumstances." What those "circumstances" are have not yet been specified.

According to Nevada Press Association Executive Director Kent Lauer, the proposal "should be dead on arrival at the Legislature because it's a blatant violation of the First Amendment. It's government censorship, plain and simple," he added.

Do you feel such legislation is a good idea or agree with Lauer that it would be a "violation of the First Amendment"? Please explain.

D. A Boston bar owner put up a supposedly racist African-themed display allegedly mocking Black History month and Martin Luther King, Jr.'s birthday. The Massachusetts Commission against Discrimination says it's illegal for businesses to say things that "ridicule or create a racial stereotype and make certain people feel unwelcome" and thus create a "hostile public accommodations environment." Therefore, the Commission is investigating whether the bar owner did this and should be punished.

Do you think the First Amendment protects his right to express his opinions—good, bad, and ugly—or should he be punished? Please explain.

DRUGS, ALCOHOL, AND TOBACCO

Although the word *drug* often makes us think of dark alleys and illegal sales, the term actually refers to any substance that causes a change in the body. This means that everything from aspirin and alcohol to cocaine and PCP are drugs. Drugs are made from plants, minerals, animals, and created synthetically in laboratories.

Some drugs, to treat illnesses like colds and allergies, are sold over the counter (OTC). Other drugs, to treat more severe ailments, can only be obtained legally with a prescription from an authorized health-care provider. Drugs known to be addictive are even more strictly controlled.

Alcohol is often referred to as the oldest drug known to humankind. Since humans discovered how to make fermented drinks about 3,500 years ago, drinking has become one of the most common social activities all over the world.

Americans, however, have always had mixed feelings about alcohol. Because of its link to violence, crime, and the destruction of families, the nation made the manufacture and sale of alcoholic beverages illegal in the 1920s. But, the public's thirst was too great and Prohibition was repealed in 1933. Today the debate is much the same. Many feel that alcohol's potential to harm individuals, families, and society is so great that it should be more tightly controlled. Others insist that when alcohol is used responsibly it is harmless and potentially beneficial.

Tobacco is one of the most widely used addictive substances in the world. Even though the first scientific studies linking smoking "with a definite impairment of longevity," appeared in the 1930s, between 1930 and 1979 per capita consumption of cigarettes in the United States almost tripled.

Attitudes about tobacco didn't begin to change until 1964, when Luther Terry, surgeon general of the United States, issued the report condemning cigarette smoking. Every surgeon general since Terry has campaigned against smoking. Even so, according to the 1999 National Youth Tobacco Survey conducted by the American Legacy Foundation and the Centers for Disease Control, tobacco products are gaining popularity among teens.

Authors in this theme provide insight into some of the issues related to drug, alcohol, and tobacco use in the United States. Each of the readings is by a different author, of a different length, and requires different tasks.

"Drugs, Alcohol, and Tobacco," Chapter 46 of *Biology*, a text by professors Kenneth Miller and Joseph Levine, opens the theme. In this chapter they detail what a drug is and the specific effects of different drugs, including alcohol and tobacco.

Next, "Alcohol—Opposing Viewpoints: Introduction" by the Editors of Greenhaven Press gives a brief review of America's continuing debate on the benefits and problems of alcohol's widespread use in contemporary society.

In "Reading the Media's Messages about Medications," Sheila Globus encourages us to thoughtfully consider what kind of drug we really need rather than buy a product because it "looks good" in a cute advertisement.

Then, four college and high school students share the results of their research in "Tobacco and Alcohol Advertisements in Magazines: Are Young Readers Being Targeted?"

And finally, Kathiann M. Kowalski provides facts and advice in "Avoiding the Lure of Tobacco, Alcohol, and Marijuana."

FEATURED SELECTION 1: "DRUGS, ALCOHOL, AND TOBACCO"

BEFORE YOU READ

About the Authors   Kenneth Miller has a Ph.D. in biology. He is a Professor of Biology at Brown University in Providence, Rhode Island, where he teaches courses in general biology and cell biology. He is a cell biologist and his research work appears in numerous journals. Joseph Levine has a Ph.D. in biology. He is an Adjunct Assistant Professor of Biology at Boston College and works on projects aimed at improving public understanding of science. Among his projects he acts as a science advisor for the PBS television series NOVA.

This chapter on drugs, alcohol, and tobacco is from "Unit 9: Human Biology," of their text *Biology*, fifth edition.

Words to Know

Key terms appear in bold type and are defined in context.

An Idea to Think About   How do you define the term *drug*? In other words, what do you think makes a substance a drug? *As you read*, find out how Miller and Levine define drug.

Chapter 46 *Drugs, Alcohol, and Tobacco*

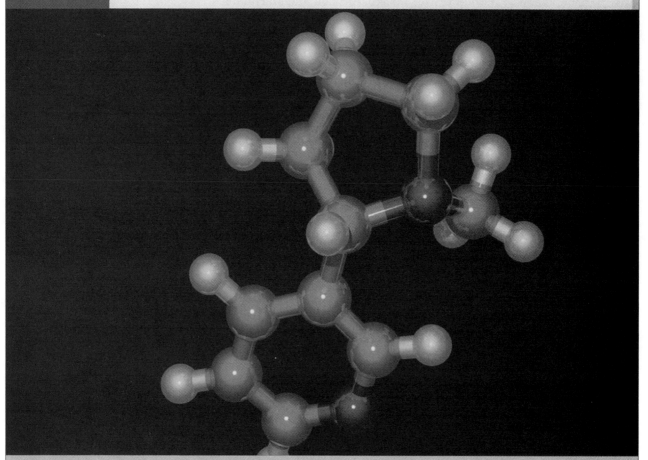

Nicotine, shown here in a computer-generated image, increases heart rate and blood pressure and, over the long term, produces physical and psychological addiction.

Chapter Inquiry Drawing Conclusions

1. Working with a partner, examine cigarette filters from smoked and unsmoked cigarettes. Describe the differences in their colors.

2. Do you think the filter "traps" all the pollutants in the smoke?

3. How might smoking unfiltered cigarettes affect a smoker's lungs?

Connect to the Main Ideas

In this unit, you have learned about the different body systems of humans. What systems are affected by tobacco smoke and nicotine? List each system, and describe the effect.

46–1   Drugs

Guide For Reading

■ What are some ways in which drugs can affect the body?

■ What is drug abuse?

By definition, a **drug** is any substance that causes a change in the body. Many substances fit that definition, including antibiotics that are used to fight infection and aspirin that is used to control pain.

All drugs affect the body in some ways. Some drugs, such as cocaine and heroin, are so powerful and dangerous that their possession is illegal. Other drugs, including penicillin and codeine, are prescription drugs and can be used only under the supervision of a doctor. Still other drugs, including cough and cold medicines, are sold over the counter,

All drugs (legal and illegal) have the potential to do harm if they are used improperly, or abused. In this section, we consider some of the most commonly abused drugs and the ways in which they affect the body.

How Drugs Affect the Body

Drugs differ in the ways in which they affect the body. Some drugs kill bacteria and are useful in treating disease. Other drugs affect a particular system of the body, such as the digestive or circulatory system. Among the most powerful drugs, however, are the ones that affect the nervous system in ways that can change behavior.

MARIJUANA   Statistically, the most widely abused illegal drug is **marijuana.** Marijuana comes from a species of hemp plant known as *Cannabis sativa.* Marijuana is commonly called

Figure 46–1 Artist Keith Haring described his attitude toward drug abuse in this anticrack mural.

Figure 46–2 *Written on this clay tablet are the world's oldest known prescriptions, dating back to about 2000 BC. The prescriptions describe the medicinal uses of certain plants.*

Figure 46–3 *Using medication after the prescription has expired is one way that even legal drugs can be abused.*

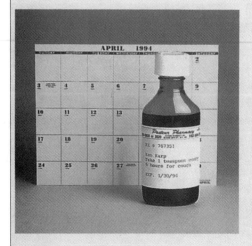

grass or pot. Hashish, or hash, is a potent form of marijuana made from the flowering parts of the plant. The active ingredient in all forms of marijuana is tetrahydrocannabinol (THC). Smoking or ingesting THC can produce a temporary feeling of euphoria and disorientation.

Short-term use of marijuana does not seem to cause immediate physical damage to the body. However, the word *seem* here is deceiving. For there is clear evidence that smoking marijuana is bad for the lungs, although the damaging effects may not be immediate. In fact, smoking marijuana is even more destructive to the lungs than smoking tobacco.

Long-term use of marijuana can result in loss of memory, inability to concentrate, and reduced levels of the hormone testosterone in males. Heavy users develop a psychological dependence (need) on the drug, which can make constructive behavior—work, sports, study, and social activities—almost impossible.

HALLUCINOGENS Some drugs affect a user's view of reality so strongly that they are known as **hallucinogens** (from a Latin word meaning "to dream"). **LSD** (lysergic acid diethylamide) is the most powerful hallucinogen. Acid, as this drug is commonly called, interferes with the normal transmission of nerve impulses in the brain. Although its effects vary from person to person, virtually all people who use LSD regularly have had a "bad trip" in which their hallucinations became frighteningly real. Some LSD users have lost touch with reality after only a single dose of the drug.

In recent years, another hallucinogen has come into use. This powerful drug, called **PCP** (phencyclidine), produces feelings of strength and great power. Also known as angel dust, PCP can result in nightmarish illusions that may last for many days. High doses of PCP produce seizures and even heart attacks. And hospital workers in emergency wards know another side effect of PCP: Users often become extremely violent and are a danger to themselves and others.

STIMULANTS A number of drugs speed up the actions of the nervous system and are therefore known as **stimulants.** The most powerful stimulants are a group of drugs called **amphetamines.** Commonly known as speed or uppers, amphetamines chemically resemble natural neurotransmitters found in the body. You may recall from Chapter 37 that neurotransmitters are compounds that pass nerve impulses from one neuron (nerve cell) to another. When a person takes a dose of amphetamine, the drug floods the body with what the body assumes are natural neurotransmitters. This causes the nervous system to increase its activity, producing a feeling of strength and energy in the user. Fatigue seems to vanish. But there is a dark side to such drugs as well.

The nervous system cannot handle the overstimulation produced by amphetamines. When a dose of the drug wears off,

Figure 46–4 Amphetamines are among the most powerful and dangerous drugs known. After it was given a small dose of amphetamine, this orb-weaver spider was unable to spin a normal web.

the user suffers from fatigue and depression. Long-term use causes hallucinations, circulatory problems, and psychological difficulties. Heavy users become so dependent on amphetamines that they are unable to function without them. They have difficulty dealing with other people and fall into a pattern of speeding up and crashing (recovering from the rapid pace of their drug-induced activities).

DEPRESSANTS   Drugs that reduce the rate of nervous system activity are called **depressants.** Among the most commonly used (and abused) depressants are the **barbiturates,** a group of compounds often found in sleeping pills. People who abuse downers, as these drugs are called, can quickly become dependent on them. When barbiturates are used with alcohol, the results are often fatal, as the nervous system can become so depressed even breathing stops.

Another danger of barbiturate abuse occurs when a user tries to stop. Unlike virtually all other abused drugs, cutting off the supply of barbiturates to the body can result in serious medical problems that must be treated immediately. Thus a barbiturate abuser needs medical attention when trying to quit.

COCAINE   The leaves of the coca plant grown in South America contain a compound known as **cocaine.** In the nineteenth century cocaine was used as a local anaesthetic to deaden pain during surgery. Today, people who abuse cocaine may sniff it, smoke it, or inject it directly into the bloodstream.

Cocaine causes the release of a neurotransmitter in the brain called dopamine. Normally, dopamine release occurs when a basic need, such as hunger or thirst, is satisfied. The release of dopamine in the brain produces a feeling of pleasure (a feeling you have probably experienced after a particularly large Thanksgiving dinner). Cocaine fools the brain into releasing dopamine, producing an intense feeling of pleasure and satisfaction.

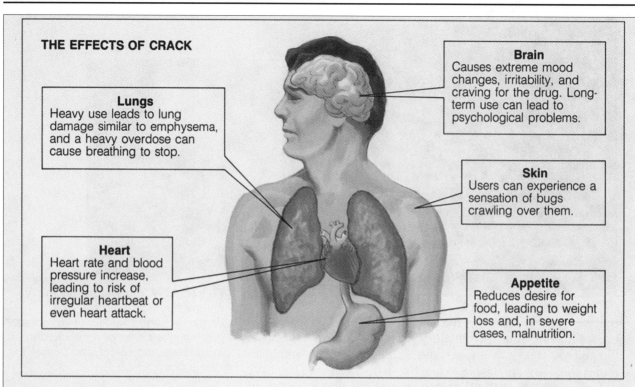

THE EFFECTS OF CRACK

Lungs
Heavy use leads to lung damage similar to emphysema, and a heavy overdose can cause breathing to stop.

Brain
Causes extreme mood changes, irritability, and craving for the drug. Long-term use can lead to psychological problems.

Heart
Heart rate and blood pressure increase, leading to risk of irregular heartbeat or even heart attack.

Skin
Users can experience a sensation of bugs crawling over them.

Appetite
Reduces desire for food, leading to weight loss and, in severe cases, malnutrition.

Figure 46–5 Crack is an extremely powerful form of cocaine. What effect does crack have on the brain?

The effects of cocaine can be so powerful that a long-term user makes obtaining the drug more important than anything else in life, including food, sleep, and a career. So much dopamine is released when the drug is used that not enough is left when it wears off. As a result, users quickly discover that they feel sad and depressed without the drug and seek to use it again and again. Thus the psychological dependence that cocaine produces is particularly difficult to break.

When cocaine reaches the bloodstream, it acts as a powerful stimulant, increasing the heartbeat and blood pressure. The stimulation can be so powerful that the heart is damaged by the drug. In some cases, even a first-time user may experience a heart attack, as happened to basketball star Len Bias.

In the late 1980s, cocaine abusers began to use a form of cocaine called **crack,** which can be smoked in a pipe. Crack is a particularly potent and dangerous form of cocaine that can become addictive after only a few doses. The drug's effect on the nervous system peaks just after smoking, producing a more rapid and powerful response than that produced by sniffing cocaine.

OPIATES   Some of the most powerful drugs are the **opiates,** a group of drugs produced from the opium poppy. The most common opiates are opium itself, which is derived directly from the opium poppy, and **morphine** and **heroin,** which are chemically refined forms of opium. All of the opiates, with the exception of heroin, can be used under a doctor's supervision to relieve severe pain. Morphine is particularly effective as a pain killer. However, all of the opiates can also result in death when taken in large doses (overdose).

Biology Update   Tobacco and Nicotine

Yes, It's Addictive, Too

The similarities of highly addictive drugs such as cocaine and heroin to transmitters in the nervous system are what make these drugs so dangerous. Although researchers have known for years of the harmful effects of tobacco, some have wondered whether tobacco is truly an addicting drug. Now, however, the results seem to be in. Tobacco contains nicotine, a chemical that mimics acetylcholine, one of the most important transmitters in the nervous system.

Effects of Nicotine

Inhaled tobacco smoke places a burst of nicotine into the blood, which quickly distributes this nicotine to the rest of the body. Nicotine stimulates the receptors on cells that would normally respond to acetycholine. The result is an increase in heart rate and blood pressure, a narrowing of blood vessels throughout the body, and a feeling of relaxation and euphoria. (Incidentally, tobacco plants synthesize nicotine as a protective insecticide. By stimulating similar receptors in the nervous systems of insects, nicotine weakens many insects and kills others.)

In other mammals, repeated nicotine use produces classic symptoms of addiction, including psychological and physical dependence. Smokers who attempt to quit experience nausea and insomnia as well as feelings of anxiety and depression.

Locating the Nicotine Receptor

Scientists have even detected the exact receptor that is responsible for this addiction. In

The nicotine patch releases a set dose of nicotine into the body. The dose can be gradually reduced in successive patches to help the person overcome the addiction to smoking.

1998, European researchers showed that they could prevent nicotine addiction in mice by "knocking out" the gene for one of the receptor proteins for acetycholine. Such experiments have proved that nicotine dependence, like addiction to other drugs, is based on the ability of nicotine to act on the central nervous system.

The practical uses of this research are beginning to show up in medicine and even in the drugstore. The sudden popularity of drugs, skin patches, and gums that ease nicotine withdrawal are testament to one of the most important facts about smoking: Tobacco is genuinely addictive. And, as with any other addictive drug, the best course of action is never to start using it.

 Get an update on tobacco and nicotine at our Internet site: *http://www.phschool.com*

Heroin, the most commonly abused opiate, is often injected directly into the bloodstream. Heroin produces a powerful, sleepy feeling of well-being that users often crave. As you might expect, heroin can result in strong psychological dependence. Opiates can also cause a strong physical dependence in which the body actually requires the drug in order to function properly. (So can barbiturates, alcohol, and tobacco.) In addition to facing many other dangers, heroin users run the risk of contracting AIDS from the use of shared needles. (See Chapter 45.)

Figure 46–6 The round yellow structure in the center of the opium poppy flower is the pod. Notice the sap, from which the opiates are derived, oozing out of the ripe poppy pod.

Drug Abuse

Each of the drugs we have discussed presents a danger to users. **Drug abuse**—the misuse of either a legal or illegal drug—is a serious problem in modern society. **Drug abuse can be defined as using any drug in a way that most doctors would not approve.** With some drugs, such as cocaine, drug abuse causes serious physical damage to the body. With other drugs, such as marijuana, drug abuse produces psychological dependence that can be strong enough to disrupt family life and schoolwork. Workers under the influence of drugs are unreliable and may commit errors of judgment that place them and their co-workers at risk.

DRUG ADDICTION   An uncontrollable craving for a drug is known as a **drug addiction.** As you have read, some drugs cause a strong psychological dependence, or need, in the user, whereas other drugs cause a strong physical dependence. (Many cause both.) In general, the term drug addiction is used to describe a physical dependence on a drug. However, as you now know, even a psychological dependence can have a chemical basis.

Opiates, such as heroin, are examples of drugs that cause a strong physical dependence. All regular users of heroin will eventually become addicted. At that point, their nervous system will become dependent on a steady supply of the drug. Any attempt at **withdrawal,** or stopping the use of the drug, will cause severe pain, nausea, chills, and fever. You may have heard the terms kick-the-habit and cold turkey applied to people who quit using heroin. These terms have a basis in fact. For during heroin withdrawal, a person develops goose bumps that make the skin resemble the skin of a turkey (cold turkey). In addition, the leg muscles of the body may jerk uncontrollably (kicking the habit). The symptoms of withdrawal are so severe that users usually seek another dose of the drug to "cure" them of withdrawal sickness.

Casual users of opiates often believe that they can control their body's need for the drug. But they are nearly always wrong. And now we know the reason why!

In the 1970s, scientists began to look for a cellular basis for opiate addiction. They found that heroin and morphine would bind to special receptors on the surfaces of nerve cells. Why should human nerve cells have receptors for compounds derived from a poppy plant native to Asia?

A group of scientists led by Candace Pert at the National Institutes of Health found the answer: The brain produces its own opiates! These morphinelike chemicals produced by the brain are called **endorphins.** There are several classes of endorphins, and not all endorphin functions are understood. But what is very clear is that endorphins produced by the brain help to overcome pain and produce sensations of pleasure.

Now we can understand how opiate addiction occurs. By coincidence, compounds such as morphine and heroin bind to the same receptors as endorphins do, producing a feeling of pleasure and blocking sensations of pain. But the abnormally high levels of opiates reached during drug use upset the normal balance of endorphins and receptors in the brain. Once the body adjusts to the higher levels of opiates, it literally cannot do without them. If the drug is withdrawn, natural endorphins cannot be supplied by the body in large enough amounts to prevent the uncontrollable pain and sickness that are characteristic withdrawal symptoms. Addiction has a cellular basis that the addict simply cannot control!

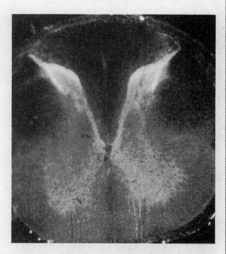

Figure 46–7 The bright spots in this cross section of the spinal cord are some of the receptors in the nervous system to which opiates bind.

46–1 SECTION REVIEW

1. Define the term drug.
2. Distinguish between drug abuse and drug addiction.
3. Compare the actions of stimulants and depressants on the nervous system.
4. **Critical Thinking—Applying Concepts**   Explain why withdrawing from an addictive drug is not simply a matter of willpower.

46–2   Alcohol

Alcohol is a drug—the oldest drug known to human culture. Written records from Egypt and Babylon show that people have made alcoholic beverages for more than 3500 years. Alcohol is produced when yeast grow in a sugar-containing liquid in the absence of oxygen. The yeast ferment the sugar to obtain energy and release alcohol and carbon dioxide as byproducts.

Effects of Alcohol

Alcohol-containing drinks are popular in nearly all cultures. They include fermented drinks, such as beer and wine, and stronger drinks made by distillation, including whiskey, vodka, scotch, and gin. The strength of different drinks depends mainly on the percentage of alcohol. Regardless of the type of drink or its strength, the form of alcohol is always **ethyl alcohol** (C_2H_5OH).

Alcohol is a small molecule that passes through cell membranes easily and is quickly absorbed into the bloodstream. High concentrations of alcohol are toxic. However, very low concentrations of alcohol can be used by the body as a source of food. This is one reason why the effects of alcohol wear off within a few hours after it enters the body.

Guide For Reading

■ What type of drug is alcohol?
■ What are some effects of alcohol on the body?
■ When does alcohol use become alcohol abuse?

Quick Lab

To reinforce the **Main Idea** of stimulant drugs, perform the Quick Lab activity called Testing the Effects of Adrenaline on p. 1112.

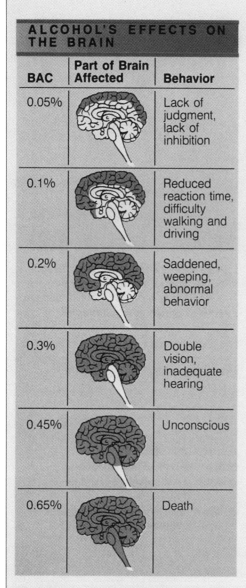

ALCOHOL'S EFFECTS ON THE BRAIN

BAC	Part of Brain Affected	Behavior
0.05%		Lack of judgment, lack of inhibition
0.1%		Reduced reaction time, difficulty walking and driving
0.2%		Saddened, weeping, abnormal behavior
0.3%		Double vision, inadequate hearing
0.45%		Unconscious
0.65%		Death

Figure 46–8 *BAC, or blood alcohol concentration, is a measure of the amount of alcohol in the bloodstream per 100 mL of blood. What happens if the BAC exceeds 0.45 percent?*

The most immediate effects of alcohol are on the nervous system. **Alcohol is a depressant.** Even small amounts of alcohol slow down the rate at which the nervous system functions. This means that any amount of alcohol slows down reflexes, disrupts coordination, and impairs judgment. Heavy drinking fills the blood with so much alcohol that the nervous system cannot function properly. People who have had three or four drinks in the span of an hour may feel relaxed and confident, but their blood contains as much as 0.10 percent alcohol, making them legally drunk in most states. They usually cannot walk or talk properly, and they are certainly not able to safely control an automobile.

Alcohol is used and accepted by cultures throughout the world. Because of this cultural acceptance, alcohol is the most dangerous and abused drug in the world. More than half of all Americans consume alcoholic beverages. Although many do so quite responsibly, a dangerously large number do not. Alcohol is the drug most commonly abused by teenagers. The abuse of alcohol has a frightening social price. One half of the 50,000 people who die on American highways in a typical year are victims of accidents in which at least one driver has been drinking. One third of all homicides are attributed to the effects of alcohol. At least $25 billion worth of damage is done to the economy in this country alone as a result of alcohol-related accidents that injure workers and damage property.

But the toll of alcohol abuse does not stop there! Women who are pregnant and drink on a regular basis run the risk of **fetal alcohol syndrome,** or damage to the developing baby due to the effects of alcohol. More than 50,000 babies are born in this country every year with alcohol-related birth defects.

Alcohol and Disease

People who have become addicted to alcohol suffer from a disease called **alcoholism.** Some alcoholics may need to have a drink before work or school—every day! They may drink so heavily that they black out and cannot remember what they have done while drinking. Other alcoholics, however, do not necessarily drink to the point where it is obvious that they have an alcohol-abuse problem. **If a person cannot function properly without satisfying the need or craving for alcohol, that person is considered to have an alcohol-abuse problem.**

Repeated bouts of heavy drinking damage the digestive system, through which the alcohol passes on its way into the bloodstream. Alcohol taken in excessive amounts can destroy neurons in the brain. Long-term alcohol use also destroys cells in the liver, where alcohol is broken down. As liver cells die, the liver becomes less able to handle large amounts of alcohol. The formation of scar tissue, known as cirrhosis of the liver, occurs next. The scar tissue blocks the flow of blood through the liver and interferes with its other important functions. Eventually, a heavy drinker may die from chronic liver failure.

You may be tempted to believe that deaths due to alcoholism are rare. If so, it might surprise you to learn that cirrhosis of the liver is the seventh leading cause of death in the United States! And although attempts have been made in the past to eliminate this drug from our society, alcohol remains with us today. Thus we must each find a way to deal with it.

As with other drugs, dealing with alcohol abuse is not simply a matter of willpower. Alcoholics often need special help and support to quit their drinking habit. Organizations such as Alcoholics Anonymous are available in most communities to help individuals and families deal with the problems created by alcohol abuse. There are even organizations for the relatives of the ten million or so alcoholics in this country. One such organization, Alateen, is for the children of people who have an alcohol problem.

46–2 SECTION REVIEW

1. What type of drug is alcohol?
2. Distinguish an alcoholic from the millions of Americans who drink but do not have a drinking problem.
3. **Critical Thinking—Making Predictions** Prohibition was a period in our nation's history (1920–1933) during which alcohol was outlawed. Would Prohibition be any more effective today than it was then? Explain.

Figure 46–9 More than 25,000 Americans die in car accidents every year in which at least one driver was under the influence of alcohol.

46–3 Tobacco

Tobacco is a plant native to North America. European explorers learned of the aromatic properties of the tobacco plant and helped to found an industry based on smoking the dried leaves. Today tobacco is used throughout the world. It may be smoked in pipes or in the form of cigarettes and cigars. Tobacco may also be used in the form of chewing tobacco or snuff.

Effects of Tobacco

Tobacco contains many substances that affect the body. **Nicotine** in tobacco smoke enters the bloodstream and causes the release of epinephrine, a stimulant that increases the pulse rate and blood pressure. Tobacco smoke also contains carbon monoxide, a poisonous gas that blocks the transport of oxygen by hemoglobin in the blood. (See Chapter 40.) Carbon monoxide decreases the body's supply of oxygen to its tissues, depriving the heart and other organs of the oxygen they need to function. **Tar**, a mixture of complex chemicals in tobacco products, includes a number of compounds that have been shown to cause cancer.

Guide For Reading

■ How do the main components of tobacco smoke affect the body?
■ What are some health problems caused by smoking tobacco?

995

Figure 46–10 *In addition to these harmful substances, there are over 4000 other compounds given off when a cigarette burns.*

When tobacco products are used or smoked regularly, the body develops an addiction to nicotine. For this reason, long-term smokers find it extremely difficult to stop.

Tobacco and Disease

Tobacco is one of the leading causes of premature death in this country. **Lung cancer, the most common form of fatal cancer in the United States, has been directly linked to smoking.** Because lung cancer may take twenty years to develop, smokers may have a false sense of security about their habit. However, even in younger smokers the signs of destruction and illness are unmistakable.

LUNG DISORDERS By age 45, the death rate from lung cancer for smokers is four times that for nonsmokers. By age 65, it is more than ten times greater. For every smoker there is a serious risk of developing lung cancer. But lung cancer is not the only risk! There are other lung disorders associated with smoking. Smoke particles become trapped in the linings of the breathing passageways. At first these linings cleanse themselves. But as smoking continues, the cells of the linings are damaged. In time, smokers may develop a persistent cough as their lungs attempt to clear themselves. Smokers also suffer higher rates of respiratory infections than nonsmokers. They often develop chronic **bronchitis,** an inflammation of the large breathing tubes (bronchi) in the lungs. Long-term smoking can lead to **emphysema,** a stiffening of the normally elastic tissues of the lung.

Figure 46–11 *This photograph shows the bronchial walls in the lungs of a nonsmoker (left). Notice the cancer cells invading the bronchial wall of a smoker (right). As you can imagine, it was too late for this person to quit.*

CIRCULATORY DISEASES   The steady inhalation of carbon monoxide seems to cause a slow poisoning of the heart. Smoking also constricts, or narrows, blood vessels. Constriction of blood vessels causes blood pressure to rise and makes the heart work harder. It is no real surprise that statistics indicate that smoking doubles the risk of death from heart disease for men between the ages of 45 and 65. Moreover, for every age group and for both sexes, the risk of death from heart disease is greater among smokers than nonsmokers.

OTHER CANCERS   Tobacco smokers also suffer from higher than normal levels of mouth and throat cancer, probably due to chemicals in tobacco tar. People who chew tobacco or inhale snuff should not be fooled into thinking these forms of tobacco are safe. Tobacco-chewers, for example, have extremely high rates of oral cancer and often fail to detect these cancers in time to prevent damage to the mouth and face.

SMOKING AND THE NONSMOKER   In recent years evidence has clearly shown that the dangers of smoking are not restricted to the smoker. Tobacco smoke in the air is damaging to anyone who inhales it, not just the smoker. For this reason, many states require restaurants to have smoking and nonsmoking sections. And in many parts of the country, smoking in public places has been restricted, if not prohibited.

Passive smoking, or inhaling the smoke of others, is particularly damaging to young children. Studies now indicate that the children of smokers are twice as likely to develop respiratory problems as are children of nonsmokers.

DEALING WITH TOBACCO   Only 30 percent of male smokers live to the age of 80. About 55 percent of male nonsmokers do. Clearly, smoking reduces expected life span. Moreover, whatever the age and no matter how long a person has smoked, a person's health can be improved by quitting. But tobacco is a powerful drug with strong addictive qualities that make it very difficult to give up. Thus, considering the cost, the medical dangers, and the chemical power of addiction, the best solution is not to begin smoking. Period!

46–3 SECTION REVIEW

1. Describe the main components of tobacco smoke and their effects on the body.

2. What are some disorders that result from smoking?

3. **Critical Thinking—Relating Cause and Effect**   What is the best advice you can give to a smoker who has not shown any ill effects, as yet, from the habit?

 IDENTIFYING SUBSTANCES IN TOBACCO

▶ *Designing an Experiment*

PROBLEM
What type of products are found in tobacco?

SUGGESTED MATERIALS (per group)

triple-beam balance	test tubes
filter paper	test-tube holder
tobacco from a ciga-	test-tube rack
rette, pipe, and cigar	Bunsen burner
cotton	matches

SUGGESTED PROCEDURE 🜂 👓 🖐 👁

1. Devise an experiment to find out some of the products that are produced when tobacco burns.
2. Write down the steps of your experimental procedure. Be sure to include a control. To begin, you may want to place each type of tobacco in a test tube and find the mass of a wad of cotton large enough to fill the opening of each test tube. Put the cotton wad into the open end of each test tube. Then, using a test-tube holder, heat the bottom of each test tube, one test tube at a time, over a Bunsen burner flame. **CAUTION:** *Be careful with open flames.* Keep the cotton pointed away from the flame, and keep the opening of the test tube away from others. After heating the tobacco for one minute, turn off the Bunsen burner and place the test tube in a rack to cool. Remove the cotton wad and measure its mass. Repeat the heating procedure for each type of tobacco.
3. Construct a data table similar to the one shown on a separate sheet of paper. Record your measurements in your data table.
4. Conduct the experiment after having your teacher approve your procedure and data table.
5. From your data, determine the type of products produced by tobacco.

OBSERVATIONS

1. What did you observe on the inside of the test tube while the tobacco was burning?
2. Did the appearance of the cotton change after it was heated?
3. Describe the appearances of tar.

ANALYSIS AND CONCLUSIONS

1. Based on its appearance, what effect would tar have on the respiratory system?
2. Which of the three types of tobacco produced the most tar? How do you know?
3. Which type produced the least tar?
4. What could be done to make these measurements more precise?

DATA TABLE

Type of tobacco	Mass of cotton before heating	Mass of cotton after heating	Difference in mass

SUMMARIZING THE CONCEPTS

The key concepts in each section of this chapter are listed below to help you review the chapter content. Make sure you understand each concept and its relationship to the theme of this chapter.

46–1 Drugs

- A drug is any substance that causes a change in the body.
- All drugs, when used improperly, have the potential to do harm.
- The most widely abused illegal drug in the United States is marijuana.
- Hallucinogens, such as LSD and PCP, are powerful drugs that change the user's view of reality.
- Stimulants, such as amphetamines, speed up the actions of the nervous system.
- Depressants, such as barbiturates, slow down the actions of the nervous system.
- Cocaine, derived from the coca plant, is a stimulant that produces very strong psychological dependence. Use of cocaine can damage the heart and cause a heart attack. Crack is a form of cocaine that is highly addictive and has many serious effects on the body.
- Opiates, such as heroin and morphine, can be used to reduce pain. Opiates are addictive and lead to strong physical dependence.
- Drug abuse can be defined as using any drug in a way most doctors would not approve.
- People addicted to drugs may suffer withdrawal symptoms when cut off from their drug supply.

46–2 Alcohol

- Alcohol is a depressant that easily passes through cell membranes. Even a small amount of alcohol acts to slow down the actions of the nervous system.
- People who are addicted to alcohol are said to suffer from a disease called alcoholism.

46–3 Tobacco

- Several substances in tobacco—among them nicotine, tar, and carbon monoxide—can lead to serious health problems, including lung cancer, other cancers, respiratory problems, and circulatory problems.

REVIEWING KEY TERMS

Vocabulary terms are important to your understanding of biology. The key terms listed below are those you should be especially familiar with. Review these terms and their meanings. Then use each term in a complete sentence. If you are not sure of a term's meaning, return to the appropriate section and review its definition.

46–1 Drugs
drug
marijuana
hallucinogen
LSD
PCP
stimulant
amphetamine
depressant
barbiturate
cocaine
crack
opiate
morphine
heroin
drug abuse
drug addiction
withdrawal
endorphin

46–2 Alcohol
ethyl alcohol
fetal alcohol
  syndrome
alcoholism

46–3 Tobacco
nicotine
tar
bronchitis
emphysema

CHAPTER REVIEW

CONTENT REVIEW

Multiple Choice

Choose the letter of the answer that best completes each statement.

1. Over-the-counter drugs include
   a. amphetamines.   c. aspirin.
   b. depressants.   d. codeine.
2. Tetrahydrocannabinol is the active ingredient in
   a. opiates.   c. alcohol.
   b. cocaine.   d. marijuana.
3. Drugs that speed up the actions of the nervous system are
   a. prescription drugs. c. depressants.
   b. stimulants.   d. opiates.
4. A drug that causes the release of dopamine in the brain is
   a. cocaine.   c. tobacco.
   b. alcohol.   d. marijuana.

5. Cirrhosis is a condition that affects the
   a. heart.   c. lungs.
   b. liver.   d. digestive system.
6. Alcohol is a
   a. depressant.   c. hallucinogen.
   b. stimulant.   d. prescription drug.
7. Which substance is found in tobacco smoke?
   a. PCP   c. LSD
   b. tar   d. THC
8. Morphine binds to the same receptor sites in the brain as
   a. cocaine.   c. THC.
   b. endorphins.   d. LSD.

True or False

Determine whether each statement is true or false. If it is true, write "true." If it is false, change the underlined word or words to make the statement true.

1. When opiate users stop using the drug, they undergo underline{dependence}.
2. Alcohol acts as a underline{stimulant} on the nervous system.
3. underline{Barbiturates} are examples of depressants.
4. underline{Carbon dioxide} is a poisonous gas found in cigarette smoke.
5. A underline{drug} is any substance that has an effect on the body.
6. The most powerful stimulants are the underline{amphetamines}.
7. Morphinelike chemicals produced by the brain are called underline{receptors}.
8. The form of alcohol used in beverages is underline{methyl alcohol}.

Word Relationships

A. *In each of the following sets of terms, three of the terms are related. One term does not belong. Determine the characteristic common to three of the terms and then identify the term that does not belong.*

1. cocaine, stimulant, barbiturate, amphetamine
2. alcohol, tobacco, barbiturate, depressant
3. ethyl alcohol, tar, nicotine, carbon monoxide
4. hallucinogen, opium, morphine, heroin

B. *Replace the underlined definition with the correct vocabulary word.*

5. Amphetamines are <u>drugs that speed up the actions of the nervous system</u>.
6. Cocaine causes the brain to release <u>a chemical that produces a feeling of pleasure</u>.
7. People who abuse heroin develop <u>an uncontrollable craving for the drug</u>.
8. Long-term smoking of tobacco can lead to <u>stiffening of the elastic tissues in the lungs</u>.

CONCEPT MASTERY

Use your understanding of the concepts developed in the chapter to answer each of the following in a brief paragraph.

1. Many people who drink alcohol state that it makes them more peppy. Explain why that is not the case.
2. Describe the physical effects of alcohol.
3. Compare psychological dependence and physical dependence.
4. Tobacco-chewers often think that their habit is much safer than tobacco smoking. Are they correct? Explain your answer.
5. Suggest some reasons why an ex-smoker should not start smoking again.
6. Not all alcoholics need to drink every day. Explain that statement.
7. Define drug abuse in your own words.
8. It has been said that no one can ever be cured of drug dependence. Explain why.
9. How is cigarette smoke related to respiratory and circulatory problems?

CRITICAL AND CREATIVE THINKING

Discuss each of the following in a brief paragraph.

1. **Relating cause and effect** Based on alcohol's effects on the nervous system, why is drinking and driving an extremely dangerous behavior?

2. **Making comparisons** Compare cocaine and crack.
3. **Expressing an opinion** How might you convince someone not to abuse drugs?
4. **Relating facts** Compare the actions on the nervous system of stimulants and depressants.
5. **Applying concepts** Explain the meaning of this ancient Japanese proverb: "First the man takes a drink, then the drink takes a drink, then the drink takes the man."
6. **Making inferences** In what ways are drug abuse and criminal acts related?
7. **Using the writing process** Choose any commonly abused drug and construct a poster designed to display the dangers of drug abuse.

FEATURED SELECTION 2: "ALCOHOL—OPPOSING VIEWPOINTS: INTRODUCTION"

BEFORE YOU READ

About the Author   The *Opposing Viewpoints* series published by Greenhaven Press is designed to promote critical thinking and assist students doing research by presenting diverse viewpoints on issues. In this excerpt from the book *Alcohol—Opposing Viewpoints*, the executive editor summarizes the contradictory nature of America's views on alcohol.

Words to Know

> *"dry" state* (¶1): a state, such as Kansas, that did not allow alcohol
> *prohibition movement* (¶2): the active group of people working to outlaw alcohol
> *banning* (¶2): prohibiting, forbidding
> *ambivalent* (¶3): uncertain, mixed feelings
> *unite* (¶4): bring together, connect
> *amplifies* (¶4): increases, expands
> *cohesion* (¶5): unity, oneness
> *substantiated* (¶5): verified, confirmed
> *prone* (¶7): inclined to, likely

An Idea to Think About   Can you name one positive effect and one negative effect of drinking? *As you read*, find out what the research says are some of the positive effects and some of the negative effects of drinking.

ALCOHOL—OPPOSING VIEWPOINTS: INTRODUCTION

Greenhaven Press, Bruno Leone, Executive Editor

Beverage alcohol, America's drug of choice, imposes enormous economic, health, and social costs on the nation each year.

—George A. Hacker and Laura Anne Stuart

In many situations drink is a joy and a privilege.

—Carey Burkett

[1]In the late 1890s, in the towns of Kansas, a woman named Carry Nation began to wreck saloons, which were illegal in that "dry" state. Using rocks and metal bars, she smashed liquor supplies, furniture, and fixtures. By the early 1900s, Nation had become famous for swinging a hatchet, which had become her signature tool, in saloons throughout New York, Washington, D.C., San Francisco, and other American cities.

[2]Having previously been unhappily married to an alcoholic, Nation was among the most visible members of the prohibition movement, who believed that alcohol should be outlawed because it contributed to violence, crime, and the destruction of families. The movement eventually succeeded; in 1920, the Eighteenth Amendment to the U.S. Constitution took effect, banning the manufacture and sale of alcoholic beverages. However,

Prohibition could not eliminate the public's thirst for beer and spirits. The law merely drove drinking underground while creating opportunities for bootleggers, dishonest government officials, and corrupt police officers to profit from the illegal alcohol trade. Widely regarded as a failure, Prohibition was repealed in 1933.

[3a]The story of Carry Nation and the prohibitionist movement illustrates America's ambivalent attitude toward alcohol. [3b]The prohibitionists were partially successful because many Americans shared their view that the excessive use of alcohol brought destructive consequences. [3c]On the other hand, the public's demand for alcoholic beverages proved stronger than the force of law. [3d]These conflicting societal forces are reflected in contemporary debates about alcohol. [3e]Many commentators and public health experts emphasize alcohol's potential to harm individuals, families, and society. [3f]Others insist that, when consumed responsibly and in moderation, alcohol can be harmless or even beneficial.

[4]On the positive side, alcohol is a key ingredient in many cultural and social customs that bring and hold people together. For example, drinks are served to break the ice and encourage social interaction at parties. At weddings, family members and friends express their shared

love and hope by offering a champagne toast to the new-lyweds. Wine is a central component in many religious rituals that unite congregations in their shared faith. In Europe, wine is commonly served to all family members—including children—when they gather for the evening meal. In the words of Ian Hindmarch, a professor of psychopharmacology at the University of Surrey in England, alcohol "eases and amplifies the joyful occasions of life." The presence of alcoholic beverages at these occasions suggests that alcohol, symbolically as well as literally, helps to hold society together.

[5]In addition to its role in promoting social cohesion, alcohol, when consumed moderately, can have a positive effect on human health. Commentators frequently refer to the "French paradox": Despite having diets high in cholesterol, the French have lower rates of heart disease than do Americans—a disparity that has been attributed to the fact that the French also drink more wine. Numerous studies have substantiated the claim that moderate drinking lowers the risk for coronary heart disease in some individuals. According to R. Curtis Ellison, "Almost every follow-up epidemiologic study has demonstrated that individuals who drink small to moderate amounts of alcohol have a lower risk than non-drinkers of dying from coronary heart disease." Based on these findings, in 1995 the U.S. government for the first time acknowledged the health benefits of alcohol in its nutrition guidelines.

[6]While alcohol offers these and other societal and health benefits, it can also be the source of significant harm. Indeed, many public health experts insist that the risks associated with alcohol far outweigh the benefits. Some commentators focus on the problem of drunk driving: Mothers Against Drunk Driving (MADD) predicts that "about two out of every five Americans will be involved in an alcohol-related crash at some time in their lives." Others focus on alcohol's role in social problems such as violent crime, suicide, domestic violence, and rape. The National Council on Alcoholism and Drug Dependence (NCADD) states that "alcohol is typically found in the offender, victim, or both in about half of all homicides and serious assaults, as well as in a high percentage of sex-related crimes, robberies, and incidents of domestic violence." Furthermore, according to the NCADD, "Alcohol-related problems are disproportionately found among both juvenile and adult criminal offenders."

[7]One of the most tragic negative consequences of alcohol abuse is addiction. Although it is believed that not all drinkers are at risk for addiction, a significant number of people do develop drinking problems. The NCADD estimates that 13.8 million adult Americans have problems with drinking and that out of this number, 8.1 million are alcoholics. Alcoholics who do not receive treatment are prone to various severe health conditions, such as liver diseases, cardiovascular diseases, and some forms of cancer. In addition to physical damage, as alcoholics continue to drink, they usually experience an increasing number of problems in their personal lives, including job loss or estrangement from family members. Families are especially strained—and are often destroyed—by the presence of a problem drinker. According to the Entertainment Industries Council, an organization that seeks to educate the public and the entertainment media about alcohol and alcohol-related problems, "Alcoholism contributes to emotional stress and instability for everyone in the family." In these cases, alcohol does not help to hold families together; instead, it tears them apart.

[8]Since alcohol brings both benefits and problems, its widespread use in contemporary society continues to provoke praise as well as criticism.

SELECTION 2 QUESTIONS

Vocabulary

Circle the letter of the best definition for the underlined word or phrase.

1. "… that the excessive use of alcohol brought <u>destructive consequences</u>." (¶3)
    a. harmful results
    b. positive effects
    c. unnatural results
    d. happy effects

2. "Wine is a <u>central component</u> in many religious rituals.…" (¶4)
    a. costly element
    b. holy sacrifice
    c. devout ceremony
    d. significant part

3. "... a <u>disparity</u> that has been attributed to the fact that the French also drink more wine." (¶5)
   a. similarity
   b. difference
   c. likeness
   d. problem

4. "... or <u>estrangement</u> from family members." (¶7)
   a. closeness
   b. emotional distancing
   c. unhappiness
   d. depression

Rephrase these passages using your own words.

5. "... experts insist that the risks associated with alcohol far outweigh the benefits." (¶6)

   _____

   _____

6. "Alcohol-related problems are disproportionately found among both juvenile and adult criminal offenders." (¶6)

   _____

   _____

Comprehension

Determine whether the statements in sentences 7 and 8 are true or false, and write your answer. Also, if the statement is false, rewrite it to make it true.

7. The public stopped drinking in 1920 when the Eighteenth Amendment to the U.S. Constitution banned the manufacture and sale of alcoholic beverages.

   _____

   _____

8. One of the most tragic negative consequences of alcohol abuse is addiction.

   _____

   _____

9. Circle the letter of the sentence that best expresses the thesis.
   a. Alcohol, when consumed moderately, can have a positive effect on human health.
   b. Alcohol can cause significant harm.
   c. Since alcohol brings both benefits and problems, its use continues to cause praise as well as criticism.
   d. Many public health experts insist that the risks associated with alcohol far outweigh the benefits.

10. Why did Carry Nation want alcohol outlawed?

   _____

11. Why was Prohibition repealed in 1933?

   _____

   _____

   _____

12. In paragraph 3, the relationship among sentences a, b, and c is:
   a. b and c develop and support a by giving examples that illustrate "America's ambivalent attitude toward alcohol."
   b. b and c develop and support a by giving the causes of the prohibitionist movement.
   c. c develops and supports a and b by giving the reasons why prohibition failed.

13. State the main idea of paragraph 6.

   _____

14. Is paragraph 1 primarily fact, opinion, or combination of fact and opinion? If it includes both, list which information is fact and which is opinion.

   _____

   _____

   _____

   _____

Vocabulary Extra

Each of these words has a prefix and/or a suffix added to the root word. (1) Break the word into its component parts (root, prefix, and/or suffix), (2) define each word part, and (3) define the whole word. For help, use the Roots, Prefixes, Suffixes table on pages 17–18 or refer to your dictionary.

1. illegal (¶1)

   root word _____

   definition _____

   prefix _____

   definition _____

   suffix _____

   definition _____

   illegal means _____

2. unhappily (¶2)

   root word _____

   definition _____

   prefix _____

   definition _____

   suffix _____

   definition _____

   unhappily means _____

3.   dishonest (¶2)

    root word _____

    definition _____

    prefix _____

    definition _____

    suffix _____

    definition _____

    dishonest means _____

4.   harmless (¶3)

    root word _____

    definition _____

    prefix _____

    definition _____

    suffix _____

    definition _____

    harmless means _____

5.   disproportionate (¶6)

    root word _____

    definition _____

    prefix _____

    definition _____

    suffix _____

    definition _____

    disproportionate means _____

FEATURED SELECTION 3: "READING THE MEDIA'S MESSAGE ABOUT MEDICATIONS"

BEFORE YOU READ

About the Author   Writer Sheila Globus's articles on health-related topics appear in many magazines. This article is from *Current Health 2*, October 1999.

Words to Know

> *hype* (subhead): to exaggerate the effects for publicity
> *sap* (¶6): weaken, exhaust
> *pharmaceuticals* (¶7): drugs
> *bombarded* (¶7): attacked with, constantly given
> *tactics* (¶7): strategies, approaches
> *conflicting* (¶11): clashing, opposing

An Idea to Think About   Has anyone in your family bought any medicine to help with a problem like a headache or a cold or allergies in the last month? If so, how did you decide which product to buy? *As you read*, find out how many Americans decide on which product to buy and why we should be careful about taking such medicines.

READING THE MEDIA'S MESSAGES ABOUT MEDICATIONS

DO THE MESSAGES WE RECEIVE FROM THE MEDIA HELP US WHEN
WE NEED RELIEF FROM ALLERGIES OR A COLD? OR ARE THEY JUST HYPE?

Sheila Globus

---

[1]The lady on TV has a throbbing sinus headache. She reaches for a bottle of a well-known pain reliever, and presto—she's out in the garden smiling and planting flowers. Switch channels.

[2]A middle-aged man lies in bed flattened with the flu. His eyes droop. His nose is red. He's stuffy, groggy, miserable. Desperate, he opens the medicine cabinet and spots the box of a nighttime cold remedy. Soon, he's resting comfortably, his smiling face nestled in the pillow.

[3]You open your favorite magazine and see a distressed Gen-Xer wondering what to do about an unsightly, blotchy rash. Turn the page, and this time she's admiring how clear and perfect her skin is, thanks to a cream "recommended most by doctors."

[4]You get the picture. The cure for everything, according to the commercials on TV, is just around the corner at your local drugstore. If only it were so simple.

[5]The truth is, taking medications is serious business. "No one should use over-the-counter (OTC) medications unless they really have to," says Michael Montagne, professor at the Massachusetts College of Pharmacy in Boston. "Just because a drug is available over the counter doesn't mean it works or has no side effects," he explains. "On the contrary, you need to be as cautious about taking it as you are about drugs prescribed by your doctor."

[6]Although prescription drugs may have more serious side effects than OTC medications, all drugs affect the body in some way. They can sap your energy, upset your stomach, dull your senses, or alter your appetite. The same drug can affect different people in different ways. "You shouldn't use OTCs without some medical supervision," says Dr. Montagne. "The difference between a prescription drug and a nonprescription drug is just its legal status."

Pill-Popping Nation

[7]Pharmaceuticals are a multi-billion-dollar industry. Drug company salespeople used to pitch the latest drugs only to doctors and nurses. Now drug companies make their pitches directly to consumers through advertising. Whether it's an ad for a cold medicine or one promising to clear up your skin in 24 hours, Americans are bombarded with drug information. "Even Saturday morning TV is full of commercials for vitamins and herbal remedies," says Dr. Montagne. Pills that work like magic on TV don't always work in real life. Still, ads for

medications can be useful. They may alert you to symptoms that need a doctor's attention, tell you about a treatment you didn't know about, or introduce you to a new product. Like all advertising, drug ads exist to get you to buy something. That's why it's helpful to know some tactics that advertisers use.

The Truth, the Whole Truth, and Nothing but the Truth?

[8]Some drug ads, for example, promise more than they can deliver. "There are no nonprescription drugs that cure," says Dr. Montagne. "They treat symptoms." Even products whose producers claim will work day and night aren't going to eliminate all your symptoms. Drugs promising instant or fast relief won't necessarily do what they say. "Your body needs time," says Dr. Montagne. "Our bodies are complex systems. Problems cannot be solved in 24 hours."

[9]Advertisements may also leave out information—or put it in hard-to-read fine print at the bottom of the screen or page. "If you're going to take over-the-counter medications," says Dr. Montagne, "read the label carefully and get the information you need from a pharmacist." Reading the label is important for another reason, too. Drugs contain more than one ingredient. If you're taking one thing for colds and another to calm your cough, and both have the same ingredient, you could be getting too much of that drug.

[10]An advertiser may claim its product is better because it's loaded with several different ingredients. All-in-one cold and allergy remedies are a good example. They may contain antihistamines, which work against allergies but do nothing for a cold. Most antihistamines can cause drowsiness, while many decongestants have the opposite effect. Still, it's hard to predict whether a product will make you sleepy or keep you awake—or neither—because reactions to drugs can vary from one person to another.

[11]Sometimes a medicine contains ingredients that have conflicting effects. Cold remedies, for example, may have one ingredient to make it easier to cough up phlegm and other ingredients that stop the urge to cough. Ask a doctor or pharmacist about choosing a product that has a single ingredient that targets your specific symptom.

[12]Some ads try to convince you to take a drug for a problem you don't even have. "It's really important to ask yourself why you're considering using a certain drug before you take it," says Dr. Montagne. "Ask yourself if its

benefits match your symptoms. If your problem is a headache, why take a cough medicine at the same time?" He also urges teens to monitor how they are using medications (at what dosage) and to have a clear idea of when they'll stop. OTCs should not be used any longer than the package directions advise. "Dependence can happen with almost any drug," he says. When you put a drug into your body, you're altering your system. When you remove that chemical, your body has to readjust.

Risky Business

[13]Because they are easily available, OTC drugs may seem harmless. But they're not.

[14]Many drugs you could once get only from a doctor are now available over the counter, Dr. Montagne explains. Because they aren't as strong as prescription drugs, people think they can take as much as they want. Sometimes they double the dose, thinking the drug will work better or make them feel better faster. "The higher the dose, the greater the toxicity [the danger of poisoning]," says Dr. Montagne. "Even at low doses, there can be problems."

[15]So what are the media's messages about medications? Since the purpose of these messages is to sell you a product, think before you buy into the pitch. Take a good look at what you need. Then decide whether that medication will help your symptoms.

SELECTION 3 QUESTIONS

Vocabulary

Circle the letter of the best definition for the underlined word.

1. "… see a distressed Gen-Xer wondering…." (¶3)
   a. sick
   b. worried
   c. lonesome
   d. underage

2. "… dull your senses, or alter your appetite." (¶6)
   a. preserve
   b. keep up
   c. maintain
   d. change

3. "… aren't going to eliminate all your symptoms." (¶8)
   a. keep
   b. get rid of
   c. hold on to
   d. reduce

Comprehension

Determine whether the statements in sentences 4–7 are true or false, and write your answer. Also, if the statement is false, rewrite it to make it true.

4. Like all advertising, drug ads exist to get you to buy something.

   _____

   _____

5. Many nonprescription drugs can cure ailments.

   _____

   _____

6. Your pharmacist can tell you if a product will make you sleepy or keep you awake—or neither—because reactions to drugs are predictable.

   _____

   _____

7. OTC drugs are harmless.

   _____

   _____

8. Circle the letter of the sentence that best expresses the thesis.
   a. Drug advertisements are misleading.
   b. The difference between a prescription drug and a nonprescription drug is just its legal status.
   c. Over-the-counter (OTC) drugs don't work.
   d. Drug advertisements are designed to sell you a product, so before you buy one make sure that the medication will help your symptoms.

9. The relationship of paragraphs 1–3 to paragraph 4 is:
   a. Paragraphs 1–3 give examples to illustrate paragraph 4.
   b. Paragraphs 1–3 give the main idea of paragraph 4.
   c. Paragraphs 1–3 give a time sequence leading up to paragraph 4.

10. The main idea of paragraph 4 is:

    _____

11. Is paragraph 13 primarily fact, opinion, or combination of fact and opinion? If it includes both, list which information is fact and which is opinion.

    _____

    _____

12. What is the purpose of drug advertisements?

    _____

13. List two ways ads for medications can be useful.

    _____

    _____

14. List two ways ads for medications might be harmful.

    _____

    _____

FEATURED SELECTION 4: "TOBACCO AND ALCOHOL ADVERTISEMENTS IN MAGAZINES"

BEFORE YOU READ

About the Authors   Lorin Sanchez and Sean Sanchez are students at Oregon Health Sciences University. Andrew Goldberg and Aaron Goldberg are high school students in Portland, Oregon. The students wrote this "Letter to the Editor" of *JAMA, The Journal of the American Medical Association*. It appeared April 26, 2000.

Words to Know

> *assess* (¶3): estimate, evaluate
>
> *(n = 195)* (¶3): the number (n) equaled 195
>
> *skewed* (¶4): misrepresented, slanted
>
> *atypical* (¶4): abnormal, unusual

An Idea to Think About   How many different brands of tobacco and alcohol are advertised in the magazines you read? Do you think there would be, or should be, more or less tobacco and alcohol ads in the magazines teenagers read? *As you read*, find out what these students discovered when they analyzed some of the magazines teens read.

TOBACCO AND ALCOHOL ADVERTISEMENTS IN MAGAZINES: ARE YOUNG READERS BEING TARGETED?

Lorin Sanchez, Sean Sanchez, Andrew Goldberg, and Aaron Goldberg

---

[1]To the Editor:

[2]As college and high school students, we were interested in previous research by Dr. King and colleagues[1] showing that cigarette brands popular among youths (aged 12–17 years) are more likely than other brands to be advertised in magazines that have high youth readership. Because the study did not include alcohol advertisements, we were motivated to extend some of the study's information.

[3]**Methods**   We selected a convenient sample of 15 magazines listed by King et al.[1] that were available in our local public library. Eleven magazines had the highest youth readership (1.9 million readers) and 4 had the smallest number of young readers (0.8 million).[2] We counted the number of pages of alcohol and tobacco advertisements to assess the volume of influence from the issue's sample (n = 195), from July 1997 to June 1998.

[4]Based on our tally, we estimated the number of advertising pages devoted to alcohol and tobacco advertisements per issue and per year. Because not all issues were available, we reduced the likelihood of obtaining a skewed sample by reassessing 4 magazines during July 1998 to June 1999 that initially had approximately 40 percent or fewer of the complete year's volumes available in our library (*Hot Rod* [n = 10], *People* [n = 46], *Sport* [n = 12], *Vogue* [n = 12]). We also reexamined the magazine with highest number of pages of alcohol and tobacco advertisements for the year to determine whether it was an atypical year for alcohol and tobacco advertisements for that particular periodical.

[5]**Results**   Based on the number of pages of all advertisements, *Rolling Stone*, a semimonthly magazine, had the greatest number of alcohol advertising pages per issue, while the monthly *Hot Rod* magazine had the largest number of pages of tobacco advertisements per issue. *Sports Illustrated*, a magazine that celebrates athletic achievement and has the highest youth readership, contained the highest number of pages per year for alcohol and tobacco advertisements. Furthermore, the sample of 1998–1999 *Sports Illustrated* issues (n = 47) showed that the number of pages of alcohol advertisements increased an average of 65 percent per issue (2.7 to 4.5), while the number of pages of tobacco advertisements increased 11 percent (2.9 to 3.2) per issue.

[6]**Comment**   A bimodal relationship between alcohol and tobacco advertisements and youth readership seems apparent in this sample. Magazines with 800,000 young readers or fewer (*New Woman*, *Ladies Home Journal*, *Harper's Bazaar*, and *Self*) had many fewer pages of advertisements per year for alcohol and tobacco than did *Time* magazine. However, *Time* magazine, with a relatively small number of alcohol and tobacco advertisements, and *Sports Illustrated*, with a high number of these advertisements, deserve comment. Both magazines have nearly identical adult (18 years) readership. *Time* magazine has 2 million readers younger than 18 years, while *Sports Illustrated* has 5.2 million young readers. We suspect that a possible reason for the greater number of alcohol (greater than 5 times) and tobacco (greater than 4 times) advertisements in *Sports Illustrated* vs. *Time* may be due to the number of youth who read *Sports Illustrated*.

[7]We acknowledge that there may be fewer young readers for certain articles and issues; thus, certain advertisements may be less visible to them, based on their placement in a particular issue. Likewise, there may be changes in youth readership from year to year, and younger readers may view only a portion of any given magazine. Despite the descriptive nature of these results, they bolster and extend previous work, suggesting that advertisers of tobacco products may target young readers.

[8]Based on the number of alcohol advertising pages in magazines with high youth readership compared with those with a small number of young readers, it appears that alcohol advertisers may target youths as well.

[9]Alcohol and tobacco use by youths has dramatically increased since 1991.[3] It may be difficult to reverse this trend in light of the high volume of tobacco and alcohol advertisements in magazines with high youth readership. Removing the likes of Joe Camel from billboards may not be sufficient.

[1] King, C., III, Siegel, M., Celebucki, C., and Connolly, G. N. "Adolescent Exposure to Cigarette Advertising in Magazines: An Evaluation of Brand-Specific Advertising in Relation to Youth Readership." *JAMA* 279 (1998): 516–520.

[2] Mediamark Research, Inc. "Youth Magazine Readership." New York, NY: Mediamark Research Inc., 1999.

[3] Monitoring the Future Study. "Trends in Prevalence of Various Drugs for 8th Graders, 10th Graders, and High School Seniors." Rockville, MD: National Institute on Drug Abuse, 1999.

SELECTION 4 QUESTIONS

Vocabulary

Circle the letter of the best definition for the underlined word.

1. *Rolling Stone* is a <u>semimonthly</u> magazine. How often is it published? (¶5)
    a. once a month
    b. twice a month
    c. every two months
    d. twice a year

2. "... they <u>bolster</u> and extend previous work...." (¶7)
    a. reinforce
    b. contradict
    c. disprove
    d. undermine

Comprehension

Determine whether the statements in sentences 3 and 4 are true or false, and write your answer. Also, if the statement is false, rewrite it to make it true.

3. *Sports Illustrated* contained the highest number of pages per year for alcohol and tobacco advertisements.

    _____

    _____

4. Magazines with older readers had fewer pages of advertisements per year for alcohol and tobacco than youth-oriented magazines.

    _____

    _____

5. Circle the letter of the sentence that best expresses the thesis.
    a. Advertisers of tobacco products may target young readers.
    b. Alcohol and tobacco use by youths has increased since 1991.
    c. It appears that alcohol advertisers as well as tobacco advertisers may target youths.
    d. Cigarette brands popular among youths are more likely than other brands to be advertised in magazines that have high youth readership.

6. Why did the students do this study?

    _____

    _____

7. What did the students discover about the number of advertising pages devoted to alcohol and tobacco advertisements in magazines that have a high youth readership?

_____

_____

8. What do the students mean by "Removing the likes of Joe Camel from billboards may not be sufficient."

_____

_____

FEATURED SELECTION 5: "AVOIDING THE LURE OF TOBACCO, ALCOHOL, AND MARIJUANA"

BEFORE YOU READ

About the Author   Writer Kathiann M. Kowalski is a frequent contributor to *Current Health 2*. This article appeared in *Current Health 2*, February 2000.

Words to Know

> *stamina* (¶5): endurance, strength
>
> *stance* (¶8): position, point of view
>
> *inhibitions* (¶13): ability to hold back on responses and emotions
>
> *impairs* (¶18): limits the ability to
>
> *derived* (¶23): made from
>
> *hinders* (¶27): prevents
>
> *correlate* (¶27): are related or connected to
>
> *subtle* (¶40): faint, difficult to identify
>
> *delusion* (¶41): mistake

An Idea to Think About   Do you know any teens who use tobacco, alcohol, or marijuana? How do you think those behaviors might effect them in 25 years? *As you read*, find out what the experts say about teens who use tobacco, alcohol, or marijuana and what the future might hold for them.

AVOIDING THE LURE OF TOBACCO, ALCOHOL, AND MARIJUANA

Kathiann M. Kowalski

[1]Devon started drinking at friends' houses at age 11. Soon, she was using marijuana, cocaine, and "whatever I could get my hands on." Before turning 16, Devon had been arrested twice for underage drinking and drug use. Eventually, an overdose of alcohol and cocaine landed the Minnesota teen in a hospital.

[2]Almost everyone who uses cocaine, heroin, and other drugs starts with tobacco, alcohol, or marijuana. In their 1998 Monitoring the Future Study, University of Michigan researchers asked teens what drugs they had used during the previous month. Among 12th graders, 35 percent said

they had smoked cigarettes, 52 percent had drunk alcohol, and 23 percent had used marijuana. Misled by billions of dollars in advertising and images in movies, experts say, teens often don't realize where these substances can lead.

Tobacco's Toll

[3]Despite health warnings on each cigarette pack, about 3,000 young people start smoking every day. The Centers for Disease Control and Prevention (CDC), a U.S. government agency, says roughly 1,000 of them will become addicted to nicotine, one of tobacco's approximately 4,000

chemicals. Before turning 18, 70 percent of teen smokers regret starting. Yet many will remain addicted until they become ill with tobacco-related diseases.

[4]Tobacco companies need young smokers. More than 400,000 Americans die each year from tobacco-related illnesses. These include lung cancer, chronic bronchitis, emphysema, heart attacks, high blood pressure, strokes, and arteriosclerosis (hardening of the arteries). Chewers risk cancers of the esophagus, mouth, and throat, and loss of teeth.

[5]But teens don't have to wait decades to get sick from tobacco. Smoking reduces lung capacity soon after a person starts, causing shortness of breath and reduced stamina. That's bad for playing sports or even just climbing stairs between classes. Smokers suffer more from asthma, as well as colds, pneumonia, flu, and other infections. Add stained teeth and fingers, foul breath, and smelly clothes. No wonder most teens prefer dating nonsmokers.

[6]And with all that negative stuff, no wonder the tobacco industry spends billions each year on advertising. Despite ads' attempts at "grown-up" images, few people start smoking after age 18. As a 1981 Philip Morris document said, "Today's teenager is tomorrow's potential regular customer."

[7]Do you doubt the power of advertising on teens? The Campaign for Tobacco-Free Kids says 86 percent of youth smokers prefer Marlboro, Camel, and Newport, the three most advertised brands. Only one-third of adult smokers prefer those brands.

[8]Even with the tobacco industry's billions of dollars in advertising, Florida's anti-tobacco stance has seen recent downturns in teen smoking rates. Teens in Florida have been clued in. Activist Christina Scelsi, age 17, credits a campaign to expose the tobacco industry by SWAT—Students Working Against Tobacco. "It encourages teens to positively rebel by not smoking and not letting the tobacco industry take them in and addict them to nicotine," says Christina.

Alcohol—Not as Advertised

[9]Like tobacco, alcohol is readily available to teens. Beavers and bar scenes in TV ads make alcohol seem fun. But for Keith Noble, Steven Donnelly, and Scott Krueger, alcohol was a killer. Many other teens have shared these college honor students' fate. Fifty college students die each year after "binge drinking"—consuming five drinks in a row for males or four for females.

[10]Alcohol is illegal in every state for people under age 21. Yet 25 percent of eighth graders in the Monitoring the Future Study already had gotten drunk. For 12th graders, the figure was 62 percent.

[11]Alcohol acts as a depressant in the body. It depresses, or slows down, the central nervous system, affecting judgment and coordination.

[12]Alicia became aware of this effect early on. She began drinking when she was 15. Over time, Alicia grew to hate the out-of-control feeling she got from alcohol's blur. Now the Ohio teen no longer drinks alcohol. "I was not really big on drinking to get drunk, and a lot of people were," Alicia says. "Why would I do something so I wouldn't be in control?"

[13]People react to alcohol differently. One drink relaxes many people. Two or three can make some people lose their inhibitions. Four or five can cause aggression.

[14]On college campuses, most fights, property destruction, date rapes, sexually transmitted diseases, unwanted pregnancies, and accidents have some link to alcohol. Even if teens don't become violent themselves, drinking makes them more vulnerable to attacks. Devon, for example, was at a drinking party when she was attacked and raped.

[15]Alcohol use—by the victim, the perpetrator, or both—is implicated in 46 to 75 percent of date rapes of college students, according to a new report by the National Center on Addiction and Substance Abuse (CASA) at Columbia University.

[16a]Sadly, people under alcohol's influence often don't realize it. [16b]"I felt like there was never an amount of alcohol that was too much for me," Jonathan recalls. [16c]After drinking all night, Jonathan crashed his car and killed his 18-year-old friend Justin. [16d]Jonathan wound up doing prison time in Georgia for vehicular homicide and driving under the influence.

No Safe Limit

[17]The more a person drinks, the higher his or her blood alcohol concentration (BAC) is. Alcohol's absorption into the body depends on gender, weight, and various other factors. In many states, an adult over 21 is legally drunk if his or her BAC is 0.8 or above. Some states have a limit of 0.5.

[18]Despite these numbers, even a single drink impairs the rapid-fire responses needed for safe driving. Generally, exceeding any detectable BAC—0.02 or less—is illegal for all drivers under age 21.

[19]Beyond its immediate effects, alcohol can cause anemia, sleep disorders, liver disease, heart disease, damage to the esophagus and pancreas, and cancer. Alcohol abuse also can have a detrimental effect on school performance and personal relationships.

[20]Of course, none of these effects show up in ads for beer or other alcoholic beverages. After all, how much alcohol would people buy if they saw ruined lives instead of smart-aleck lizards?

[21]Alcohol and tobacco are legal drugs for adults, and they are easily available. But another drug, marijuana, is illegal for everyone. Yet it's accessible to everyone—adults and teens.

Marijuana—Don't Buy the Hype

[22]Marijuana goes by many names: pot, grass, reefer, roach, smoke, dope, joint, Mary Jane, and others. Because marijuana is illegal, it's not advertised directly. But at least a half-dozen movies last year portrayed marijuana as cool. Real life is nothing like the movie hype.

[23]Derived from a hemp plant called cannabis sativa, marijuana contains hundreds of chemicals. A main ingredient responsible for marijuana's "high" is delta-9-tetrahydrocannabinol, or THC.

[24]Most people who smoke or eat marijuana want to get high. Some users feel relaxed or detached. Others get giddy or silly. But marijuana's health effects are anything but silly.

[25]Marijuana is at least as bad for your lungs as tobacco. Smoking marijuana can cause lung cancer and other respiratory diseases. It causes temporary increases in heart rate. And it can affect the immune system—the body's defenses against disease.

[26]Beyond this, marijuana affects the brain. Studies of college students showed decreased ability to concentrate and remember things. Even after highs wore off, marijuana users consistently scored lower on various tests. With college admissions or job interviews ahead, the last thing any teen needs is something that interferes with memory, reasoning, and even understanding simple ideas. Marijuana also blunts coordination and concentration, making driving, sports, and other activities very dangerous.

[27]Marijuana alters users' moods. Even if a user avoids paranoia and hallucinations, marijuana's high hinders good judgment. "That puts you at risk for making poor life decisions," stresses Alan Leshner, director of the National Institute on Drug Abuse (NIDA). Unprotected sexual activity (with risks of AIDS and sexually transmitted infections), use of other drugs, and impaired driving are just a few dangerous behaviors that correlate with marijuana use.

[28]As if that's not enough, marijuana is illegal. Getting high isn't worth the risk of jail time, a huge fine, and a criminal record. Nor is it worth the risk of getting knocked off a sports team or being rejected for a job. Since traces remain in the body for a long time, many schools and businesses use testing to screen out people who use marijuana and other drugs.

[29]Last year CASA announced that more teens and children entered treatment for marijuana abuse than for all other drugs—-more than 87,000 in 1996. Movie makers wouldn't pull in such huge profits if they replaced silly stoned characters with real-life suffering teens.

Opening the Door to Other Addictions?

[30]Why do so many teens keep using tobacco, alcohol, and marijuana? And might they lead to use of other drugs?

[31]"The truth is, if you don't use alcohol, tobacco, or marijuana by the time you're 21, the probability of ever becoming addicted to anything is virtually zero or is tremendously reduced," says NIDA's Leshner. "And the earlier you use substances, the greater the probability of becoming addicted to other things."

[32]It's not necessarily a direct causal connection, notes Leshner. For example, many teens addicted to nicotine, alcohol, or marijuana have other emotional and psychological problems. Those problems, genetics, or other factors could explain the high correlation.

[33]Nonetheless, the statistics are startling. "Among teens who report no other problem behaviors, those who used cigarettes, alcohol, and marijuana at least once in the past month are almost 17 times likelier to use another drug like cocaine, heroin, or LSD," says CASA's president, Joseph A. Califano, Jr.

The Brain's Response

[34]How are these drugs linked to harder drugs? Important clues lie in how nicotine, alcohol, and THC affect the brain. At first the substances produce pleasant feelings. The body's response reinforces, or rewards, continued use. Over time, users develop a tolerance. They need more and more to get the same feeling. Soon, users become addicted to the substance.

[35]Nicotine, for example, travels to the brain within 8 seconds. There it mimics effects of a neurotransmitter called acetylcholine. Neurotransmitters travel from nerve cell to nerve cell and cause responses. Acetylcholine affects muscle movement, breathing, heart rate, learning, memory, and hormone levels.

[36]Nicotine also affects levels of another neurotransmitter called dopamine, which is associated with feelings of pleasure and reward. The pleasant feelings encourage the smoker to use tobacco again. Alcohol and marijuana likewise affect levels of dopamine and other neurotransmitters.

[37]Cocaine, heroin, and other drugs also change levels of dopamine and other chemicals in the brain. These changes in brain chemistry suggest a link between tobacco, alcohol, and marijuana and other drugs. "While scientists have not yet discovered the smoking gun," says Califano, "they have certainly found the trigger finger."

[38]"Adolescence is a particularly important period of life because of all the social, emotional, and physical development going on," notes Harvard Medical School's Elena Kouri. Beyond their effects on thinking and emotional functions, drugs can interfere with teens' motivation to develop to their full potential. "All drugs that have reinforcing properties (the ones that make you feel good) have the potential to become addictive," says Kouri. "Every time a person uses a drug or alcohol, the likelihood of the person becoming addicted to it increases."

[39]Addiction becomes harder to escape when withdrawal symptoms hit. Cigarette smokers feel restless, hungry, depressed, or suffer headaches. Problem drinkers get shaky, anxious, nauseous, and sweaty when they can't drink.

[40]With heavy marijuana use, "the withdrawal syndrome is subtle, and oftentimes individuals don't associate it with marijuana," says Kouri. "Instead, they feel cranky, irritable, a little anxious." Even if withdrawal doesn't interfere with daily activities, Kouri says, "it is often severe enough to drive individuals to smoke marijuana again."

[41]Hormones associated with the withdrawal response might make some teens crave something stronger. Or, while they're drunk or stoned, teens may experiment with other drugs. But it's a delusion for anyone to think they can control their use of addictive substances.

[42]"The determinant of whether you become addicted is unknown," stresses NIDA's Leshner. Genetics, for example, may make you vulnerable without your knowing it. "Therefore, nobody is immune … and you need to protect yourself from the risks."

Far-Reaching Effects

[43]Tobacco, alcohol, and marijuana don't affect just the people who use them. They affect family members and all the people with whom users come in contact. "A lot of my family members smoke," says 14-year-old Brittany from Runnemede, New Jersey, "and I have a hard time because I have asthma." Secondhand smoke also leads to other lung problems and increased infections.

⁴⁴Tobacco, alcohol, and marijuana strain relationships. Users may lie about use, steal from family members to support their habit, or become abusive to people they should love and trust.

⁴⁵Strangers get hurt too. Driving under the influence of alcohol or marijuana kills and injures thousands each year. And all of society suffers from the costs of higher health care expenses, destruction from violence, and lost opportunities from what users might have achieved.

⁴⁶Teens face enough challenges without the health hazards of tobacco, alcohol, and marijuana. "Nobody thinks they're going to get addicted. Nobody thinks they're going to get in trouble," says Alyse Booth, CASA's director of communications. "But on the other hand, why take the risk if you really value yourself and your future?"

Getting Help

⁴⁷Devon was one of the lucky ones. After her hospital stay, she got treatment for her drug and alcohol addiction. Then Devon enrolled at Sobriety High, an alternative school in Edina, Minnesota, for recovering teen substance abusers.

⁴⁸Even for less serious substance abuse problems, it's never too early to get help. "We're not against smokers; we're against the tobacco industry," says SWAT's Christina Scelsi. At a program in her county, teens can get counseling and classes to help them stop smoking. With parental permission, they can also use patches to wean themselves away from nicotine. Ask your doctor or contact the American Lung Association to find out about programs in your area.

SELECTION 5 QUESTIONS

Vocabulary

Circle the letter of the best definition for the underlined word.

1. "… drinking makes them more <u>vulnerable</u> to attacks." (¶14)
   a. energetic
   b. forceful
   c. defenseless
   d. surprised

2. "… abuse also can have a <u>detrimental</u> effect on school performance.…" (¶19)
   a. good
   b. harmful
   c. positive
   d. definite

3. "Marijuana also <u>blunts</u> coordination and concentration.…" (¶26)
   a. dulls
   b. intensifies
   c. brightens
   d. strengthens

4. "… it <u>mimics</u> effects of a neurotransmitter.…" (¶35)
   a. imitates
   b. reverses
   c. controls
   d. contradicts

5. "… nobody is <u>immune</u> … and you need to protect.…" (¶42)
   a. positive
   b. exempt
   c. able to fight
   d. responsible

Comprehension

Determine whether the statements in sentences 6–8 are true or false, and write your answer. Also, if the statement is false, rewrite it to make it true.

6. The earlier you use addictive substances, the greater the probability of becoming addicted to other things.

    _____

    _____

7. All drugs that make you "feel good" have the potential to become addictive.

    _____

    _____

8. People always know when they've had too much to drink.

    _____

    _____

9. Circle the letter of the sentence that best expresses the thesis.
    a. Teens must realize that the harmful effects of using tobacco, alcohol, and marijuana are far reaching.
    b. People under age 21 shouldn't drink alcohol.
    c. About 3,000 young people start smoking every day.
    d. Marijuana is illegal.

10. According to the 1998 Monitoring the Future Study, what percentage of 12th graders said that during the previous month they had:
    a. smoked cigarettes   _____ percent
    b. drunk alcohol   _____ percent
    c. used marijuana   _____ percent

11. Does the information Kowalski presents lead you to believe advertising influences teen use of tobacco, alcohol, and marijuana? Please list two specific statements from the article to support your answer.

    _____

    _____

12. State the main idea of paragraph 16.

    _____

13. In paragraph 16, what is the relationship of sentences b–d to sentence a?
    a. Sentences b–d give the cause of sentence a.
    b. Sentences b–d provide a change in direction of thought from sentence a.
    c. Sentences b–d give an example to support and develop sentence a.

14. Is paragraph 29 primarily fact, opinion, or combination of fact and opinion? If it includes both, list which information is fact and which is opinion.

_____

_____

_____

CROSSWORD PUZZLE

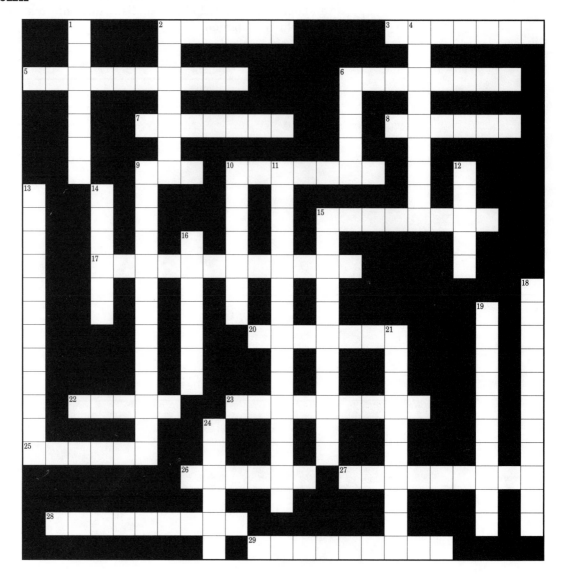

ACROSS

2 position, point of view
3 prohibiting, forbidding
5 defenseless
6 abnormal, unusual
7 prevents
8 imitates
9 weaken, exhaust

10 limits the ability to
15 unity, oneness
17 emotional distancing
20 made from
22 bring together, connect
23 get rid of
25 misrepresented, slanted

26 faint, difficult to identify
27 corrupt
28 difference
29 attacked

DOWN

1 reinforce
2 endurance, strength
4 increases, expands
6 change
9 verified, confirmed
10 unlawful

11 drugs
12 inclined to, likely
13 results
14 estimate, evaluate
15 clashing
16 strategies

18 harmful
19 uncertain, mixed feelings
21 worried
24 dulls

WORD LIST (NOT ALL USED)

alter	destructive	prone
ambivalent	detrimental	sap
amplifies	dishonest	skewed
assess	disparity	stamina
atypical	disproportionate	stance
banning	distressed	substantiated
blunts	eliminate	subtle
bolster	estrangement	tactics
bombarded	hinders	unite
cohesion	illegal	vulnerable
conflicting	impairs	
consequences	mimics	
derived	pharmaceuticals	

LOG ON TO THE WEB

There are hundreds of Web sites with general health information plus many additional sites specifically about drugs, alcohol, or tobacco. Sites include:

> The National Clearinghouse for Alcohol and Drug Information (NCADI) and the Substance Abuse and Mental Health Services Administration's (SAMHSA) PREVLINE site at <http://www.health.org>.
>
> The Bureau of Alcohol, Tobacco and Firearms' site at <http://www.atf.treas.gov>.
>
> The National Institute of Health's Health Information site at <http://www.nih.gov/health>.
>
> Students against Drugs and Alcohol (SADA) at <http://www.sada.org>.
>
> The National Institute on Alcohol Abuse and Alcoholism (NIAAA) at <http://www.niaaa.nih.gov>.
>
> Action on Smoking and Health at <http://www.ash.org.uk>.
>
> The National Academy of Science's "Taking Action to Reduce Tobacco Use" at <http://www.nap.edu/readingroom/books/tobacco>.

Log on to one of these sites and use the information there, use one of their links to a related site, or use a search directory/engine to locate a site with information about "drug, alcohol, or tobacco use."

Read one report, article, or story. Write down: (1) the address (http://www. ...), (2) the name of the person or company who sponsors and maintains the site, (3) the name of the person who wrote the information, (4) what you know about the writer, and (5) one important thing you learned from the information on "drug, alcohol, or tobacco use."

IDEAS FOR WRITING AND DISCUSSION

A. Think back over the articles you read in this theme. What do you think would be a good over-all statement about "using drugs, alcohol, and tobacco" that most of the authors would agree with? Please explain.

B. In March 1999, a nationwide Gallup poll found that when asked
    whether they would vote for or against a law to make marijuana legal
    when used to "reduce pain or suffering," 73 percent said they would
    vote in favor, 25 percent said they would vote against, and 2 percent
    had no opinion.

    What do you think are some of the reasons people would vote in favor
    of such a law? What do you think are some of the reasons people would
    vote against such a law? How would you vote?

C. In July 2000, a jury in Miami-Dade County, Florida, ordered the tobac-
    co industry to pay almost $145 billion in punitive damages (fines,
    penalties) to some 500,000 sick Florida smokers. The public and legal
    debate about the award is expected to continue for years.

    Were you surprised by the jury ordering the tobacco industry to pay
    such a large amount of money? What might have been some of the rea-
    sons the jury awarded such a large amount of money? What could be
    some reasons the tobacco industry wouldn't have to pay the full
    amount?

D. One of the most common social activities all over the world is drinking
    alcoholic beverages. Current evidence suggests that moderate drinking
    is associated with a lower risk for coronary heart disease in some indi-
    viduals. However, drinking often contributes to accidents and domestic
    violence incidents.

    How much of a role do you think the government should have in reg-
    ulating and restraining drinking, such as increasing the tax on alcohol
    or prohibiting television advertising of alcoholic beverages?

Tips for Preparing for
and Taking Standardized Reading Tests

Although many of these ideas may help you prepare for and take any type of test, they are specifically for standardized reading tests for which you cannot study specific content. Tips for preparing for and taking content exams are available on the Companion Website at http://www.prenhall.com/mcgrath.

BEFORE THE TEST

FAMILIARIZE YOURSELF WITH THE TEST; KNOW HOW LONG IT IS AND WHAT KIND OF QUESTIONS ARE ON IT

A typical state standardized reading test consists of six-to-eight reading selections of about 300 to 750 words each. The selections represent a variety of subject areas and are similar to material you are likely to read in college. After each selection, you answer five-to-six multiple-choice questions about the selection.

Each multiple-choice question consists of two parts:

1. The Stem—the statement or question. These are designed to test your ability to do things like: (a) determine the meaning of words and phrases, (b) understand the main idea and supporting details, (c) identify an author's purpose and point of view, (d) analyze the relationships among ideas, (e) use critical reasoning skills to evaluate information, (f) organize and summarize information, and (g) interpret graphic information.
2. The Choices—also known as alternatives. From three or four possible answers, you select the option that best completes the thought expressed in the stem. You may refer back to the selection to answer the questions.

PRACTICE WHAT YOU WILL BE DOING ON THE TEST

The single most effective way to prepare for any test is to practice what you will do on the test. Get sample test questions or a copy of a practice test from the testing center or on the Web. For example, The Texas Academic Skills Program (TASP) Web site at http://www.tasp.nesinc.com/index.htm includes a TASP® Practice Test with typical readings and questions.

BE PREPARED TO TAKE THE TEST

Get adequate rest the night before the test. Eat and exercise on your regular schedule. Have all the supplies you need, such as pencils and a watch, with you. Arrive at the test room early. Select a seat that has good lighting and where your view of students leaving the room is minimized. Be calm and alert. Plan to do well.

LISTEN TO AND READ ALL DIRECTIONS CAREFULLY BEFORE STARTING THE TEST

Know what you need to do, how to mark your answer sheet, and how long you have to complete the test. Calculate how much time you can allow for each selection and budget your time to allow time to complete all the selections.

KNOW HOW THE TEST IS SCORED

If there is no penalty for guessing, answer every question. If, however, you are penalized for wrong answers, blind guessing will probably hurt your score.

DURING THE TEST

READ A SELECTION BEFORE YOU ATTEMPT TO ANSWER THE QUESTIONS

Although this point gets a lot of debate, I suggest you first read the passage to determine the main idea. Then, read and answer the questions, referring back to the passage as needed for specific details. Remember, however, that the order of information requested in the questions does not necessarily correspond to the order of information in the reading selection.

READ THE QUESTION AND ANSWER IT IN YOUR MIND; THEN LOOK FOR THE MATCHING ANSWER

- Read the question—the stem.
- Think about a phrase that would answer the question.
- Compare each choice—alternative—to your answer.

By thinking of the answer first, you are less likely to be fooled by a wrong answer.

LOOK AT ALL THE ANSWERS BEFORE YOU MARK AN ANSWER

It is important to read all the alternatives before you select one, and not just take the first answer you think is correct.

WATCH FOR WORDS SUCH AS ALWAYS, NEVER, EVERY, ABSOLUTELY, AND ONLY

These absolute-type words make statements apply to everything all of the time, not just 99 percent of the time. Statements that use words like these are often incorrect because there are very few statements that have no exceptions (but there are a few).

WATCH FOR WORDS SUCH AS SOMETIMES, OFTEN, SELDOM, MAY, AND GENERALLY

Unlike the absolute words that make a statement true 100 percent of the time, qualifying words like these are so vague they often make an answer difficult to disprove. This means they may be included in a statement that is correct.

IF THE QUESTION IS DIFFICULT OR LONG AND COMPLEX, TRY TO MAKE IT MORE CLEAR

Try the following tactics:

- Underline the subject and verb to focus your attention.
- Mark key words. To help find the key words, ask yourself what, who, where, when, and how?
- Restate the question in your own words, but be sure you don't change the meaning of the question.

DO NOT SPEND TOO MUCH TIME ON ANY ONE QUESTION

Every minute counts. If you do not know the answer, make a guess, circle the question number and go on to the next question. When you finish all the questions you do know, go back to your circled questions.

MARK YOUR ANSWER SHEET CAREFULLY AND NEATLY

Make sure the number you are marking on your answer sheet corresponds to the number of the question you are answering. If you skip a question, be sure to leave the space for that question blank. Carefully fill in the entire answer space and completely erase any changes.

WHEN YOU DON'T KNOW THE ANSWER, MAKE AN EDUCATED GUESS

If there is no penalty for guessing, never leave an answer blank. Use strategies like these to help you analyze the answer choices and select the correct alternative.

- *Cross out any of the answers you know are wrong.* By carefully eliminating answers you know must be wrong, you can increase your chances of guessing correctly.
- *Look for the most general alternatives.* Since the most general alternative includes the most information, it is often the correct answer.
- *See if two alternatives mean the same.* If two alternatives mean the same thing, and there is only one correct answer, eliminate both of them. Neither will be correct. Make your choice from those remaining.
- *See if two alternatives are similar, but different.* If two alternatives mean almost the same thing, one of them will often be correct. Look for the word or concept that makes them different and determine which one is correct.
- *See if two alternatives state the opposite of each other.* The correct alternative is probably one of a pair of direct opposites. If you notice that two alternatives have opposite meanings, one of them is probably correct.
- *Check for singular and plural words in the stem.* If the stem uses the word "is," then the correct alternative will most likely be a singular word. If the stem has the word "are," look for an alternative with a plural, or a word that means more than one object.

DO NOT KEEP CHANGING YOUR ANSWER

Although this point also generates debate, I suggest that unless you have a serious reason to change, your first impression is likely to be the right one. Only change your answer if you are absolutely sure you made a mistake.

AFTER YOU HAVE FINISHED THE TEST, GO BACK TO ANY QUESTIONS YOU CIRCLED

Take as much time as you have. Never leave a test early, unless you are sure you have answered every question correctly.

SAMPLE READING: "ADVICE TO BEGINNING WRITERS"

ADVICE TO BEGINNING WRITERS

Robert L. McGrath

---

[1]Countless successful writers—and some not so accomplished—have tried to unlock the secret of their triumphs to share it with others. Obviously, there is no patented method to achieve success. What works for one person may be a washout for others. But here's a method that works for me, and perhaps it will be helpful to you. I call it SWAP—a four-part approach to achievement in your writing efforts.

[2]S—Studying. Writing requires a lifetime of study. Your study may be concentrated at local colleges that offer writing courses at various levels, along with occasional seminars and local writers' groups. Or it may involve reading all the books about creative writing you can find. Constant review of magazines such as *Byline*, *Writer's Digest*, *The Writer*, and others will contribute immeasurably to your study program. Read the type of material you aspire to write. Saturate yourself with it. Have at hand several basic tools: a good dictionary, a thesaurus, a market list, books on technique covering the categories you hope to sell. Use them!

[3]W—Writing. This, of course, is the only way to succeed. A writer must write; otherwise, he is not a writer, and cannot lay claim to the appellation. Study courses, either in classroom situations or by correspondence, can be helpful, combining study with actual writing by requiring a certain amount of discipline—otherwise often elusive. I like an additional formula: SOP-2-SOC—seat of pants to seat of chair. So Hemingway stood at the mantel to write...do it your way, but do it. Pen, pencil, typewriter, word processor—they're all good tools. Use them! Form the habit of writing, every day if possible. Time or place do not matter. Just do it!

[4]A—Ambition. Set realistic goals for yourself. Be practical. Your first effort probably won't be The Great American Novel. But an expressive poem just might find print in an obscure journal and set you on your way. Or you might be a winner in one or more of the many *Byline* contests. You'll need a certain amount of self-confidence, for without it, you'll never reach those goals. Know that you have the native ability to put words on paper—words that will be worthwhile not only to you, but to others as well. Another formula comes to mind: SYI—scratch your itch. You have that urge to write. So write ... write ... write.

[5]P—Perseverance. Never give up on something you believe in. You can succeed, but only if you refuse to toss in the towel. My files contain irrefutable proof of the value of hanging in there. My short story, "Payment Received," won tenth place in the 1955 *Writer's Digest* contest. I figured it had to be a worthy piece. But on thirty-nine trips to various editors, it failed to make the grade. The fortieth submission was to a magazine that previously had rejected it. I goofed; otherwise, I probably wouldn't have resubmitted it to *Alfred Hitchcock's Mystery Magazine*. It was later published in a hardcover collection of Hitchcock yarns, and reprinted in two separate paperback editions of the same anthology. It was read over a South African radio station (for which I was paid). It was the subject of a *Writer's Digest* experience report. Perseverance caused its sale. Other stories have parallel records. One sold to prestigious *Stories* magazine on its fifty-fifth trip out. The record for me is a sale on the eightieth trip to an editor's desk. Believe in yourself—persevere!

[6]Try the SWAP plan. Results aren't guaranteed, but it's worth a try.

SAMPLE READING QUESTIONS

1. Which of the following best expresses the main idea of the selection?
   a. No one really knows the keys to being a successful writer.
   b. Although it's not guaranteed, study, practice, self-confidence, and perseverance can help you become a successful writer.
   c. All successful writers write something every day.
   d. SWAP is a four-part approach that guarantees writing success.

2. The writer's main purpose in writing this selection is to do the following:
   a. Outline the steps you should use when writing an essay.
   b. Describe the writing process.
   c. Provide advice to writers who want to sell their work.
   d. Explain the differences between writing for pleasure and writing for publication.

3. In paragraph 5 the author writes, "You can succeed, but only if you refuse to toss in the towel." In this context, what does the author mean by <u>you refuse to toss in the towel</u>?
   a. You won't give up.
   b. You reject the idea of rewriting.
   c. You decline to listen to critics.
   d. You won't stop to do the laundry.

4. Which of the following sets of topics best organizes the information in the selection?
   a. **Advice**
      Study
      Write
      Never Give Up
   b. **Tips for Success**
      Read what you want to write
      Write every day
      Set realistic goals
      Believe in yourself
   c. **SWAP**
      Studying
      Writing
      Ambition
      Perseverance

5. In describing the story that sold on the eightieth trip to an editor's desk, the author wanted to illustrate which of the following ideas?
   a. A writer should never give up.
   b. Editors can never make up their mind.
   c. Some stories never sell.
   d. A good story always sells on the first try.

6. Which of the following best defines the word <u>appellation</u> as it is used in paragraph 3?

   a. money

   b. reward

   c. discipline

   d. title

7. Which of the following is a valid conclusion based on the information in paragraph 5?

   a. The author has sold more than one piece of writing.

   b. The author only writes mystery stories.

   c. The author has never sold any of his writings.

   d. The author has been writing for about ten years.

8. Which of the following statements from the selection is presented as a fact rather than an opinion?

   a. Writing requires a lifetime of study.

   b. Form the habit of writing, every day if possible.

   c. Your first effort probably won't be The Great American Novel.

   d. My files contain irrefutable proof of the value of hanging in there.

9. Which of the following is the best assessment of this writer's credibility?

   a. The author's enthusiasm for writing raises a serious question about his credibility.

   b. The considerable amount of factual detail the author presents inspires faith in his credibility.

   c. Because the writer is offering suggestions based on his own experience, his credibility is good.

   d. Although the selection provides useful information about writing, the writer's credibility is weakened by his failure to say how much he gets paid for his work.

GLOSSARY

antonym   A word that means the opposite of another word.

appendix   A special section located toward the end of a book that contains extra or supplemental information. The plural of appendix is appendices.

compare; comparison   Giving the likenesses between or among things, ideas, or people.

context   The meaning of words as understood from their surrounding text; words or phrases that can help a reader understand a term or concept; how words are used in conjunction with other words.

context clue   Information an author provides within the sentence or paragraph to help the reader understand important words.

contrast   Giving the differences between or among things, ideas, or people.

controlling thought   What the author wants the reader to know or understand about the topic.

directly stated main idea   The topic and controlling thought of a paragraph stated in a sentence; often called a topic sentence.

fact   Statements of fact tell about people, places, things, and events objectively, without value judgements or personal interpretations.

general   Broad, comprehensive; including everything.

glossary   An in-book dictionary that contains the meanings of important words used in the book.

implied main idea   An indirectly stated main idea that leaves it up to the reader to piece together the information from all the sentences and to infer, or put together, the main idea.

infer   To reach a reasoned conclusion based on the information given.

inference   The best reasoned conclusion based on the information given.

index   An alphabetical list (located at the end of a book) of the topics covered in a book and their page numbers.

irrelevant information   Information that is interesting, and sometimes important, but does not support or develop the main idea in a paragraph.

major supporting detail   A specific piece of information that directly supports and explains the main idea.

minor supporting detail   A very specific piece of information that supports and explains a major detail.

multi-paragraph selection   A group of related paragraphs, each with a main idea, that supports and explains one thesis, or overall main idea—for example, an essay or text chapter.

opinion   Statements of opinion tell about people, places, things, and events subjectively from the author's point of view. An opinion is not right or wrong, or good or bad. However, depending on the amount and type of evidence the author considered before forming the opinion, it can be valid or invalid.

outline   A type of graphic organizer that uses differing amounts of indentation to create a picture of the relationships among the ideas.

paragraph   A group of related sentences that supports and explains one main idea.

paraphrase   Restating information in your own words.

pattern of organization   How an author develops and supports the thesis or main ideas; the structure he or she gives the information. Six common methods of organization are examples or listing, comparison and/or contrast, time order or steps in a sequence, definition, classification, and cause and effect. In addition, authors often combine two patterns.

preface   An introductory letter from the author located in the first few pages of some textbooks.

prefix   A word part added to the beginning of a root word to change its meaning.

preview   To look at or see in advance; in reading, the term means to survey, or examine, reading material in an orderly way *before* you begin to read.

purpose for reading   Specific reasons for reading based on what you need to know when you have finished reading.

reasoned judgment   Thoughtful, coherent evaluations that informed individuals make from the available evidence.

root word   The basic part of a word.

signal word   Words or phrases an author uses to point the reader in a specific direction of thought or to alert the reader to particular types of information; often called transitions.

specific   Limited; individual; narrow in scope.

strategy   An action a reader consciously selects to achieve a particular goal; strategies are means to an end.

structural organizers   Parts of an article or essay like titles and subtitles that you read during preview to give you an overview of the content.

suffix   A word part added to the end of a root word to change its meaning or the way it can be used in a sentence.

synonym   A word that means the same, or nearly the same, as another word.

table of contents   Located in the first few pages of a textbook, it lists the titles, and often the subtitles, of the chapters and the page number on which they begin.

thesaurus   A book of words and their synonyms.

thesis   The primary idea of a multi-paragraph selection that combines the main ideas of all the paragraphs; the frame that holds the paragraphs of the essay or chapter together.

topic   The who or what the author is writing about.

transition word   See *signal word*.

word analysis   Defining a word by defining its root and any prefixes and/or suffixes.

Suggested Answers for Odd-Numbered Practice Exercises and Crossword Puzzles

Chapter 1

EXERCISE 1.1 (PAGE 2)

1. page 6
2. Chapter 2
3. page 209
4. Two appendices:
   Finding Web Sites That Have Moved
   What to Look for When Purchasing a Computer
5. First three major sections in Chapter:
   Internet Navigation Using Browsers
   Learning Adventure Using Browsers to Surf the Net
   Multimedia-Oriented Web Environments

EXERCISE 1.3 (PAGE 3)

1. Leshin says the Internet is a powerful medium for "finding information, sharing information, and interacting with others."
2. List two ways the Internet is a valuable tool:
   - finding the latest information on a subject for research papers
   - collecting data from others online
   - collaborating with others who share your research interests
   - cross-cultural exchanges with Netizens worldwide
   - meeting and learning from subject matter experts on virtually any topic
   - access to resources such as dictionaries, encyclopedias, and library catalogs worldwide
   - access to literature such as the classics and novels
   - access to news publications and electronic journals with resources for researching their databases for past articles
   - access to databases of diverse information at universities and government agencies
   - learning about companies by visiting their Web sites

3. In addition to helping you succeed in school, Leshin thinks understanding the Internet "provides you with important skills that employers value."

EXERCISE 1.5 (PAGE 4)

1. Leshin taught computer literacy and Internet classes at Arizona State University and Estrella Mountain Community College.
2. Leshin's doctorate is in educational technology.

EXERCISE 1.7 (PAGE 5)

1. Information about importing bookmarks: pages 33–34
2. For information on "address" see "URLs"

EXERCISE 1.9 (PAGE 5)

1. Appendix contains information on how to find Web sites that have moved

EXERCISE 1.11 (PAGE 7)

1. The term *bookmark* means "a feature providing the user with the opportunity to mark favorite pages for fast and easy access."
2. A *cookie* means: "Cookie technology allows the storage of personal preferences for use with Internet information and communication tools. A text file is created of a user's preferences, saved in their browser's folder, and stored in RAM while the browser is running."

CHAPTER 2

EXERCISE 2.1 (PAGE 12)

1. c. fire
2. d. without germs
3. b. sharp
4. c. centers of activity
5. a. working together
6. b. hurt
7. d. honest
8. a. good influence
9. d. for a brief time
10. c. deserted

EXERCISE 2.3 (PAGE 16)

Answers will vary.

EXERCISE 2.5 (PAGE 19)

1. gerontophobia: fear of aging
2. achievable: able to be achieved, attained
3. enrich: make richer, better
4. interactions: connections between
5. chronologically: according to the number of years lived
6. credibility: trustworthiness
7. maladjusted: unstable, not well adjusted
8. portable: easily moveable
9. empowering: authorizing, giving power to
10. manual: doing work with your hands

EXERCISE 2.7 (PAGE 23)

1. (3) bleak; desolate; barren
2. (5) an aspect, as of something viewed or considered; point of view
3. (2) to help to grow or develop; stimulate; promote
4. (3) a crucial turning point affecting action, opinion, etc.
5. (2) to be kind or helpful to, but in a haughty or snobbish way, as if dealing with an inferior
6. (1) a pad of folded cloth, sometimes medicated or moistened, for applying pressure, heat, cold, etc. to some part of the body
7. (4) moderate or reasonable; not extreme
8. (2) disagreement or conflict because of differences of opinion, temperament, etc.
9. (2) more than enough; abundant
10. (vt1) to enter in a catalog

EXERCISE 2.9 (PAGE 27)

Answers will vary.

EXERCISE 2.11 (PAGE 29)

1a. site
1b. cite
1c. sight
2a. angle
2b. angel
3a. you're
3b. your
4a. stationery
4b. stationary
5a. accept
5b. except

EXERCISE 2.13 (PAGE 31)

1. interpersonal relationships: connected relationships between/among people
2. derived: gotten and/or adapted from
3. rustic: unsophisticated, rough
4. collaborating: working together, cooperating on
5. complement: supplement, complete
6. sedentary: inactive
7. hospitable: friendly, livable
8. differentiates: distinguishes between, contrasts
9. quandary: dilemma, problem
   cartographers: people who make maps
10. incised: cut or carved into

CHAPTER 2 CROSSWORD PUZZLE (PAGE 39)

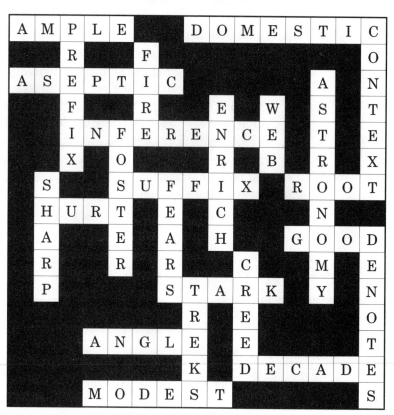

CHAPTER 3

EXERCISE 3.1 (PAGE 42)

1. animal
2. money
3. fish
4. drink
5. fabric
6. sport

EXERCISE 3.3 (PAGE 43)

You need <u>any</u> two examples of the category. These are just samples.

1. car, truck, motorcycle
2. teacher, truck driver, banker
3. hamburger, chicken, pizza
4. sweater, jeans, shirt
5. aspirin, Tylenol, vitamin
6. soda, beer, water

EXERCISE 3.5 (PAGE 46)

1. sundial
2. lightning
3. sun's rays
4. college costs
5. con artist
6. library
7. climate
8. speak well
9. dictionary
10. solar eclipse

EXERCISE 3.7 (PAGE 49)

1. *topic*: smoking
   controlling thought: many people find it very hard to stop
   main idea: Many people find it very hard to stop smoking.
2. *topic*: weather
   controlling thought: it has a big influence on our lives
   main idea: Weather has a big influence on our lives.
3. *topic*: online auction sites
   controlling thought: there are hundreds of general and specialized ones
   main idea: There are hundreds of general and specialized online auction sites.

4. *topic*: 2000 Arena Football League season

   controlling thought: will be played

   main idea: The 2000 Arena Football League season will be played.

5. *topic*: people-watching

   controlling thought: is fun

   main idea: People-watching is always fun.

6. *topic*: technology

   controlling thought: is rapidly changing the way we communicate

   main idea: Technology is rapidly changing the way we communicate.

7. *topic*: Salzburg, Austria

   controlling thought: you can still visit the places that were used in the movie version of *The Sound of Music*

   main idea: In Salzburg, Austria you can still visit the places that were used in the movie version of *The Sound of Music*.

8. *topic*: takeout meals

   controlling thought: food industry's fastest growing segment

   main idea: Takeout meals are the food industry's fastest growing segment.

9. *topic*: *My Dog Skip*

   controlling thought: is a nearly perfect piece of bedtime reading for kids and their parents

   main idea: *My Dog Skip* is a nearly perfect piece of bedtime reading for kids and their parents.

10. *topic*: salt cedar

    controlling thought: is a serious threat to native plants and wildlife across much of the Southwest

    main idea: The salt cedar is a serious threat to native plants and wildlife across much of the Southwest.

EXERCISE 3.9 (PAGE 56)

1. c
2. a
3. a
4. c
5. a
6. b

EXERCISE 3.11 (PAGE 59)

1. Led Zeppelin should be considered the first great heavy metal band.

2. Although tornadoes and hurricanes are nature's most awesome storms, lightning and flash floods are responsible for the greatest number of weather-related deaths.

3. Online investing can help you be more efficient or lose your money quickly.
4. For you to reach your ultimate potential at school and/or at work, you must work with your team and not against it.
5. While you may find a lot in common with others, you alone possess your unique personality.
6. You can expect your best recall shortly after a learning session.

CHAPTER 3 CROSSWORD PUZZLE (PAGE 65)

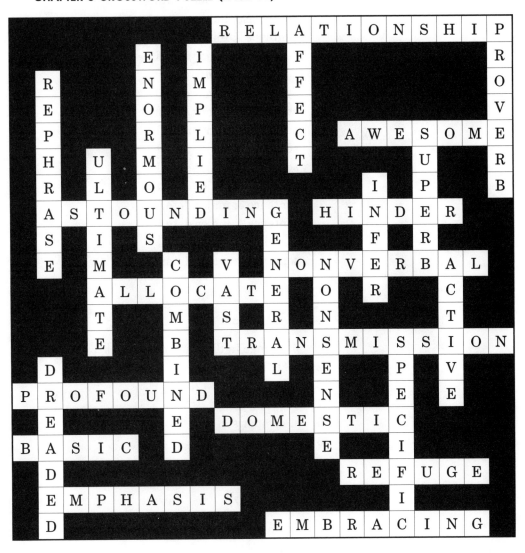

CHAPTER 4

EXERCISE 4.1 (PAGE 70)

1. sentence 2: major detail
   sentence 3: minor detail
   sentence 4: major detail
2. sentence 2: major detail
   sentence 3: major detail
   sentence 4: major detail
   sentence 5: minor detail
   sentence 6: major detail
   sentence 7: minor detail
3. sentence 2: major detail
   sentence 3: minor detail
   sentence 4: minor detail
   sentence 5: minor detail
4. sentence 2: major detail
   sentence 3: major detail
   sentence 4: major detail
5. sentence 2: major detail
   sentence 3: major detail
   sentence 4: major detail
6. sentence 2: major detail
   sentence 3: major detail

EXERCISE 4.3 (PAGE 85)

1. b. change in direction of thought
2. c. definition
3. b. summary
4. b. example
5. a. comparison
6. b. contrast

EXERCISE 4.5 (PAGE 87)

1. a. Main idea: Johnson lacked Lincoln's winning personal qualities.
   b. Organization: comparison/contrast
   c. Read to find: how Lincoln was more charming than Johnson
2. a. Main idea: In the generation following the Civil War, three developments made it possible for fresh beef and pork to be shipped long distances without spoilage.
   b. Organization: cause/effect
   c. Read to find: the three reasons (causes) why it became possible to ship meat without spoiling

3. a. Main idea: America has had many "Wests."
   b. Organization: example
   c. Read to find: examples of the many "Wests"

4. a. Main idea: The term vegetarian means different things to different people.
   b. Organization: definition/example
   c. Read to find: the various definitions of vegetarian

5. a. Main idea: The drought of 1988 was one of North America's worst droughts in this century.
   b. Organization: cause/effect
   c. Read to find: the effects of the drought

6. a. Main idea: Weather and climate mean different things.
   b. Organization: contrast
   c. Read to find: how weather and climate are different from one another

7. a. Main idea: Because they are relatively easy to learn and can play both melody and harmony together, instruments with keyboards have been popular for several hundred years.
   b. Organization: example
   c. Read to find: examples of keyboard instruments through the years

8. a. Main idea: Several factors caused the breakup of the Beatles.
   b. Organization: cause/effect
   c. Read to find: the causes for the breakup

9. a. Main idea: The differences between Los Angeles and San Francisco are striking.
   b. Organization: contrast
   c. Read to find: how Los Angeles and San Francisco are different from one another

10. a. Main idea: The development of the photographic process involved several people over a period of years.
    b. Organization: time sequence
    c. Read to find: who helped develop the photographic process and when

CHAPTER 4 CROSSWORD PUZZLE (PAGE 100)

```
. . T . . . . . . . . I . . . . . . V
. D R O U G H T . M A N D A T E D . A
. . A . V . . . . . . T . . . . E . R
. . N . I . R . V . . E . . . . P . I
C . S . D . I . O . . N . . . . L . A
O . F A T A L I T I E S . . . . E . T
M . O . . . . . . . . E . . . . T . I
P E R C E P T I B L E . . . . . E . O
A . M . S . . . . P R E C E D I N G S
R . S S E Q U E N C E . . . . . . . S
E . . S . . L . . . R A D I C A L . .
. . . . V I T A L . C O N T R A S T .
. . . . I . . . . . D . . . . E . . .
C . M . . . . . . . I N C L I N E D .
A . L . . . I . . . . . . . . E . . .
U . . . . . O . . . . . . . . V . . .
S . . . . . U . . . . . . . . E . . .
E . . . . . O . . . F L A T T E R Y .
S . . C O P E S . . E F F E C T S . .
```

Across: DROUGHT, MANDATED, FATALITIES, PERCEPTIBLE, PRECEDING, SEQUENCE, RADICAL, VITAL, CONTRAST, COMPARABLE, INCLINED, FLATTERY, COPES, EFFECTS

Down: TRANSFORMS, INTENSE, VARIATIONS, DEPLETE, COMPARE, CAUSES

CHAPTER 5

EXERCISE 5.1 (PAGE 104)

1. O
2. F
3. F
4. F
5. O
6. F
7. O
8. F
9. F
10. O

EXERCISE 5.3 (PAGE 105)

1. a. Sentence 1: fact
    b. Sentence 2: combination—fact: Made in 1964, starring Julie Andrews and Christopher Plummer; opinion: it is one of the best movies of all time
2. a. Sentence 1: combination—fact: attract more than 11 million participants a year; opinion: the flashiest winter sports
    b. Sentence 3: fact
3. a. Sentence 1: fact
    b. Sentence 5: opinion
4. a. Sentence 3: fact
    b. Sentence 5: fact
5. a. Sentence 1: opinion
    b. Sentence 5: opinion
6. a. Sentence 2: fact
    b. Sentence 5: opinion

EXERCISE 5.5 (PAGE 111)

1. b. There is a need for people to become blood donors.
2. a. People who live in Arizona have more chance of seeing several different kinds of hummingbirds than those who live in New York.
3. b. For those who can exercise, aerobic exercise has several beneficial effects.
4. c. Play is a valuable activity for children.
5. a. The amount of sleep a person needs varies with each individual.
6. b. A number of factors contribute to being overweight.

EXERCISE 5.7 (PAGE 114)

A1. We can infer that Barra: b. likes Costas's book
    Barra said that the book "puts you more in mind of a good conversation during a rainout that makes you forget the game is on hold."
A2. We can infer that Barra: a. thinks Costas is a good writer
    Barra said that Costas "makes his points with neat, forceful prose," and that he argues persuasively.
B1. We can infer I recommend: a. annotating more than highlighting
    I said that annotating is an active process that requires thinking while highlighting is a passive activity that postpones reading.
B2. We can infer I believe: b. Students learn more from rephrasing ideas in their own words than from highlighting a sentence.
    I said that students often "don't even understand the material they highlight," while "rephrasing an idea into your own words makes you think the idea through and process its meaning."

CHAPTER 5 CROSSWORD PUZZLE (PAGE 123)

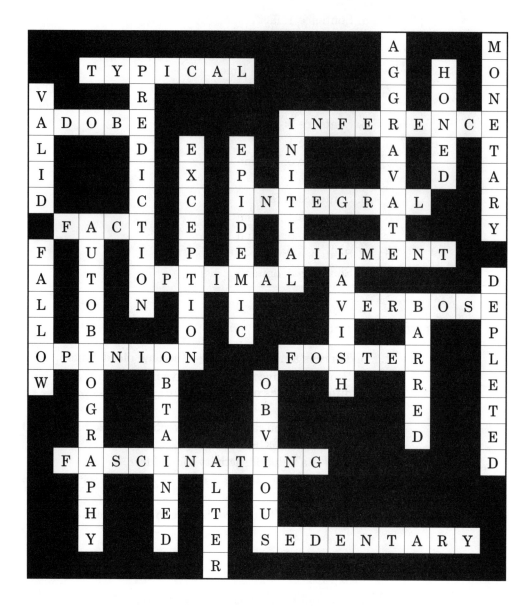

CHAPTER 6

EXERCISE 6.1 (PAGE 128)

1. Title: Your Role as a Nursing Assistant
2. Two important ideas in the Introduction could include:
   - A nursing assistant is an important member of the health care team.
   - Duties may include a variety of direct and indirect patient care tasks.
   - Specific job descriptions vary among institutions.
   - In addition to job duties, nursing assistants are expected to demonstrate good interpersonal and organizational skills.
   - A personal code of ethics and awareness of legal aspects of nursing are essential.

3. Two things readers will be able to do when they complete the chapter could include the following:
   - display qualities that are desirable in a good patient/nursing assistant
   - identify duties and role functions of nursing assistants
   - practice good personal hygiene
   - behave ethically
   - keep confidences to themselves
   - work accurately
   - be dependable
   - follow rules and instructions
   - develop cooperative staff relationships
   - show respect for patients' rights
   - explain how laws affect them and the patients they care for
   - report incidents
4. There are fourteen key terms listed for this chapter.

EXERCISE 6.3 (PAGE 130)

1. The chapter's title, heading, and subheadings:
   Your Role as a Nursing Assistant
       The Nursing Assistant: An Important Caregiver
       Role of the Nursing Assistant
       Duties and Functions of the Nursing Assistant
2. The paragraphs under the subheading "Role of the Nursing Assistant" probably contain information on what nursing assistants do and who they work with and report to.
3. Wolgin defines *accountable* as "to be answerable for one's behavior; legally or ethically responsible for the care of another."
4. The margin note *Key Idea* highlights an important idea.

EXERCISE 6.5 (PAGE 132)

1. Important ideas in the Summary that were in the Introduction could include the following:
   - A nursing assistant is an important member of the health care team.
   - In addition to job duties, nursing assistants are expected to demonstrate good interpersonal and organizational skills and good hygiene.
   - A personal code of ethics and awareness of legal aspects of nursing are essential.
2. Ideas in the Summary that were not in the Introduction could include the following:
   - Nursing assistants will be ensuring that patients do not suffer any extra pain and will be making their stay easier.
   - Always remember that patients are entitled to respect for their human rights.
   - Patients must be kept safe and properly cared for at all times.
   - Laws protect both the patients and the workers.

3. Answer to the Chapter Review's Fill in the Blank Question 1: "accountable"

   The answer is in the margin vocabulary note on page 16.

EXERCISE 6.7 (PAGE 133)

Answers for questions 1–7 will vary.

EXERCISE 6.9 (PAGE 138)

1. c. breakdown
2. b. protection
3. T
4. F—A person affected by hypothermia usually ~~asks for help immediately~~ denies that anything is wrong.
5. F—It's important to wear ~~gloves~~ a knit cap because more than half the body's heat can be lost through the ~~hands~~ head.
6. c. X-cold can be deadly so take immediate steps to reverse it or prevent it.
7. List any four of these warning signs of hypothermia:
   - Chattering teeth and shivering
   - Slow, hard-to-understand speech
   - Forgetfulness, confusion
   - Fumbling hands
   - Stumbling, difficulty in walking
   - Sleepiness (the person going to sleep may never wake up)
   - Exhaustion (if the person can't get up after a brief rest, X-cold has taken over)
8. List any four of these positive actions:
   - Find shelter
   - Build a fire
   - Get the victim out of wind, rain, snow
   - Strip off wet clothing and put on dry clothes or wrap up in a sleeping bag
   - Give warm drinks
   - Avoid medicines
9. c. cause
10. Main idea of paragraph 5: X-cold reduces reasoning power and judgment because of lack of oxygen to the brain.

CHAPTER 6 CROSSWORD PUZZLE (PAGE 165)

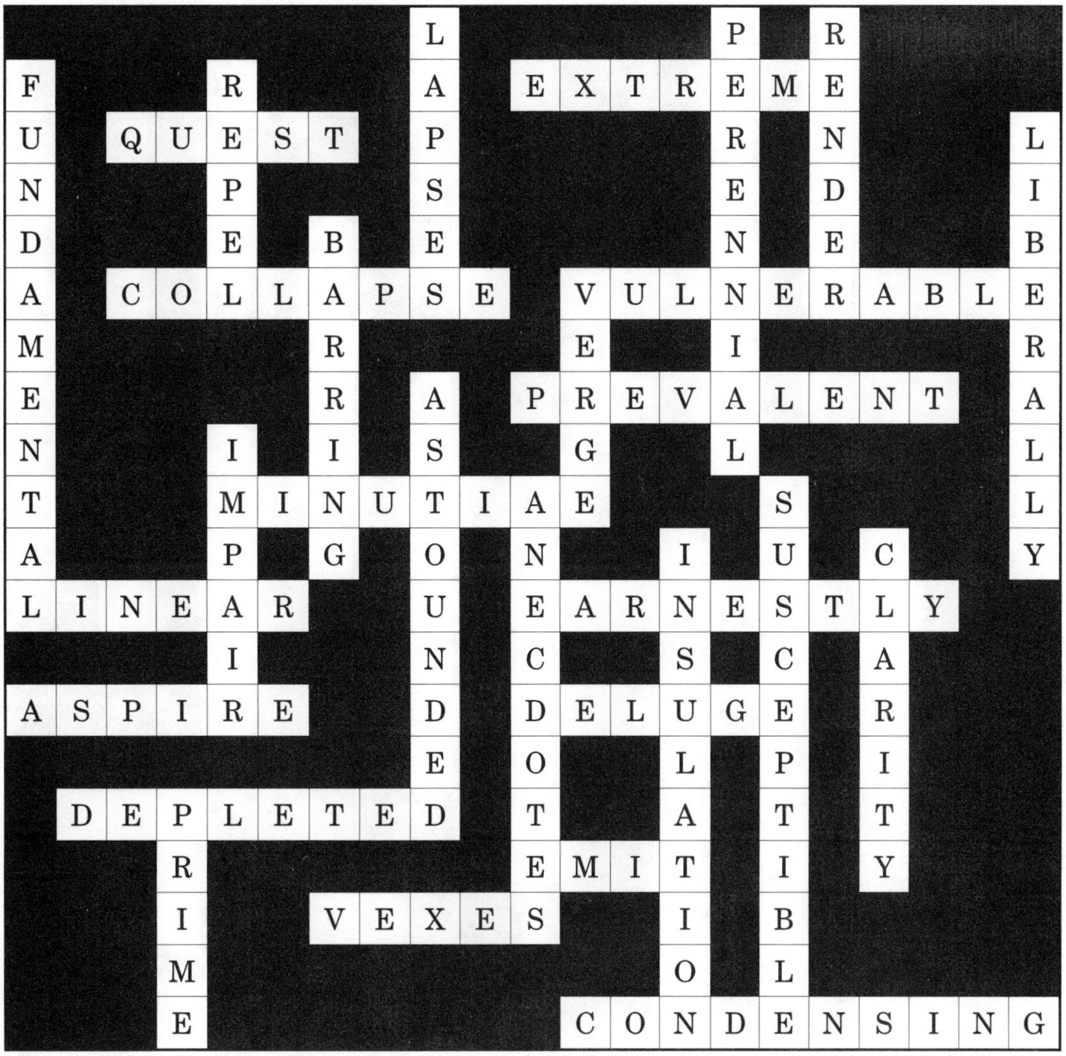

THEME 1 CROSSWORD PUZZLE (PAGE 198)

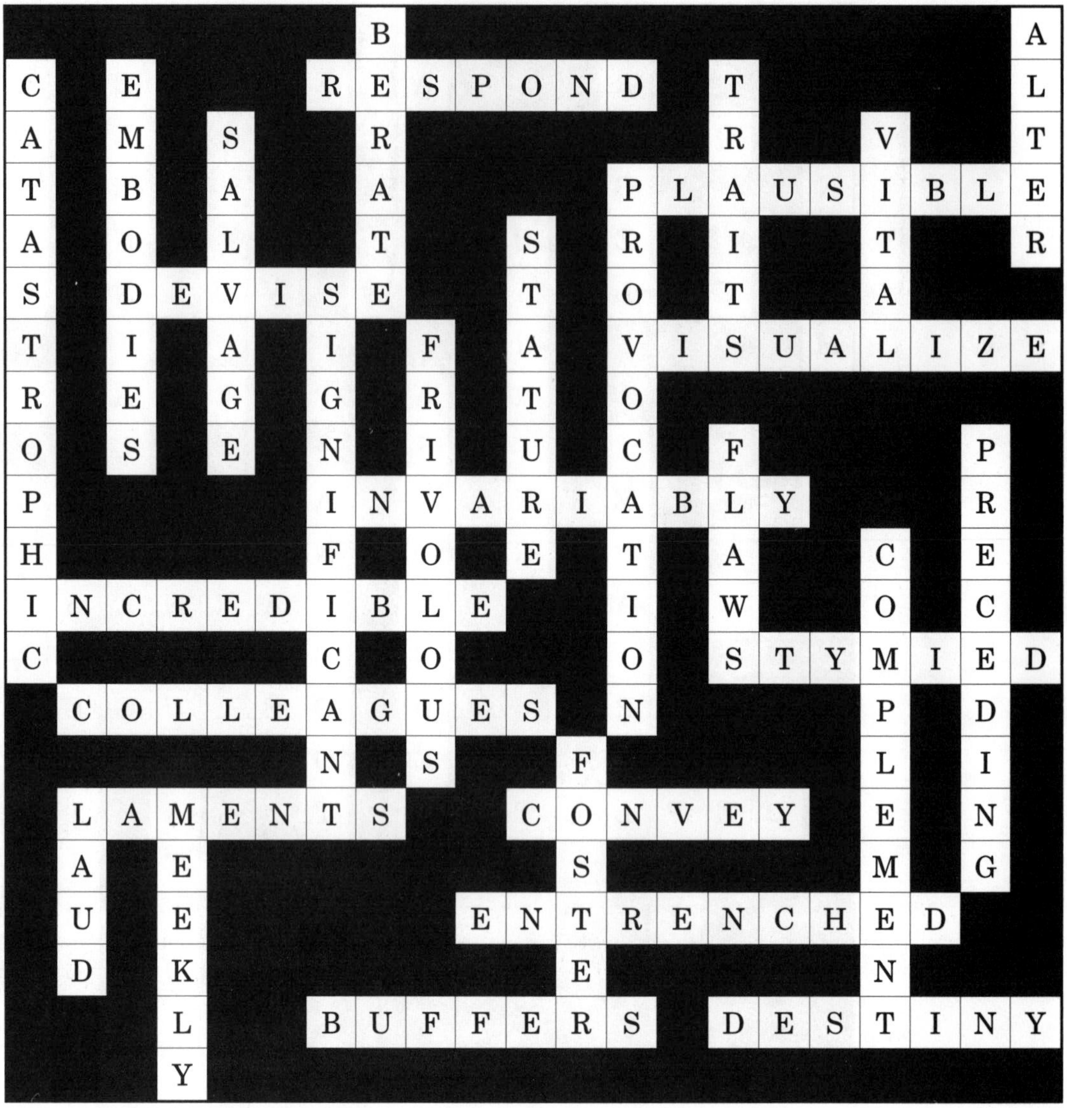

THEME 2 CROSSWORD PUZZLE (PAGE 245)

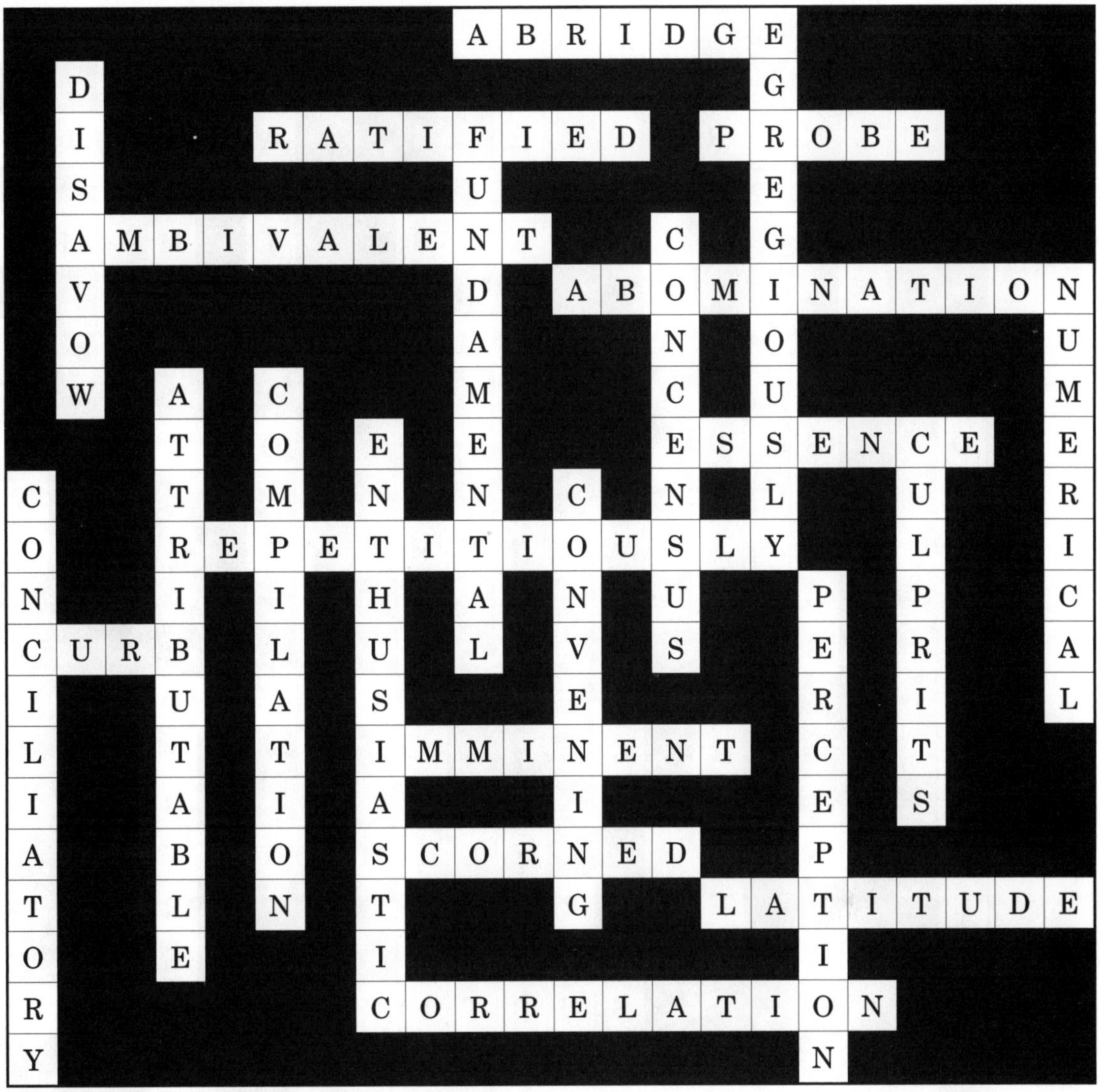

THEME 3 CROSSWORD PUZZLE (PAGE 282)

STANCE
BANNING
VULNERABLE
ATYPICAL
HINDERS
MIMICS
SAP
IMPAIRS
COHESION
ESTRANGEMENT
DERIVED
UNITE
ELIMINATE
SKEWED
SUBTLE
DISHONEST
DISPARITY
BOMBARDED
BOLSTER
STAMINA
AMPLIFIED
ALTER
SUBSTANTIATED
ILLEGAL
PHARMACEUTICALS
PRONE
CONSEQUENCES
ASSESS
TACTICS
CONFLICTING
DISTRESSED
AMBIVALENT
DETRIMENTAL
BLUNTS

CREDITS

CHAPTER 1

Excerpts from *Student Resource Guide to the Internet* by Cynthia B. Leshin, © 1998. Reprinted by permission of Prentice-Hall, Inc., Upper Saddle River, NJ.

CHAPTER 2

Cincinnati Post Editorial Cartoon by Jeff Stahler, reprinted by permission of Newspaper Enterprises Association, Inc.

Cartoon from *Mother Goose and Grimm* by Mike Peters © Tribune Media Services, Inc. All rights reserved. Reprinted with permission.

Cartoon from *Family Circus*, May 4, 2000. Reprinted with special permission of King Features Syndicate.

CHAPTER 6

Excerpts from *Being a Nursing Assistant* by Francie Wolgin. Copyright © 1999. Reprinted by permission of Pearson Education, Inc., Upper Saddle River, NJ.

"Getting Organized," from *Adjustment and Human Relations* by Tricia Alexander. Copyright © 2000. Reprinted by permission of Prentice-Hall, Inc., Upper Saddle River, NJ 07458.

"When X-Cold Strikes" by Robert L. McGrath. Reprinted by permission of Robert L. McGrath.

"Healthy Aging: A Lifelong Process," from *Access to Health*, Fifth Edition by Rebecca J. Donatelle and Lorraine G. Davis. Copyright © 1998 by Allyn & Bacon. Reprinted by permission.

"Change Your Bad Habits to Good" by Robert Epstein. Copyright © 1998 by Dr. Robert Epstein. Reprinted with permission of the author.

"How to Write Clearly" by Edward T. Thompson. Reprinted by permission of the author.

"Think Quick!" by Daniel R. Foster. Reprinted from *Choices for Living Magazine*, Spring 1997.

Excerpt from "The Kennedy and Johnson Years," from *America: Pathways to the Present* by Andrew Clayton, Elisabeth I. Perry, Linda Reed and Alan M. Winkler. © 2000 by Prentice-Hall, Inc. Used by permission of Pearson Education, Inc.

THEME 1

"Attitudes," from *Strengthening Your Grip* by Charles R. Swindoll (Nashville, TN: Word, Inc: Anaheim, CA: Insight for Living, © 1982). All rights reserved. Used by permission of The Meredith Agency (714-993-9469).

"Is It Time for an Attitude Adjustment?" by Barbara K. Bruce and Denise Foley. Reprinted from *USA Today Magazine*, September 1998. Copyright ©) 1998 by the Society for the Advancement of Education.

"Choosing a Positive Attitude: Your Survival Strategy for Balancing Work and Personal Life" by Renee Magid, from The Life Station of Initiatives, Inc. Reprinted by permission.

"Hold On to Your Positive Attitude" by Elwood N. Chapman and Sharon Lund O'Neil, from *Your Attitude Is Showing*, Ninth Edition. Copyright © 1999. Reprinted by permission of Pearson Education, Inc., Upper Saddle River, NJ.

"'Little Engine' Holds a Valuable Life Lesson" by Ana Veciana-Suarez, *Miami Herald*. Copyright © 1995 by Miami Herald. Reproduced by permission of Miami Herald in textbook format via Copyright Clearance Center.

THEME 2

"Civil Liberties: First Amendment Freedoms" from *Magruder's American Government*, 2000 Edition by William A. McClenaghan. © 2000 by Mary Magruder Smith. Published by Prentice-Hall, Inc. Used by permission of Pearson Education, Inc.

"State of the First Amendment 2000" by Kenneth A. Paulson (Nashville, TN: First Amendment Center, June 29, 2000). Copies of the full report are available free of charge from the First Amendment Center by calling 1-800-830-3733 and requesting Publication No. 00-F03.

"Well, Would You Rather Have an Unfree Press?" by Bill Thompson, *The Fort Worth Star–Telegram*, July 7, 1999. Reprinted by permission.

"You Be the Judge" by Chip Rowe, *Playboy*, August 1999. Reprinted by permission of Playboy, Inc.

THEME 3

"Drugs, Alcohol, and Tobacco" from *Biology*, Fifth Edition by Kenneth Miller and Joseph Levine. © 2000 by Prentice-Hall, Inc. Used by permission of Pearson Education, Inc.

"Alcohol" by Bruno Leone, from the *Opposing Viewpoints* Series. Copyright © 1998 by the Gale Group. Reprinted by permission of the Gale Group.

"Reading the Media's Messages about Medications" by Sheila Globus, from *Current Health 2* © 1999 by Weekly Reader Corporation. All rights reserved.

"Tobacco and Alcohol Advertisements in Magazines: Are Young Readers Being Targeted?" by Lorin Sanchez, et al., *Journal of the American Medical Association*, 283: 2106–2107. Copyright © 2000. Reprinted by permission.

"Avoiding the Lure of Tobacco, Alcohol, and Marijuana" by Kathiann M. Kowalski, from *Current Health 2* © 2000 by Weekly Reader Corporation. All rights reserved.

APPENDIX

"Advice to Beginning Writers" by Robert L. McGrath. Reprinted by permission of Robert L. McGrath.

PHOTOS

CHAPTER 6

page 161: FRENT
page 162: John F. Kennedy Presidential Library
page 164: John F. Kennedy Presidential Library

THEME 2

page 203: © B & J McGrath/The Picture Cube
page 205: AP/Wide World Photos
page 206: AP/Wide World Photos
page 209: © John O'Connor/Monkmeyer Press
page 210: © Miro Vintoniv/Stock Boston
page 212: © Paul Conklin
page 214: © Frank Siteman/The Picture Cube
page 218: © Bob Rashid/Monkmeyer Press
page 220: © Ura Wexler/Folio
page 221: © Randy Taylor/Sygma
page 225: © The Bettmann Archive
page 227: © Mike Mazzaschi/Stock Boston

THEME 3

page 250: © LagunaDesign/Science Photo Library/Photo Researchers, Inc.
page 251: R. B. Sanchez/The Stock Market
page 252, top: The University Museum, University of Pennsylvania
page 252, bottom: Ken Karp Photography
page 253, left: Howard Sochurek Inc.
page 253, right: J. H. Robinson/Photo Researcher's, Inc.
page 255: © Jim Sleby/Science Photo Library/Photo Researchers, Inc.
page 256, top: Dr. Jeremy Burgess/Science Photo Library/Photo Researchers, Inc.
page 256, bottom: Michael Hardy/Woodfin Camp & Associates
page 257: National Institute of Health
page 259: Bobby Holland/READER'S DIGEST FOUNDATION
page 260, left and right: © Lennart Nilsson, The Incredible Machine, National Geographic Society
page 265: Ted Russell/The Image Bank

INDEX